A2-Level Geography

This book is packed with thorough notes and detailed case studies covering everything you need to know for AQA A2-Level Geography.

It's also got plenty of stuff to help you prepare for the exams. There are warm-up and exam-style practice questions for every topic, plus an Exam Skills section full of notes on the graph, map and statistical skills you'll need.

And of course, we've done our best to make the whole thing vaguely entertaining for you.

Complete Revision and Practice

Exam Board: AQA

Published by CGP

Editors:
Luke Antieul, Claire Boulter, Ellen Bowness, Joe Brazier, Anthony Muller, Jo Sharrock.

Contributors:
Helen Nurton, Sophie Watkins.

Proofreaders:
Harriet Broadbent, Duncan King, Rosie McCurrie.

ISBN: 978 1 84762 879 4

With thanks to Laura Collar for the copyright research.

With thanks to Science Photo Library for permission to use the images on pages 7 and 19.

With thanks to iStockphoto.com for permission to reproduce the photographs used on pages 9, 12, 16, 17, 20, 23, 38, 44, 59, 61, 64, 73, 75, 78, 85, 87, 110 and 128.

Graph of UK temperature and rainfall on page 28 © Crown copyright reproduced under the terms of the Open Government Licence.

Maps of UK annual temperature, rainfall and wind speed 1971-2000 on pages 28 and 29 © Crown copyright reproduced under the terms of the Open Government Licence.

Map showing the course of the Great Storm with pressure readings on page 32 © 2007 Risk Management Solutions, Inc.

With thanks to Rex Features for permission to use the images on pages 40 and 92.

Graph showing climate change in Greenland over the last 20 000 years on page 46 reproduced with thanks to the NOAA for the graphic and to the Alley (2000) paper for the underlying data.

Last 1000 years of climate change graph on page 46 reproduced with kind permission from Climate Change 2001: The Scientific Basis, Contribution of Working Group I to the Third Assessment Report of the Intergovernmental Panel on Climate Change, SPM Figure 1. Cambridge University Press.

Graph showing temperature change over the last 110 years on page 46 © Crown copyright 2009, the Met Office.

Image of an offshore wind farm near Barrow-in-Furness on page 51 © Copyright David Dixon and licensed for reuse under the Creative Commons Licence.

Data used to construct the Average Climate in a Tropical Rainforest graph on page 60 from the U.S. National Climatic Data Center.

Data used to construct the map showing global urban population on page 77 © 2011 Human Development Report, United Nations Development Programme.

Map of LTGDC developments on page 89 adapted from http://ltgdc.org.uk/

Graph of methods of waste disposal in the UK on page 94 © Crown copyright reproduced under the terms of the Open Government Licence.

Data used to compile the table on page 101 © Central Intelligence Agency.

Page 115 — Apple Inc. is a registered trademark in the U.S. and other countries.

Pie chart of the UK's population by ethnic group in 2001 on page 132 © Crown copyright reproduced under the terms of the Open Government Licence.

Map of the UK's non-white population by area in 2001 on page 132 contains National Statistics data © Crown copyright and database rights 2012.

Graph of the regional distribution of the UK's non-white population on page 133 © Crown copyright reproduced under the terms of the Open Government Licence.

Pie chart of the population of Bradford by ethnic group in 2001 on page 135 contains National Statistics data © Crown copyright and database rights 2012.

Data used to construct the map on page 136 from the United Nations Millennium Goals Report 2007.

Data used to construct the map on page 137 © WHO, 2011. All rights reserved. World Health Organisation, http://www.who.int/whosis/whostat/EN_WHS2011_Full.pdf

Page 148 — Mapping data reproduced by permission of Ordnance Survey® on behalf of HMSO © Crown copyright (2012). All rights reserved. Ordnance Survey® Licence No. 100034841.

Every effort has been made to locate copyright holders and obtain permission to reproduce sources. For those sources where it has been difficult to trace the copyright holder of the work, we would be grateful for information. If any copyright holder would like us to make an amendment to the acknowledgements, please notify us and we will gladly update the book at the next reprint.

Groovy website: www.cgpbooks.co.uk
Jolly bits of clipart from CorelDRAW®
Printed by Elanders Ltd, Newcastle upon Tyne.

Based on the classic CGP style created by Richard Parsons.

Contents

Section 1 — Plate Tectonics

Section 2 — Weather and Climate

Section 3 — Ecosystems

Section 4 — World Cities

Section 5 — Development and Globalisation

Section 6 — Contemporary Conflicts and Challenges

Exam Skills

Plate Tectonics Theory

The ground beneath your feet is moving all the time — but fear not, it's moving really, really, really slowly (about the same speed as your toenails grow. Yuk, toenails). Plate tectonics theory explains this movement...

*Part of the Earth's **Mantle** is **Semi-molten***

1) At the **centre** of the Earth is the **CORE**, which is split into an **inner** core and an **outer** core:
   - The inner core is a **solid ball** containing lots of **iron and nickel**.
   - The outer core is **semi-molten** and also contains lots of **iron and nickel**.
2) Around the core is the **MANTLE**, which is mostly made of **silicate rocks** (rocks that have loads of the element silicon in them):
   - The part of the mantle **nearest the core** is **quite rigid**.
   - The **layer above** this, called the **asthenosphere**, is **semi-molten** (it can flow).
   - And the **very, very top bit** of the mantle is **rigid**.
3) The **outer layer** of the Earth is called the **CRUST**.
4) The **rigid top part** of the **mantle** and the **crust** together are called the **LITHOSPHERE**.
5) There are **two types** of crust — **CONTINENTAL** and **OCEANIC**:
   - **Continental** crust is **thicker** (30-70 km thick) and **less dense**.
   - **Oceanic** crust is **thinner** (6-10 km thick) and **more dense**.

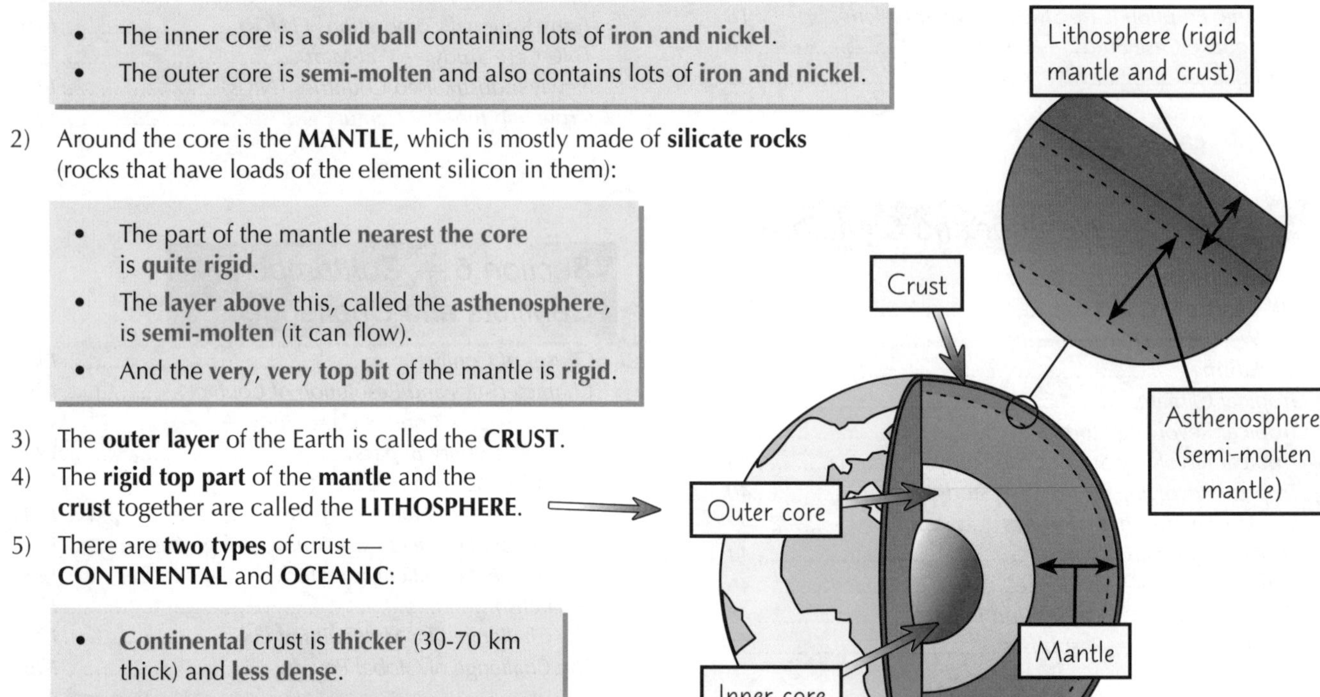

*The **Earth's Surface** is **Separated** into **Tectonic Plates***

1) The lithosphere is **divided** into lots of slabs called **tectonic plates**.
2) The plates are **moving** due to **convection currents** in the **asthenosphere** (see the next page).
3) The places where plates meet are called **boundaries** or **plate margins**.

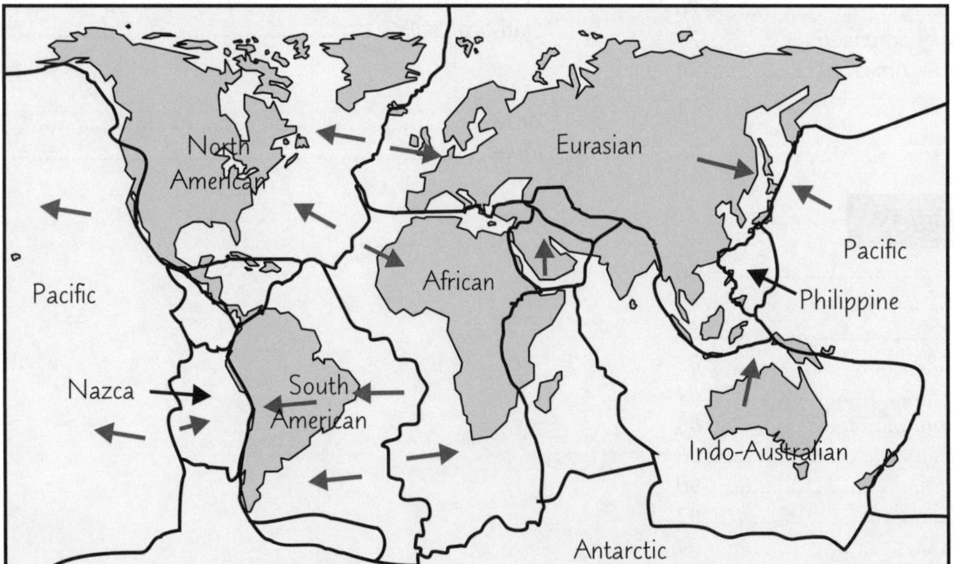

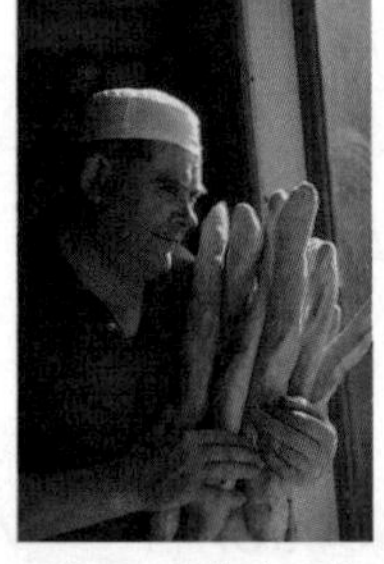
Pierre really loved continental crust.

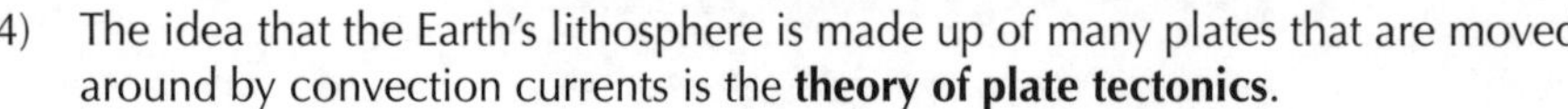
4) The idea that the Earth's lithosphere is made up of many plates that are moved around by convection currents is the **theory of plate tectonics**.

Plate Tectonics Theory

The Tectonic Plates **Move** due to **Convection Currents** in the **Mantle**

1) **Radioactive decay** of some elements in the mantle and core, e.g. uranium, generates a **lot of heat**.
2) When **lower parts** of the **asthenosphere heat up** they become **less dense** and slowly **rise**.
3) As they move towards the **top** of the asthenosphere they **cool down**, become **more dense**, then slowly **sink**.
4) These **circular movements** of semi-molten rock are called **CONVECTION CURRENTS**.
5) Convection currents in the asthenosphere **create drag** on the **base** of the **tectonic plates** (which are solid and rigid) — and this causes them to **move**.

The Earth's core is extremely hot — it's over 4000 °C.

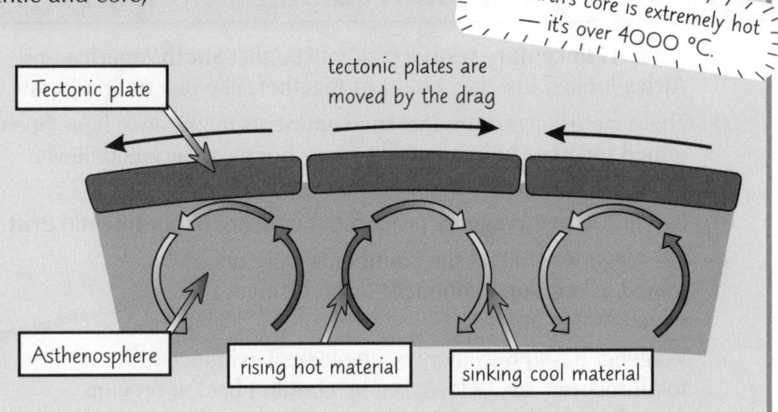

New crust formation at mid-ocean ridges doesn't happen at the same speed everywhere — at some it's less than 10 mm per year and at others it's more than 100 mm per year.

Crust is **Created** When **Plates** Move **Apart**

1) **Rising convection currents diverge** (move apart) at the base of the lithosphere.
2) The drag of the convection currents causes the **plates** above them to **diverge too**.
3) **Magma rises up** to fill the gap created, then **cools** to form **new crust**.
4) Over time, the **new crust** is **dragged apart** and even **more new crust forms** between it.
5) When this happens at a plate margin under the sea the **sea floor gets wider**.
6) This **process** is called **sea floor spreading**... imaginative name.
7) It creates structures called **mid-ocean ridges** — ridges of higher terrain on either side of the margin.
8) A similar process of spreading occurs at **land margins** where the plates are moving apart.
9) When plates move together, sometimes the crust is **destroyed** and sometimes it's pushed up into **mountains** (see p. 6 for more).

Lava cools to form new crust
Mid-ocean ridge
Plate
magma
Asthenosphere

Practice Questions

Q1 What is the asthenosphere?

Q2 What is the lithosphere?

Q3 Briefly describe sea floor spreading.

Exam Questions

Q1 Describe the structure of the Earth. [8 marks]

Q2 Describe and explain how convection currents cause tectonic plates to move. [8 marks]

Plate tectonics — it's a cracking theory...

What a lovely couple of pages to ease you in gently, but don't think you can get away without knowing this stuff inside out. If you don't get the basics, the rest of this section will be more painful than stubbing your toe on a slab of oceanic crust. A bit of work now will help make the rest of plate tectonics a piece of Victoria sponge. You'd better get learning...

Plate Tectonics Theory

The theory of plate tectonics is widely accepted by scientists. It grew out of the theory of continental drift — which a clever bloke called Alfred Wegener came up with early in the 20th century...

The **Theory of Plate Tectonics** started with **Alfred Wegener**

1) In the **17th centur**y people first noticed that **South America** and **Africa** looked like they could **fit together**, like pieces of a **jigsaw**.
2) There were suggestions that the **continents** might once have been **joined together** before moving apart, but most people believed the continents were fixed in place.
3) In 1912 **Alfred Wegener** proposed the theory of **continental drift**.
4) He suggested that **all the continents** were once **joined** as **one supercontinent** (called **Pangaea**) which drifted apart.
5) Wegener based his theory on **geological evidence** and **fossil records** (see below), but he **couldn't** back it up with a **mechanism** that explained how the continents **moved**.
6) But in the **1950s**, **palaeomagnetism** (see the next page) provided **evidence** that supported continental drift.
7) And in the **1960s** the process of **sea floor spreading** (see previous page) was discovered — it provided the **mechanism** for continental drift.
8) The continental drift theory was **developed further** by scientists after these findings. It grew into the **theory of plate tectonics**.

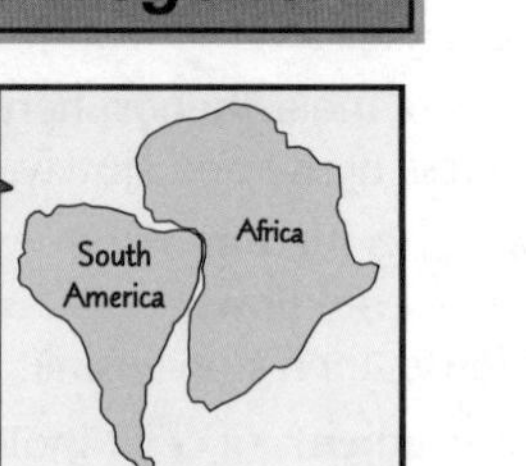

Ethel and Walter remembered the good ol' days back in Pangaea...

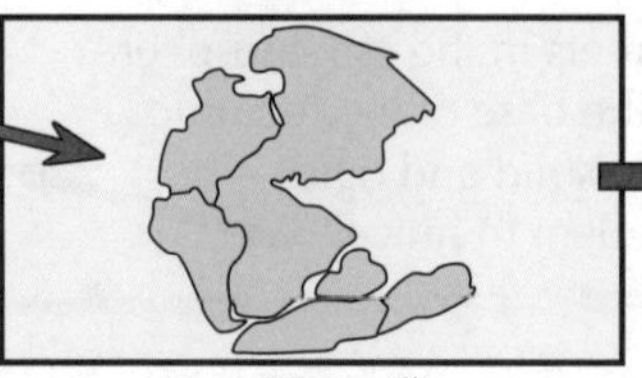

Pangaea, about 250 million years ago

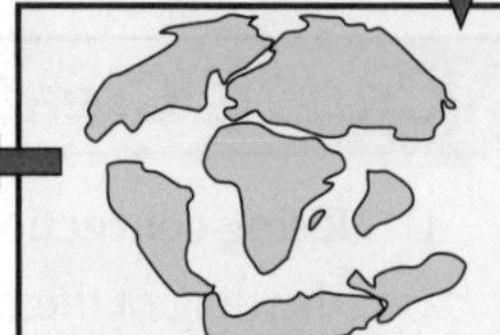

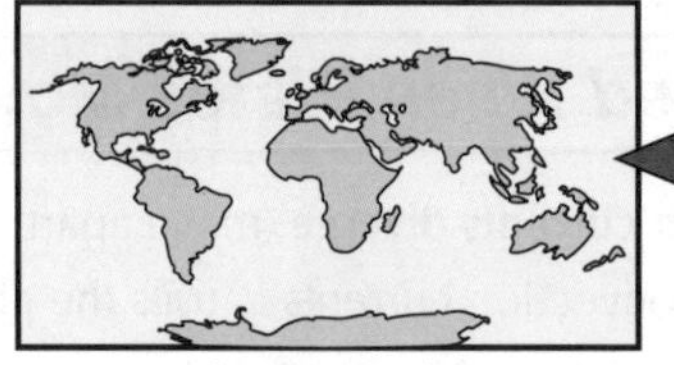

The present day

There's **Plenty of Evidence** for the Theory

Geology

1) Areas of **South America** and **Africa** have **rocks** of the **same age and composition** — if you fit these continents together, the **distribution** of the rocks **matches up**.
2) You can also **match up** the age, rock type and distribution of some **mountain ranges**, e.g. mountains in **Scotland**, **Norway**, **Sweden** and **Finland** are similar to those on the **east coast of North America**.
3) These rocks and mountains must have formed under the **same conditions** and in the **same place** in order to match so well — this would **only be possible** if the **continents were once joined**.

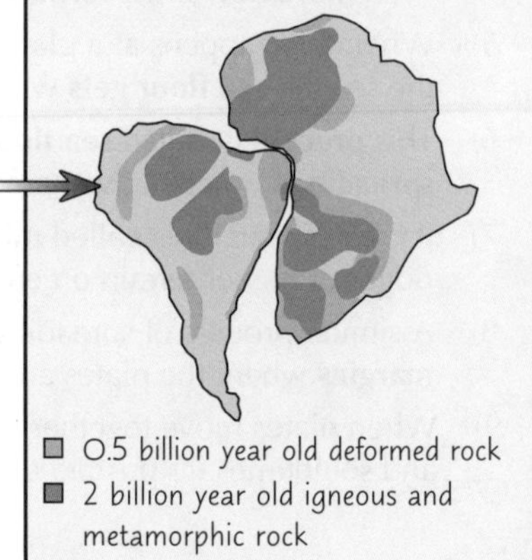

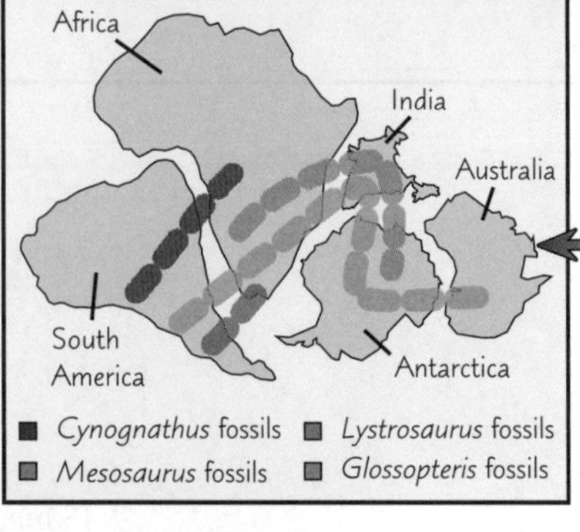

Fossil Records

1) By fitting land masses together you can **match up** the **distribution** of some **fossils**, e.g. fossils of *Lystrosaurus*, *Cynognathus*, *Mesosaurus* (all reptiles) and *Glossopteris* (a plant).
2) It's **very unlikely** that these species **migrated** across thousands of miles of water, or that they **evolved** in different places.
3) So the fossil records **suggest** that these places were **joined together** when these organisms were alive — **hundreds of millions of years ago**.

Living Species

1) The same living organisms can also be found on **different continents** — like with the fossilised organisms above, it's **unlikely** that some of them **migrated** across the oceans, or **evolved** in different locations.
2) For example, **earthworms** of the family *Megascolecidae* are found in **New Zealand**, parts of **Asia** and **North America**. This suggests that the **continents were once joined**, allowing the earthworms to travel between them.

Plate Tectonics Theory

Climatology

There's evidence that the **past climates** of some continents were **similar**, despite being **thousands of miles apart** now. This suggests that they were **located together** and in a **different place** on Earth to where they are now. Here are a **couple of examples**:

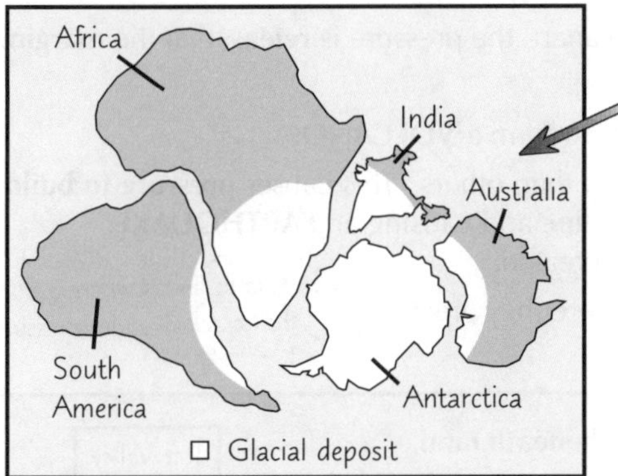

1) Similar **glacial deposits** are found in **Antarctica, Africa, South America, India** and **Australia.** By fitting these places together you can **match up the distribution** of the deposits, which suggests that they were **joined together** millions of years ago and located **close to the South Pole.**
2) Large **coal deposits** that were **formed in tropical conditions** have been found in **North America** and parts of **Europe.** This suggests these regions were once **closer to the equator** than they are now — they've drifted over time.

Palaeomagnetism

1) **Palaeomagnetism** is the study of the history of the **Earth's magnetic field**.
2) **Once every 200 000 years** or so, the Earth's magnetic field **reverses polarity** (the magnetic north and south poles switch).
3) Palaeomagnetism has provided evidence for the process of **sea floor spreading** (see page 3).
4) As **magma erupts** from mid-ocean ridges, **magnetic minerals** in the molten rock **align themselves** with the direction of the **Earth's magnetic field**.
5) When the new crust has **solidified**, the **alignment** is **fixed**.
6) The magnetic minerals in crust created in periods of **normal polarity** (magnetic north near the North Pole) are aligned in the **opposite direction** to those in crust created in periods of **reverse polarity** (magnetic north near the South Pole).
7) This creates a series of **alternating magnetic stripes** along the sea floor. The stripes show that the **crust** is **older** the **further away** from a **mid-ocean ridge** you go — this means that the **plates are moving apart**.

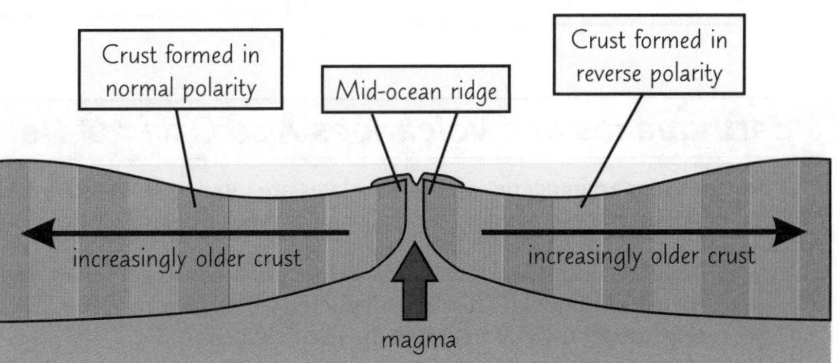

Practice Questions

Q1 Describe the theory of continental drift.

Q2 Name five sources of evidence for the theory of plate tectonics.

Exam Question

Q1 Describe the different types of evidence for the theory of plate tectonics. [40 marks]

Increasingly older crust usually goes hard and grows green stuff...

Two things to bear in mind when you're learning this little lot. Firstly, despite it being called a theory, plate tectonics is pretty much accepted as fact — there's an overwhelming amount of evidence that proves the plates are moving around. Secondly, continental drift takes place over hundreds of millions of years — it's unlikely that the UK will be nestled next to Australia any time soon...

Types of Plate Margin

The next couple of pages build on some of the stuff you should have learnt at GCSE. It's not the most difficult of topics (I'm saving those for later...) but it's vital nonetheless — so put on your favourite revision hat and get ready to take it all in.

***Earthquakes** and **Volcanoes** Occur at **Constructive** Margins*

1) A **constructive margin** occurs where two plates are moving **APART** (diverging).
2) The mantle is under **pressure** from the plates above. When they move apart, the pressure is **released** at the **margin**.
3) The release of pressure causes the mantle to **melt**, producing **magma**.
4) The magma is **less dense** than the plate above, so it **rises** and can **erupt** to form a **VOLCANO**.
5) The plates **don't** move apart in a **uniform way** — some parts move faster than others. This causes **pressure to build up**. When the pressure becomes **too much** the plate **cracks**, making a **fault line** and causing an **EARTHQUAKE**. **Further earthquakes** may also occur along the fault line once it's been created.
6) Constructive margins create **two different landforms**, depending on where they are:

A fault line is where a plate has cracked under pressure.

MID-OCEAN RIDGE

1) Where diverging plates are **underwater**, a **mid-ocean ridge** forms (see page 3). For example, the **Mid-Atlantic Ridge** is where the **Eurasian plate** and **North American plate** are moving apart.
2) **Underwater volcanoes** erupt along mid-ocean ridges and they can **build up** to be above sea level. For example, **Iceland** has been formed by the build-up of underwater volcanoes along the Mid-Atlantic Ridge.

RIFT VALLEY

1) Where plates diverge **beneath land**, rising **magma** causes the continental crust to **bulge** and **fracture**, forming **fault lines**.
2) As the plates keep moving apart, the **crust** between parallel faults **drops down** to form a **rift valley**. For example, the **East African Rift System** is a series of rift valleys that stretches from **Mozambique** to the **Red Sea** — about 4000 km. It's formed because the **Nubian** and **Somalian** plates are diverging. Some parts of the system are hundreds of metres deep and thousands of metres wide.
3) **Volcanoes** are found around rift valleys. For example, **Mount Kilimanjaro** and **Mount Kenya** (the two highest mountains in Africa) are volcanoes in the **East African Rift System**.

***Earthquakes** and **Volcanoes** Also Occur at **Destructive** Margins*

A **destructive margin** occurs where two plates are moving **TOWARDS EACH OTHER** (converging). What happens at these margins depends on the **types of plates** converging:

Oceanic-Continental

1) Where **continental crust** and **oceanic crust** converge, the **more dense oceanic** crust is **forced under** the **less dense continental** crust (it's **subducted**). This forms a **DEEP SEA TRENCH** (a very deep trench in the sea — e.g. the **Peru-Chile trench** in the Pacific Ocean).
2) **FOLD MOUNTAINS** also form where the plates meet. They're made up of **sediments** that have accumulated on the continental crust, which are **folded upwards** along with the **edge** of the **continental crust**.
3) The oceanic crust is **heated** by **friction** and **contact** with the upper mantle, which melts it into **magma**.
4) The magma is **less dense** than the continental crust above and will **rise** back to the surface to form **VOLCANOES**.
5) As one plate moves under the other they **can get stuck**. This causes **pressure** to **build up**. When the pressure becomes **too much** the plates **jerk** past each other, causing an **EARTHQUAKE**.

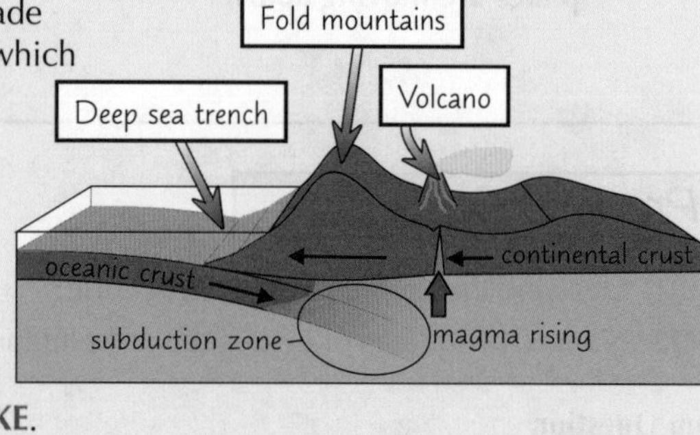

Oceanic-Oceanic

1) Most of the same processes occur where two plates of **oceanic crust** are moving towards each other — the **denser** of the two will be **subducted**, forming a **DEEP SEA TRENCH** and triggering **EARTHQUAKES** and **VOLCANIC ERUPTIONS**.
2) **Volcanic eruptions** that take place **underwater** (e.g. when two plates of oceanic crust converge) create **ISLAND ARCS** — clusters of islands that sit in a curved line, e.g. the **Mariana Islands**.

Types of Plate Margin

Continental-Continental

1) Where two plates of **continental crust** move towards each other, **neither** is subducted so there **aren't any volcanoes** — but the pressure that builds up between them can cause **EARTHQUAKES**.
2) **FOLD MOUNTAINS** form when continental crusts converge. E.g. the **Himalayas** were created in this way.

Only Earthquakes Occur at Conservative Plate Margins

1) A **conservative margin** occurs where two plates are moving **PAST EACH OTHER**.
2) The two plates get **locked together** in places and **pressure builds up**. As with destructive margins, this causes the plates to **jerk** past each other (or to **crack**, forming **fault lines**), releasing the **energy** as an **EARTHQUAKE**.
3) For example, the **Pacific plate** is moving past the **North American plate**. Many earthquakes occur along this margin and along its fault lines, e.g. along the **San Andreas fault** in **California**.

©PETER MENZEL / SCIENCE PHOTO LIBRARY

*Here's a **Summary** for Each Plate Margin — Learn It*

Have a look back at the map on page 2 — it'll tell you where the plates are.

Type of margin		Example	Landforms	Earthquakes?	Volcanoes?
Constructive		Eurasian plate and North American plate	• Mid-ocean ridges (when underwater) • Rift valleys (when under land)	Yes	Yes
Destructive	Oceanic-Continental	Nazca plate and South American plate	• Deep sea trenches • Young fold mountains	Yes	Yes
	Oceanic-Oceanic	Pacific plate and Philippine plate	• Deep sea trenches • Island arcs	Yes	Yes
	Continental-Continental	Indo-Australian plate and Eurasian plate	Fold mountains	Yes	No
Conservative		North American plate and Pacific plate	Low ridges	Yes	No

Practice Questions

Q1 Name the two landforms that are created at constructive margins.

Q2 Explain what happens when two continental plates meet.

Q3 Name the two types of plate margin where no volcanic activity takes place.

Q4 Give one example of each type of plate margin.

Exam Questions

Q1 Describe the features of constructive plate margins. [8 marks]

Q2 Compare and contrast margins where two oceanic plates are converging with margins where two continental plates are converging. [8 marks]

Tectonic plates are great — but they do have their faults...

Well that wasn't too bad at all, and you even got out of a 40-mark exam question. Hmm, maybe I've been a bit lenient with you — too much carrot and not enough stick. Right then, before you can move on to the next couple of pages you have to know every little bit about each of these types of plate margin, as well as an example. And yes, I do mean every little bit — get learning.

Volcanic Activity

These pages cover all your classic eruption-style volcanic activity, but they also go that little bit further. Yep, not all lava's the same you know, and we're also talking bubbling pools of mud, fountains of steam and plumes of magma.

Volcanic Activity can be Intrusive or Extrusive

1) The **high pressure** inside the Earth keeps rocks in some parts of the mantle **semi-molten**.
2) When this pressure is **released**, e.g. at constructive boundaries, the rocks become **molten**. The hot molten rock is called **magma**.
3) Because magma is **less dense** than the rock around it, it **rises up** towards the Earth's surface.
4) **Most** magma **doesn't reach the surface**, but some does — the type of **volcanic activity** depends on where the magma ends up:

Once magma erupts from the Earth's surface it's called lava.

INTRUSIVE volcanic activity
- This takes place **BENEATH** the **Earth's surface**.
- It includes the formation of **large magma chambers** and **magma** being **forced into the crust** (through cracks in the rock).

EXTRUSIVE volcanic activity
- This takes place **ON** the **Earth's surface**.
- The **major form** of this activity is **volcanic eruptions** of **lava** and other material.
- **Minor types** of extrusive volcanic activity include **hot springs**, **geysers** and **boiling mud pools**.

Intrusive Volcanic Activity forms Dykes, Sills and Batholiths

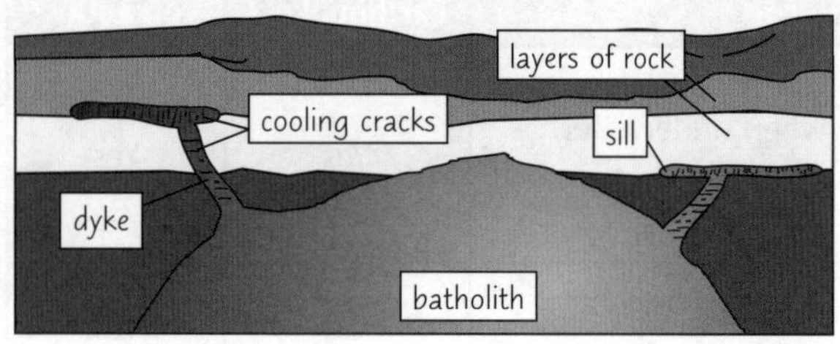

1) When large chambers of magma **cool underground** they form domes of igneous rock called **batholiths**.
2) Where the magma has flowed into **gaps** in the surrounding rock and cooled it forms vertical **dykes** (across the layers of rock) and horizontal **sills** (between the layers of rock).
3) Cracks may form as the magma cools — these are called (wait for it...) **cooling cracks**. In a sill they're **vertical**, and in a dyke they're **horizontal**.

Batholiths (e.g. the Sierra Nevada batholith in the US) can become exposed if the rock layers above them are eroded away.

Lava Eruptions are a form of Extrusive Activity

1) There are **three** main types of lava:

- **BASALTIC lava** is made at **CONSTRUCTIVE** plate margins.
- **ANDESITIC lava** is made at **DESTRUCTIVE** plate margins.
- **RHYOLITIC lava** is made at **DESTRUCTIVE** plate margins.

2) The **different types** of lava have **different chemical compositions** — and it's the chemical composition that controls the **viscosity** (thickness) and **temperature** of the lava:

	BASALTIC LAVA	ANDESITIC LAVA	RHYOLITIC LAVA
Silica content	Low	Medium	High
Viscosity	Low (runny)	Medium	High (thick and sticky)
Temperature of eruption	Over 950 °C (usually 1100 - 1200 °C)	750 - 950 °C	Less than 750 °C

3) **Basaltic lava** has a **low viscosity** so it flows easily and gas can escape from it easily. As a result, eruptions of basaltic lava **aren't violent**. Basaltic lavas usually erupt **frequently** and for **long periods** of time.
4) **Andesitic** and **rhyolitic lavas** have a **higher viscosity** than basaltic lava. They flow less easily, and often form **blockages** in volcanic vents. Also, volcanic gases can't escape easily from viscous lava. **Pressure** builds up because of the lava blockages and trapped gases, until the blockages are cleared by a **violent eruption**. Andesitic and rhyolitic lavas usually erupt **intermittently** (every once in a while) and the eruptions are **short-lived**.

Volcanic Activity

There are Lots of **Different Types** of **Volcano**

DOME VOLCANO

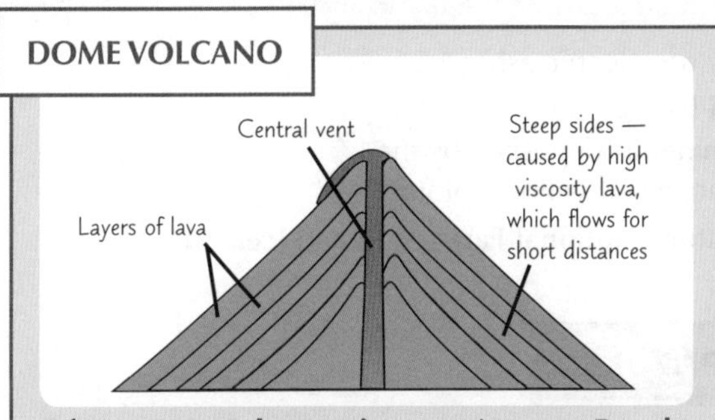

Often occur at **destructive** margins, e.g. **Puy de Dome in France**. The lava from dome volcanoes tends to be either **rhyolitic** or **andesitic**.

A composite volcano (or stratovolcano) is similar to a dome volcano except that it has layers of lava alternating with layers of ash and cinders.

SHIELD VOLCANO

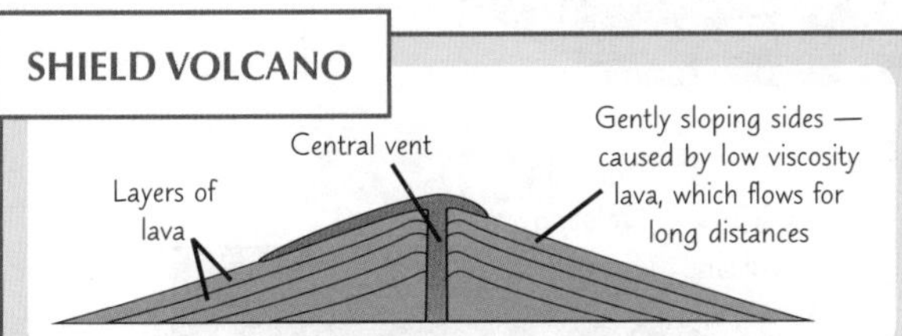

Often occur at **constructive** margins or **hotspots** (see p. 10), e.g. **Mauna Loa** in **Hawaii**. Shield volcanoes usually produce **basaltic lava**.

CALDERA

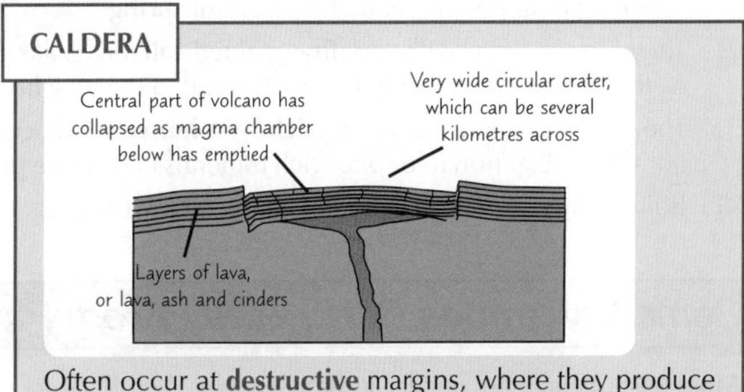

Often occur at **destructive** margins, where they produce **andesitic** and **rhyolitic lavas**, e.g. **Aira Caldera** in **Japan**.

FISSURE VOLCANO

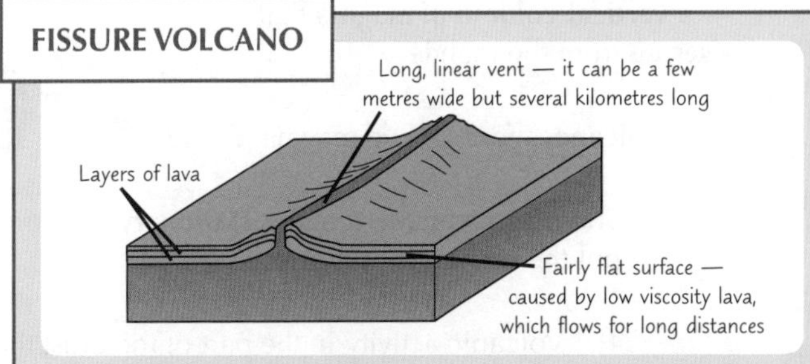

Also called a fissure vent or volcanic fissure. Often occur at **constructive** margins, e.g. **Laki Fissure System** in **Iceland**. Fissure volcanoes usually produce **basaltic lava**.

Hot Springs are **Springs**... of **Hot Water**

1) **Springs** are places where **groundwater** emerges at the **surface**.
2) If the **groundwater source** of a spring flows **close** to an area of recent **intrusive volcanic activity**, the water is heated and the spring becomes a **hot spring**.
3) The **temperature** of hot springs varies from around **20 °C** to over **90 °C**.
4) Hot spring water often has a **high mineral content** because hot water can hold a lot of dissolved solids.
5) Hot springs are found **all over the world** and are often popular with **tourists**, e.g. the springs in **Rio Hondo** (Argentina) and **North Island** (New Zealand).

Geysers are **Hot Springs** where the **Water Erupts**

Hot springs, geysers and mud pools are often called geothermal features.

1) Geysers are a type of hot spring where **hot water** and **steam** are ejected from the surface in a **fountain**. They form in areas of **intense volcanic activity** — this is what happens:
   - **Groundwater** is **heated** to above **boiling point** by **magma** deep in the crust.
   - The hot water becomes **pressurised** and forces its way to the surface along **cracks** in the rocks. Finally, the hot water and steam spray out from a **vent**.
2) Geysers **erupt periodically**. This is because they only erupt when the **pressure** has built up enough to **force** the water **out of the ground**.
3) Examples of geysers are **Strokkur** (Iceland) and **Old Faithful** in Yellowstone National Park (USA).

The Strokkur Geyser in Iceland

Volcanic Activity

Boiling Mud Pools... you guessed it... are Pools of Boiling Mud

1) A **boiling mud pool** is another type of **hot spring**.
2) They form in areas with **very fine-grained soil** (e.g. soil rich in clay or volcanic ash) — the hot spring water **mixes** with the soil to create a **hot muddy pool**.
3) The pools sometimes contain **brightly-coloured mud** because of **minerals** deposited by the hot water. E.g. iron and sulfur-rich minerals can create purple, orange and yellow colours.
4) Boiling mud pools can be found all over the world, e.g. in **Yellowstone National Park** (USA) and **Iceland**.

Some Volcanoes Occur Away From Plate Margins

Most volcanic activity occurs at **plate margins**, but there are some areas of **intense volcanic activity** that **aren't** near any plate margins. These areas are called **hot spots**:

1) A hot spot is caused by a **magma plume** — a **vertical column of magma** that **rises up** from the mantle.
2) **Volcanoes** form above magma plumes.

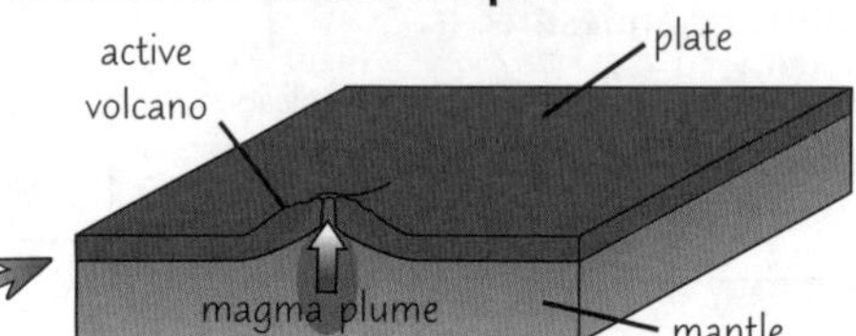

3) The **magma plume** remains **stationary** over time, but the **crust moves** above it.
4) Volcanic activity in the part of the crust that **was** above the hot spot **decreases** as it moves away.
5) **New volcanoes** form in the part of the crust that is **now above** the hot spot.

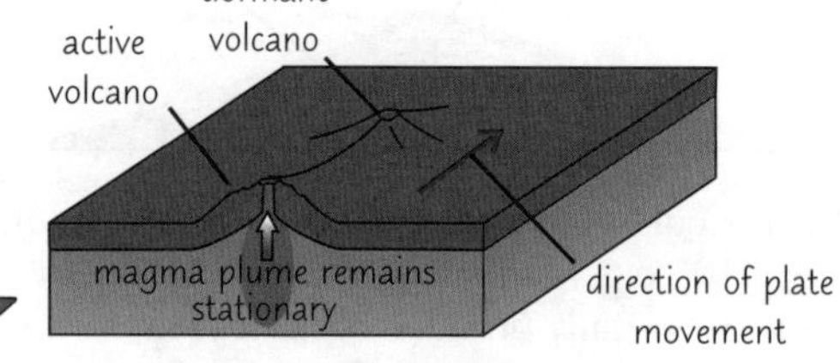

6) As the crust continues to move, a **chain of volcanoes** is formed.
7) There's a hot spot in **Hawaii** (USA).

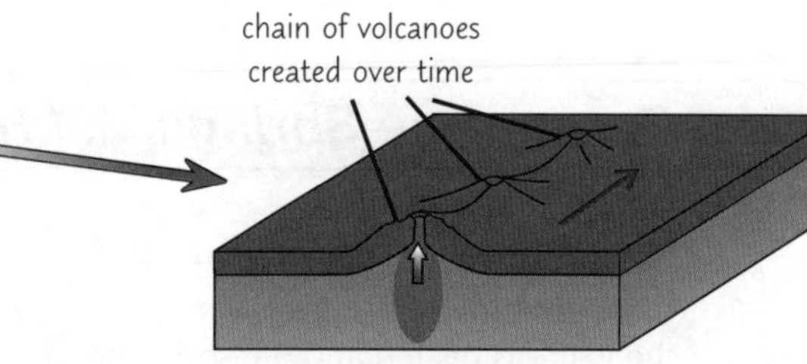

Yep, Hawaii's definitely Kevin's idea of a hot spot.

Practice Questions

Q1 What is intrusive volcanic activity?

Q2 Describe how batholiths, sills and dykes are formed.

Q3 Briefly describe the characteristics of the three main types of lava.

Q4 What type of lava is made at constructive plate margins?

Kauai — around 6 million years old

Oahu — around 3 million years old

Maui — around 1.3 million years old

Hawaii — around 500,000 years old

N

Exam Questions

Q1 The diagram shows the names and estimated ages of some of the Hawaiian islands. Describe and explain the distribution of the islands in relation to hotspots. [7 marks]

Q2 Yellowstone National Park contains many features such as geysers and boiling mud pools. Explain how these features form. [8 marks]

Mr Basil Tic is one hot guy...

*Ooh, lots to learn here — yes indeed. No need to panic though — just take it slowly, one type of volcano and one type of lava at a time. Try quickly scribbling out diagrams of the different types of volcano to get it all clear in your mind. My challenge to you, dear reader, is to know it all before you turn the page. And your prize for knowing every last fascinating scrap of it will be...**

*er, a slightly bigger brain.

Seismic Activity

Earthquakes happen more often than you think. Obviously there are the big ones that cause loads of damage and make the headlines on the news, but there are also lots of weak earthquakes every year that hardly anyone notices. Sneaky.

Earthquakes are ***Caused*** *by* ***Tectonic Plate Movement***

1) Earthquakes are caused by the **tension** that builds up at **all three** types of **plate margin** — see pages 6 and 7.
2) When the plates **jerk past each other** it sends out **SEISMIC WAVES** (vibrations). These vibrations are the **earthquake**.
3) The seismic waves **spread out** from the **FOCUS** — the place **in** the lithosphere where the earthquake **starts**. The focus doesn't have to be a single point — for example, it could be along a **fault line**. Near the focus the waves are **stronger** and cause **more damage**.
4) The **EPICENTRE** is the point **on the Earth's surface** where the earthquake is **felt first**. It's **straight above** the **focus**.

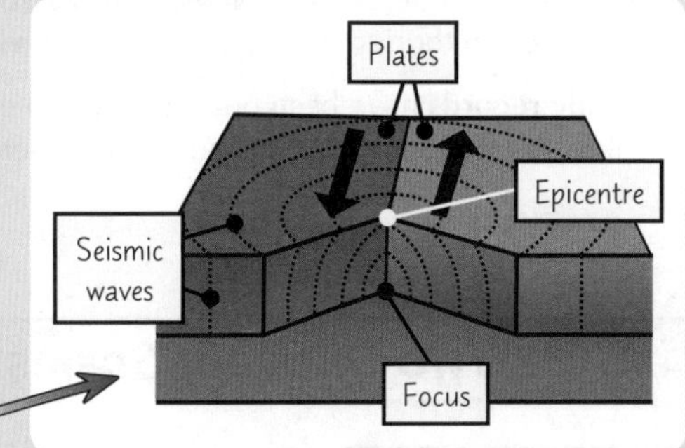

Although **most** earthquakes are caused by movement at **plate boundaries**, there are **other** possible **causes**:

- **Reactivation** of **old fault lines** that have not been active for a long time.
- **Subsidence** (when the ground sinks) as a result of **deep mining**.
- **Pressure on surface rocks** from water in large **reservoirs**.

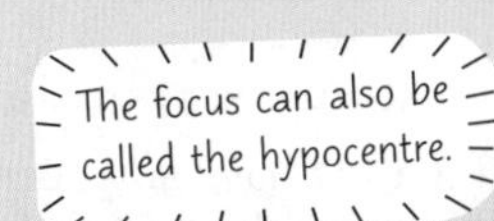

5) Earthquakes cause **damage** in various ways — they can cause structures to **collapse** (e.g. buildings, bridges), cause **tsunamis** (see next page), **avalanches**, **landslides** or **liquefaction** (where waterlogged soil behaves like a liquid).

There are ***Three*** *Main Types of* ***Seismic Wave***

Some seismic waves travel through the **interior** of the Earth:

P (or primary) **waves** can travel through **solids** and **liquids**. The waves **push and pull** the earth in the **same direction** as the wave is **travelling**. They travel **faster** than other types of seismic wave.

Compression

Vibrations in same direction as wave is travelling

S (or secondary) **waves** can travel through **solids** but **not liquids**. The waves move the earth at **90°** to the **direction of travel**. These waves can cause a **lot of damage** because of their **shearing effect**.

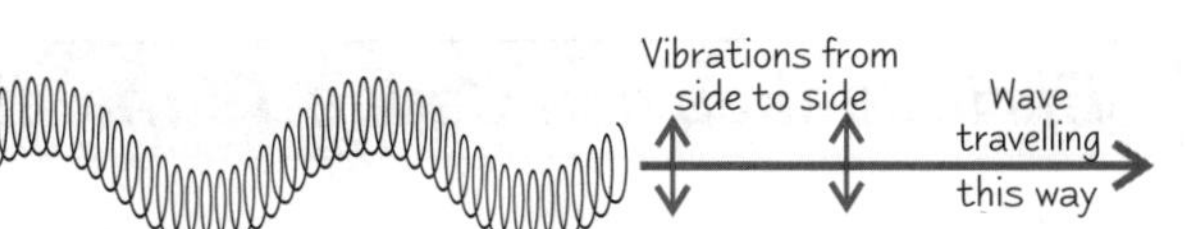

Others can only travel near the Earth's **surface** (in the **crust**):

Surface waves come in two varieties and travel **more slowly** than P and S waves.

- **Love waves** can only travel through **solids**. They move the surface from **side to side**. These waves also cause a **lot of damage** because of their **shearing effect**.
- **Rayleigh waves** can travel through **liquids** and **solids**. They move the surface in a **rolling motion** — just picture a wave moving across an ocean.

Seismic Activity

*Earthquakes can be **Measured** Using **Seismometers***

1) The amount of **energy released** by an earthquake can be measured using a **seismometer**.
2) Seismometers measure the **magnitude** (strength) of earthquakes — the amount of energy they release. They also measure the **duration** and **direction** (horizontal or vertical) of the **vibrations**.
3) **Seismic records** have been built up over time, which allow us to look at the **frequency** of earthquakes in different areas.

Seismometers are also called seismographs or seismoscopes.

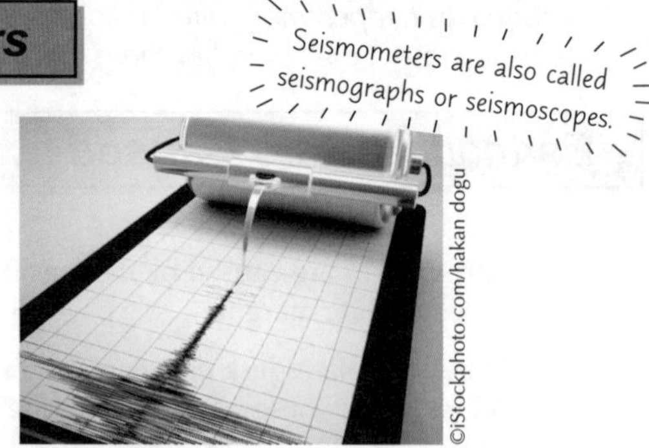

©iStockphoto.com/hakan dogu

*There are **Two Different Scales** for **Measuring Earthquakes***

THE RICHTER SCALE

1) The **Richter scale** measures the magnitude of an earthquake.
2) It doesn't have an upper limit and it's **logarithmic** — this means that an earthquake with a magnitude of **5** has an amplitude (wave size) **ten times greater** than one with a magnitude of **4**.
3) Each value on the scale also represents about **30 times more energy released** than the previous value.
4) Most people **don't feel** earthquakes of magnitude **1-2**. **Major** earthquakes are **above 7**.

THE MERCALLI SCALE

1) The **Mercalli scale** measures the **impacts** of an earthquake (see diagram on right).
2) The impacts are measured using **observations** of the event (e.g. reports and photos).
3) The scale is between **1 and 12**, with **1** being an earthquake that's only detected by **instruments**, and **12** being an earthquake that causes **total destruction**.

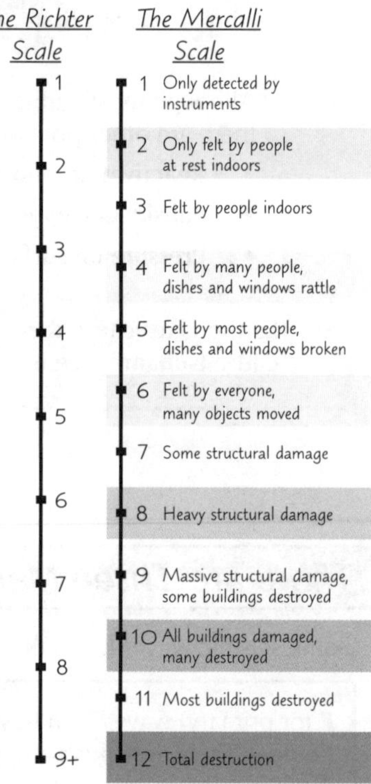

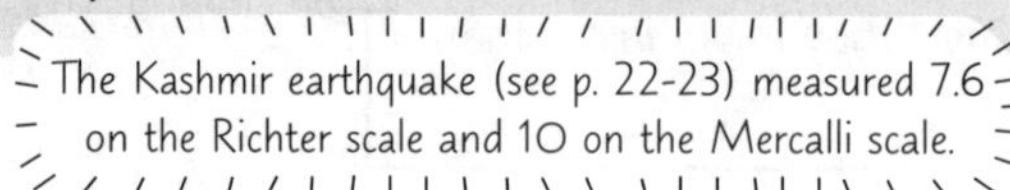

The Kashmir earthquake (see p. 22-23) measured 7.6 on the Richter scale and 10 on the Mercalli scale.

Earthquakes** can **Cause Tsunamis

1) Tsunamis are **large waves** caused by the **displacement** of large volumes of **water**.
2) They can be triggered by **underwater earthquakes**. The earthquakes cause the seabed to move, which displaces water. Waves **radiate** out from the **epicentre** of the earthquake. The **greater** the **movement** of the sea floor, the greater the volume of water displaced, and the **bigger** the **wave** produced.
3) **Volcanic eruptions** and **landslides** that slide into the sea can also displace large volumes of water and **cause tsunamis**.
4) A tsunami will usually be **more powerful** if it starts **close to the coast**. This is because the waves **lose energy** as they travel towards land. So, the closer to the coast the waves start, the less energy they will lose.
5) The waves travel **very fast** in deep water so they can hit the shore **without much warning**. This means that they can cause a **high death toll**.

The word tsunami comes from the Japanese words 'tsu' meaning harbour and 'nami' meaning wave.

Seismic Activity

Tsunami Waves **Increase** in **Height** When They Get **Close To Land**

1) Tsunamis **don't** just affect the **surface** of the water — they affect the **whole column** of water from the surface down to the seabed.
2) In the **open ocean** where the water's **very deep**, the waves travel at **high speeds** of 500-950 km/h. They have a **long wavelength** of about 200 km, and a **small amplitude** (wave height) of about 1 m.
3) **Closer to land** the water gets **shallower**. This causes the waves to get **compressed** (squashed together) and their **energy** becomes **more concentrated**. The waves **slow down** to less than 80 km/h, their **wavelength decreases** to less than 20 km, and their **amplitude increases** to many metres.
4) Just before the tsunami reaches the **coast**, the water **withdraws** down the shore (this is called drawback).
5) The wave then hits with **great force**, but only travels a **short distance inland**.

Aidan was unimpressed with the energy of Santa's wave.

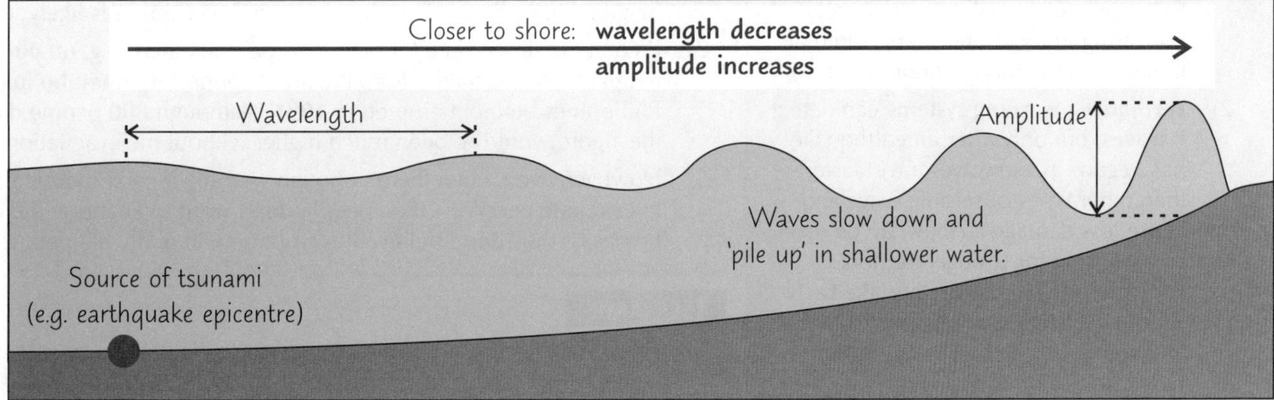

Practice Questions

Q1 Describe what the focus of an earthquake is.

Q2 What is the epicentre of an earthquake?

Q3 Apart from movement at plate boundaries, give three other possible causes of earthquakes.

Q4 Why are seismic records useful?

Q5 What is the Richter scale?

Q6 What scale is used to measure the impacts of an earthquake?

Exam Questions

Q1 Describe the different types of seismic wave. [8 marks]

Q2 Describe the causes and characteristics of tsunamis. [8 marks]

The Beach Boys' seismometer — great for picking up good vibrations...

The problem with tsunamis is that they travel so fast — even if you knew one was coming, you wouldn't have much time to get out of its way. That's one of the reasons why the Indian Ocean tsunami caused so much loss of life back in 2004. It goes without saying then, that managing the impacts of tsunamis is a tad tricky — which brings us neatly to the next page...

Managing the Impacts of Tectonic Hazards

Dear me, all this talk of volcanoes, earthquakes and tsunamis is a bit alarming. Panic ye not — a bit of management can help.

*The **Impacts** of **Hazards** caused by **Tectonic Processes** can be **Managed***

1) A **hazard** is something that's a **potential threat** to **human life** or **property**.
2) **Tectonic hazards** (e.g. **earthquakes**, **volcanoes** and **tsunamis**) are hazards **caused** by **movement of tectonic plates**.
3) Tectonic hazards can have **many impacts** on people and their environment. However, some of these impacts can be reduced by **management strategies** such as **prediction**, **building techniques**, **planning** and **education**.

Predicting When and Where a Hazard Will Occur Really Helps

EARTHQUAKES

1) It's currently **impossible** to **predict when** an earthquake will happen, but there can be **clues** that an earthquake is about to happen, e.g. small tremors, cracks appearing in rocks and strange animal behaviour (e.g. rats abandoning nests).
2) **Earthquake warning systems** can detect **P waves**, but only **after** an earthquake has **begun**. These waves travel faster than other types of seismic wave and cause less damage so they can be used as a **warning** for stronger tremors. For example, **Japan's Earthquake Early Warning system** was set up in 2007 and warns people by **TV** and **radio**. However, even far away from the epicentre the warnings may only arrive a **few seconds** before the **strong tremors**.
3) It's **possible** to **predict where** future earthquakes may happen using **data** from **past earthquakes** — these places can **prepare themselves** for the **impacts** of an earthquake.

VOLCANOES

1) Unlike earthquakes, it's **possible** to **roughly predict when** a **volcanic eruption** will happen. For example, **tiny earthquakes** and **changes** in the **shape** of the volcano (e.g. bulges in the land where magma has built up under it) can mean an **eruption** is **likely**.
2) Prediction allows time for people to be **evacuated**, e.g. **60 000 people** were evacuated from the area around **Mt. Pinatubo** in the Philippines before it erupted in **1991**. Although 800 people died, this figure would've been much higher without the evacuation.
3) However, even when there's enough warning it can be **difficult** to **evacuate** people. Often people **don't want** to abandon their homes or they **don't believe** the eruption will really happen.

TSUNAMIS

1) **Tsunami warning systems** rely on **earthquake detection systems**. If an **earthquake** occurs in a place that's **likely** to cause a **tsunami** (e.g. under an ocean), a **warning** is issued.
2) There are **tsunami warning centres** all around the world. For example, The USA's National Oceanic and Atmospheric Administration (**NOAA**) runs centres in **Alaska** and **Hawaii**.
3) Early warnings give people **time to evacuate**. However, they rely on **good communication systems**. If people **don't receive** the warning message they **won't evacuate**. Also, if an earthquake happens **very close to land**, the tsunami will **reach the coast very quickly** and people won't be warned early enough to evacuate.

Building Techniques can Physically Protect People

Building techniques can be used to **protect people** from some of the effects of tectonic hazards. However, they're **more expensive** than standard building techniques.

EARTHQUAKES

1) **Buildings** can be **designed** to **withstand earthquakes**, e.g. by using strong materials like reinforced concrete or building special foundations that absorb an earthquake's energy.
2) **Construction laws** in some earthquake-prone countries (e.g. Japan and the US) have become **stricter** in recent years — this means that **newer buildings** are more likely to be able to **withstand earthquakes**.

VOLCANOES

1) Buildings **can't be designed** to **withstand lava flows**. However, they can be **strengthened** so they're **less likely** to **collapse** due to the weight of falling ash.
2) It's sometimes possible to **divert** the lava from a volcano **away from settlements** using **barriers**. For example, when **Etna** in Italy erupted in 1983 a **rubble barrier** 10 m high and 400 m long was built on its slopes, which **successfully diverted** the lava flow. However, this is only possible where the **lava** is **slow moving** and there's sufficient **warning**.

Managing the Impacts of Tectonic Hazards

TSUNAMIS

1) **Buildings** designed with **raised, open foundations** and made of strong materials such as **concrete** are less likely to be damaged by the force of the water during a tsunami.
2) In some places, e.g. Hokkaido (Japan), **tsunami walls** have been built **around settlements** to protect them. They're not always effective though, e.g. some tsunamis have overtopped them.

Planning and *Education* can be *Cost Effective Methods*

1) **Future developments**, e.g. new houses, can be **planned** to **avoid** the **areas most at risk**, e.g. close to an active volcano.
2) **Emergency services** can **train** and **prepare** for disasters. For example, **FEMA** in the USA train emergency personnel to deal with all sorts of disasters.
3) Governments can plan **evacuation routes**. For example, in **Oregon** (USA) leaflets are provided containing evacuation route maps in case of a tsunami.
4) **Governments** and other **organisations** can **educate people** about **what to do** if there's a disaster and **how to evacuate**. For example, earthquake and tsunami **drills** are practised regularly in **Japan**.
5) All these methods are **very cost-effective** ways of reducing the impacts.

Rupert wasn't keen on education. He did have a plan though.

Some Factors can *Increase* the *Severity* of the *Impacts*

DEVELOPMENT LEVEL OF A COUNTRY

1) The impacts are **higher** in **less developed countries** than in more developed countries. The main reason is that they **don't have the money** for disaster preparation or response, e.g. they have no money to spend on training emergency teams.
2) Also, the **buildings** are **poorer quality** than in more developed countries, so are **more easily damaged** by hazards.
3) **Infrastructure** is often **poorer**, making it **more difficult** for **emergency services** to **reach affected areas**.
4) **Health care isn't as good** in less developed countries, so they **struggle** to **treat large numbers** of **casualties**.
5) **Many people depend on agriculture** in less developed countries, which is often badly affected by eruptions or tsunamis.
6) However, the **economic impact** is often **higher** in **more developed** countries as the **buildings** and **infrastructure** damaged are **worth a lot of money**.

POPULATION

1) Obviously, the **more people** in an **area**, the **more people** will be **affected** by a disaster.
2) **Densely populated areas** such as cities have a lot of **buildings**. **Collapsing** buildings pose a big risk to life, particularly during **earthquakes**.
3) It can be difficult to **evacuate large numbers** of people because the **routes** are often **limited**. For example, if everyone in an area tries to drive away from a volcano the roads will quickly become clogged and people will be trapped.

TIMING

1) **When** in the **day** or **year** a disaster happens can have an effect on the severity of its impacts.
2) For example, if an earthquake occurs in the **middle of the night** most people will be **asleep**, so they **don't** get out of buildings as **quickly** and more people are hurt.
3) Also, if an earthquake occurs during **winter**, people can freeze to death before they can be rescued.

Practice Questions

Q1 How can the development level of a country affect the severity of the impacts of tectonic hazards?

Q2 Explain why the timing of a tectonic hazard may affect the severity of its impacts.

Exam Question

Q1 Critically evaluate the strategies used to manage the impacts of tectonic hazards. [40 marks]

If in doubt — run...

These two pages may seem a bit daunting at first, but it's worth putting the effort in to learn it all — this is just the kind of stuff that you could get a long essay question about. In fact, just look at the practice exam question — what are the chances...

Volcanic Eruption Case Study — Montserrat

Get your brain into gear and get ready to learn some facts and figures — it's case study time.

*The **Soufrière Hills** Volcano in **Montserrat** Erupted on **25th June 1997***

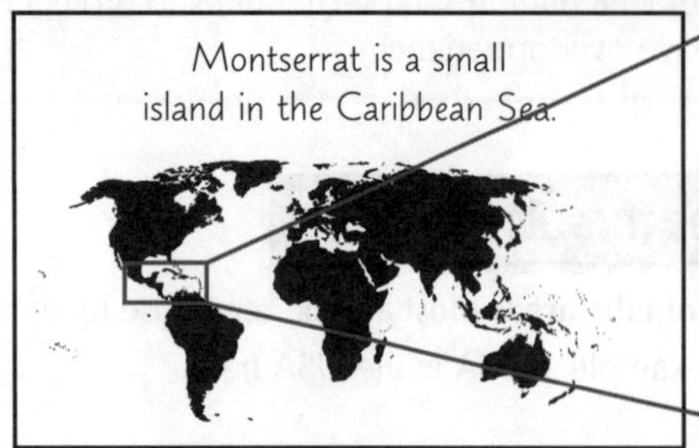

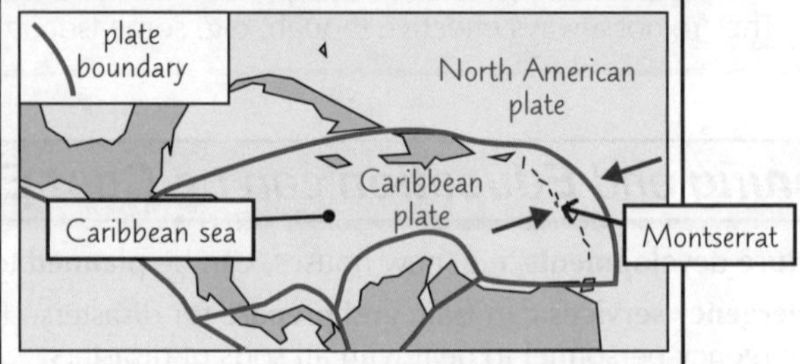

1) The **Soufrière Hills volcano** is a **composite volcano** in Montserrat.
2) Montserrat is above a **destructive plate margin**, where the **North American plate** is being **forced under** the **Caribbean plate**.
3) In **1995**, **earthquakes**, **small eruptions** and **lahars** started. These continued until 1997.
4) On **25th June 1997** there was a series of **small earthquakes**. This was followed by **pyroclastic flows** (fast flowing streams of hot volcanic material and gases).

©iStockphoto.com/MichaelUtech

5) After more earthquakes the **main eruption** happened. About **4-5 million m³** of material was released over a **20 minute period**. **Pyroclastic flows** covered several square kilometres and reached within **50 m** of the airport, which was 5.5 km north of the volcano. The eruption also produced a **large ash cloud**.
6) There were **further eruptions** over the next **few months** and the airport was destroyed by a **pyroclastic flow** on 21st September 1997.

Lahars are mudflows — volcanic material mixed with water.

*There were **Many Impacts***

ECONOMIC IMPACTS

1) The **total loss in value** of people's homes and investments was estimated to be about **£1 billion**.
2) Over **20 villages** and **two thirds of homes** on the island were **destroyed** by **pyroclastic flows**.
3) **Tourists stayed away** and **businesses** were **destroyed**, disrupting the **economy**. However, **tourism** on the island is now **increasing** as people come to **see the volcano**.
4) **Schools, hospitals**, the **airport** and the **port** were **destroyed**.

SOCIAL IMPACTS

1) **19 people died** and seven were injured.
2) **Hundreds** of people **lost** their **homes**.
3) **Fires destroyed** many buildings, e.g. local **government offices**, the **police headquarters** and **petrol stations**.
4) The **population has declined** — **8000** of the island's 12 000 inhabitants **have left** since the eruptions began in **1995**. Around **4000** of those came to the UK.

ENVIRONMENTAL IMPACTS

1) **Large areas** were **covered** with **volcanic material** — the capital city **Plymouth** was buried under **12 m of mud and ash**.
2) **Vegetation** and **farmland** were **destroyed**.
3) **Volcanic ash** from the eruption has **improved soil fertility**.

Volcanic Eruption Case Study — Montserrat

Responses Included Help from the Emergency Services and Aid

The responses to the eruption were both short-term and long-term:

1) **People** were **evacuated** from the south to **safe areas** in the north. The first evacuations took place in **1995**.
2) **Shelters** were **built** to house evacuees.
3) Temporary **infrastructure** was also built, e.g. **roads** and **electricity supplies**.
4) The **UK** provided **£17 million** of **emergency aid** (Montserrat's an overseas territory of the UK).
5) **Local emergency services** provided support units to **search** for and **rescue** survivors.
6) A **risk map** was created and an **exclusion zone** is in place. The south of the island is **off-limits** while the volcano is **still intermittently active**.
7) The **UK** has provided **£41 million** of long-term aid to develop the north of the island — **new docks**, an **airport** and **houses** have been built with this.
8) The **Montserrat Volcano Observatory** has been set up to try and **predict** future eruptions.

Little Management Before the Event Increased the Severity of the Impacts

1) **Scientists** had studied the volcano in the **1980s** but their report wasn't given a lot of attention.
2) There was **no disaster management plan** for a volcanic eruption. So when the volcano started erupting the **responses** were **slow**.
3) Also, in the **1990s** key **infrastructure** had been built in areas at **risk**, so when the volcano erupted it was **destroyed** — this further hampered the response.

©iStockphoto.com/Sean Hannah

The city of Plymouth in Montserrat buried under ash and mud by the eruption.

Practice Questions

Q1 In which year did the main Soufrière Hills volcano eruption occur?

Q2 What type of volcano is the Soufrière Hills volcano?

Q3 Give two economic impacts of the eruption.

Q4 Give one environmental impact of the eruption.

Q5 Briefly describe the responses to the eruption.

Q6 Describe one way in which hazard management affected the severity of the event.

Exam Question

Q1 With reference to an example you have studied, describe the impacts of a volcanic event and the responses to it. [8 marks]

Maybe Caribbean islands aren't so idyllic after all...

The scientists at the volcano observatory on Montserrat monitor loads of things all over the volcano. For example, they take thermal images of the dome to see how hot different bits are, they measure earthquakes in the area and they monitor how the ground is bulging using lasers. If things look like they're hotting up they issue alerts so everyone knows to hightail it out of there. Eeek.

Volcanic Eruption Case Study — Mt St Helens

As if one volcano case study wasn't enough, it's time for a second one. It doesn't matter if you've studied different volcanoes in class — if you have, learn those instead. Just make sure you know all about two different case studies.

Mount St Helens** Erupted on **18th May 1980

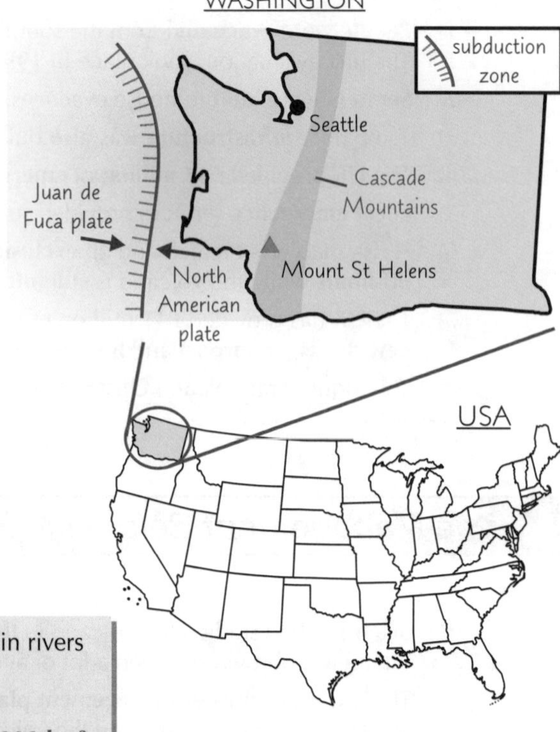

1) **Mount St Helens** in **Washington** (USA) is one of several volcanic peaks in the Cascade Mountains.
2) The Cascade Mountains are above a **destructive plate margin**, where the **Juan de Fuca plate** is being **forced under** the **North American plate**.
3) Mount St Helens is a **composite volcano**.
4) From March 1980, there were **signs** that an **eruption** could happen soon — there were small **earthquakes**, a **bulge** appeared on the side of the volcano and **ash** and **steam** were released.
5) On **18th May** 1980 there was a **large earthquake** of magnitude **5.1** followed by a massive **eruption** of **volcanic material** — including **rocks**, **ash**, **hot gases**, **steam** and **lava**.
6) The eruption covered a **600 km² fan-shaped area** north of the volcano (**the blast zone**). Almost all **vegetation** and **buildings** were **destroyed** in the blast zone which reached up to about **30 km** away from the volcano.
7) **Pyroclastic flows**, **lahars** and **floods** (due to material being dumped in rivers and lakes, displacing water) were caused by the eruption.
8) Shortly afterwards there was another eruption of **ash** and **steam**. About **540 million tonnes of ash** were deposited over an area of **57 000 km²**.

*The Eruption was the **Most Economically Destructive** Ever in the **USA***

ECONOMIC IMPACTS

1) The **total cost** of the damage was around **$1.1 billion**.
2) Over **200 homes and cabins** were **destroyed** and many more were **damaged**.
3) **Airports** were temporarily **closed** (some for up to two weeks) because of reduced visibility. Over **1000 commercial flights** were **cancelled**.
4) A lot of money had to be spent on **clearing ash** from roads and runways, e.g. it cost **$2.2 million** to clear the ash in Yakima (a city 135 km from the volcano).
5) **27 bridges**, **24 km of railways** and around **300 km of roads** were destroyed.
6) **River traffic** and **shipping** was disrupted, and 31 ships were stranded because **mudflows** dumped huge amounts of **sediment** in rivers.
7) The **timber industry** was severely affected by the destruction of forest.

SOCIAL IMPACTS

1) **57 people** were **killed** — mostly by inhaling volcanic ash.
2) **Hundreds** of people **lost** their **homes**.
3) **Unemployment** rose **tenfold** at first — although this did return to normal once clean-up operations began.
4) **Social facilities** and **recreational sites** were **destroyed**.
5) Some people experienced **emotional stress**.

ENVIRONMENTAL IMPACTS

1) Almost **240 km²** of **forest** was **destroyed**.
2) **Wildlife** suffered — around **7000 big game animals** (e.g. deer, elk and bear) and many thousands of **birds** and **small mammals** were **killed**. Around 12 million young salmon were also killed.
3) **Sediment** dumped in **Spirit Lake** raised the lake bottom by over 90 m and the water level by over 60 m.
4) **Water quality** was temporarily **reduced**.

Volcanic Eruption Case Study — Mt St Helens

Responses Included Emergency Shelters and Ash Clearance

Emergency responses were **coordinated** by **FEMA** (Federal Emergency Management Agency) and involved both **national organisations** (e.g. the US Army Corps of Engineers) and **local services** (e.g. local emergency services).

- **Face masks** were distributed in some areas to protect people from breathing in ash.
- **Emergency shelters** were set up for stranded and homeless people.
- **Ash clean-up operations** were organised — around **900 000 tonnes** of ash were removed from **roads**, **buildings** and **airports**.
- **Shipping channels** were cleared of sediment to restore shipping and some **new channels** were cut.
- **45 500 acres** of land have been **replanted** with more than **18.4 million trees**.
- **Domestic water supplies** were monitored to ensure they weren't contaminated.

The ash clean-up operation near Mount St Helens.

Mount St Helens was declared a 'National Monument' in 1982. 445 km^2 is now a protected and preserved area — it's used for scientific study, education, recreation and tourism.

Good Management Meant That Hazardous Areas Were Evacuated

1) When the earthquakes began in March, the **USGS** (United States Geological Survey) started a round-the-clock **monitoring system**. It included **gathering seismic data** and measuring the **rate of bulge growth**, **ground temperature** and **sulfur dioxide gas emissions**. Volcanic and seismic activity **reports** were **issued daily**.
2) USGS scientists issued **warnings** to people living in the area and made **recommendations** about the **locations of hazardous zones**.
3) Based on these recommendations, in **March** access to the volcano was **restricted** and the evacuation of around **2000 people** was started.
4) Despite the monitoring data, scientists **couldn't accurately predict** the eruption — on the **day of the eruption** there were **no unusual changes** that could be taken as warning signs.

Practice Questions

Q1 When did Mount St Helens erupt?

Q2 What type of plate boundary is Mount St Helens situated on?

Q3 What type of volcano is Mount St Helens?

Q4 What were the warning signs that Mount St Helens was going to erupt?

Exam Question

Q1 With reference to two volcanic eruptions you have studied, contrast how managing the hazard affected the severity of its impacts. [10 marks]

Hmm, Juan de Fuca — there must be a joke in there somewhere...

When it comes to case studies, it's the details that count. When examiners ask about them, they're looking for answers packed with specific facts and figures — vague waffle just won't cut it, I'm afraid. So go through this case study again and get learning the when, the why, how many, how big, how small, how long, how short, how wide, how narrow, how fast, how slow, how's your father...

Earthquake Case Study — L'Aquila

Italy — the home of pasta, pizza, Pisa... and a surprising number of earthquakes.

The **L'Aquila Earthquake** Happened on **6th April 2009**

1) **L'Aquila** is a city in **central Italy** with a population of around **70 000 people**.
2) The area is **prone to earthquakes** because of a **major fault line** that runs **north-south** along the **Apennine mountain range**. There's also an **east-west fault line** across the centre of Italy.
3) The fault lines are close to the **destructive plate margin** between the **Eurasian** and **African plates**.
4) The L'Aquila earthquake occurred at **3.32 am** (local time) on **6th April 2009**.
5) It measured **6.3** on the **Richter scale**.
6) The earthquake only lasted a few seconds but it was **felt throughout central Italy**.
7) The **focus** of the earthquake was at a **depth** of about **5 miles** and the **epicentre** was close to **L'Aquila**.
8) It was **caused** by movement along the **north-south fault line**.
9) Several **aftershocks** were felt in the days following the main earthquake — some of them measured around **5** on the **Richter scale**.

The **Social Impacts** Were **Bigger Than Expected**

ECONOMIC IMPACTS

1) It's been estimated that the earthquake cost Italy **$15 billion** in total.
2) **Thousands of buildings**, both historic and modern, were **damaged** or **destroyed**. These included part of the city **hospital**, a dormitory at the **university** and **L'Aquila Cathedral**.
3) A **bridge** near the town of Fossa **collapsed**, and a **water pipe** was **broken** near the town of Paganica.
4) **Fires** in some collapsed buildings caused **more damage**.

A house destroyed by the earthquake.

SOCIAL IMPACTS

1) There were around **300 deaths**, mostly caused by **collapsed buildings**.
2) About **1500 people** were **injured**.
3) **70 000 people** were made **homeless**.
4) The **aftershocks** hampered **rescue efforts** and caused **more damage**.
5) **Thousands of people**, many of them young people, have had to **move away** from the area to other parts of Italy to find **jobs** after buildings were destroyed.

The timing of the earthquake may have made things worse. It happened at around three in the morning when most people would have been asleep — so they'd have been slow to react.

ENVIRONMENTAL IMPACTS

1) An area of about **1000 km²** was affected by **surface ruptures** (cracks in the ground), **rockfalls** and **landslides**.
2) The **broken water pipe** near the town of Paganica also caused a **landslide**.
3) **Wildlife habitats** were affected by the earthquake.

Earthquake Case Study — L'Aquila

The **Responses** Included **Rescuing** and **Rehoming People**

1) **Camps** were set up for **homeless people** with **water**, **food** and **medical care**.
2) **Ambulances, fire engines** and the **army** were sent in to **rescue survivors**.
3) **Cranes** and **diggers** were used to **remove rubble**.
4) **International teams** with **rescue dogs** were sent in to look for **survivors**.
5) **12 000 rescue and support workers** were brought in to help with the response.
6) **Money** was provided by the **government** to **pay rent**. **Mortgage payments**, and **gas** and **electricity bills** were suspended.
7) The Italian Prime Minister promised to build a **new town** to replace L'Aquila as the **capital** of the area.
8) By the end of 2009, **4500 new buildings** had been put up to **house 12 000 people** who had been made homeless.

Some of the **Management Strategies Didn't** Have **Much Effect**

Although L'Aquila itself **hadn't** suffered from a **major earthquake** for 300 years, the area around the Apennines experiences regular minor earthquakes. So, there were some **management strategies** in place:

BUILDING TECHNIQUES

Because of the risks, there were **strict building regulations** to ensure that **newer buildings** were **designed** and **built** to **withstand earthquakes**. However, **some** of the newer buildings that were **supposed** to meet the regulations had been **poorly built** and they were **severely damaged** or **destroyed**.

For example, the **San Salvatore Hospital** in west L'Aquila was built in **2000**. It **should** have been able to **withstand** the earthquake, but it actually **collapsed** and the **patients** had to be treated in **tents outdoors**. An investigation was set up to look into why so many modern buildings, like the hospital, collapsed.

PREDICTION

Seismologists were **monitoring** the area prior to the event. Some people felt that the earthquake hazard could have been managed better — in August 2009 a group of **local residents** made a formal complaint that six **seismologists** working in the area **didn't predict** the earthquake. The residents blamed the scientists for the number of people killed and requested a **criminal investigation**. However, it's currently **impossible to predict exactly** when and where an earthquake may occur.

PLANNING

Italy has a **Civil Protection Department** that trains **volunteers** to help with things like **rescue operations**.

Practice Questions

Q1 When was the L'Aquila earthquake?

Q2 Which plate margin is L'Aquila close to?

Q3 What were the social impacts of the L'Aquila earthquake?

Exam Question

Q1 With reference to at least one example you have studied, critically evaluate the strategies used to manage earthquake hazards. [10 marks]

Darling, did you feel the Earth move... er, yes actually, I did...

L'Aquila wasn't unprepared for an earthquake — Italy experiences quite frequent earthquakes and it had management strategies in place to deal with the impacts. The problem was that when it came to crunch time, those strategies didn't seem to help much.

Earthquake Case Study — Kashmir

Aha, the last case study of the section — no dozing off at the back...

The **Kashmir Earthquake** Happened on **8th October 2005**

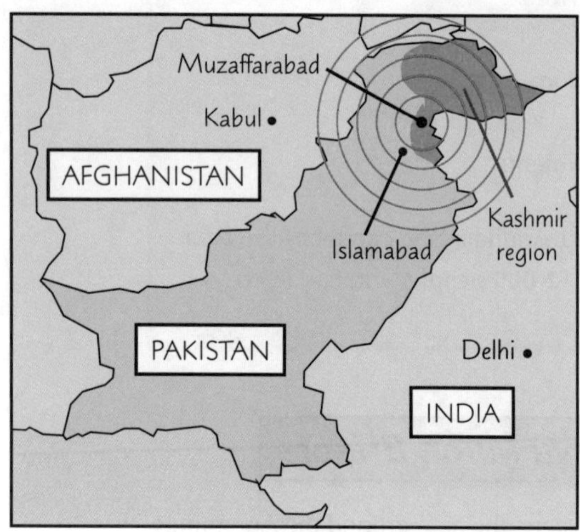

1) The **Kashmir region**, to the north of **Pakistan**, sits on a **destructive plate margin** where the **Indian plate** is being forced under the **Eurasian plate**.
2) An earthquake occurred in the Kashmir region on **8th October 2005**.
3) It happened at **8.50 am** (local time) and measured **7.6** on the **Richter scale**.
4) The **focus** of the earthquake was at a **depth** of about **16 miles** and the **epicentre** was close to **Muzaffarabad**.
5) The earthquake resulted from **movement** along the **plate margin**, which caused a **75 km long** crack in the Earth's surface to form.
6) The earthquake caused **damage** to an area of **30 000 km²** — it was felt as far away as **Kabul** in **Afghanistan** and **Delhi** in **India**.
7) By **27th October 2005** there had been **978 aftershocks** measuring at least **4** on the **Richter scale**.

The **Earthquake** was the **13th Most Destructive** on Record

ECONOMIC IMPACTS

1) It's been estimated that the earthquake cost around **US$5 billion** in **total**.
2) **Whole villages** and **thousands of buildings** were **destroyed**. For example, **80%** of the town of **Uri** was destroyed. Even in some areas up to 25 km from the epicentre, nearly 25% of buildings collapsed and 50% were severely damaged. The **total cost of rebuilding** has been estimated to be **US$3.5 billion**.

SOCIAL IMPACTS

1) There were around **80 000 deaths**, mostly caused by **collapsed buildings**. This is the **13th highest death toll** of any earthquake on record.
2) **Hundreds of thousands** of people were **injured**, including around **6000** in **India**.
3) Around **3 million people** were made **homeless**.
4) **Water pipelines** and **electricity lines** were **broken**, cutting off supplies.
5) **Landslides** buried **buildings** and **people**. They also **blocked access roads** and cut off **water supplies**, **electricity supplies** and **telephone lines**.
6) **Diarrhoea** and **other diseases** spread due to little **clean water**.
7) **Freezing winter conditions** shortly after the earthquake caused **more casualties** and meant **rescue** and **rebuilding operations** were **difficult**.

ENVIRONMENTAL IMPACTS

1) **Landslides** and **rockfalls** occurred throughout the region. Most landslides were relatively small but there were **two major landslides** that each affected an area of more than **0.1 km²** — one in **Muzaffarabad** and one in the **Jhelum Valley**.
2) The Jhelum Valley landslide was the **biggest** — it was over **1 km wide** and the debris reached over **2 km** from the top of the slide. The debris created a **dam** at the bottom of the valley that **blocked two rivers** where they joined.
3) As a result of the earthquake and surface rupture, the **ground shifted** by more than **5 m** in some areas of Kashmir.

Earthquake Case Study — Kashmir

The **Response** was **Delayed** in **Many Areas**

1) **Help didn't reach** many areas for **days** or **weeks**. People had to be rescued by hand without any equipment or help from emergency services.
2) **Tents, blankets** and **medical supplies** were distributed within a **month**, but **not to all areas** affected.
3) The Pakistani government set up the **Federal Relief Commission** (FRC) and the **Earthquake Reconstruction and Rehabilitation Authority** (ERRA) to **coordinate activities** with other international agencies and non-governmental organisations.
4) **International aid** and **equipment** such as helicopters and rescue dogs were brought in, as well as **teams** of people from **other countries**.
5) Around **40 000 people** have been **relocated** to a **new town**, from the destroyed town of Balakot.
6) **Government money** has been given to people whose homes had been destroyed so they can **rebuild them themselves**.
7) **Training** has been provided to help rebuild more buildings as **earthquake resistant**.
8) New **health centres** have been set up in the area.

The terrain in the Kashmir region and the winter conditions made the rescue operation more difficult.

An estimated $5.8 billion of foreign aid was provided by the international community in response to the disaster. Some of this was for long-term development.

There was **No Hazard Management**

1) There was **no** local **disaster planning** in place.
2) **Buildings** were **not** designed to be **earthquake resistant**. Many **houses** were **structurally poor** because people **couldn't afford** better buildings. However, even **government buildings** in areas such as Muzaffarabad were **structurally unsound** and so were damaged in the earthquake.
3) **Communications** were **poor**. There were **few roads** and they were **badly constructed**.

Practice Questions

Q1 When was the Kashmir earthquake?
Q2 The movement of which two tectonic plates caused the earthquake?
Q3 Give one economic impact of the earthquake.
Q4 Describe three social impacts of the earthquake.
Q5 Give two environmental impacts of the earthquake.

Exam Question

Q1 With reference to at least two examples you have studied, compare and contrast the responses to an earthquake. [10 marks]

Nope, sorry — it's just not very funny...

So, you've reached the end of the Plate Tectonics section. It's really been quite a journey — almost to the centre of the Earth. Well, not really, but 'a journey a bit below the Earth's surface' sounds less dramatic. And, let's face it, this section is all about drama.

Climate Basics

Hurricanes, monsoons, the gaseous composition of the atmosphere — yep, climate's a pretty thrilling topic...

Weather and Climate are Two Different Things

- **WEATHER** is the **SHORT-TERM atmospheric conditions** in a particular place — e.g. temperature, cloud cover, precipitation type, wind speed.
- **CLIMATE** is the **LONG-TERM atmospheric conditions** in a particular place — **average measurements** of temperature, precipitation etc. over a **long period** of time.

The Atmosphere is a Mixture of Gases that Surrounds the Earth

1) The atmosphere contains **dry air** and **water vapour**. **Dry air** is a **mixture** of **gases**, including **nitrogen** (78%), **oxygen** (21%) and **other gases** such as **carbon dioxide** and **methane** (0.04%).
2) The atmosphere is made up of **four layers**:

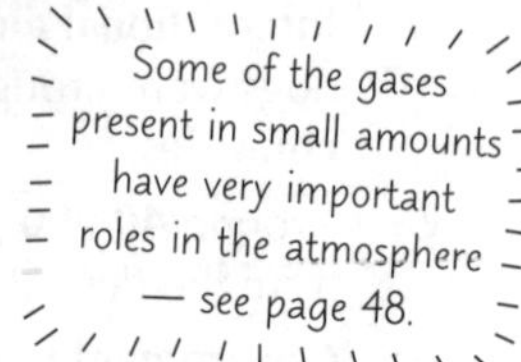

1 TROPOSPHERE

- The troposphere extends from the **Earth's surface** to about **12 km** up on average.
- **Temperature decreases** with **altitude** in the troposphere. This is because the Earth's surface warms the troposphere, so the further away from the surface the cooler it gets.
- There's lots of **turbulence** (air movement) because **warm air rises** through the layer and **cool air sinks**.
- The troposphere has lots of **clouds**. This is because there's a lot of **water vapour** that has evaporated from the Earth's surface.
- The **tropopause** is the **boundary** between the **troposphere** and **stratosphere**. **Jet streams** (fast moving currents of air) are found just below the tropopause.

Altitude is the height above sea level.

2 STRATOSPHERE

- The **stratosphere** extends from around **12 km** to about **50 km** up.
- **Temperature increases** with altitude in this layer because the **ozone layer** is found in the lower stratosphere — it absorbs UV radiation, which warms the upper stratosphere.
- The stratosphere **isn't turbulent** and there **aren't** many **clouds**.
- The **stratopause** is the **boundary** of the **stratosphere** and **mesosphere**.

3 MESOSPHERE

- The **mesosphere** extends from around **50 km** to **85-90 km** up.
- **Temperature decreases** with altitude in the mesosphere. This is because the mesosphere is **warmed** by the **stratosphere** — the further away from the stratosphere the cooler it gets.
- The **mesopause** is the **boundary** of the **mesosphere** and **thermosphere**.

4 THERMOSPHERE

- The **thermosphere** extends from **85-90 km** to around **1000 km** up.
- **Temperature increases** with altitude in the thermosphere. This is because small amounts of **oxygen** in this layer **absorb UV radiation**, warming the thermosphere.

Air pressure decreases with **altitude** through the **atmosphere**.

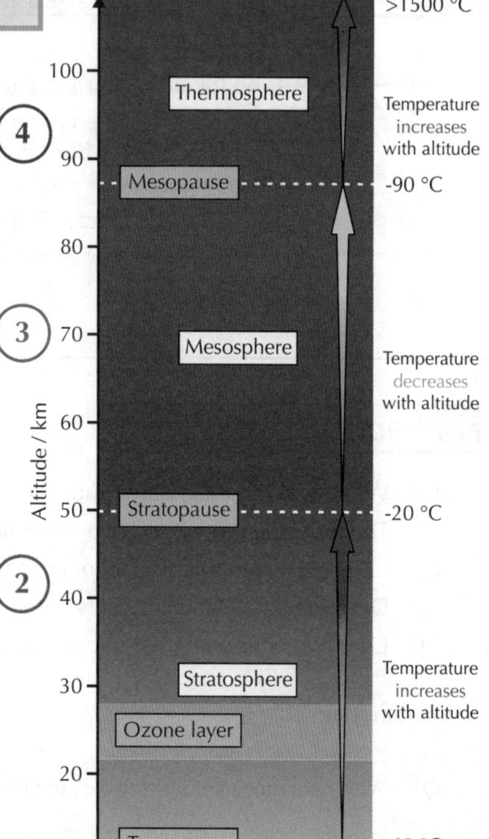

Climate Basics

The Atmospheric Heat Budget is Heat Gained and Lost by the Earth

1) We get **energy from the sun** in the form of **shortwave solar radiation**. This is also known as **insolation**.
2) About **50%** of insolation is **absorbed** by the **surface** of the Earth and then released as **longwave radiation**, i.e. **infrared** or **heat energy**. This radiation heats up the **troposphere**.
3) The other **50%** of incoming solar radiation is split three ways:
    - About 25% is **reflected back into space** by the air and clouds in the **atmosphere**.
    - About 20% is **absorbed** by the air and clouds in the **atmosphere**.
    - About 5% is **reflected back into space** by the Earth's **surface**.

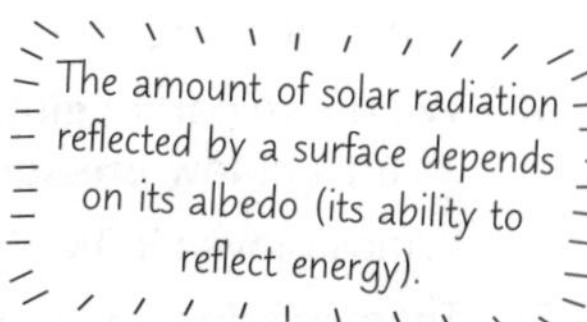

Four Main Factors Affect How Much Solar Radiation the Atmosphere Receives

1) The **SOLAR CONSTANT** is the amount of solar radiation we get from the sun. It **varies slightly** with the **sun's activity**. When the sun is **more active**, the Earth receives **more solar radiation**.
2) **EARTH'S DISTANCE FROM THE SUN** changes as it orbits. When Earth is **closer to the sun** it receives **more solar radiation**.
3) The **HEIGHT OF THE SUN IN THE SKY** varies with **latitude**:
    - Near the **Equator** the sun is **higher** in the sky and incoming solar radiation is **spread over a smaller surface area**.
    - Near the **poles** the sun is **lower** in the sky and incoming solar radiation is spread **over a larger surface area**. This means there's **less solar radiation per m² at higher latitudes**.
4) **LENGTH OF DAY AND NIGHT**. This varies with the seasons, which are more pronounced at higher altitudes. In **winter** there are **fewer hours of daylight** — so **less solar radiation**.

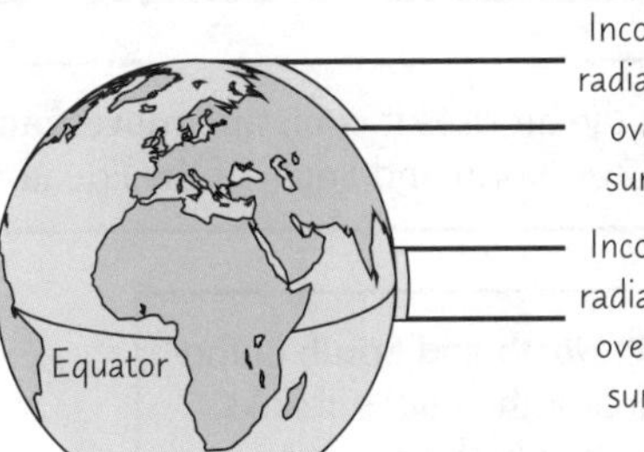

Higher Latitudes and Higher Altitudes are Colder

Latitude is the distance (in degrees) north or south of the Earth's Equator.

1) Higher **latitudes** are colder because:
    - They receive **less solar radiation** because the sun is **lower in the sky** (see above).
    - They receive **less solar radiation** because there are **fewer hours of daylight in winter** (see above).
2) Higher **altitudes** are colder because:
    - The Earth's surface heats the atmosphere through **conduction**, so the temperature is greatest close to the heat source and decreases away from it (upwards).
    - **Air pressure** decreases with altitude — there are fewer air molecules and they move more slowly. This means they create less **heat**, which means lower temperatures.

Practice Questions

Q1 Describe the difference between weather and climate.

Q2 Briefly explain why only 50% of incoming solar radiation reaches the surface of the Earth.

Q3 What are the four main factors that affect how much solar radiation the atmosphere receives?

Exam Question

Q1 With particular reference to temperature, describe and explain the vertical structure of the atmosphere. [8 marks]

Solar radiation won't give you superpowers — just really bad sunburn...

Who'd have thought that something you can't see could be so complicated. I made up a little mnemonic to remember the layers of the atmosphere, it's about a boy I used to know who liked to wear small swimming trunks — we called him Tight Shorts Mike Turner...

Climate Basics

So the Equator gets more solar radiation than the poles, but the Equator doesn't keep getting hotter and the poles don't keep getting colder... I always assumed this was down to the heat elves, but apparently it's wind and ocean currents.

Energy *is* ***Redistributed*** *from the Equator to the Poles by* ***Winds...***

1) **Winds** are **large scale movements of air** caused by **differences in air pressure.**
2) Differences in air pressure are caused by **differences in atmospheric heating** between the **Equator** and the **poles.**
3) Winds are part of **global atmospheric circulation cells.** These cells have a body of **warm rising air** which creates an area of **low pressure**, and a body of **cool falling air** which creates an area of **high pressure.**
4) Winds move **FROM** the areas of **high pressure TO** the areas of **low pressure.**
5) There are **three main types** of global atmospheric circulation cells — **Hadley**, **Ferrel** and **Polar Cells.**
6) Here's how it all works:

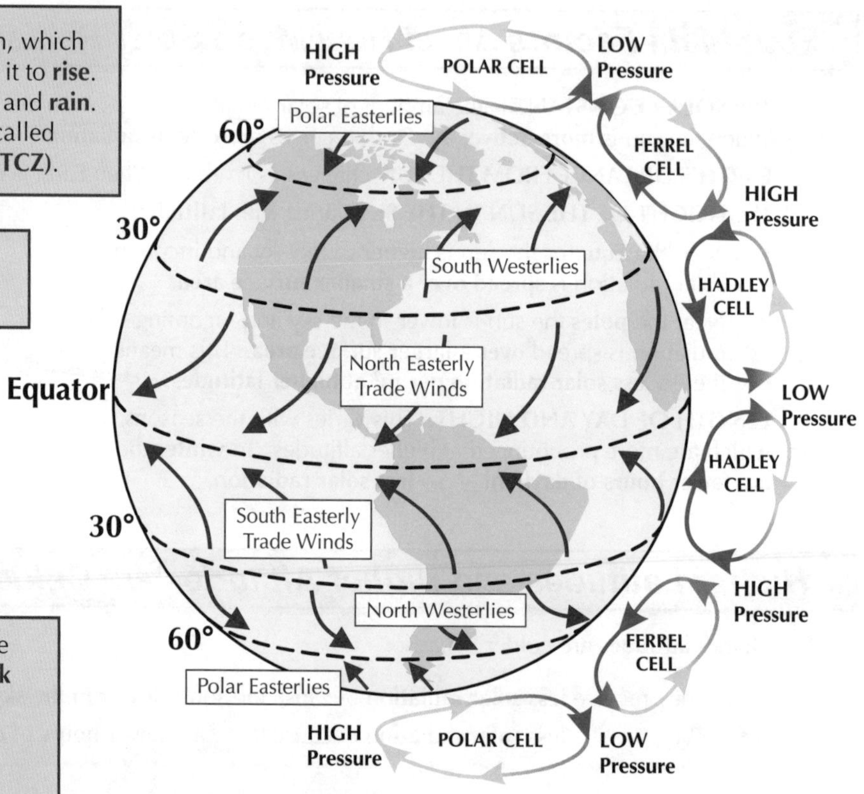

1) At the **Equator** the **sun warms** the Earth, which transfers heat to the air above, causing it to **rise.** Rising air creates **low pressure, clouds** and **rain.** This low pressure zone of rising air is called the **Intertropical Convergence Zone (ITCZ).**

2) As the air rises it **cools** and **moves out** to 30° North and South of the Equator.

3) **30° North and South** of the Equator the **cool air sinks**, creating **high pressure. Sub-tropical jet streams** are found here (jet streams are fast moving currents of air).

4) The cool air reaches the ground surface and moves as surface winds either **back to the Equator** or **towards the poles**:
- Surface winds blowing towards the **Equator** are called **trade winds.**
- They blow from the SE in the southern hemisphere and from the NE in the northern hemisphere. At the Equator, these **trade winds meet** (converge) in the **ITCZ**, and are heated by solar radiation. This causes them to rise, condense and form **clouds.**
- Surface winds blowing towards the **poles** are called **westerlies.** They blow from the NW in the southern hemisphere and from the SW in the northern hemisphere.

Winds are deflected to the right in the northern hemisphere and to the left in the southern hemisphere because of the Earth's rotation.

5) **60° North and South of the Equator** the warmer surface winds meet colder air from the poles. The warmer air is less dense than the cold air so it **rises**, creating **low pressure.**

6) Some of the air joins the Ferrel cell and **moves back** towards the Equator, and the rest joins the polar cell and moves towards the **poles.**

The polar front jet stream is found around 60° North and South of the Equator.

7) At the **poles** the **cool air sinks**, creating **high pressure.** The high pressure air is drawn back towards to the Equator in **surface winds.**

Climate Basics

...and by Ocean Currents

1) Ocean currents are **large scale movements of water** caused by **differences** in **water density**. Density depends on **water temperature** and **salinity**.
2) Currents are affected by **surface winds**, the **position of land masses** and **other currents**.
3) Ocean currents **transfer heat energy** from **warmer** to **cooler** regions. **Warm** ocean currents **raise air temperature**, which warms the **land** nearby. **Cool** ocean currents **lower air temperature**, which cools the **land** nearby.
4) Ocean currents form **giant loops** that travel **clockwise** in the **northern hemisphere** and **anti-clockwise** in the **southern hemisphere**. This is because of **surface winds** — e.g. trade winds push water west along the Equator, and westerlies push water east between 30° and 60° North and South.
5) Here's a rough guide to the main ocean currents. **Red arrows** are **warm currents** and **blue arrows** are **cold**.

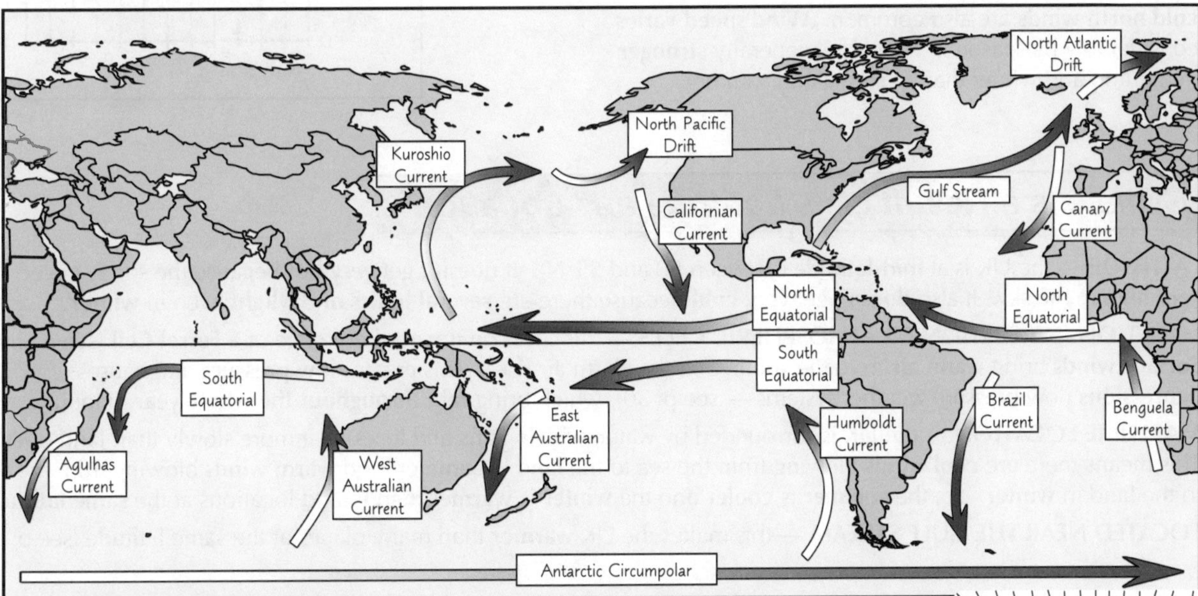

You don't need to memorise this map, but make sure you learn the main patterns of ocean currents (e.g. the direction the loops move in each hemisphere) and how they move energy (e.g. from the Equator towards the poles along the west side of the oceans).

6) Ocean currents **affect the climate** of many regions. For example:

- The **Gulf Stream** carries **warm** water from the Caribbean Sea along the east coast of America and across the Atlantic to **Western Europe**.
- The Gulf Stream keeps Western Europe **much warmer** than it would otherwise be.
- Water in the Gulf Stream **cools** in the northern hemisphere and becomes **more dense**. Some of this water **sinks** and is carried back to the Equator by the **Canary Current**, which **cools** the west coast of Africa.

Practice Questions

Q1 What are winds?

Q2 How is air pressure affected by a) rising warm air and b) sinking cool air?

Q3 Define trade winds and westerlies.

Q4 What causes ocean currents?

Q5 Briefly explain how ocean currents affect climate.

Exam Question

Q1 Describe how energy is redistributed from the Equator to the poles by winds. [8 marks]

I thought current affairs were something completely different...

*The diagrams on these pages are incredibly complicated. Don't worry, you won't be expected to know the diagram on ocean currents in too much detail, but you **do** need to learn the diagram on atmospheric cells. That's all the cells, winds and pressures...*

UK Climate

The climate of the UK is quite temperamental — it ranges from lovely and warm to cold and 'orrible.

*UK Climate is **Temperate** — **Cool**, **Wet Winters** and **Warm**, **Wet Summers***

1) **Temperature** in the UK **varies** with the **seasons**. It's **coldest in winter**, it warms up through spring, is **hottest in summer**, and then cools down again through autumn.
2) Temperature ranges from an average of **5 °C in January** to **20 °C in August**.
3) **Rainfall** in the UK is **fairly high all year round**, but it also **varies** with the **seasons**. It's **higher** in autumn and winter (an average of 120 mm in January) and **lower** in spring and summer (an average of 65 mm in May).
4) **Winds** in the UK are mostly **warm south westerlies**, but **cold north winds** are also common. **Wind speed varies** considerably by season — winds are generally **stronger** in autumn and winter than in spring and summer.

UK AVERAGE TEMPERATURE AND RAINFALL

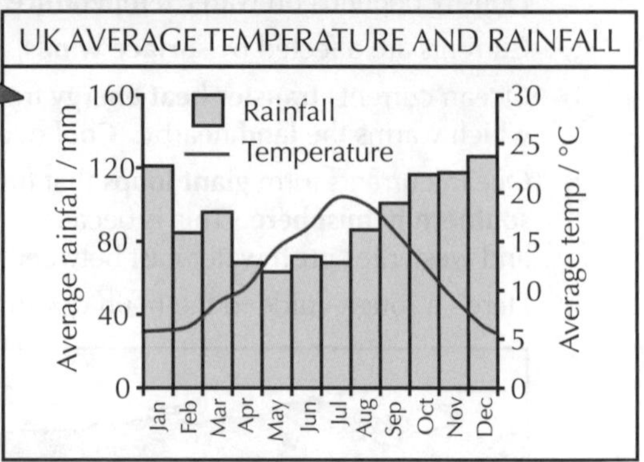

*UK Climate is a **Result** of its **Latitude** and **Location***

1) **LATITUDE** — the UK is at **mid-latitude** (between 50 and 55°N). It **doesn't** get **very hot** because the sun is never **very high** in the sky. It also **doesn't** get very **cold** because there are **several hours of daylight** even in **winter**.
2) **LOCATION IN RELATION TO ATMOSPHERIC CELLS** — the UK is on the northern edge of a **Ferrel Cell** (see p. 26). **Surface winds** bring **warm air** from the south, and the warm air rises. This creates **low pressure** and causes **depressions** (low pressure weather systems — see p. 30), which bring **rain throughout the whole year**. Hooray...
3) **MARITIME LOCATION** — the UK is surrounded by water, which gains and loses heat more slowly than land does. This means there are **cool winds** blowing from the sea to the land in **summer**, and **warm winds** blowing from the sea to the land in **winter**. So, the **summer** is **cooler** and the **winter** is **warmer** than inland locations at the **same latitude**.
4) **LOCATED NEAR THE GULF STREAM** — this makes the UK **warmer** than many places at the same latitude (see p. 27).

*Climate **Varies Within** the UK*

UK ANNUAL TEMPERATURE 1971-2000

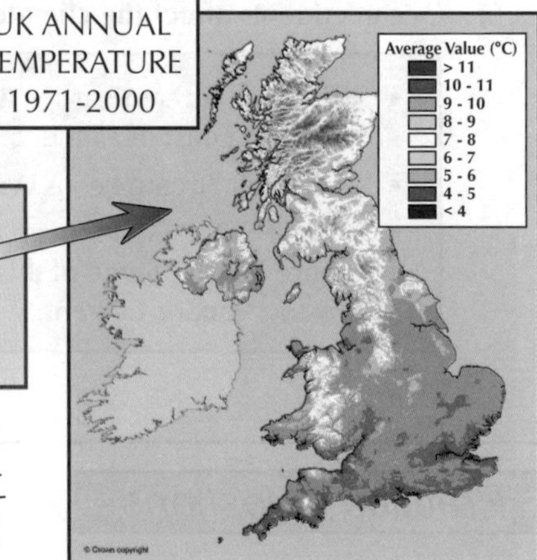

TEMPERATURE

It's warmer in the south because there's **more insolation** (more solar radiation reaching the ground). This is because the sun is **higher in the sky** and there are **more hours of daylight** than in the north (see p. 25). E.g. annual average maximum temperature is 13.6 °C in Cornwall, and 9.3 °C in the north of Scotland.

The UK's maritime setting is important too — the climate is different inland compared to on the coast (see above).

UK ANNUAL RAINFALL 1971-2000

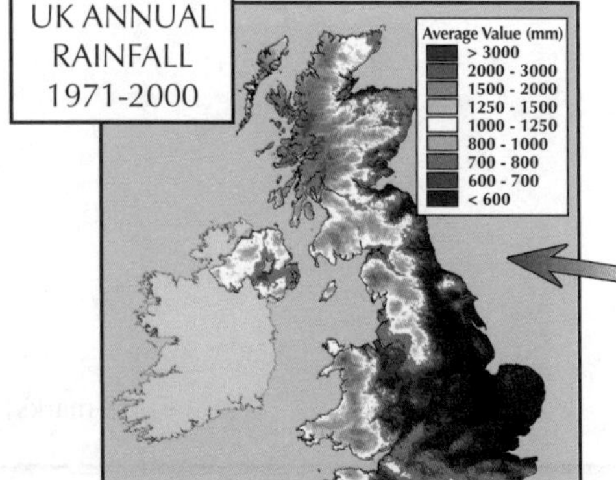

PRECIPITATION

It's **wetter** in the **west** than the **east**, e.g. annual average rainfall is 871 mm in Blackpool (on the west coast), and 565 mm in Cleethorpes (on the east coast). This is because **south westerly surface winds** bring **warm, wet air** from the **Atlantic Ocean**. The air reaches the **west side** of the UK, and it's forced upwards **over the land**. The **air cools**, the **water vapour condenses** and it **rains**. This is known as **orographic** or **relief rainfall**. The west of the UK is generally **more mountainous** than the east, so the air masses lose most of their moisture in the west. The area to the east of the mountains, where less rain falls, is called the **rain shadow**.

UK Climate

WIND

1) Winds are stronger in the **west**, e.g. the annual average wind speed is 21.7 km/h in St. Mawgan (on the south west coast), and 16.7 km/h in Marham (on the east coast). This is because **south westerly surface winds** come over the **ocean** — the ocean is **flat** so there's **nothing to slow the winds down**. When the **winds hit land**, they're affected by hills and they become weaker.
2) Winds are **stronger** at **higher altitudes** because there are **fewer obstacles to slow them down.**

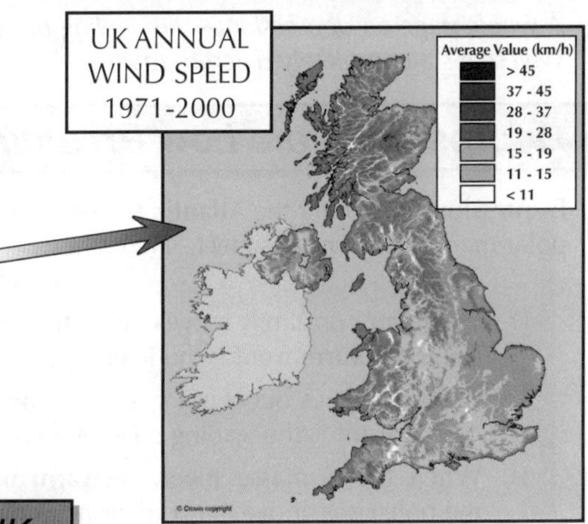

*There are **Five Main Air Masses** that Affect the UK*

1) Air masses are **large volumes of air** with a **similar temperature** and **water vapour content**.
2) They cover **large areas** (several hundred km^2) and can **travel long distances**.
3) They're classified by the region they form over:
   - **Arctic** or **Polar** air masses form at **high latitudes** (so they're **cooler**).
   - **Tropical** air masses form at **low latitudes** (so they're **warmer**).
   - **Maritime** air masses form over **oceans** (so they've got a **higher water vapour** content).
   - **Continental** air masses form over **land** (so they've got a **lower water vapour** content).
4) The UK is affected by **five different air masses**. Each air mass brings a **different type of weather**, which is one of the reasons why the **UK's weather** is so **variable**:

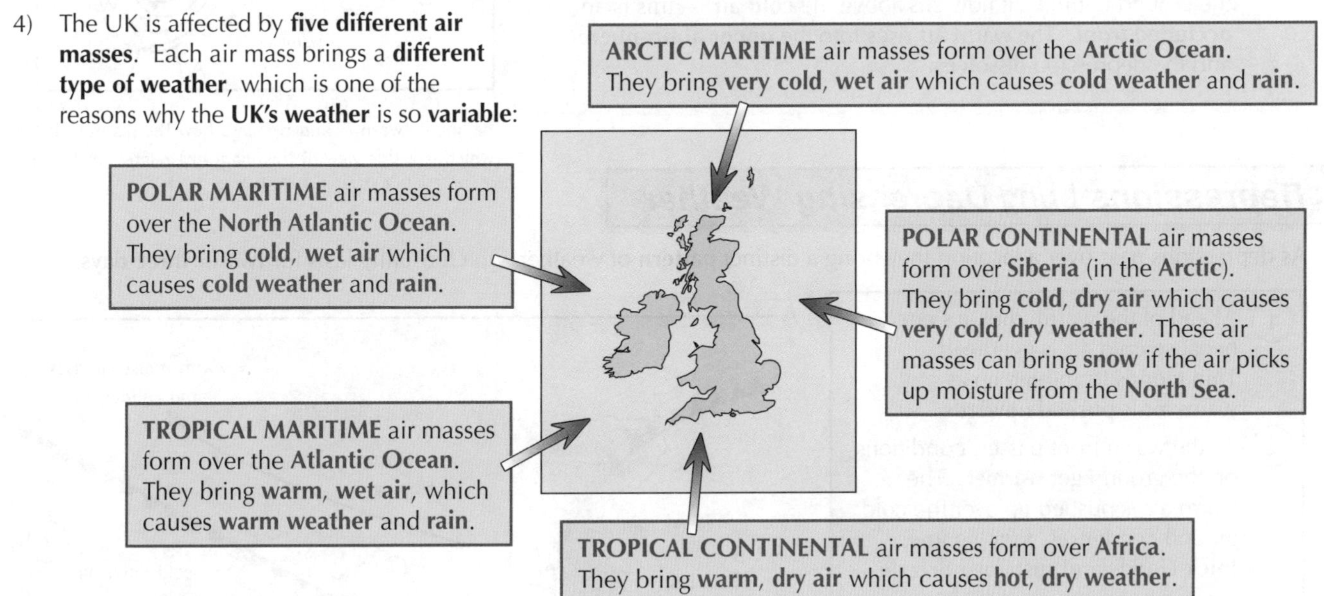

Practice Questions

Q1 Describe how temperature and rainfall in the UK vary with the seasons.

Q2 Why is it warmer in the south of the UK than in the north?

Q3 Why is it wetter and windier in the west of the UK than in the east?

Q4 What are air masses?

Exam Question

Q1 Discuss how the climate of the UK is a result of its position on the Earth. [8 marks]

Learn these pages and you'll never be lost for small talk again...

"It's a nice day today, isn't it?", "Yes it is, and here's why... blah blah blah". You can bore the socks off anyone you meet with the information here. Surely that's motivation enough to get revising. And if not, just think about all those lovely exam marks...

UK Weather Systems

A whole page on depression — I'm feeling pretty miserable just thinking about it. Oh, hang on... depressions you say. Well that's a completely different matter — I love a good low pressure weather system. Let's get cracking.

Depressions are Low Pressure Weather Systems

Depressions form over the **Atlantic Ocean**, then move **east** over the UK. They usually form when the tropical maritime and polar maritime air masses meet. Here's how:

1) **Warm air** constantly moves out of tropical areas, **towards** the **poles**. A **warm front** is the **leading edge** of a **warm air mass**.
2) **Cold air** moves out of polar regions, **towards** the **tropics**. A **cold front** is the **leading edge** of a **cold air mass**.
3) Where the air masses **meet**, the **warm air** heading towards the pole **rises** above the cold air heading towards the tropics (because **warm air** is **less dense** than cold air).
4) The rising **warm air** means that atmospheric **pressure** is **reduced**.
5) **Strong winds** blow from surrounding areas of high pressure towards this area of low pressure and the whole system **rotates** as air continues to rise.
6) **Cold fronts move more quickly** than warm fronts, so the cold front **catches up** with the **warm front**.
7) When this happens the **warm air** behind the warm front is **undercut** by the incoming cold front and is **lifted** away from the ground entirely. It now sits **above** the **cold air** — this is an **occluded front**. The warm air rises into the **upper atmosphere** and the depression **dissolves**.

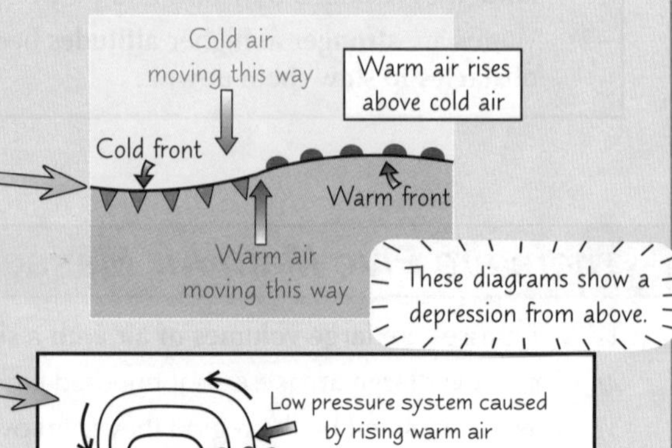

These diagrams show a depression from above.

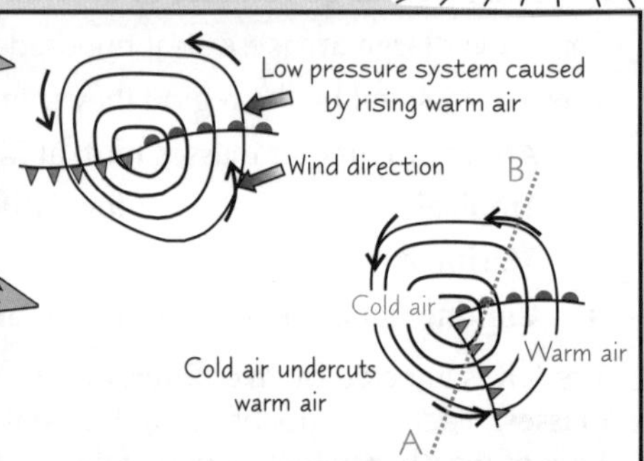

The line between A and B shows how the diagram below (which is a side view of this diagram) relates to this one.

Depressions bring Depressing Weather

As depressions pass over a location they bring a distinct **pattern** of weather, which usually lasts for **two** or **three days**:

1. Ahead of the warm front, it's **cool** because cold air is **overhead**. **Thin clouds** form high up as warm air is pushed **upwards**.
2. As the warm front passes, conditions on the ground get **warmer**. The warm air is pushed up over the cold air and **condenses**, forming **low, thick clouds** and **sustained drizzle**.
3. When the warm air is overhead, it's **warm**. There's no **cloud** because warm air holds a lot of **water vapour**.
4. As the cold front passes, cool air brings the **temperature down** again. The cold dense **air behind** the cold front **undercuts** the warm air mass in front. This forces the warm air to rise rapidly and condense, **forming clouds** and **heavy showers**. Rapidly rising air makes it **very windy** at the surface.
5. When the cold front catches up with the warm front, all of the warm air has been **squeezed upwards** so there's **no warm air left** at the bottom. There's **less rain** because the uplift of air has decreased. There is **little condensation**, so **cloud cover decreases**. **Wind speed** also **decreases**, but **air pressure rises** as the dense cold air replaces the uplifted air and the depression dies out.

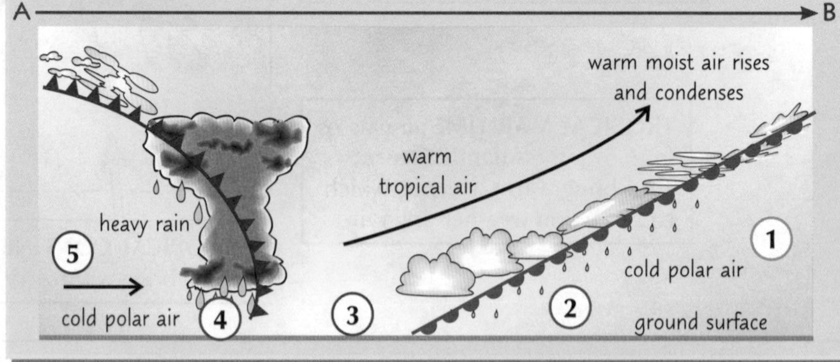

	5 Cold air overhead	4 As the cold front passes	3 Warm air overhead	2 As the warm front passes	1 Ahead of the warm front
Rain	Showers	Heavy showers	None	Sustained drizzle	None
Clouds	High, broken	Towering, thick	None	Low, thick	High, thin
Pressure	Rising	Suddenly rising	Steady	Falling	Falling
Temperature	Cold	Falling	Warm	Rising	Cool
Wind speed	Decreasing	Strong	Decreasing	Strong	Increasing
Wind direction	NW	SW to NW	SW	SE to SW	SE

UK Weather Systems

Anticyclones are *High Pressure Weather Systems*

1) The UK also experiences **anticyclones** — areas of **high atmospheric pressure** caused by a large mass of **falling air**.
2) The air falls from the **upper atmosphere**, and **warms** on its way down. This causes humidity to decrease because air masses can hold more moisture as they get warmer. This means **clouds don't develop**, and conditions are very **dry**.
3) In anticyclones there's **not much difference** in **air pressure** between the centre and edges. Because the **pressure is similar**, the winds are weak, and flow gently outwards. In the **UK**, the winds flow **clockwise** around the centre.
4) Anticyclones cause **different weather** in winter than in summer:

WINTER WEATHER

- **Low** temperatures during the day (from below freezing to 5 °C), because the sun is at a **low angle**.
- **Extremely cold** overnight temperatures (below freezing) with frosts, because clear skies allow **loss of heat** through **radiation**.
- **Low level cloud** and **radiation fogs** — radiation fog forms overnight. As the ground cools, moisture in the air close to the ground condenses, forming fog.
- **High levels of atmospheric pollution** in urban areas — pollutants are trapped by **temperature inversions** (when the air at **higher altitudes** is **warmer** than the air at **lower levels**). A lack of wind means pollutants aren't dispersed.

SUMMER WEATHER

- The **absence of clouds** leads to intense **insolation**, which means it's **hot**, **sunny** and there's **no rain**.
- Rapid **radiation** at night can cause **temperature inversions**, dew and morning mist.
- **Coastal areas** may get **fogs** and **strong breezes**. Highlands may experience **strong winds** due to heating of valley sides, which causes a **pressure gradient**.
- After **several days** there's a risk of **thunderstorms**, due to large amounts of rapidly rising warm air.

5) Some anticyclones are described as **'blocking'**. Blocking anticyclones can sit over the UK and remain there for **many days**. Depressions that would normally travel across Britain are forced around the upper edge of the anticyclone. **Extreme weather conditions** are likely, e.g. heatwaves in summer and dry, freezing weather in winter.

Make Sure You can *Read Synoptic Maps*

Synoptic maps have **lines** called **isobars**. These **link** together **points** of **equal atmospheric pressure**, which is measured in **millibars** (mb). Here are **two synoptic charts**, one showing a **depression** and the other an **anticyclone**.

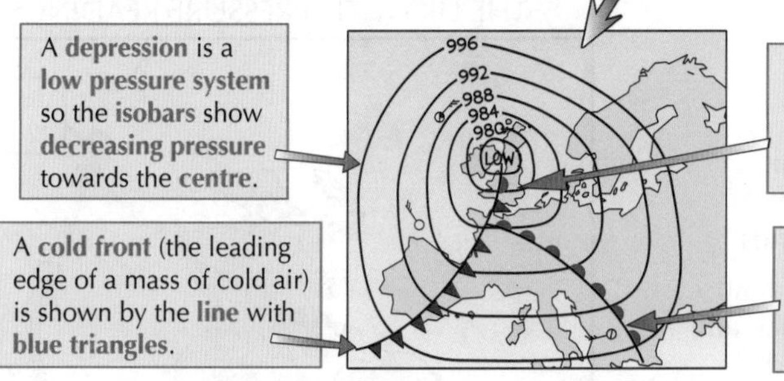

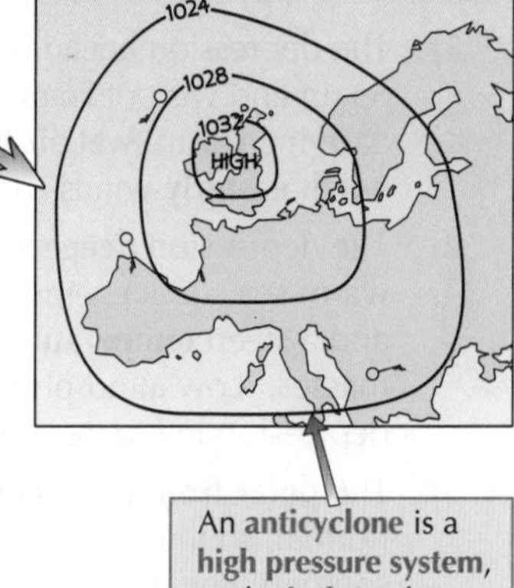

Winds blow almost **parallel** to the **isobars**, not straight across them. This means that winds move in a spiral fashion **into** the **centre** of a depression and **out** of the **centre** of an anticyclone.

Practice Questions

Q1 Write a short description of how a depression forms.

Q2 Give three differences between anticyclones and depressions.

Exam Question

Q1 Describe, and give reasons for, the changes in weather as a depression passes over the UK. [8 marks]

I've been anti-cyclones ever since my house blew away...

*There's **a lot** of information on these pages. Unfortunately it's all important, so you'll have to learn it. You could do some drawing to take your mind off it. How about a nice diagram of a depression cross section? It's doubly fun if you label it too...*

UK Storms

People are scared of things they don't understand. If you're scared of temperate storms then this is the page for you... You need to know how storms form in temperate climates, and learn the details of one case study of a temperate storm.

Storms that Hit the UK are Temperate Storms

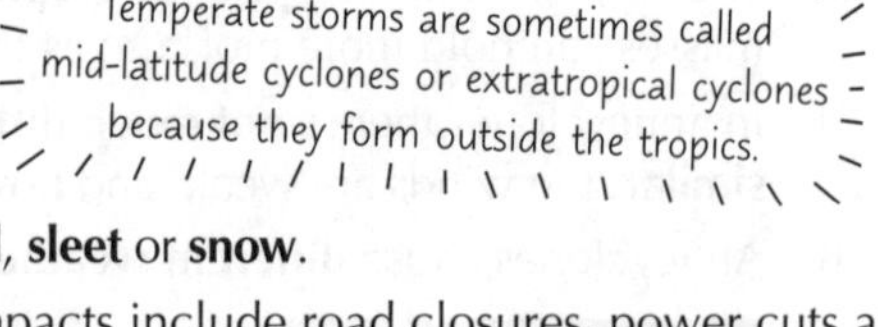

1) Temperate storms occur in **temperate climates** — these are climates that are found at **mid-latitudes, 30-60° north** or **south** of the Equator.
2) They range from **mild** (e.g. rain showers and 15-30 km/h winds) to **severe** (e.g. thunderstorms and 120 km/h winds). They can bring **strong winds**, **rain**, **hail**, **sleet** or **snow**.
3) They generally cause **less damage** than **tropical storms** (see p. 36). Typical impacts include road closures, power cuts and damage to trees. Occasionally temperate storms can be very severe, with winds strong enough to damage buildings.
4) Temperate storms are caused by **depressions**:

- Depressions often form **over the sea** in **autumn** when the water is warm — **warm surface water** leads to warm, moist air which rises. When this **warm** air meets the polar front it rises rapidly above the **cold polar air** creating an area of **low pressure**, along with **condensation** and **heavy rain**.
- A steep **pressure gradient** between the two air masses drives **strong winds**, which **spiral around the depression**.
- **Steep temperature gradients** in a depression affect the storm's strength — a strong temperature gradient means there is also a stronger **pressure gradient** (warm air has lower atmospheric pressure than cold air) which drives **strong winds**.

"Shall I compare thee to a temperate storm? Thou art more stormy and less temperate." "Ooh Trevor, you're such a romantic."

The Great Storm Hit the UK in 1987

On the night of the **15th October 1987** the **UK** and **France** were hit by a severe **temperate storm**...

The Storm was Caused by a Depression with Rapidly Falling Air Pressure

1) The depression began over the Bay of Biscay (north of Spain and west of France) as **south westerly** winds carrying **warm, wet air** from the **North Atlantic** met **north easterly** winds carrying **cold air** from the **Pole**.
2) The depression **deepened rapidly** due to unusually warm sea surface temperatures in the Bay of Biscay and a steep **temperature gradient** between the two air masses. Low atmospheric pressure in the core of the depression led to the development of **very strong winds**.
3) The **polar front jet stream** was located **further south** than normal, so the depression formed over northern France and southern England, rather than to the north of Scotland.
4) On the 15th October, pressure in the **centre** of the depression **fell** from 970 mb at midday to 953 mb at midnight (much lower than the average air pressure in the UK — 1013 mb).
5) The storm hit the **south coast** of **Cornwall** and **Devon** shortly after midnight, moved **across the Midlands**, and reached the **Humber Estuary** on the **east coast** at around 5.30 am on the 16th October.
6) The **South East** suffered **especially severe winds** between 3 and 6 am, with gusts up to 196 km/h at Gorleston in Norfolk. The highest hourly mean wind speed was recorded at Shoreham-by-Sea, where winds of 136 km/h blew for 20 minutes continuously.
7) After 6 am the depression began to weaken and **moved away** over the **North Sea**.

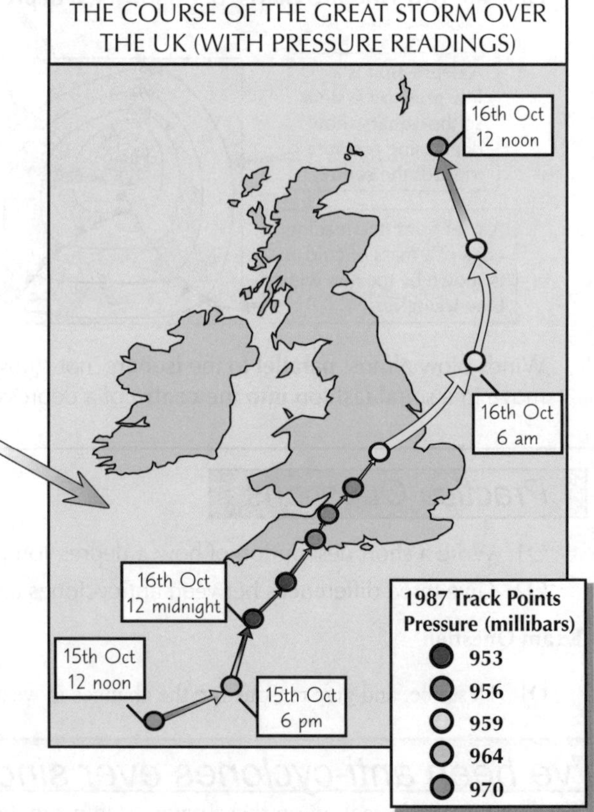

UK Storms

Impacts included *Deaths*, *Infrastructure Damage* and *Economic Costs*

SOCIAL IMPACTS

- **18 people died** in England, and another **4** in **France**.
- **Power** and **telephone lines** were knocked down (mostly by falling trees). **150 000 homes** lost their **telephone connection**, and **several hundred thousand** people had **no electricity** for more than 24 hours.
- Some **historical buildings** were **damaged** or **destroyed**, e.g. Shanklin pier on the Isle of Wight was destroyed by waves.

ECONOMIC IMPACTS

- Over **1 million buildings** were **damaged**. Insurance claims totalled **£1.4 billion**.
- **Transport** was **disrupted** as fallen trees **blocked roads** and **railways**.
- **Gatwick airport closed** because it had lost power.
- Thousands of **boats** were **wrecked**. MV Hengist, a cross channel ferry, was **beached**.

ENVIRONMENTAL IMPACTS

- About **15 million trees** were blown down.
- Some areas lost **97%** of their trees, causing a **loss** of woodland **habitat**.

Responses included *Clean Up Operations* and *Improved Forecasting*

1) During the storm **emergency authorities** (e.g. fire, police, ambulance, and coastguard) dealt with huge numbers of emergency calls — four months' worth of calls in one night.
2) After the storm a massive **recovery** and **clean up operation** began:
   - **Phone companies** and **electricity boards** worked round the clock **repairing** and **replacing equipment** until phone lines and power were restored.
   - **Highways agencies** began **clearing roads**, and **railway companies** cleared **railways**.
   - **Forestry workers** began **collecting the fallen trees** in forests (around 4 million m^3 of timber needed recovering). It took hundreds of workers **over two years** to collect and store all the timber.
   - The **Forestry Commission** established the **Forest Windblow Action Committee** to help woodland owners **recover fallen trees** and offer advice on **replanting**.
3) The **Met Office** were **criticised** for how they **forecast** the storm and **issued warnings**:
   - **Severe storm warnings** were only issued about **three hours** before the storm hit.
   - The **Ministry of Defence** were only warned that **military assistance** might be needed to help deal with the impacts of the storm at around 1 am on 16th October.
4) There was an **inquiry**, and changes were made:
   - **More observations** of weather systems are now made by **ships**, **aircraft** and **satellites**.
   - **Improved computer models** are now used to forecast weather.
   - The **government** established a **national severe weather warning service** to improve the way severe weather warnings are made and issued.

Practice Questions

Q1 What sort of weather system causes temperate storms?

Q2 What types of weather might a temperate storm cause?

Q3 Describe some of the typical impacts of temperate storms.

Exam Question

Q1 Describe the impacts of, and responses to, one temperate storm that you have studied. [10 marks]

The Great Storm — not so great, and actually quite scary...

Even if you're using a different case study, these pages are a good guide to the kind of facts and figures that you'll need to remember if you want to do well in the exam. Those examiners love specific details, so give them what they want.

Tropical Climates

For your exam you need to learn about the climate of one tropical region. There are three examples here — pick the one you've studied in class and revise that. "Just one?" I hear you cry... Sorry, but knowing all three won't get you any extra marks.

All Tropical Climates *are* ***Hot****, and* ***Most*** *are* ***Wet***

1) They're hot because the sun is **overhead** (high in the sky) — lots of **solar radiation** reaches the surface.
2) They're usually wet because they're affected by the **ITCZ** (**Intertropical Convergence Zone**). In this zone, NE and SE **trade winds** meet and create a **low pressure zone** of rising air that **cools** and **condenses**, forming **frequent heavy rainstorms**.
3) They're also wet because of travelling low pressure systems such as **subtropical cyclones**. Subtropical cyclones are **spinning storms** with a **low pressure centre** that form **outside the tropics**. They often move towards the Equator, bringing cooler air, winds and rain. (Tropical cyclones form in the tropics and are covered on p. 36-37.)

Equatorial Climates *are* ***Hot*** *and* ***Wet All Year***

Equatorial climates are found **between the Equator** and **5° north** and **south** of the Equator.

Characteristics of an Equatorial climate include:

- **Hot temperatures** all year round (about 26-32 °C). Often the daytime temperature doesn't vary by more than about 2 °C, although it can drop by up to 10 °C at night.
- **High rainfall** all year round (about 1600-3600 mm a year), with a fairly **even distribution** throughout the year. It rains **every day**, usually in the **afternoon**.
- **Winds** are mostly **warm trade winds**, and vary in strength over the year.

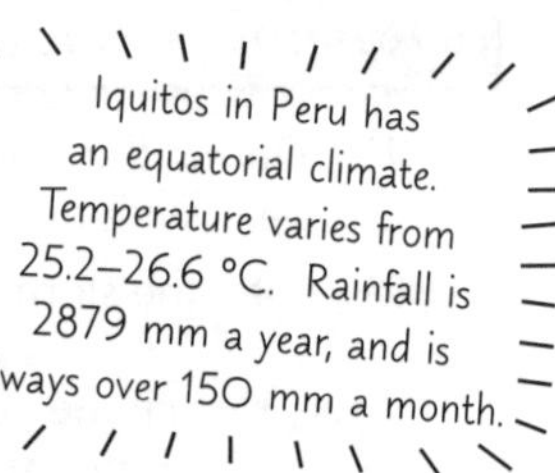

The climate is like this because:

1) The sun is **overhead all year** round.
2) The **ITCZ** influences the weather **all year round**, bringing **rain** every day.
3) **Strong convection** (heating of surface air) causes **regular afternoon rains**. The sun warms the ground, which warms the air above it and evaporates surface water. The warm, wet air rises, cools again, and the water vapour condenses into rain.

Tropical Savanna Climates *are* ***Hot*** *with a* ***Wet Season*** *and a* ***Dry Season***

Tropical savanna climates are found between **5** and **20° north** and **south** of the Equator, between the **ITCZ** and zones of **subtropical high pressure**.

Characteristics of a tropical savanna climate include:

- **Hot temperatures** all year round (between 18 and 30 °C). Often daytime temperature doesn't vary by more than about 2-4 °C (although it can drop by 10-15 °C at night).
- **Medium annual rainfall** (from around 500 mm to over 1700 mm a year). Rainfall is **seasonal** — **most** of the rain falls in the **wet season**, and **little** falls in the **dry season**.
- **Winds** are mostly **trade winds**.

Lagos in Nigeria has a tropical savanna climate. Temperature varies from 24.9–28.2 °C. Rainfall is 1740 mm a year, and it varies from 25 mm in December to 414 mm in June.

The climate is like this because:

1) The sun is **overhead all year** round.
2) The wet and dry seasons are caused by a **seasonal shift** in the position of the **ITCZ**:
   - In January, the ITCZ moves **south**. The northern hemisphere tropical savannas lie under the **high pressure zone**, so they get **little rain**.
   - In July, the ITCZ moves **north**. This brings **low pressure** and **heavy rainfall** to the tropical savannas in the northern hemisphere.

JANUARY — DRY SEASON

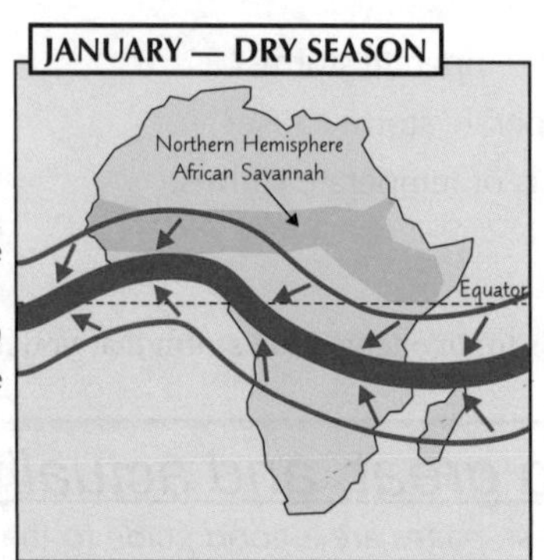

JULY — WET SEASON

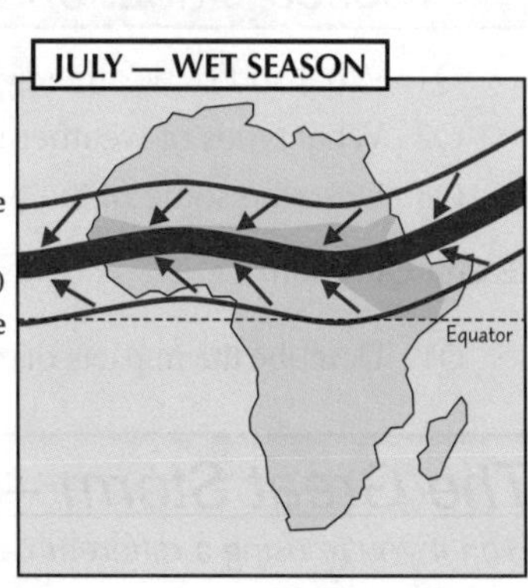

Tropical Climates

Monsoon Climates have *Hot, Wet Summers* and *Cooler, Dry Winters*

Monsoon climates are found in **coastal regions** between **5** and **20° north** and **south** of the Equator, **between the ITCZ** and a zone of **subtropical high pressure.**

Characteristics of a monsoon climate include:

- **Hot temperatures** all year round (about 18-30 °C), varying by up to 10 °C between summer and winter.
- **Rainfall is high** (around 3000 mm a year). **Most** of the rain falls in the **wet season**, and little falls in the dry season.
- **Winds change direction with the seasons** — in the wet season the winds blow towards the land and in the dry season they blow towards the sea.

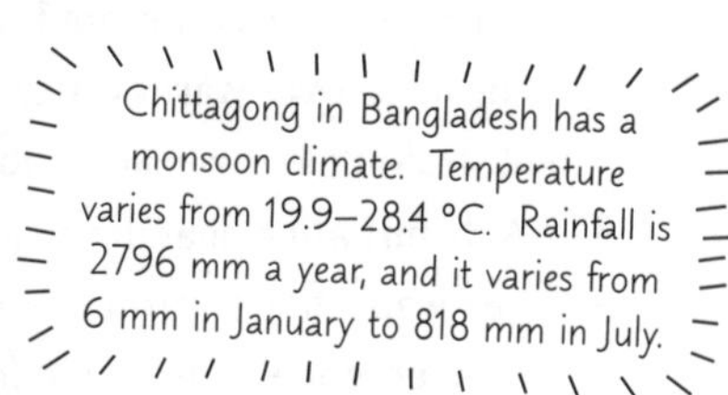

The climate is like this because:

1) The sun is **overhead all year** round.
2) Seasonal changes in **rainfall**, **temperature** and **wind direction** are caused by a **seasonal shift** in the position of the **ITCZ** and zones of **high pressure**. E.g. on the Indian subcontinent:

In the **cool**, **dry** season:

- The ITCZ moves **south**. Northern hemisphere tropical monsoon areas lie under the **high pressure zone**, so they get **little rain**.
- The ITCZ is **over the ocean**, and a zone of high pressure is **over the land**. This forces winds **from** the land to the ocean.
- The land is cooler than the ocean (land cools down faster than water), so these **NE winds** are **cool** and bring lower temperatures.

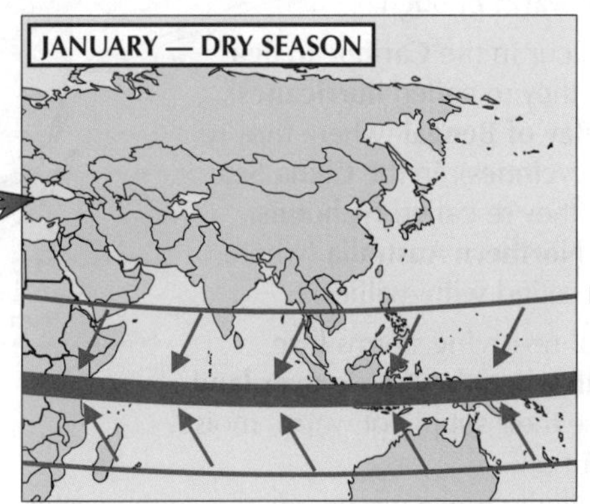

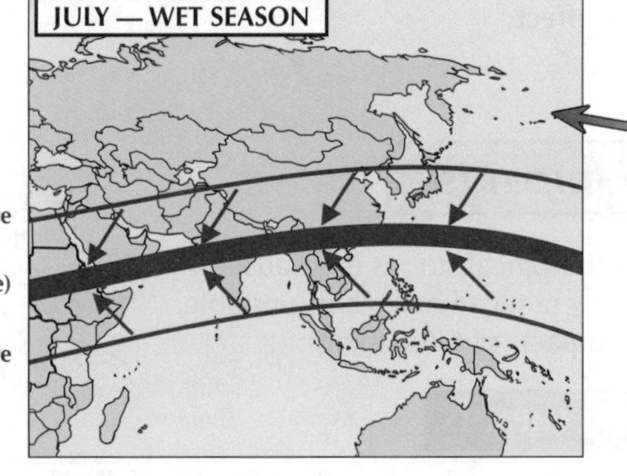

In the **warm**, **wet** season:

- The ITCZ moves **north**. This brings **low pressure** and **heavy rainfall** to the tropical monsoon areas in the northern hemisphere.
- The ITCZ is **over the land**, and a zone of high pressure is **over the ocean**. This forces the winds **from** the ocean to the land.
- The ocean is warmer than the land (water cools down slower than land), so these **SE winds** are **warm** and bring higher temperatures.

Practice Questions

Q1 Why are tropical climates hot?

Q2 What is the ITCZ?

Q3 What type of weather does the ITCZ bring?

Q4 What type of weather do subtropical cyclones bring?

Exam Question

Q1 Describe and explain the climate in one tropical region. [8 marks]

A-Level high pressure belt — found in the exam convergence zone...

Ah the tropics — white sand beaches, azure seas, swaying palm trees, monsoon rain... Hmmm, the holiday brochure didn't mention that last one. Maybe I'll just stick to sandy sandwiches and a can of pop in the good old British drizzle...

Tropical Revolving Storms

The weather in tropical areas is generally a darn sight better than it is here, but things can get ugly...

Tropical Revolving Storms Form Over Warm Water in the Tropics

1) Tropical revolving storms are **huge spinning storms** with **strong winds** and **torrential rain**.
2) They develop over **warm water**. As warm, moist air **rises** and **condenses**, it **releases energy** that increases wind speed.
3) Scientists don't know exactly **how** they're formed but they do know the **conditions needed**. These include:
   - A **disturbance** near the sea-surface that triggers the storm (e.g. an area of low pressure).
   - **Sea water** that's **warm** (above **26.5°C** to **at least 50 m** below the surface), so lots of water will evaporate.
   - **Convergence of air** in the **lower atmosphere** — either within the ITCZ or along the boundary between warm and cold air masses. This forces warm air to **rise**.
   - A location at least **5° from the Equator**. They **don't form 0-5° either side** of the Equator because the **Coriolis effect** isn't strong enough to make them spin.

The Coriolis effect is a force caused by the Earth's rotation. It deflects the path of winds but it's weak at the Equator.

4) So tropical revolving storms form in the **tropics** because the water there is **warm enough**.
5) They occur in the **Caribbean Sea** (where they're called **hurricanes**), in the **Bay of Bengal** (where they're called **cyclones**), in the **China Sea** (where they're called **typhoons**) and in **Northern Australia** (where they're called **willy-willies**).
6) Tropical revolving storms **lose strength** when they move **over land** because their supply of warm, moist air is cut off.
7) They initially **move westwards** due to the **easterly winds** in the **tropics**, e.g. the trade winds move cyclones west across the Atlantic Ocean.
8) They **move away** from the **Equator** because of the **Coriolis effect**.

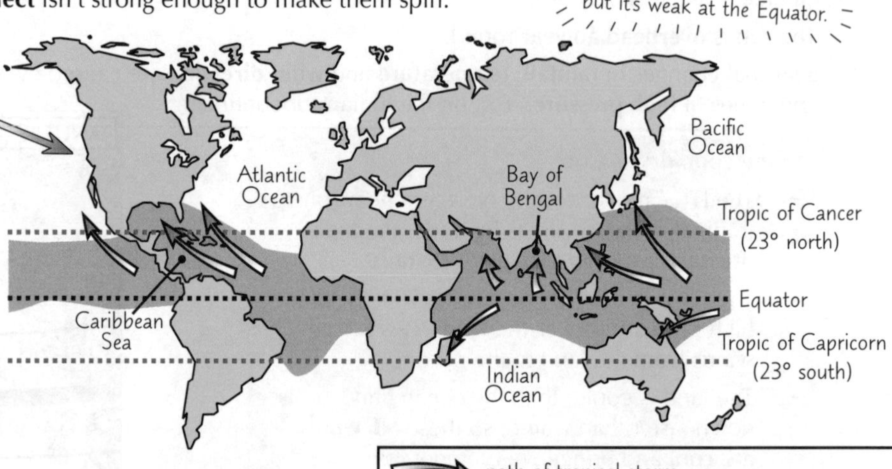

Tropical Revolving Storms Have a Lot of Impacts

The **strong winds**, **high rainfall** and **storm surges** that come with tropical storms can cause havoc. High rainfall and storm surges cause **flooding** (and heavy rain can make hills unstable, causing **landslides**). Here are a **few examples** of the **possible impacts** of these things:

Storm surges are large rises in sea level caused by the low pressure and high winds of a storm.

ENVIRONMENTAL IMPACTS

1) **Beaches** are **eroded** and **coastal habitats** (e.g. coral reefs) are **damaged**.
2) **Environments** are **polluted** by all sorts of things, e.g. salt water, oil, chemicals spilled from factories damaged by the storm.

ECONOMIC IMPACTS

1) **Buildings, bridges, roads, railways, ports** and **airports** are **damaged** or **destroyed**. These cost a huge amount to **rebuild**.
2) **Business premises** are **damaged** or **destroyed**, so they **can't trade**.
3) **Agricultural land** is **damaged**, affecting **commercial farming**.

SOCIAL IMPACTS

1) People may **drown**, or be **injured** or **killed** by **debris** that's blown around or carried in flood water.
2) People are left **homeless**.
3) **Electricity supplies** are **cut off** because cables are damaged.
4) Flooding causes **sewage** overflows which **contaminate water supplies**.
5) The **shortage** of **clean water** and **lack** of proper **sanitation** makes it easier for **diseases** to spread.
6) In **poorer countries** there's often a **shortage** of **food** because **crops** are damaged and **livestock** is killed.
7) **Unemployment increases** because **businesses** are damaged or destroyed.
8) **Damaged roads** make it very difficult for **aid** and **emergency vehicles** to get through.

Tropical Revolving Storms

The **Impacts** are Usually **Higher** in **Less Developed Countries**

There are several reasons why the impacts of a tropical storm are **higher** in **less developed countries**:

- They **don't have the money to respond**, e.g. there is little money for flood defences or training emergency teams.
- The **buildings** are **poorer quality** compared to more developed countries, so are **more easily damaged** by storms.
- **Evacuation** can be **difficult** to organise, particularly when there is **limited access to transport** or when **rural populations** live in **remote areas** with poor communications.
- **Health care isn't as good** in less developed countries, so they **struggle** to **treat large numbers** of **casualties**.
- **Many people depend on agriculture** in less developed countries, which is often badly affected.
- **Infrastructure** is often **poorer**, making it **more difficult** for **emergency services** to **reach affected areas**.

However, the **economic impact** is often **higher** in **more developed** countries, as the **buildings** and **infrastructure** damaged are **worth a lot of money**.

Learn the Main **Responses** to **Tropical Revolving Storms**

EVACUATION

1) **When** and **where** tropical storms will hit land can be **predicted**. Scientists use **data** from things like **radar**, **satellites** and **aircraft** to **track** the storm. **Computer models** are then used to **calculate** a **predicted path**. For example, the **National Hurricane Center** in the USA tracks and predicts hurricanes using these techniques.
2) Predicting where and when a tropical storm is going to strike **gives people time** to **evacuate**. It also gives them time to **protect** their **homes** and **businesses**, e.g. by **boarding up windows** so they don't get smashed.
3) Evacuation can be a **very effective** response, e.g. a cyclone in Bangladesh in 1997 only killed around 100 people because of a successful evacuation. However, it's not effective if people don't receive the evacuation order.
4) Also, if forecasters get it wrong and areas are **evacuated unnecessarily** it **wastes a lot of money**.

PLANNING and EDUCATION

1) **Future developments**, e.g. new houses, can be **planned** to **avoid** the **areas most at risk** (e.g. right on the coast).
2) **Emergency services** can **train** and **prepare** for disasters. For example, in the USA **FEMA** (Federal Emergency Management Agency) train emergency personnel to deal with disasters such as floods and hurricanes.
3) Governments can plan **evacuation routes** to **get people away from storms quickly**. For example, in **Florida** evacuation routes are signposted all along the coast.
4) **Governments** and other **organisations** can **educate people** about **how to prepare** for a tropical storm (e.g. by stockpiling water and food) and **how to evacuate**.
5) All these methods are very **cost-effective**.

BUILDING TECHNIQUES

1) Buildings **can be designed** to **withstand tropical storms**, e.g. by using **reinforced concrete** or by **fixing roofs securely** so they don't get blown off. Buildings can also be **put on stilts** so they're safe from floodwater. For example, homes along the **Gulf Coast** of the USA are built on stilts.
2) **Flood defences** can be built **along rivers** (e.g. levees) and **coasts** (e.g. sea walls).
3) These methods **are effective**, but **don't guarantee** buildings **won't be damaged**. For example, levees in New Orleans broke during Hurricane Katrina, flooding the city.

AID

Aid sent by **governments** or **organisations** can be **very effective**, but there are often **problems** with **getting the aid to the people who need it**, e.g. due to **damaged roads** or **political problems**. For example, Burma's government initially refused to let aid workers in after Cylone Nargis in 2008.

Aid includes lots of things, e.g. tents, food, medicine, rescue teams.

Practice Questions

Q1 Give two social impacts and two environmental impacts of tropical revolving storms.

Q2 Give three reasons why the impacts of tropical revolving storms are usually higher in less developed countries.

Exam Questions

Q1 Describe the characteristics of tropical revolving storms. [7 marks]

Q2 Comment on the effectiveness of responses to tropical revolving storms. [8 marks]

My response to this page is aaaaaaaaaaaagggggggghhhhh...

There's a whopping amount to learn on these two pages, so stop eyeing up the TV remote (I saw you) and get learnin'.

Tropical Revolving Storm Case Study — Katrina

And now time for the inevitable case studies — first up, a little madam called Katrina...

Hurricane Katrina *Struck the* ***South East USA*** *on* ***29th August 2005***

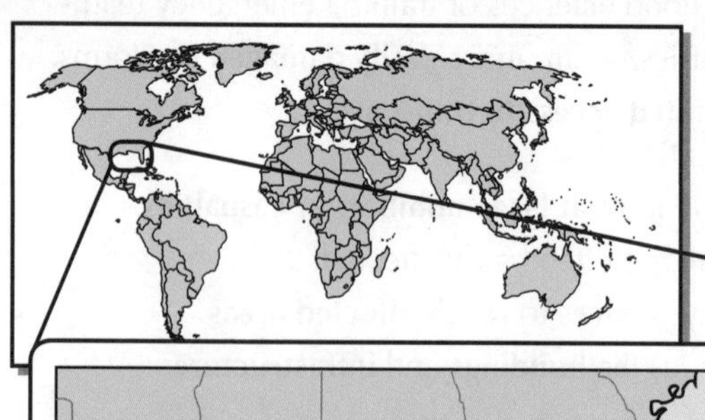

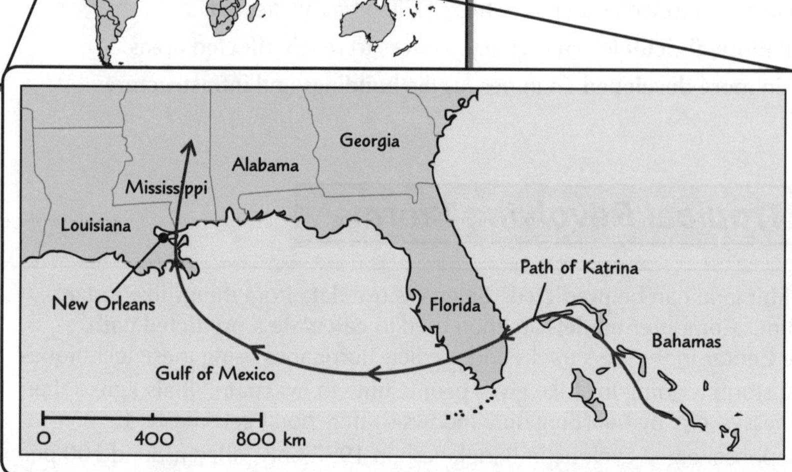

1) A storm **formed** over the **Bahamas** on the **23rd August**.
2) It moved **north west** and **strengthened into a hurricane** just before it went over the southern tip of **Florida** into the **Gulf of Mexico**.
3) As it travelled over the warm water of the Gulf of Mexico it **strengthened** from a **Category 1** hurricane to a **Category 5** hurricane.

Hurricanes are classified using the Saffir-Simpson Scale, which is based on wind speed. Category 5 is the strongest (with winds over 250 km/h) and 1 is the weakest (with winds of 120-150 km/h).

4) On the night of the **28th August** it **weakened** to a **Category 3** hurricane.
5) On the **morning** of the **29th** it struck land, bringing winds of around **200 km/h** and **200-250 mm** rainfall in **Louisiana** and a **storm surge** of up to **8.5 m** in **Mississippi**.
6) It **travelled over 240 km inland** before the winds dropped enough for it to be **downgraded** from a hurricane to a storm.

The Hurricane had a ***Huge Economic Impact***

1) The coast of **Louisiana** and **Mississippi** bore the brunt of the hurricane, but south Florida and Cuba were also affected. The city of **New Orleans** was very badly damaged. The storm surge and heavy rainfall **overwhelmed the levees** which should have **protected** the city. This caused **widespread flooding** (over **80%** of the city was **underwater**) which hugely increased the **number of deaths** and **level of damage**.
2) The **high winds**, **storm surge** and **flooding** had the following impacts:

SOCIAL IMPACTS

- **1836** people were **killed**.
- **300 000 houses** were **destroyed**.
- **Hundreds of thousands** of people were made **homeless**.
- **3 million** people were left **without electricity**.
- One of the main routes out of New Orleans was closed because parts of the **I-10 bridge collapsed**.
- **Water supplies** were **polluted** with sewage, chemicals and dead bodies. **Five people died** from **bacterial infections** caught from the contaminated water (although this was far less than feared).
- The **education** of hundreds of thousands of children suffered when schools were damaged or destroyed, e.g. **18 schools** in **New Orleans** were **destroyed** and **74** were badly **damaged**.

ECONOMIC IMPACTS

- **230 000 jobs** were **lost** from businesses that were damaged or destroyed.
- The total **cost of damage** is estimated at around **$300 billion**.
- **30 oil platforms** in the Gulf of Mexico were **damaged** or **destroyed** and **nine oil refineries** had to **close**, disrupting the oil industry.
- **5300 km² of forest** was destroyed in **Mississippi**, severely affecting the **logging industry** (the loss of income was estimated to be about **$5 billion**).
- Many **ports** were **damaged**, e.g. **Gulfport** in Mississippi. This disrupted the **shipping industry**.

Damage from Hurricane Katrina.

ENVIRONMENTAL IMPACTS

- **Coastal habitats** such as **sea turtle breeding beaches** were **damaged**.
- Some **coastal conservation areas** were **destroyed**, e.g. around **half of Breton National Wildlife Refuge** in **Louisiana** was **washed away**.
- Flooding damaged oil refineries in Louisiana, causing massive **oil spills**.
- Permanent flooding of **salt marshes** in **Louisiana** caused loss of habitat.

Tropical Revolving Storm Case Study — Katrina

*Effective **Warning Systems** Helped the USA **Respond Rapidly***

WARNINGS

1) The USA has a **sophisticated monitoring system** to **predict** if (and where) a hurricane will hit. The **National Hurricane Center** (**NHC**) in Florida tracks and predicts hurricanes using things like **satellite images**, and **'hurricane hunter' planes** that collect weather data on approaching storms.
2) On **August 26th** the NHC issued a **hurricane warning** for **Louisiana**, **Mississippi** and **Alabama**. It continued to track the hurricane, updating the government on where and when it would hit.

RESPONSES BEFORE IT HIT

1) The Federal Emergency Management Agency (**FEMA**) **coordinated** the **response**.
2) A **state of emergency was declared** in **Louisiana** on the evening of the **26th August**, and in **Mississippi** on the **27th**. FEMA and various other organisations **started preparing** for the hurricane, for example:
   - The **US Coast Guard** positioned **helicopters** and **boats** around the area likely to be affected.
   - **FEMA** organised teams and supplies, e.g. **mortuary teams** with refrigerated trucks to deal with bodies.
3) On the morning of **August 28th** the mayor of New Orleans ordered a **mandatory (compulsory) evacuation** of the city. It's estimated that around **80%** of New Orleans residents **were evacuated** before the hurricane reached land. This reduced the number of people killed because lots of people had left the areas where the hurricane hit.
4) **Voluntary** or **mandatory evacuation orders** were also issued in **other places** along the coast.

RESPONSES DURING/AFTER

1) Around **100 000 people didn't evacuate**, either because they wanted to **stay and protect their property**, or because they **didn't have enough money** or **didn't have any transport**. **Emergency shelters** were set up for these people, e.g. the **Louisiana Superdome** in New Orleans sheltered **26 000 people** during the hurricane.
2) The coastguard, police, fire service and army **rescued over 50 000 people** after the hurricane hit.
3) Lots of organisations sent **teams** and **supplies** into the area after the hurricane:
   - **FEMA** sent **search and rescue** teams, **medical** teams, **water**, **ice** and **ready meals**.
   - 58 000 **National Guard troops** (reserve military troops) were deployed from all over the US and were responsible for rescuing 17 000 people and evacuating 70 000.
   - **Charities** collected over **$4 billion** of donations from the public to provide aid to victims of Katrina, e.g. the Salvation Army provided 5.7 million hot meals to people in and around New Orleans in the days after the storm.

Responses** to the Disaster Have Been **Criticised

The national response **reduced the impact** of the hurricane, but it was subject to **criticism**:

1) Some **emergency shelters weren't properly prepared** for the number of people needing shelter, e.g. the National Guard delivered enough food to the Louisiana Superdome to feed 15 000 people for 3 days, but 26 000 turned up.
2) Widespread **looting** took place in many areas, e.g. in New Orleans, because there **weren't enough police** or **troops**.
3) Most people agree that the evacuations ordered saved many lives, but the evacuations were **criticised** for **not helping people without transport** to get out, e.g. poorer New Orleans residents without a car.

Practice Questions

Q1 On what date did Hurricane Katrina hit the South East USA?

Q2 Give two social impacts, two economic impacts and two environmental impacts of Hurricane Katrina.

Exam Question

Q1 With reference to one example, discuss how the impacts of a tropical revolving storm are affected by the preparation for and response to the event. [10 marks]

You need to know what happened, the impacts and the responses...

The US was pretty prepared for a hurricane, but the sheer size and strength of Hurricane Katrina and the fact that New Orleans received a direct hit caused problems. The death toll was way, way higher than anybody expected for such a developed country.

Tropical Revolving Storm Case Study — Nargis

And for your second helping of case study it's... drum roll please... Cyclone Nargis.

Cyclone Nargis** Struck **Burma** on **2nd May 2008

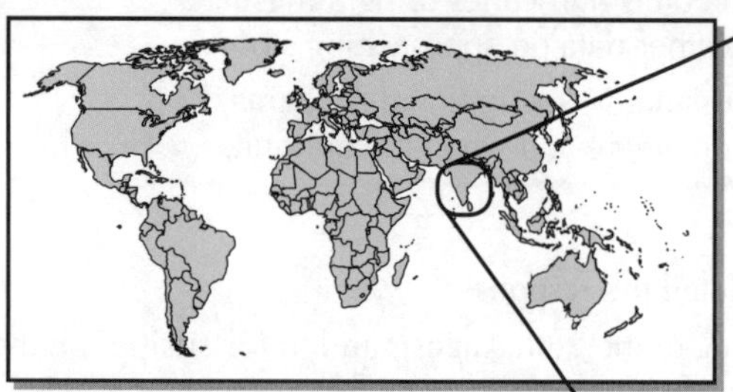

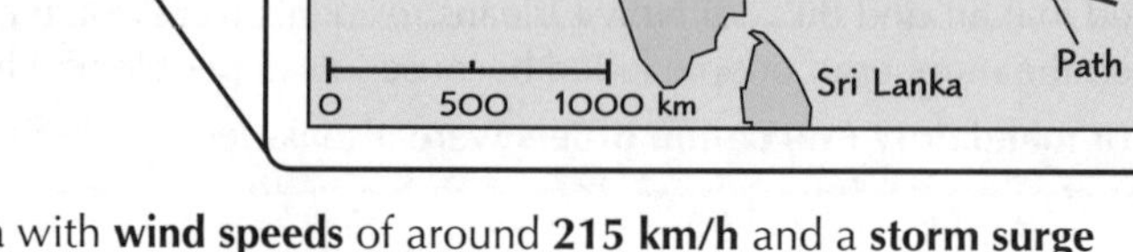

1) A storm **formed** in the **Bay of Bengal** during the **last week** in **April**.
2) On the **28th April** it had **strengthened** enough to be **upgraded** to a **cyclone**.
3) As it **approached the coast of Burma** it strengthened to **Category 4** on the Saffir-Simpson scale (p. 38).
4) On **May 2nd** it **hit the coast of Burma** with **wind speeds** of around **215 km/h** and a **storm surge** of **5 m** (storm waves added another 2 m on top of this).
5) It **weakened** as it **moved inland** and was **downgraded** from a cyclone to a storm on the **3rd May**.

*The Cyclone had a **Huge Social Impact***

1) The **Irrawaddy Delta** in Burma was the hardest hit area because the cyclone hit it head on. A large proportion of it is only just above sea level and over **14 000 km²** of land was **flooded**.
2) **Sri Lanka** was also affected by heavy rainfall, which led to **flooding** and **landslides**.
3) Across the region, the **high winds**, **storm surge** and **flooding** had the following impacts:

SOCIAL IMPACTS

- More than **140 000** people were **killed**.
- **450 000 houses** were **destroyed** and **350 000** were **damaged**.
- **4000 schools** were **destroyed** or severely **damaged**.
- **75%** of **health facilities** were **destroyed** or **severely damaged**.
- Up to **2.5 million** people were left without **shelter**.
- **43%** of **freshwater ponds** (valuable sources of fresh water for local people) were **damaged** by salt water.
- **Almost 70%** of the population **had no access** to **clean water**.
- A lot of people suffered from **diseases** caused by **poor sanitary conditions** and **contaminated water**, e.g. **dysentry, diarrhoea**.
- Many people suffered **mental health problems** afterwards, e.g. up to 30% of the people treated by one aid agency had mental health problems caused by the cyclone.

A house damaged by Cyclone Nargis.

ENVIRONMENTAL IMPACTS

- **38 000 hectares** of **mangrove forests** were **destroyed**.
- The flooding caused **erosion** and **salination** (increased salt content) of land.

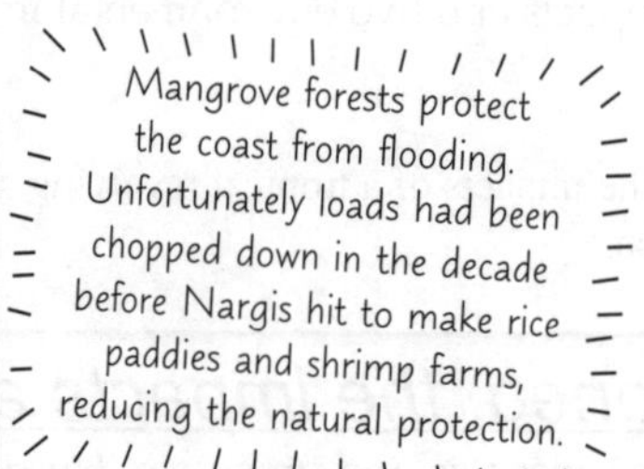

ECONOMIC IMPACTS

- Over **600 000 hectares** of **agricultural land** was damaged, including around 65% of rice paddies in the region.
- **Crops** were **lost**, **200 000 farm animals** were **killed** and over **40%** of **food stores** were **destroyed**. This had a huge impact on the **agricultural industry**.
- **Millions** of people **lost their livelihoods**, e.g. many **fishing boats** were destroyed.
- The **total cost** of the damage was around **$4 billion**.

Tropical Revolving Storm Case Study — Nargis

Burma Wasn't Prepared for Cyclone Nargis

1) **Burma doesn't have** a dedicated **hurricane monitoring centre.** However, **Indian** weather agencies **warned** the Burmese Government that Cyclone Nargis was likely to hit the country **48 hours before** it did.
2) **Burmese weather forecasters** did **give warnings** the cyclone was coming via **TV** and **radio**, but it's claimed that they **didn't** say how **severe** it would be or give any advice about **how to prepare** or **evacuate**. This **increased** the number of people **killed** because people didn't know what to do or where to evacuate to.
3) There were **no emergency preparation plans, no evacuation plans** and the country **didn't** have an **early warning system.**

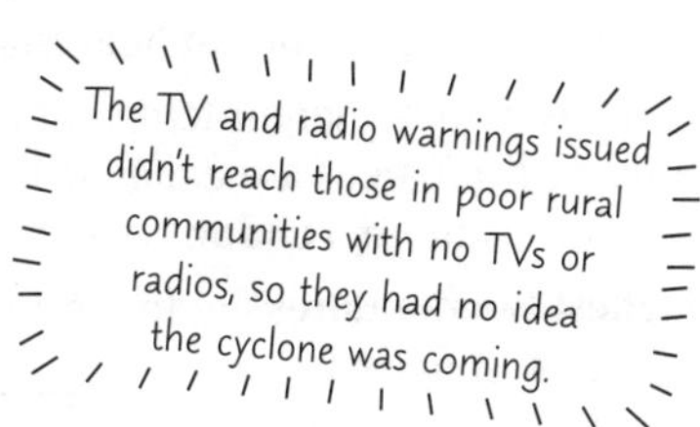

The Response was Really Slow

1) **Burma's government** initially **refused** to accept any **foreign aid.**
2) On the 9th May they decided to **accept aid donations** of things like food and tents, but **wouldn't** let in **aid workers.** Some countries and organisations sent aid that helped **reduce** the impacts of the cyclone, for example:
   - The **UN refugee agency** (UNHCR) sent in 22 tonnes of tents and other supplies from Thailand.
   - **Charities** sent aid e.g. **Muslim Aid** distributed water purification tablets, blankets and food parcels.
   - **Italy** sent 25 tonnes of **emergency equipment**, e.g. **shelters, first aid kits** and **water purifiers.**
3) This helped a lot, but there were **still problems**, e.g. a French Navy ship carrying 1500 tonnes of supplies was refused entry because the Burmese government thought it was a warship.
4) Also, some **aid** was **seized** by the **military**, delaying its delivery to the people who needed it, e.g. two shipments of high-energy biscuits were seized.
5) On the 19th May, **ASEAN** (Association of South East Asian Nations) held an emergency summit to discuss the situation. Following this, Burma decided to **allow aid workers** from **ASEAN member countries** in to help.
6) After talks between the **UN Secretary General** and the **Burmese leader** Than Shwe, **all aid workers** were **allowed in** on the **23rd May** — **three weeks after** the disaster occurred.
7) The **government response** to the disaster has been **heavily criticised** by other countries — the delay in accepting international aid greatly increased the number of deaths because help for some people **came too late.**

Practice Questions

Q1 On what date did Cyclone Nargis hit Burma?

Q2 What category was Cyclone Nargis when it hit Burma?

Q3 Describe the timeline of Cyclone Nargis.

Q4 Which area of Burma was worst hit?

Q5 Give two social impacts, two economic impacts and two environmental impacts of Cyclone Nargis.

Exam Question

Q1 With reference to two examples, discuss how the impacts of a tropical revolving storm are affected by the level of economic development of the country it affects. [40 marks]

Make sure you learn all about Cyclone Nargis...

Disasters tends to have a higher social impact in less developed countries, and a higher economic impact in more developed countries. This is the same whether you're studying a tropical storm, an earthquake or a volcano, so make sure you understand why it is.

Urban Climate Characteristics

Urban climate characteristics — or 'what the weather's like in cities' to you and me. Geographers and their fancy names...

Urban Areas are Warmer than the Surrounding Rural Areas

1) The phenomenon of urban areas being warmer than rural areas is called the **urban heat island effect.**
2) Urban areas with higher air temperatures than the surrounding rural areas are called **urban heat islands** (UHIs). For example, **London** has a clearly defined UHI.
3) The **highest temperatures** are found in **industrial areas** and in the most **densely built up** areas, e.g. the **CBD** (Central Business District).

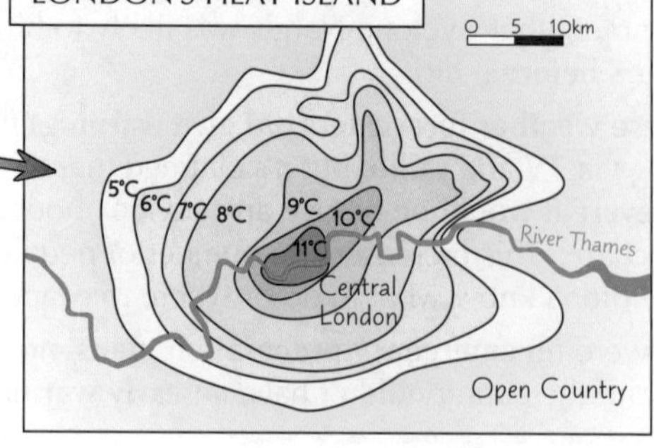

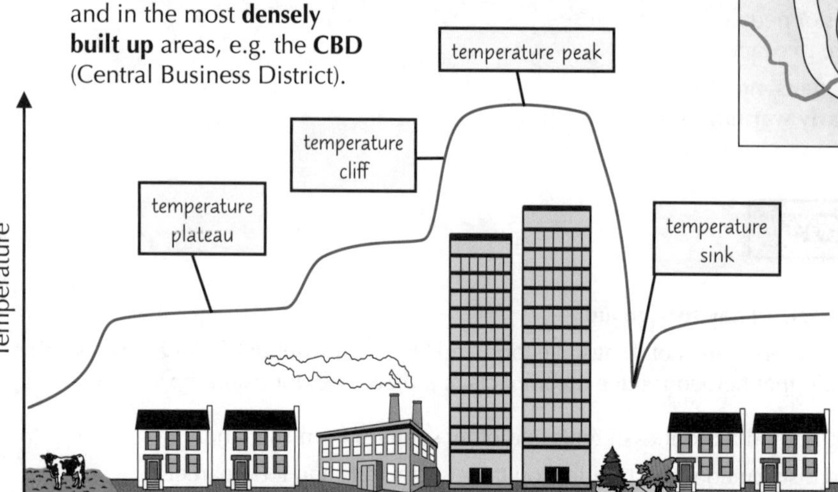

4) There are **pockets** of **cool air** above **parks** and **bodies of water** (e.g. rivers or ponds). These are called temperature '**sinks**'.
5) Areas within the city with the **same land use** (e.g. industry) generally have the **same temperature**. These are called temperature '**plateaus**'.
6) Temperature can **change rapidly** when **land use changes** (e.g. from inner city housing to CBD high rise buildings). Rapid changes are referred to as temperature '**cliffs**'.

There are Four Main Causes of the UHI Effect

Urban surfaces have a low albedo (p. 25) — they absorb lots of energy instead of reflecting it.

1) **ABSORPTION OF HEAT BY URBAN SURFACES:**
Concrete, brick and tarmac surfaces **absorb** and **store heat from the sun** during the **day**. They slowly **release** the heat as **long wave radiation** — this is most noticeable at **night**, when it warms the air.
2) **AIR POLLUTION:**
Air pollution from cars and factories **increases cloud cover** over the city. It also creates a '**pollution dome**' — a layer of pollution over the city. Both these things **trap outgoing heat radiation** and **reflect it back** to the surface.
3) **HEAT FROM HUMAN ACTIVITY:**
Cars, factories, offices, central heating, air conditioning units and people themselves all release heat.
4) **LESS EVAPOTRANSPIRATION:**
When it rains the water's quickly removed by **drainage systems**, so there's **little surface water** to **evaporate**. Also, there isn't much **vegetation**, so there's **little transpiration**. **Evapotranspiration** uses heat energy, so less evapotranspiration means higher temperatures.

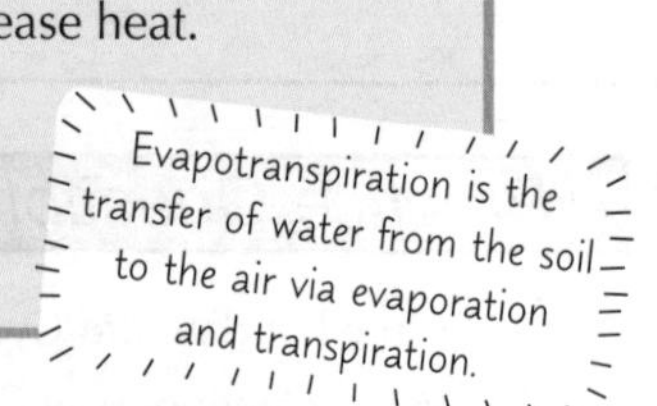

The Effect Varies Seasonally and Diurnally (between Day and Night)

1) The UHI effect is stronger at **NIGHT**. Urban **daytime** temperatures are on average **0.6 °C warmer** than surrounding rural areas, but **night time** temperatures can be **3-4 °C warmer**. This is because rural areas cool down at night, but **urban areas don't cool as much** because **urban surfaces continue to release heat** that they've absorbed during the day.
2) It's stronger in **SUMMER** (in mid-latitude cities like London). Average **winter** temperatures can be **2 °C warmer**, but average summer temperatures can be up to **5 °C warmer**. This is because there's **more solar radiation in summer**, so urban areas absorb more heat.
3) It's stronger when there's an **ANTICYCLONE**. Anticyclones cause **clear skies** and **low winds** (see p. 31). If there are no clouds, **more solar radiation** reaches and heats the ground. **Low winds** mean **warm air isn't blown away**.

Urban Climate Characteristics

Winds are Affected by Buildings in Urban Areas

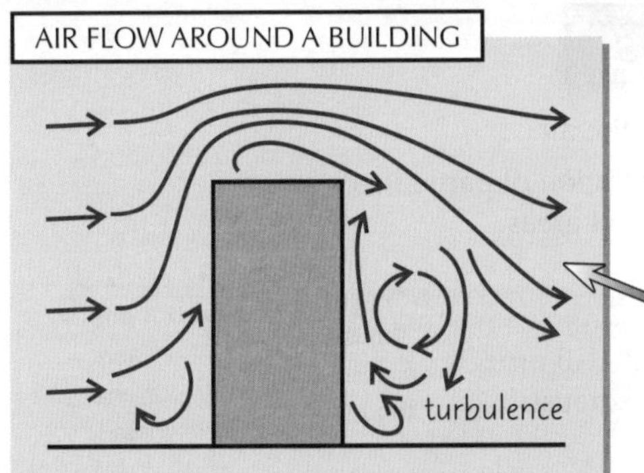

1) **Average wind speed** is usually **lower** in cities than in rural areas. This is because **tall buildings create friction** that slows down the moving air.
2) There are areas where **wind speed** is **zero**, because some areas are **totally sheltered** from wind by **buildings**.
3) You get **turbulence around buildings**. This happens when **wind hits** the **face** of a **building** — some of it's **deflected down**, some **around the sides** and some **over the top**. When these winds hit other buildings or the ground they causes **vortices** (bodies of swirling air).
4) You get **powerful gusts** of wind when wind is **channelled down streets** — this is known as the **canyon effect**.

The canyon effect has implications for building design and town planning, e.g. positioning of buildings, and the location of doorways on larger buildings.

There's More Rain, Fog and Thunderstorms...

1) It **rains more often** in urban areas than in the surrounding countryside.
2) The rain is also **more intense** and there are **more thunderstorms**.
3) There are **two** main reasons for these things:

- The **UHI effect** means the air in urban areas is warm, and warm air can hold more water. The **warm, moist air rises** — this is called **convectional uplift**. As it rises it **cools**, the **water vapour condenses** and it **rains**. This type of rain is called **convectional rainfall**.
- Urban areas generate huge amounts of **dust** and **pollution**. Particles of dust and pollution floating about in the air act as **condensation nuclei** (they trigger water to condense around them). This **encourages clouds** to form, rather than allowing the warm, moist air to disperse.

4) The higher concentration of **condensation nuclei** in urban areas also **increases** the **frequency** of **fog**.

...but Less Snow and Frost

1) It **doesn't snow as often** in urban areas, and when it does snow the **snow melts faster**. This is because it's **warmer** due to the **UHI effect**.
2) Urban areas have **fewer days of frost** for the same reason.

Darn that UHI effect — now I've gone and got my sleigh stuck.

Practice Questions

Q1 What is the urban heat island effect?

Q2 Briefly describe the four main causes of the urban heat island effect.

Q3 Explain why the urban heat island effect is stronger at night than during the day.

Q4 What effect do urban structures have on average wind speed?

Q5 Why is fog more frequent in urban areas than in rural areas?

Exam Question

	City A	City B
Annual average rainfall (mm)	1200	1300
Average July temperature (°C)	21	23
Average number of thunderstorms per year	18	25
Average number of days with fog	17	23
Average number of days without cloud cover	180	120

Q1 Study the table, which shows climate data for two cities.
Describe and suggest reasons for the differences between the two urban climates. [7 marks]

UHI — I'm sure you can buy cream for that...

If you know what causes the UHI effect, you should be able to use your common sense to answer any exam question on it, e.g. if you're asked why parks are cooler than built up areas, talk about the fact that they have more vegetation and less tarmac. If you're asked why one city has a stronger UHI than another think about whether it might be more polluted, or more built up.

Urban Air Quality

*Urban air pollution causes a range of pretty horrible health problems. Today, *cough* — sorry. Today, most pollution comes from road traffic. Cities all over the world have tried to solve the pollution problem simply by reducing traffic.*

There's a lot of **Particulate Pollution** in Urban Areas

1) **Particulates** are **tiny pieces** of **solids** and **tiny droplets** of **liquids** floating in the air.
2) **More** particulates are found in **urban areas** than in rural areas. The concentration of particulates in urban areas is around 10-40 μg/m³, compared to less than 10 μg/m³ in rural areas.
3) **Sources** of particulates include:

A microgram (μg) is a one thousandth of a gram and a micrometre (μm) is a one thousandth of a millimetre.

- **Vehicle exhausts** — they produce very **fine particulates** (0.01 μm-1.0 μm). About **80%** of fine particulates in urban areas are from vehicle exhausts.
- **Burning** of refuse, cigarettes and fuel, e.g. coal — this produces both **fine** and **coarse particulates**, e.g. sulphates, nitrates, soot and ash.
- **Construction**, **mining** and **quarrying** — these activities produce **coarse particulates** (10 μm-100 μm), e.g. tiny fragments of rock, brick and cement dust.
- **Plants and moulds** — also generate **coarse particulates**, e.g. pollen and mould spores.

4) Particulates can cause **health problems**. **Coarser particulates** are usually **filtered out** by the nose and throat, but **finer particulates less than 10 μm** in diameter (often called PM10) can enter the **lungs**. PM10 could **cause** or **make worse** problems like asthma, bronchitis, lung cancer and heart disease.

Other Types of Pollution Lead to **Photochemical Smog**

1) Pollutants such as **nitrogen oxides**, **sulfur oxides** and **hydrocarbons** come from **burning fossil fuels** (e.g. in vehicles and factories).
2) When these **pollutants** come into contact with **sunlight**, the **UV light** causes them to **break down** into **harmful chemicals** (e.g. ozone) which form **photochemical smog**.
3) Photochemical smog is a **problem** in **many cities**, e.g. Los Angeles (USA), Beijing (China), Mexico City (Mexico) and Barcelona (Spain). It's more common in places with **hot** and **sunny climates** because there's **more sunlight**.
4) These locations often have a **temperature inversion** (a layer of warm air trapped below denser cooler air), which keeps the pollutants at **ground level**.
5) Photochemical smog is linked to **health problems** such as **breathing difficulties** (coughing, shortness of breath), **respiratory disorders** (e.g. asthma) and **headaches**.

©iStockphoto.com/Phototreat

Smog over Mexico City.

Ozone is useful in the upper atmosphere (protecting us from UV radiation), but when it's in the lower atmosphere it causes health problems.

There are Lots of Different Ways to **Reduce Air Pollution**

Lots of cities have tried to **reduce pollution** by **reducing traffic**. There are various ways that this can be done:

CONGESTION CHARGING

- **People** are charged if they **use their vehicles** in **certain places** at **certain times**.
- This reduces pollution by **reducing road traffic**. In **Central London** congestion charging has reduced traffic and emissions in the congestion zone by **up to 15%** since 2003.
- However, some people **travel around** the edge of **zones** to avoid being charged, which increases traffic in these areas.
- It's difficult to enforce the charge because the **volume of traffic** is so large that it's hard to process all the fines correctly.

PEDESTRIANISATION

- **Vehicles are restricted** from **entering certain places** at **certain times**. It reduces pollution by **reducing road traffic**.
- Many cities have pedestrianised zones — including London, Cardiff, Manchester and Liverpool.
- Pedestrianisation can lead to shops receiving **fewer customers** because people can only get to them on foot.

Urban Air Quality

PUBLIC TRANSPORT IMPROVEMENTS

- Encouraging people to **use public transport** instead of their cars reduces pollution. For example, many cities have:
  - **Improved bus services** to make bus journeys cheaper, faster and more efficient. E.g. many cities have introduced bus lanes so buses don't get caught in slow-moving traffic.
  - **Park and ride schemes** (car parks on public transport routes) to make it easier to **access public transport**.
  - **Trams** and **light railway services** which run on lines, so they don't get caught in **road congestion**. They also **pollute less** than **buses**. E.g. The Metrolink in Manchester opened in 1992. It links the city centre to the suburbs and has been very successful — the line to Bury and Altrincham has taken about **2.6 million** cars off the roads.
- Public transport improvements are often **expensive** — e.g. construction of the Metrolink has cost over £1 billion.
- New developments can also cause problems — e.g. **park and ride schemes** can shift traffic problems to rural areas.

OTHER SCHEMES FOR REDUCING TRAFFIC

- In **Mexico City** drivers are **banned** from using their cars **one weekday** per week, based on the last digit of their number plate, e.g. number plates ending in 5 or 6 can't be used on Mondays. However, some richer households get around the system by **buying two cars**.
- **Birmingham**, **Bristol** and **London** have council-run **car sharing** schemes to encourage people making the same journey to share a car. However, some people find car sharing inconvenient, or are worried about sharing a car with a stranger.

There are **larger scale** ways of tackling urban air pollution too. For example:

LEGISLATION (LAWS)

Laws aim to **reduce pollution** by **limiting emissions** and setting **air quality standards**. For example:

- The **UK Clean Air Acts** of 1956 and 1968 reduced domestic pollution by introducing **smoke control areas** where only smokeless fuels could be burned, and **reduced industrial pollution** by introducing the use of **tall chimneys** (which mean that pollutants are dispersed higher in the atmosphere, so they're less harmful to people in the city).
- The **Road Vehicles Regulations** reduce exhaust emissions by ensuring cars pass an **emissions test** in their MOT.
- In Scotland, legislation allows local authorities to do **roadside emission tests**, where they can **issue fines** if the vehicle fails. Throughout the UK, local authorities can issue fines to people who leave their engines running unnecessarily.

ALTERNATIVE FUELS

Petrol and diesel are replaced with **cleaner fuels** that **pollute less**. For example:

- **Biofuels** (e.g. **bioethanol** and **biodiesel**) are produced from **plants**. They can **directly replace** petrol and diesel, and have **lower particulate emissions**. However, growing the crops needed to make biofuels can **reduce biodiversity**, e.g. biofuels like corn-based ethanol need a lot of land to grow, which means clearing other vegetation.
- **Liquefied petroleum gas** (**LPG**) is a **gas** produced from **fossil fuels** that has **lower emissions** than petrol or diesel. However, cars have to be **converted** to use LPG, and **service stations** have to be **adapted** to distribute it.
- **Electric vehicles** have **lower emissions** because they run off **batteries**, rather than **conventional fuel**. Electric vehicles need **recharge points**, and **producing** and **disposing** of the **batteries** can cause environmental problems.

Practice Questions

Q1 What are particulates?

Q2 How is photochemical smog produced?

Q3 Why is photochemical smog more common in hot climates?

Exam Question

Q1 Describe how air pollution in urban areas can be reduced. [8 marks]

Country Mouse came to visit Town Mouse... and died due to poor air quality

Ah, the lesser known version of the classic tale. The health and environmental problems associated with urban air pollution really are serious — make sure you learn about the potential solutions and their drawbacks. If only we could all live in the countryside...

Climate Change — Evidence

In the exam you could well be asked to write about climate change and the evidence for it. You need to know specifics, it's no use saying, 'Well, it feels a bit warm today.' Even if it does, you won't make Mr Examiner a very happy man. No sir.

Climate Change is any *Long Term* change in *Weather*

1) **Climate change** is any **significant** change in the **weather** of a region over a period of at least **several decades**. E.g. increasing average **temperature** or **rainfall**, or a change in the usual **wind direction**.
2) The climate **constantly changes**, it **always has**, and it **always will**.
3) For the last 2.5 million years, global temperature has shifted between **cold glacial periods** that last for around 100 000 years, and **warmer interglacial periods** that last for around 10 000 years. We're in an **interglacial period now**.
4) **20 000 years ago** the Earth was cold. Around **15 000** years ago it started to warm up — this was the end of the last glacial period.
5) There was a brief **return** to **cold conditions** between **13 000 and 11 500 years ago**, before a period of **rapid warming**.
6) Over the last **10 000 years** the climate has been **warm** with **minor fluctuations**.

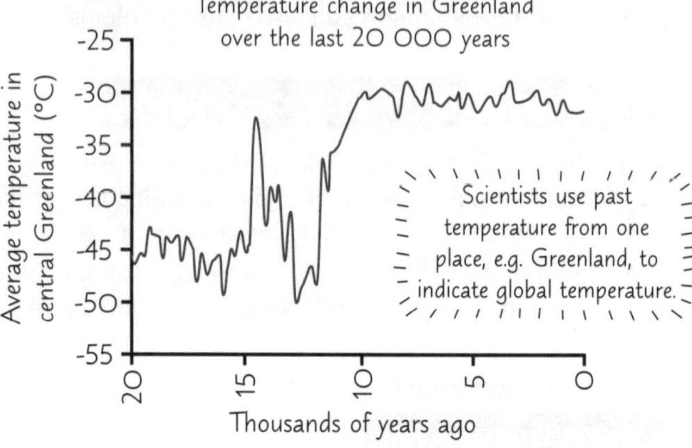

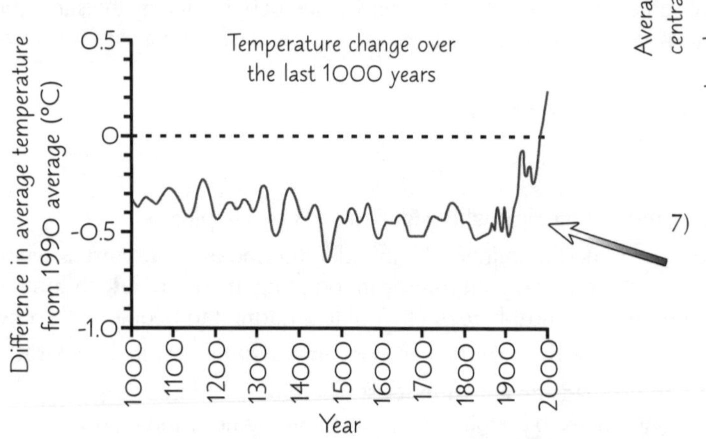

7) Over the last **1000 years** the climate has been fairly **constant** with small fluctuations (+/– 0.2 °C) in annual temperature.

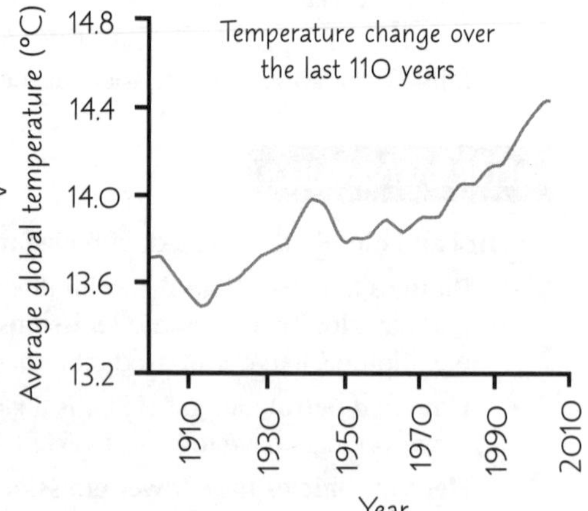

8) Over the **last century global temperature** has **increased rapidly**. This is called **global warming**. There's been a **sharp rise** in average temperature (**0.7 °C** between **1900** and **2000**).
9) Global temperatures **rose steadily** from the **early 20th century** until the **1940s** (from **13.5 °C** to **14 °C**), then **dropped**. Scientists thought there would be another **glacial period**, but temperatures have **risen even more rapidly since** the 1970s (from **13.8 °C** to **14.4 °C**).
10) The **temperature increase** over the last century has been **very fast**. There is a **consensus** among scientists that the **changes** in **climate** over the last century are a result of **human activities**.

Evidence for *Climate Change* comes from *Many Sources*

Observations

1) **HISTORICAL RECORDS:**
   - Historical records can **indirectly** show **different conditions** in the past. For example, **agricultural reports** (such as harvest times) show changing conditions throughout **human history**.
2) **WEATHER RECORDS:**
   - Details of **weather conditions** have been consistently **collected since 1861**.
   - These can be used to show detailed **climate changes** over the short time period they've been collected.

Climate Change — Evidence

Physical Evidence

1) **ICE CORES:**
   - Scientists drill deep into **ice sheets (huge masses of ice)** to extract **cores of ice**. Ice sheets are made up of **layers** of ice — **one** layer is formed **every year**. So the ice at the bottom of the core is really, really old.
   - By analysing **gases** trapped when the ice formed and the **chemistry of the ice** they can tell what the **temperature** was each year and work out how it has **changed over time**. Carbon dioxide (CO_2) and oxygen are key indicators:
     - **High CO_2** levels in ice indicate a **warm climate** at that time.
     - **Oxygen** has two main isotopes — **O-18** and **O-16**. O-16 is **lighter** than O-18. In cold periods there is **less energy** for evaporation, so water molecules containing the lighter O-16 evaporate more **easily**. This O-16 rich water vapour is carried to the poles and falls as snow. This is recorded in ice cores — **high** levels of **O-16** compared to O-18 indicate a period of **cold climate**.
2) **SEA FLOOR SEDIMENTS:**
   - Sediments deposited on the sea floor record the chemical composition of seawater when they were deposited.
   - Like ice cores, sediments contain **oxygen isotopes**. During periods of cold climate water molecules containing O-16 are more easily evaporated, so the ocean becomes **richer** in O-18. This is recorded in sea floor sediments — sediments with **high** levels of **O-18** indicate a period of **cold climate**.
3) **SEA LEVEL CHANGE:**
   - **Sea level** is affected by things like the volume of water **stored as ice**.
   - As the climate warms, ice caps **melt** and sea level **rises**. Some **valleys** formed above sea level are now **submerged** (e.g. Poole Harbour in Dorset and Lough Swilly in Ireland), showing that sea level is **higher** than it used to be.
4) **RETREATING GLACIERS:**
   - Scientists can tell **how big** a glacier was and how far it **extended** by looking at historical photos and at the position of **rocks deposited** by the glacier. These rocks can be **dated** to show when they were deposited.
   - The **distance** of the rocks from the current glacier **indicates climate change**. E.g. if the front of the glacier is now miles away from the rocks it indicates that **temperatures** have **increased** over that period of time.

Biological Evidence

1) **POLLEN ANALYSIS:**
   - **Pollen** is often **preserved** in **sediment**. Scientists study the preserved pollen and **identify** the plant it came from. They also **date** the sediment the pollen is found in so they know when it was **deposited**.
   - Scientists know the **climatic conditions** that plants live in now. When they find preserved pollen from similar plants, it helps them understand what the climate was like when that pollen was **produced**.
2) **COLEOPTERA:**
   - **Coleoptera** are **beetles** whose remains are easily preserved in **sediments**. Different **species** of Coleoptera live in different **climatic conditions**. Scientists can identify the species of Coleoptera in a sediment, and use it to build up a **picture of the climate** when the sediment was laid down.
3) **TREE RINGS (DENDROCHRONOLOGY):**
   - As a tree grows it forms a new **tree ring** each year — the tree rings are **thicker** in warm, wet conditions.
   - Scientists take **cores** and count the rings to find the **age** of a tree. The **thickness** of each ring indicates what the climate was like **each year**. Tree rings can reliably **show** and **date** climate conditions up to **10 000 years ago**.

Practice Questions

Q1 Define climate change.

Q2 Briefly explain what is meant by 'global warming'.

Exam Question

Q1 Outline the sources of evidence for climate change. [8 marks]

All scientists care about is evidence — what about truth, beauty, and love...

All these graphs can be mighty confusing, especially when people manipulate the data to try and show that climate change isn't happening. Basically, the climate has always been changing, but global warming is an unusually large and rapid change.

Climate Change — Causes and Impacts

Pretty much everyone agrees that global warming is a bad thing, but not many people know exactly how wide ranging its impacts could be. Time for you to become one of the privileged few...

Most Scientists** Agree that **Human Activity** is **Causing Global Warming

1) The recent **rise** in **global temperature** (**global warming**) and the **rate** of this increase is **unheard of** in **historical terms**.
2) There's a **scientific consensus** that this temperature rise is **caused** by human **enhancement** of the **greenhouse effect**.
3) The **greenhouse effect** is where greenhouse gases absorb **outgoing long-wave radiation**, so less is **lost** to space. It's **essential** for keeping the planet **warm**.
4) But **too much** greenhouse gas in the atmosphere means **too much** energy is trapped and the planet **warms up**.
5) **Increasing** amounts of **CO_2** and **methane** are the main contributors towards the recent **rise** in **temperature**, but other greenhouse gases include **nitrous oxide**, **water vapour** and **ozone**.
6) **Humans** are increasing the **concentration** of greenhouse gases by:

Ozone is a greenhouse gas in the lower atmosphere. Don't get it confused with the ozone layer higher in the atmosphere.

Burning Fossil Fuels

- **CO_2 is released** into the atmosphere when **fossil fuels** like coal, oil, natural gas and petrol are **burnt**, e.g. in power stations or in cars.
- Since the industrial revolution in the mid-19th century levels of **atmospheric CO_2** have **increased** from **280 ppm** (parts per million) to **380 ppm**. The level had been **broadly stable** for the previous 10 000 years.

Deforestation

- **Plants remove CO_2** from the atmosphere and convert it into **organic matter** using photosynthesis. It's also stored in the soil as **dead organic matter**.
- When trees and plants are chopped down, they stop taking in CO_2.
- CO_2 is also **released** into the atmosphere when trees are **burnt** as fuel or to make way for agriculture.

Farming

- Using nitrogen-based **fertiliser** to grow crops increases **nitrous oxide** emissions.
- **Farming** of **livestock** produces a lot of **methane** — cows love to fart...
- **Rice paddies** contribute to global warming, because **flooded fields** emit **methane**.

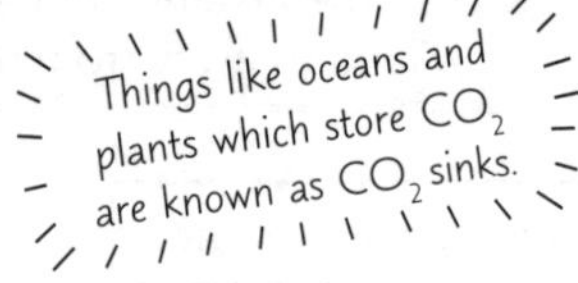

Global Warming** Could Have **Huge Impacts Globally

Temperature is expected to **increase** by **1.4-5.8 °C** between **1990** and **2100**. This would have major impacts:

Global Climate would Change

The **pattern of precipitation** is expected to change:

- **Wet areas** are expected to get **wetter** (e.g. **mid** to **high latitudes**, especially North America and Europe).
- **Precipitation** is expected to **decrease** by 5-20% in **other areas** due to changes in **ocean circulation** and **wind patterns**. **Dry areas** are expected to get **drier** (e.g. the **subtropics**, especially southern Africa, Central America and Australia).

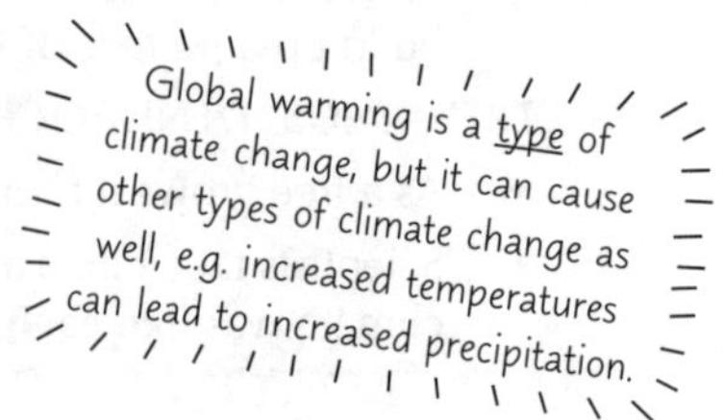

Glaciers, Sea Ice and Ice Caps would continue to Melt and Sea Level to Rise

- Arctic sea ice has **decreased** by **10-15%** since the **1950s**, and there's been **widespread reduction** of **non-polar glaciers** (e.g. in the Alps). This will continue as temperature rises, and many polar and glacial **habitats** could be **lost**.
- Average global sea level is expected to **rise** by 0.09-0.88 m between 1990 and 2100. This will **flood coastal** and **low lying areas** (e.g. areas of **SE Asia** and islands in the **Pacific** and **Indian** Oceans).

More Extreme Weather Events

- **Storms**, **floods** and **droughts** are likely to occur **more often** and be **more severe** due to **changes in ocean circulation** and **wind patterns**.
- **Less developed countries** are expected to be **worst affected** as they are **less able** to deal with the impacts.

Climate Change — Causes and Impacts

The Incidence of Some Illnesses and Diseases could Increase

- **More people** are likely to suffer from **heat-related illnesses** (e.g. heat stroke) — especially **very old** and **very young** people.
- **Breathing problems** are likely to **increase** as **air pollution** in **cities rises** (higher temperatures cause an increase in photochemical smog — see p. 44).
- **Disease vectors** (e.g. mosquitoes that carry malaria) may **spread** to **regions currently too cold** to support them.
- **Food-borne illnesses** may **increase** as temperature rises.

Conflicts over Water Resources could Increase

- In some areas **higher temperatures** and **reduced rainfall** would **reduce river flow** and **groundwater**, and cause **reservoirs** to **dry up**.
- In some areas water supply is expected to **decrease** by **10%** by 2050. This will affect hundreds of millions or even billions of people.
- This reduction of water supply means it will become a much more **valuable resource**. There may be increased **conflict** over it.

Patterns of Agriculture would Change

- **Agricultural productivity** (how much food farmers can produce) will **decrease in some areas**. E.g. reduced rainfall and droughts in Africa and Australia may reduce productivity.
- **Agricultural productivity** may **increase in other areas**. E.g. increased temperature and rainfall may increase productivity in North America and Europe.
- There may be **changes** in the **types of crops** grown. Crops that **prefer warmer conditions** (e.g. grapes and melons) could be grown further **north**, and crops that **prefer cooler conditions** (e.g. potatoes) would be less successful in their current locations and produce **lower yields**.
- **Agricultural pests** and **diseases** may **increase** in some areas. E.g. the range of the European Corn Borer (a pest of maize) is shifting northwards due to increased temperatures.

Species Distributions would Change and Biodiversity could Decrease

- The **geographical range** of some species will **change**. E.g. the range of some plants, insects, birds and fish will **shift** towards the **poles**, in line with temperature change, as they try to stay in the type of climate they're suited to. Other ecosystems may be damaged by the **invasion** of **new species**.
- **Some species** will **disappear** from some areas as they're **unable to cope** with **changes in climate**.
- **Some habitats** will be **damaged** or **destroyed**, e.g. polar habitats are being destroyed by sea ice melting, and coral reefs and mangrove swamps are threatened by sea level rise.
- Species that are adapted to living in these areas may become **extinct**.

Global Warming will also have Impacts in the UK

1) **UK CLIMATE WILL CHANGE:**
   - **Temperature** will **increase**. The increase is expected to be greatest in Southern England, where the average summer temperature is projected to increase by 3.9 °C by 2080.
   - **Winter rainfall** is expected to **increase** in many areas — by up to 35% in parts of the western side of the UK.
   - **Summer rainfall** is expected to **decrease** in many areas — by up to 49% in parts of Southern England.
2) **SEA LEVEL WILL RISE** — sea level is expected to rise by 13-76 cm by 2095. The areas **worst affected** by flooding would be towns and cities on estuaries (e.g. Hull, Cardiff, Portsmouth and London) and **low lying areas near the coast** (e.g. large areas of Norfolk). **Housing** and **agricultural land** may be lost in these places and people may have to **move away**.
3) **DROUGHTS MAY INCREASE** — droughts are expected to be more **frequent** and **intense**, especially in **Southern England**.
4) **PATTERNS OF AGRICULTURE ARE EXPECTED TO CHANGE:**
   - **Temperature increase** and a **longer growing season** may increase **productivity of some crops**, e.g. asparagus, onions, courgettes, peas and beans.
   - **Types of farming** may **shift northwards**. E.g. dairy farming and arable crop farming may increase in the north.
   - New **crops adapted** to **warmer climates** could be grown in **Southern England**, e.g. soya, peaches and grapes.
   - **Reduced rainfall** and **droughts** in **Southern England** would increase the need for irrigation and water storage schemes.
5) **HABITATS WILL CHANGE** — some species have already left their original habitats and moved **north** to find **cooler temperatures** (e.g. the comma butterfly). This can affect **ecosystems** and lead to **species extinction**.

Climate Change — Causes and Impacts

Climate will Change in *Tropical Regions*

You only have to learn about **one** tropical region (see p. 34-35).

Equatorial areas

- **Equatorial areas** are expected to get **hotter**, e.g. temperature in the Amazon basin is predicted to increase by 2-3 °C by 2050. The Amazon basin is likely to receive **less rainfall** overall, and rain may be more **seasonal.**
- This would cause **ecosystems** to change — e.g. large areas of the **Amazon rainforest** may **become savanna** due to **reduced rainfall** during the dry season. Species are expected to become **extinct**, so biodiversity will decrease.
- A longer dry season would **decrease agricultural productivity** and increase the risk of **forest fires**.
- Sea level rise along the Amazon delta would increase **erosion** and threaten **mangrove forests**.

Tropical savannas

- **Tropical savanna** areas are also likely to get hotter, e.g. the average annual temperature in Australia is projected to rise by 0.4-2 °C by 2030. This would result in **higher evapotranspiration** and **drought**.
- **Close** to the **Equator**, rainfall is likely to **increase**. This may cause **flooding** and an increase in **water-borne diseases**, e.g. cholera. However, it may also **increase agricultural productivity**.
- **Further** from the **Equator**, rainfall is likely to **decrease**. This would **increase drought** and result in ecosystem changes, including **extinction** of **savanna species**.
- **Rainfall** is likely to become **more variable**, with more extreme events and flooding during the wet season.
- **Increasing sea level** is likely to flood low-lying areas and increase coastal erosion, while **increased sea temperatures** may damage coral reefs due to coral bleaching (see p. 70).

Monsoon areas

- **Monsoon areas** are expected to get **hotter**, e.g. the average temperature in Bangladesh is projected to increase by 2-4 °C by 2100.
- **Seasons** are expected to become more **pronounced**, e.g. Bangladesh could experience **longer winter droughts**, but **more rain** during the **summer monsoon**.
- Intense rainfall may cause flooding, landslides and crop damage.
- **Tropical cyclones** may **increase** in frequency and **intensity**.
- Higher intensity cyclones would cause stronger **storm surges** and more **flooding**.
- **Sea level rise** will flood many islands and coastal areas. E.g. in Bangladesh sea level is predicted to rise by 30-100 cm by 2100, which would submerge up to 18% of the land surface. Millions of people would have to **migrate** from flooded areas. Mass migration, e.g. from Bangladesh to India, would cause **overcrowding** and **tension** between nations.
- **Agricultural productivity**, e.g. rice production, will **decline** due to loss of land caused by sea level rise.
- Areas that suffer from **increased flooding** would be more vulnerable to illnesses such as **cholera** and **hepatitis**.

Paolo was prepared for rapid sea level rise.

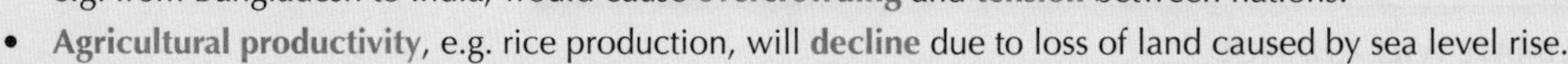

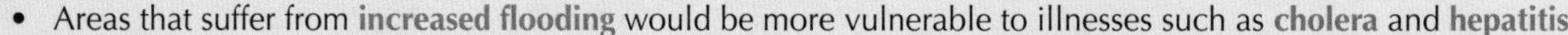

Practice Questions

Q1 List three human activities that cause global warming.

Q2 How will global climate change as a result of global warming?

Q3 Explain why global warming may increase agricultural productivity in North America.

Q4 Give two ways in which global warming is likely to affect the climate of the tropical region you have studied.

Exam Question

Q1 Describe the potential impacts of global warming in the UK. [8 marks]

I thought that switching from °F to °C would reduce global warming...

Global warming is a bit of a misleading name — it's not just about temperatures rising. Learn the specifics of the climate changes that will affect the UK and the tropical region you've studied (equatorial, tropical savanna or monsoon). You won't regret it...

Climate Change — Responses

I bet you're sick of hearing about global warming by now, but guess what — there's more. This 'ere bit's about the responses to climate change. There are things the world can do, things that nations can do, and things you can do too...

Responses to Global Warming can be International

The Kyoto Protocol aimed to reduce emissions...

1) The Kyoto Protocol is an **international agreement** formed in 1997. **190 countries** have joined the agreement, which involves pledging to **monitor** and **reduce** greenhouse gas emissions.
2) The agreement divided the countries into two groups — **developed** and **developing**.
3) **Developed countries** agreed to **cut emissions** (by 5% of their 1990 emissions levels) between 2008 and 2012.
4) **Developing countries** didn't have to cut emissions, but needed to **monitor** and **report** their emissions.
5) One of the incentives for countries to reduce their emissions was the introduction of **carbon credits.** Countries and businesses are given a **limit** on the **emissions** they can produce — if they produce **less** they can **sell** the extra carbon credits, if they produce **more** they need to **buy** more credits.
6) They can also gain credits by helping to **reduce emissions** in developing countries — this encourages developed countries to **invest** in developing countries to help them develop in a **sustainable way**.

...but there were problems with it

1) **Four countries** with **high emissions** (the USA, Australia, China and India) **didn't sign up** for the original agreement. The **USA** and **Australia** felt that signing would affect their **economies** and that the developing countries should have targets **as well**. **China** and **India** thought it would slow their **rate of growth**.
2) Australia, India and China have now joined the agreement, but there's still lots of **criticism**. Some people think the targets aren't **high enough**, and others think there's no point if the highest polluters **aren't included** (the **USA** still hasn't **fully** joined). In addition, countries have **failed** to meet their targets — in many cases emissions are actually **increasing**.

The Kyoto Protocol ends in **2012** and world leaders met in 2009 to reach a **new agreement**. The **Copenhagen Accord** was agreed, with each country allowed to set its **own targets** for cutting emissions (e.g. the USA agreed to cut emissions by 17% compared to 2005 levels). However, the accord is **not legally binding** and there are **no penalties** for countries who miss their targets.

Responses can also be Made at a National Level

In the UK, 73% of electricity is generated by fossil fuels, 17% by nuclear power, 8% by renewable energy sources and 2% from other sources.

Changing the Energy Mix of a Country

- The **energy mix of a country** is the mix of energy sources used to meet its energy needs — e.g. **fossil fuels** (oil, gas and coal), **nuclear power** and **renewable energy** (e.g. hydroelectric and wind power). France gets over three quarters of its energy mix from nuclear power, while the UK gets most of its energy from fossil fuels.
- **Replacing** fossil fuels with nuclear power and renewable energy can help reduce climate change by **reducing** greenhouse gas emissions from **power stations**.
- In the UK, around **40%** of emissions reductions by **2020** will be achieved by changing the energy mix. The aim is to generate **30%** of our electricity from **renewable sources** by **2020**.
- More **offshore wind farms** are being built, several **wave** and **tidal power projects** are planned, and more electricity is being generated using **solar panels**, **wind turbines** and **biomass burning**.
- The UK government is encouraging **small scale renewable energy projects**, e.g. by **relaxing** planning laws to make it easy for people to install solar panels.

BUT...

- There needs to be more investment in nuclear power and renewable energy before these sources can meet all our **energy needs**, so countries still have to rely on **other forms** of energy, e.g. fossil fuels.
- There are also **environmental problems** associated with nuclear power and renewable energy, e.g. nuclear power creates **dangerous waste**, and tidal power can **disrupt coastal ecosystems**.

An offshore wind farm near Barrow-in-Furness, Cumbria.

Climate Change — Responses

Using New Technologies to Cut Emissions from Power Stations

- **Carbon Capture and Storage (CCS)** is a new technology designed to reduce climate change by **reducing emissions** from **power stations**.
- CCS involves **capturing carbon dioxide** and **transporting it** to places where it can be stored safely, e.g. in deep geological formations.
- CCS has the potential to reduce emissions from power stations by **90%**.

BUT...

- The technology is still at the **developmental stage** and several problems have been identified. CCS **uses fuel** and **increases the cost of energy**. There's also the risk of stored **carbon dioxide leaking**.

CCS could reduce emissions from power stations.

Encouraging Energy Conservation at Home

- Encouraging energy conservation **reduces domestic fuel consumption**. This also **reduces emissions** from power stations, because less energy needs to be produced.
- In the UK, around 15% of emissions reductions by 2020 will be achieved by making homes more energy efficient. Government strategies in the UK include **providing energy efficiency grants** to help people pay for energy saving improvements (e.g. new boilers and insulation).
- **Financial incentives** are also being offered to encourage people to **generate their own electricity** from **renewable sources** (e.g. by installing **solar panels** or a **wind turbine**).
- Homes being sold need an **Energy Performance Certificate** that shows how energy efficient the home is, and how efficient it can be. This helps to make people **more aware** of energy use and conservation.

BUT...

- Energy saving improvements can have a **high initial cost** (but this could be **offset** by **reduced fuel consumption**).
- It's **difficult** to work out how energy efficient some houses are.
- There are regulations **restricting** the improvements that can be made to **listed buildings**.

Reducing Emissions from Transport

- In the UK, around 20% of emissions reductions by 2020 will be achieved by **reducing emissions from transport**. Strategies include **encouraging people** to **buy lower emissions vehicles**, e.g. **road tax** is free for cars emitting up to 100 g CO_2/km, but costs £475 a year for cars emitting over 255 g CO_2/km.
- **Financial incentives** are also being offered to encourage people to buy less polluting **electric** and **hybrid cars**, e.g. a government grant of up to £5000 is available for people buying cars that emit less than 75 g CO_2/km.

BUT...

- There are still lots of **older cars** with **higher emissions** on the roads, which will stay on the roads for many years.
- **Producing** hybrid and electric cars uses complex technologies, which use lots of **energy** and **produce emissions**.

*There are also **Local Responses** to **Global Warming***

Recycling Waste

- Recycling waste helps reduce climate change because it usually requires **less energy** to recycle material than to create a product from scratch. It also **reduces landfill waste** (landfills generate greenhouse gases like methane).
- In the UK, **recycling prevents the release of 10-15 million tonnes** of **carbon dioxide** every year. This is the equivalent of taking 3.5 million cars off the road every year.

BUT...

- There are some **problems** associated with recycling schemes. For example, **transporting products** to be recycled **creates transport emissions**. This is why it is important to develop **local recycling facilities**.

Climate Change — Responses

Using Cars Less

- **Using cars less** (e.g. by **walking** or **cycling** more, using **public transport** and **car sharing**) reduces climate change by **reducing transport emissions**.
- The **average car produces 2.7 tonnes** of **carbon dioxide every year** in the UK. Millions of tonnes of carbon dioxide could be saved every year if people walked or cycled journeys of less than 5 miles.

BUT...

- Many people **prefer using a car** to the alternatives, because they feel **safer** in their car, and it is often **faster** and more **convenient**.

With cars going out of fashion, Elena had to find something new to drape herself over.

Buying Local

- **Buying local produce** reduces climate change by **reducing transport emissions**. Many fruits and vegetables are **flown** to the UK, and **aircraft have very high emissions** per mile compared to other methods of transport, e.g. shipping.
- **Heated greenhouses** (used to grow produce out of season) have a **high energy consumption**. Eating **seasonal products** and **importing less food** could save millions of tonnes of carbon dioxide every year.

BUT...

- Many people like to have access to a **variety** of foods **all year round**.

Local responses are mostly carried out by individuals, but governments and councils can encourage them, e.g. by subsidising buses in rural areas, or improving recycling facilities.

Choosing Energy Efficient Appliances

- Energy efficient appliances **reduce fuel consumption**, which **reduces emissions** from power stations because less energy needs to be produced.
- Many **modern appliances** are **50% more efficient** than **older models**. If everyone in the UK upgraded their fridges and freezers it would prevent the release of around 3.7 million tonnes of carbon dioxide every year.

BUT...

- Throwing away old appliances creates lots of **waste**.
- Making new appliances uses **energy**, which increases emissions.
- People may be reluctant to spend **money** on buying new appliances.

Practice Questions

Q1 How does recycling reduce climate change?

Q2 Why might people choose to use cars instead of public transport?

Q3 How does buying local help reduce climate change?

Q4 What are the problems involved in upgrading appliances?

Exam Questions

Q1 Evaluate one or more international responses to climate change. [8 marks]

Q2 'Replacing fossil fuels with renewable energy is the most effective way for the UK to reduce its greenhouse gas emissions.' To what extent do you agree with this statement? [40 marks]

Responses to weight change — use cars less and buy low-cal...

There's a lot to remember on these pages — for your exam you need to know about responses to climate change on all scales. Unfortunately, these responses are stuffed full of information that you'll just have to learn if you want to bag top marks.

Ecosystem Basics

Don't fret — you haven't picked up your biology book by accident. These two pages cover the basics of ecosystems, so don't skip them unless you want to be exceptionally confused by the end of the section.

Make Sure You Know the **Difference** Between an **Ecosystem** and a **Biome**

- An **ECOSYSTEM** is a set of **relationships** between **all** the **organisms** and **non-living factors** in a particular area, e.g. a forest ecosystem includes the **trees**, **animals** and **microorganisms** as well as the **water**, **soil**, **rock** and **air**.
- The organisms that live there are called **biotic factors** and the non-living objects are **abiotic factors**.
- The **organisms** depend on **physical factors** and **each other** to survive, so **relationships** between organisms are **important**.
- Ecosystems **vary in size** — they can be small (e.g. a pond) or large (e.g. a forest, mountainside or ocean).

- A **BIOME** is an area with a distinctive **climate** and **vegetation**, e.g. a tropical rainforest or arctic tundra.
- Biomes can contain **different ecosystems**, e.g. within a tropical grassland biome there could be areas of open woodland, areas of swamp, lakes and grassland plains.
- Biomes usually cover a **large area**, often spanning multiple countries.

Energy Moves Between the **Organisms** in an **Ecosystem**

1) **Energy enters** an ecosystem by **photosynthesis** — plants use **energy** from **sunlight** to **grow** and **reproduce**.
2) The energy is **stored** in the **plant** and **passed** up the food chain when the plant is **eaten**.
3) This process continues throughout the **ecosystem** — when one organism eats another it receives the energy from that organism. This means that **energy flows** between all the **organisms** in an **ecosystem**.

Food Chains and **Food Webs** Show How **Energy Moves** Through an Ecosystem

1) Each **stage** in a food chain or web is called a **trophic** (feeding) **level**.
2) **Producers** (autotrophs, e.g. **plants**) occupy the **first trophic level**. They make their own food.
3) **Primary consumers** (**herbivores** or **omnivores**) occupy the next level — they **eat producers**.
4) **Secondary consumers** (**carnivores** and **omnivores**) occupy the next level — they **eat consumers**.
5) **Tertiary consumers** (**top carnivores** and **omnivores**) occupy the next level — they **eat consumers**.
6) **Biomass** (the total mass of living matter) **decreases** at each **trophic level** e.g. a **field of dandelions** feeds a **family of rabbits**, which can all be scoffed by **one hungry fox**.

Herbivores eat plants, carnivores eat meat, and omnivores eat plants and meat.

7) **Food chains** tend to over-simplify the relationships — a lot of **consumers** don't just fit in **one trophic level**, e.g. a bird will eat seeds from a plant and also eat the insects that feed on the plant. **Food webs** are more complicated:

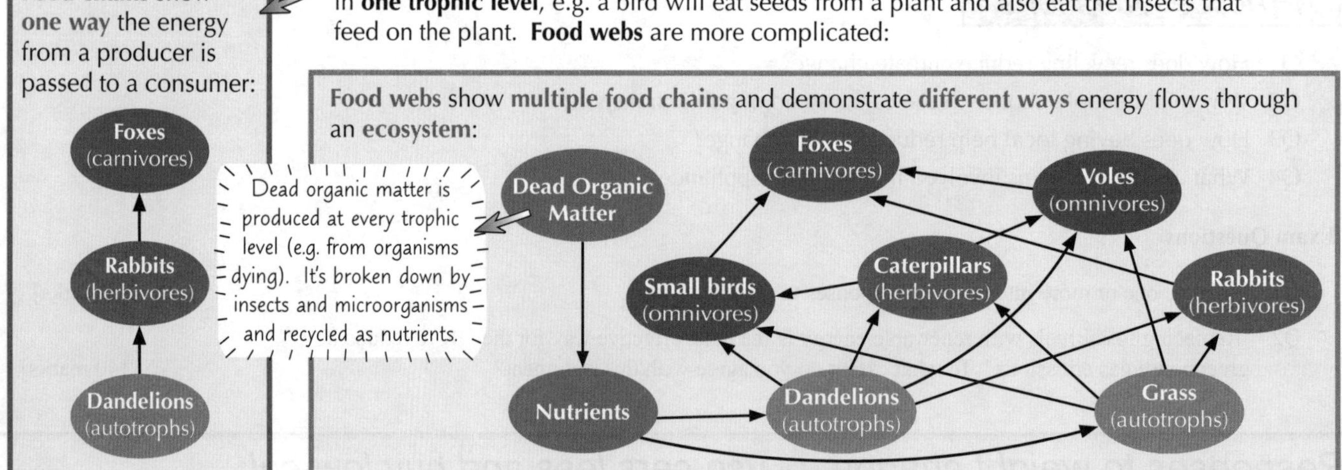

Ecosystem Basics

Some Energy is Lost at Each Level in a Food Chain

As you go up the trophic levels in a food chain, the **amount of energy** at each level **decreases**. Around 90% of energy is lost at each trophic level. Here are some reasons why:

50% → Dandelions (autotrophs) → 10% → Rabbits (herbivores) → 10% → Foxes (carnivores)

1 Energy lost between sunlight and the autotroph

Less than 50% of sunlight is actually used in **photosynthesis**, for example:

- Some will fall on areas of the plant that **don't photosynthesise**, e.g. the stem or trunk.
- The plant can only use certain wavelengths of light.

2 Energy lost by the consumers

Only about 10% of the energy stored by the **autotrophs** is passed to the **herbivores**, and 10% of the energy stored by the herbivores is passed to the carnivores:

- **Some parts** of the organisms **aren't eaten**, e.g. the **roots**, **bones** or **fur**, and not all of what is eaten is used for energy.
- Some energy is lost as **waste**, e.g. droppings.
- Consumers use some of the **energy** for **movement** and generating **body heat**, so it's not passed to the next level.

Nutrients are Constantly being Recycled in Ecosystems

Living organisms need large quantities of **carbon**, **hydrogen**, **oxygen**, **nitrogen** and **sulfur**, among other things. These elements are constantly being **recycled** through **ecosystems** — they're recycled between plants, animals and the atmosphere.

1) Plants take **carbon dioxide** from the **air** and **nutrients** from the **soil**, e.g. **nitrogen**. They use these to create **plant material**.
2) These nutrients get passed along food chains by **feeding**.
3) When plants and animals die they're broken down by **decomposers** (e.g. bacteria). **Nutrients** (e.g. nitrogen) are **returned** to the **soil** to be used again by plants.
4) Plants, animals and decomposers all release **carbon dioxide** back into the air through **respiration**.

Photosynthesis uses carbon dioxide and gives out oxygen — respiration does the opposite.

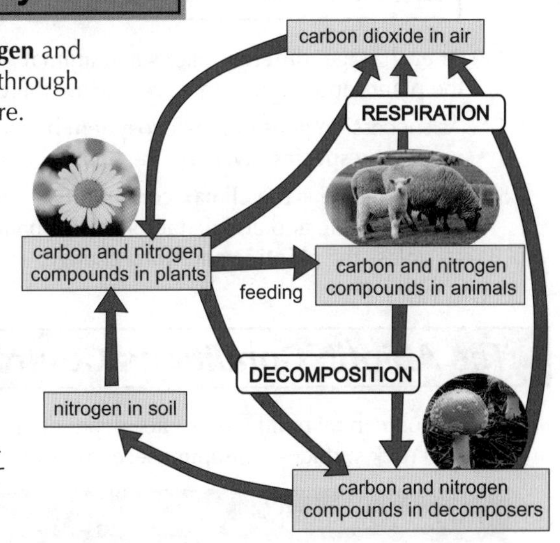

Practice Questions

Q1 What is an ecosystem?

Q2 What is meant by the term 'trophic level'?

Exam Question

Q1 Look at the food web on the right.

Describe how energy is transferred through the food web, and how it is lost.

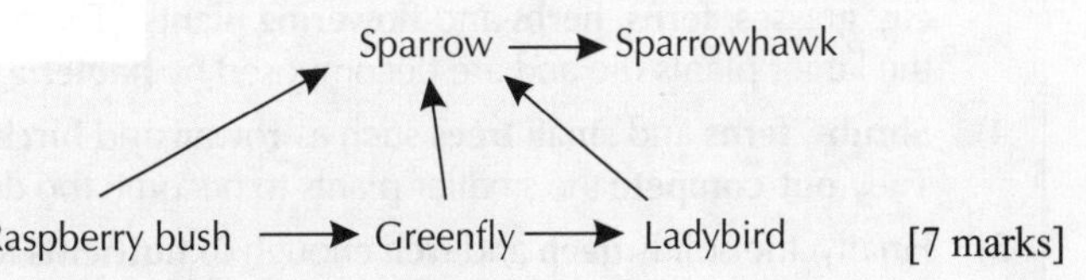

[7 marks]

I bet Lewis Hamilton has a fair few auto trophies...

Food webs and food chains are the kind of diagrams examiners love. You might be given one to explain in your exam, so make sure you understand them. Remember the arrows show the transfer of energy up the trophic level — in other words, who is eaten by who.

Succession

Leave any surface sitting there for long enough and some plant or other will start colonising it. For your exam you only need to know about one of the ways that this happens, but I'm feeling keen so I've covered four for you here...

Succession** is the **Process of Ecosystem Change

1) **Succession** is the process by which an **ecosystem changes** over **time**. The **biotic conditions** (e.g. **plant** and **animal life**) change as the **abiotic conditions** (e.g. **water availability**) change.
2) Succession occurs in **stages** called **seres**. There are **two** types of succession:

Primary succession

This happens on land that's been **newly formed** or **exposed**, e.g. where a **volcano** erupts and forms a **new rock surface**.

- The **abiotic conditions** are **harsh**, e.g. there's no soil to **retain water**. **Seeds** and **spores** are blown in by the **wind**.
- The **first species** to colonise the area are called **pioneer species** — this is the **first sere**. Pioneer species can **grow** because they're **specialised** to cope with the harsh conditions, e.g. **marram grass** can grow on sand dunes near the sea because it has **deep roots** to get water and can **tolerate** the salty environment.
- The pioneer species **change** the **abiotic conditions** — they **die** and **decompose**, which forms a **basic soil**.
- This makes conditions **less hostile**, e.g. the basic soil helps to **retain water**, which means **new organisms** can grow. These then die and are decomposed, adding **more** organic material and making the soil **deeper** and **richer in minerals**. This means **larger plants** like **shrubs** can start to grow in the deeper soil, which retains **even more** water.

Secondary succession

Secondary succession happens on land that's been **cleared** of all the **plants**, but where the **soil remains**, e.g. after a **forest fire**. **Secondary succession** happens in the **same way** as primary succession, but because there's already a **soil layer** succession starts at a **later sere** — the pioneer species in secondary succession are **larger plants**, e.g. shrubs.

3) At each stage, **different** plants and animals that are **better adapted** for the improved conditions move in, **out-compete** the plants and animals that are already there, and become the **dominant species** in the ecosystem.
4) As succession goes on, the ecosystem becomes **more complex**. New species move in **alongside** existing species, which means the **species diversity** (the number of **different species** and the **abundance** of each species) tends to **increase**.
5) The **final sere** is the **climax community** — the ecosystem is supporting the **largest** and **most complex** community it can, and the biotic and abiotic factors are **in balance**. This is known as the **climatic climax** and it **won't change** much more — unless the **abiotic conditions change**.

*The **Abiotic Conditions Control** the **Type of Community** that **Develops***

Succession can take different routes depending on the **abiotic conditions** at the start of the process. A **lithosere** occurs on exposed rock surfaces, a **psammosere** on sand, a **hydrosere** on water and a **halosere** in saline conditions.

Lithosere example — bare rock to woodland

1) **Pioneer species**, e.g. **lichens**, **colonise** the rocks because they can live with **very little water** and few nutrients. Lichens **break down** rock, which **releases minerals**. As the rock is broken down, its **surface** becomes uneven, which helps to retain **water**.
2) As the rocks get more **damp**, **mosses** begin to grow and **weather** the rock surface. Lichens and mosses **die** and **decompose**, forming a **thin soil**.
3) As the soil **deepens**, **larger plants** that need **more water** move in e.g. **grasses**, **ferns**, **herbs** and **flowering plants**. The soil **gets deeper** as the larger plants die and are decomposed by **bacteria** to form **humus**.
4) **Shrubs**, **ferns** and **small trees** such as **rowan** and **birch** begin to grow. They **out-compete** the smaller plants to become the **dominant** species.
5) Finally, the soil is **deep** and **rich** enough in **nutrients** to support slow-growing **large trees** like **ash** and **oak**. These become the dominant species, and the **climax community** is formed.

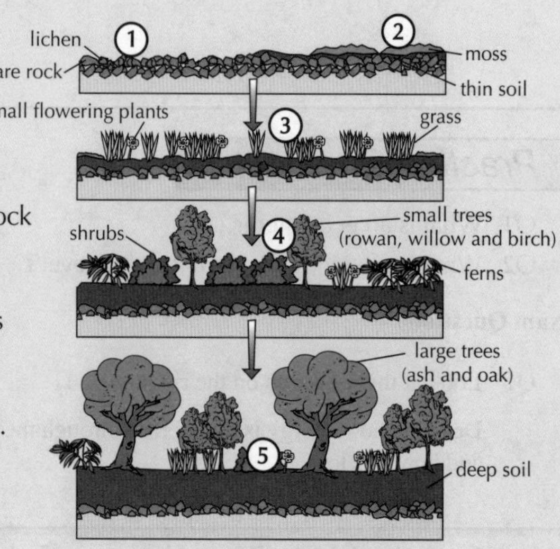

The four examples of succession on these pages are all for the temperate climate zone. Different successions occur in different climate zones.

Succession

Psammosere example — bare sand (e.g. coastal sand dune) to woodland

1) Pioneer species colonise the bare sand, e.g. **lyme grass** and **marram grass** have a **high salt tolerance** and leaves that retain **moisture**. The **roots** of these plants **bind** the sand together.
2) The pioneer species **die** and **decompose**, helping to form a **thin soil**. Other species move in, e.g. **sand dune screw moss** and **sand sedge**. At first the soil is very **alkaline** because it contains **shell fragments** and **salt** from seawater.
3) The soil **deepens** and becomes **less alkaline** as more **organic matter forms**. Small plants (e.g. **hawkweed** and **evening primrose**) and larger plants (e.g. **gorse** and **heather**) move in.
4) The soil continues to deepen as larger plants die and decompose. Shrubs and small trees (e.g. **hawthorn** and **elder**) move in and **out-compete** the smaller plants.
5) The soil can eventually **support large trees**. Fast-growing trees (e.g. **pine** and **birch**) move in first, followed by slower growing **ash** and **oak**. These gradually become the **dominant climax species**.

Animals (e.g. rabbits) move in as plant cover increases and their droppings help to improve soil quality.

Hydrosere example — fresh water (e.g. lake) to woodland

1) Pioneer species (e.g. **algae** and floating plants such as **duckweed**) colonise the **water surface**. They die and sink to the bottom, where they accumulate along with other **sediments** (e.g. sediments deposited by rivers).
2) The water gets shallower as sediments and decomposing plant material **accumulate**. Aquatic plants move in, e.g. **elodea** and **starwort**. They are **rooted** in the lake bed and trap and hold **more sediment** on the bottom.
3) The water becomes **very shallow**, and **swamp** and **marsh plants** (e.g. **reeds** and **rushes**) move in. Marsh plants generate lots of leaf litter, which builds up and forms a **wet soil**.
4) Larger plants (e.g. **ferns**) and tree seedlings (e.g. **willow** and **alder**) move in. These plants decrease soil moisture by transpiration, until the soil is no longer water-logged.
5) The **soil deepens** and becomes drier as larger plants die and decompose. This provides suitable conditions for **large climax tree species**, e.g. oak and beech, which become dominant.

Halosere example — salt water (e.g. estuary) to woodland

1) Pioneer species that can tolerate being submerged in saltwater, e.g. **eelgrass** and **cordgrass**, colonise the **intertidal zone** (the bit of the beach exposed at low tide). Their roots **trap mud** brought in by **tidal water**, causing it to accumulate.
2) Pioneer species die and **decompose**, forming a **thin soil**. This **accumulation** of decaying material and mud makes the ground level **rise** above all but the **highest tides**, so less salt water reaches the soil. Species that can tolerate a bit of salt water move in (e.g. **sea lavender** and **sea aster**). Their roots **trap** and **hold more sediment**.
3) The ground level continues to rise and soil **deepens** as more decomposing plant material builds up. Shrubs and small trees (e.g. **rowan** and **alder**) move in and **out-compete** the smaller plants.
4) The **soil deepens** further and **large climax tree species** (e.g. **oak** and **ash**) become dominant.

Practice Questions

Q1 What is the difference between primary and secondary succession?

Q2 What is a pioneer species?

Q3 What is meant by the term 'climatic climax'?

Exam Question

Q1 Describe and explain the characteristic features of one example of a primary plant succession. [8 marks]

I'll have a chicken korma, pilau rice and a vegetable psammosere please...

Each sere follows a similar pattern from bare surface to climatic climax, but it's remembering the details that will get you top marks in your exam — you need to talk about specific species and the abiotic changes they cause, and use the scientific terms correctly.

Succession

When an ecosystem reaches a climatic climax, it settles down and just gets on with life. That is, until humans come along and mess with things, and then succession can take an unexpected turn...

You Need to Know the Characteristics of the UK Climatic Climax

The UK climatic climax is a **temperate deciduous woodland** biome. It has these characteristics:

The **canopy layer** is made up of **trees** (e.g. oak, elm and beech) that grow to around **30 m** tall. These are the dominant species.

Trees grow wider at the crown (top) and have **broad** leaves.

The **trees** are **deciduous**, which means they **lose** their **leaves in autumn**. This **reduces water loss** from leaves in the winter months, when roots struggle to take **water** from the **frozen soil** and when **low light** slows the rate of **photosynthesis**.

Epiphytes, e.g. **lichens** and **mosses**, grow on the **trunks** and **branches** of trees in **all layers**.

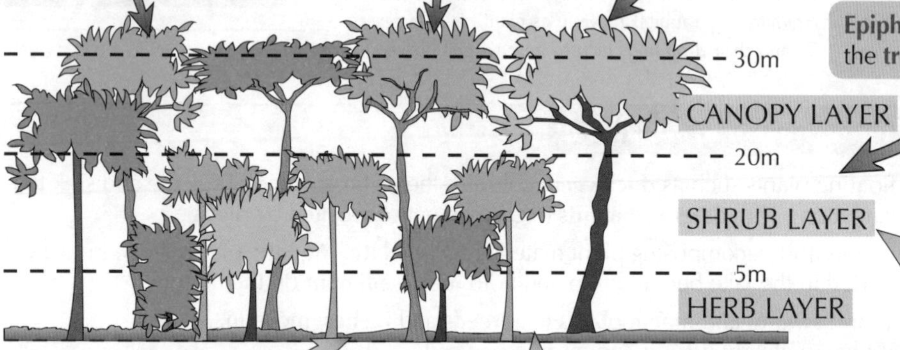

At the **shrub layer** there are **smaller trees**, such as hazel, rowan and hawthorn. They're about **5 to 20 m** tall and tend to be fairly shade-tolerant.

At **ground level**, **mosses** and **leaf litter** create a thick carpet on the forest floor. This is broken down by **decomposers**, e.g. **bacteria**, living in the soil. This returns the **nutrients** to the soil and keeps it **fertile**.

If enough light gets through, the undergrowth can be **dense** with shade-tolerant plants, e.g. **grasses** and **ferns**. **Flowering plants** (e.g. **bluebells**) can grow on the forest floor in the spring, because the trees have not yet **re-grown** all their leaves. This period of time before the canopy develops fully is called the **spring window**.

Human Activity Can Stop or Deflect Succession

Human activities can **stop succession** or **redirect** it towards a different climax. When this happens a climax that's different to the normal **climatic climax** forms — this is called a **plagioclimax**. For example:

Human activity	Why it's carried out	Why it prevents the climatic climax being reached	Characteristics of the resulting plagioclimax
Deforestation	To get **wood** for **timber** or **fuel**, or to make **space** for **farming**.	Removing trees **reduces soil quality** because it takes nutrients out of the ecosystem that would otherwise be returned to the soil by **leaf fall** or **tree death**. **Fewer** types of **plants** can **grow** in the poor soil.	**Hardy shrubs**, e.g. heather.
Animal grazing	Domesticated **animals** kept for **meat** (or other **products**) often **graze** for their food.	**Small plants** and saplings are **eaten** or **destroyed** by trampling before they get a chance to grow.	**Fast** growing **grasses** and **plants** (e.g. dandelions). Very few trees and shrubs.
Clearance by fire	To **clear** an area for **farming**, to **control** the **plants** growing in an area, or to **improve** the **soil** in an area (ash is a fertiliser).	All the **plants** are **destroyed**, and the **fastest growing** types of plants **re-colonise** the area.	**Fast-growing plants**, whose roots aren't damaged by fire, e.g. heather.
Afforestation (planting trees)	To plant trees for **timber**.	The **trees** in an area may be **cleared** to make way for the **new saplings**. Only **one species** is planted and managed (monoculture), so this species **dominates**.	In **managed areas** like forestry plantations **humans control** the **plagioclimax**, e.g. a planted pine forest.

Succession

Plagioclimax Case Study — North York Moors: Heather Moorland

Heather moorland is an area of **open country** mostly covered in **heather**. It's a **plagioclimax** because it's created by human activity. The **North York Moors** are the **largest area** of heather moorland in England, covering **1436 km²** of land.

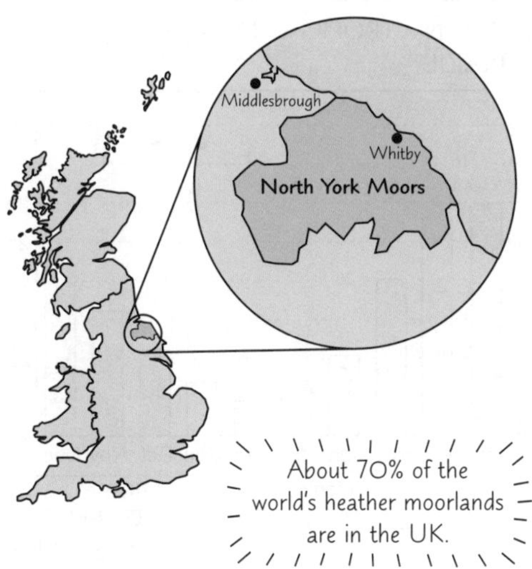

The moors were created by human activities:

1) The moors used to be an **oak forest** (a temperate deciduous woodland biome), where only **small amounts** of **heather** grew at ground level.
2) Up to about **5000 years ago** people hunted and gathered in the woodland for food. As the population grew, people began to **clear** the most fertile areas of **woodland** to keep animals and **grow crops**.
3) From around **4000 to 2000 years ago**, the remaining woodland was cleared. Clearing trees **reduced soil quality** — when an area was no longer fertile enough for farming, people moved on.
4) Few types of plants were able to grow in the **poor quality soil**. Heather is a **hardy shrub** — it was able to grow, and it flourished because there was **less competition** from other plants.
5) Around **1000 years ago**, sheep **grazing** became a major form of agriculture in North Yorkshire. This **prevented the re-growth** of other plants (as saplings were eaten or trampled before they got a chance to mature), which **reduced** the level of **competition**. Heather is **fast growing** so it was able to cope with being grazed, and soon it dominated the area.

The moors are also maintained by human activities:

1) The **North York Moors** are a **national park** and the moorland is carefully maintained for **environmental** and **economic** reasons. The moors are an **important habitat** for **rare plants**, e.g. sundew and common spotted orchid, and **birds**, e.g. merlin and golden plover. The moors are also used for **sheep grazing** and **grouse shooting**.
2) Without **active management** the heather moorland would eventually return to a **temperate deciduous forest**, and the **moorland plants** and **animals** would **lose their habitat** and **move on** or **die out**.
3) Although **sheep grazing** helps to maintain the moorland, **controlled burning** is the primary management technique. A few sections are burned each year in an **8-15 year rotation**. If left alone heather becomes **tough** and **woody** and eventually collapses, but burning **encourages** new heather shoots to **grow**, which provides better grazing for sheep and grouse. Burning also **destroys less fire-resistant plants**, which helps to ensure that the heather remains **dominant**.

Heather moorlands in Yorkshire.

Practice Questions

Q1 Name the three layers in the temperate deciduous woodland biome.

Q2 What is a plagioclimax?

Q3 Give three ways in which human action can prevent a climatic climax being reached.

Exam Question

Q1 With reference to one plagioclimax you have studied, explain how it was created, and how and why it is maintained. [10 marks]

A plagioclimax on both your houses...

Ecosystems are made of pretty stern stuff — you can burn them down, flood them out or plant trees all over them and they just keep coming back for more. It's a bit like you and this revision guide really, you just can't keep away (because it's so great, obviously).

Tropical Ecosystems — Characteristics

You need to know about one tropical biome. The next few pages cover tropical rainforests — if you've covered another biome in a tropical region in class, dig out your notes and have a look at them instead.

*The **Climate** in **Tropical Rainforests** is **Hot** and **Wet** All Year*

1) Tropical equatorial rainforests have a distinctive climate.
2) It's hot (mean monthly **temperature** is generally between **20-28 °C** and only varies by a few degrees over the year). This is because tropical rainforests are found near the **equator**, where the sun is **overhead all year** round.
3) **Rainfall** is **high all year round**, around 2000 mm per year. It rains every day (usually in the afternoon) because the high temperature creates **convectional rainfall**:
   - The sun **warms** the ground, which conducts this heat to the air above and **evaporates** surface water.
   - The **warm air** can hold lots of **water vapour**.
   - The warm, wet air **rises** — and as it rises it **cools**.
   - The cooler air can hold **less water vapour**, so water condenses to form clouds and then **rain**.
4) The **soil moisture budget** (the balance between water inputs and outputs in the soil) is high, because **precipitation** is higher than **potential evaporation**.

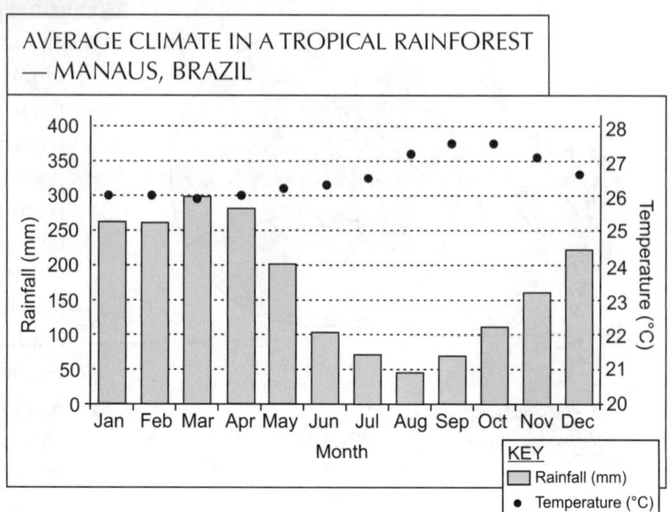

*Tropical Rainforests have **Four Layers** of **Vegetation***

Tropical rainforests have a **layered structure**. Different amounts of **sunlight** reach the **different levels** of vegetation. The **trees** have differently **shaped crowns** to absorb **as much light** as they can.

The **canopy layer** is a **continuous** layer of **trees** around **30 m** high. It absorbs about **80%** of **incident light** (direct sunlight that hits the leaves) and **shades** the rest of the forest.

The **tallest trees** are called **emergents**. They can reach around **40 m** and poke out of the main canopy layer. They have **straight trunks** and **widely spaced branches** only at their **crown** where **most light** reaches them. This makes them look **umbrella-shaped.** The emergents receive the **most direct light** of all the layers in the rainforest.

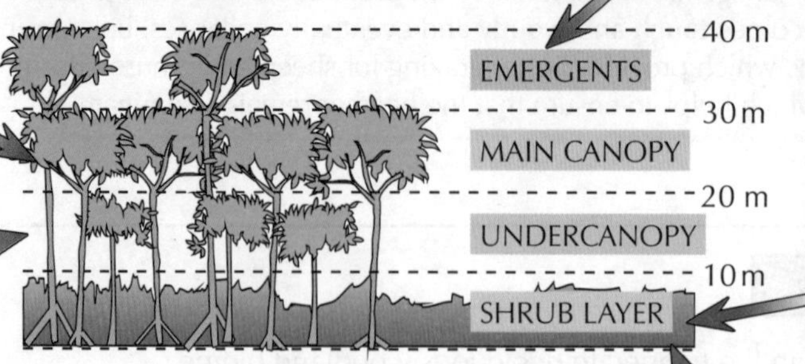

Trees in the **undercanopy layer** are about **half** the **height** of the canopy layer.

The **shrub layer** is nearest the ground at around **10 m high.** **Only 5%** of **direct light** reaches this layer, so shrubs have very **large, broad leaves** to absorb as much of the **available light** as they can.

Rainforest soils are known as **latosols**. They are **very nutrient poor** because:

1) Although there is a constant supply of new **leaf litter** and **dead organic matter** onto the soil surface, it is broken down **very quickly** because the **warm, wet climate** is ideal for micro-organisms.
2) The growing season continues all year, so as soon as **dead organic matter** is broken down the nutrients are **re-absorbed** by plants. This means that few nutrients remain in the soil.
3) Nutrients are also **leached** down the soil column by heavy rainfall.

There is a **thin layer** of nutrients in the **top layer** of soil, where organic matter is **decaying**. Trees make the most of this by keeping their **roots** very close to the **soil surface**.

Tropical Ecosystems — Characteristics

The **Organisms** that Live There are **Adapted** to the **Abiotic Conditions**

PLANT ADAPTATIONS

1) Plants are **adapted** to the **heavy rainfall** — they have thick, waxy leaves with **pointed tips** (called **drip-tips**). The drip-tips channel the water so it **runs off** quickly to prevent **fungi** and **bacteria** growing on the leaves.
2) Some plants, e.g. Anthurium, have leaves that **rotate** to follow the sun, so they can absorb as much **light** as possible.
3) Tree trunks **only** have **branches** and **leaves** at the top of the canopy where they can absorb **sunlight**. They **grow quickly** to reach the sunlight. Plants in the lower layers have **broad leaves** to maximise **photosynthesis**.
4) Tall trees have big roots called **buttress roots** to keep them upright.
5) The trees are **deciduous** — they **drop** their **leaves** throughout the year because there is **no winter season**. This means they can keep on growing **all year** round.
6) **Lianas** root in the soil and **climb** up trees, while **epiphytes** like orchids and bromeliads grow **on the trees**. These adaptations help plants to reach the **light**.
7) Organisms such as bacteria and fungi are adapted to take **nutrients** from **dead organic matter**. There's lots of dead organic matter in the rainforest because of **high rates** of **leaf fall**. In return, these organisms make **nutrients** (e.g. **carbon** and **nitrogen**) **available** to the **other organisms** in the ecosystem. The **rainforest nutrient cycle** depends on these species **recycling nutrients**, because the quality of the **soil** is so **poor**.

Buttress roots of the Santinay tree.

When organisms support one another and depend on the existence of the other to survive it is called a symbiotic relationship.

ANIMAL ADAPTATIONS

1) Many animals are adapted to living in the **canopy** because there's plenty of food there (e.g. **plants** and **fruits**). For example, **red-eyed tree frogs** have **suction cups** on their toes to help them climb trees, and **flying squirrels**, **flying geckos** and **flying lemurs** have **flaps of skin** that they use for **gliding** between trees. These adaptations also help them to **escape predators**.
2) **Jaguars**, **sloths** and **vampire bats** are **nocturnal** — they sleep through the day and are active during the night. This means they can **save energy** by hunting and feeding at night when it's **cooler**.
3) **Camouflage** is an important way of **avoiding predation** for some animals, e.g. **leaf-tailed geckos** are the same colour and texture as tree bark. **Predators** are also camouflaged to help them **hunt**, e.g. tigers' stripes make them less visible in the shadows.
4) Some animals are adapted to the **low light** conditions in the undercanopy. **Tapirs** and **anteaters** have **excellent senses** of hearing and smell, so they can **detect predators** without **seeing** them.
5) Many **rainforest** animals can **swim**. This allows them to **cross river channels** and cope with **flooding** of the forest floor. For example, **pond turtles** have **webbed feet** to help them move through water.

Smoky and Mr Jump had definitely drawn the short straw in their symbiotic relationships.

Practice Questions

Q1 Briefly describe the climate of a tropical rainforest.

Q2 What are the four layers of vegetation in a tropical rainforest?

Q3 Name one plant that is adapted to living in the rainforest, and explain how it is adapted.

Exam Question

Q1 Explain how climate affects the organisms living in a tropical region that you have studied. [10 marks]

Very few species in the rainforest are adapted to exam conditions...

All these adaptations are certainly very clever, but no matter how webbed your feet are or how good your hearing is, you won't do well in your exam unless you take a bit of time to learn all the snazzy ways that plants and animals cope with life in the jungle.

Tropical Ecosystems — Human Activity

Rainforests are one of the most important biomes on Earth — they produce oxygen, provide habitats for countless species and they're a great place to make a nature documentary. But human activity is a serious threat in all sorts of ways.

Deforestation is the Main Threat to Tropical Rainforests

There are lots of reasons why rainforests are chopped down:

Small scale farming — trees are cleared to set up small **subsistence farms**. Often the "slash and burn" technique is used — **vegetation** is **cut down** and left to dry, then **burnt**. Increasing **populations** mean more forest is being cleared.

Cattle farming — forest is cleared to make room for **cattle grazing**.

Commercial agriculture — trees are felled for planting **crops** like **palm oil** and **soya**.

Other — for example, land is cleared for **mineral extraction** (e.g. of gold and iron ore) and for **new settlements**. Building **dams** to generate **hydroelectric power** floods large areas of forest.

Commercial logging — wood is used for **timber**, **pulp** and **paper**. **Road building** for logging also makes new areas of forest accessible for **agriculture**.

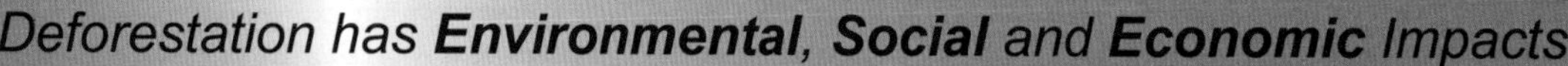

Deforestation has Environmental, Social and Economic Impacts

ENVIRONMENTAL

1) **Deforestation** causes **habitat loss**. This **reduces biodiversity** — if organisms can't **move** or **adapt** they may **become endangered** or **extinct** (e.g. in **Brazil** the number of **endangered species** grew from **218** in **1989** to **628** in **2008**).
2) Deforestation causes increased **surface run-off** and **flooding**. In **deforested areas** there is no tree canopy to intercept rainfall, so more water reaches the ground surface. There is too much **water** to soak into the soil. Instead the **water** moves to rivers as **surface run-off**, which increases the risk of **flooding**.
3) Deforestation degrades the **rainforest soil**. Without **roots** to **hold the soil** together, heavy rain **washes away** the **nutrient rich** top layer of soil.
4) Deforestation **removes nutrients** from the ecosystem. Most of the nutrients in the rainforest are **stored** in the trees and plants. When these are removed, nutrients are **lost**. There is also less **leaf litter**, so humus isn't formed. These changes mean the soil cannot support **new growth**.
5) Deforestation reduces the **rate** of **evapotranspiration** (see p. 42) — this means less water vapour reaches the atmosphere, **fewer clouds form** and **rainfall** is **reduced**. This means there's an increased risk of **drought**.
6) **Deforestation** is a major cause of global warming. Trees **remove CO_2** from the atmosphere and store it, so fewer trees means more atmospheric CO_2, which enhances the greenhouse effect (see p. 48).

SOCIAL

1) **Quality of life** for some local people improves as there are **more jobs**.
2) The **traditional livelihoods** of some local people are **destroyed** — deforestation can cause the loss of the **plants** and **animals** that they rely on to make a living. For example, **Brazilian rubber tappers** have lost their livelihoods as **rubber trees** have been **cut down**.
3) Some **native tribes** are **forced to move** when their land is cleared, e.g. the **Guarani** tribe in **Brazil** were evicted so their land could be used for **cattle ranching** and **sugar plantations**.
4) Local people are at **risk** because they're not **immune** to **western diseases** introduced by incomers. E.g. the population of the **Nukak** people in the rainforest of the **Amazon basin** has been more than **halved** since **1988**, after outsiders brought in **flu** and **malaria**.
5) There can be **conflict** between native people, landowners, mining companies and logging companies over **use of land**. In **Peru** more than 30 **native people** were **killed** in 2009 in riots over **rainforest destruction**.

ECONOMIC

1) Logging, farming and mining **create jobs**, e.g. at least **50 000 people** are employed in **gold mining** in Peru.
2) A lot of money is made from selling **timber**, **mining** and commercial **farming**. E.g. in 2008, Brazil made **$6.9 billion** from **cattle trading**.
3) In the long term, deforestation destroys the **resources** that countries depend on, e.g. timber.

Tropical Ecosystems — Human Activity

Humans are Damaging Tropical Rainforests in Other Ways too

OVERHUNTING

- **Indigenous people** living in the rainforest have always hunted and fished for their **own use**. For many people living in the rainforest, meat from wild animals (**bushmeat**) is an **important** part of their diet.
- As populations **increase**, there is a higher demand for bushmeat.
- Hunting is becoming **commercialised**, e.g. people working in the logging industry have access to **weapons** and **transport**. This means they are **equipped** to hunt and take bushmeat to towns outside the forest **to sell**.

POACHING

- Poaching is when **wild animals** and **plants** are taken or killed **illegally**, e.g. for food or as pets.
- Tropical rainforests are home to a huge variety of animals. Many of these species are attractive to poachers because their **skins**, **tusks** and other body parts are **valuable** for sale as **ornaments** or **medicines**.
- Poaching is a big problem in many areas. For example in the Bouba N'Djida conservation reserve in Cameroon **200 elephants** (half the population in the reserve) were killed for their ivory in January 2012.

CLIMATE CHANGE

1) **Climate change** can severely impact tropical rainforests. In some areas **temperature** is increasing and **rainfall** is decreasing, which leads to **drought**. The **Amazon** had **severe droughts** in **2005** and **2010** — the worst in 100 years.
2) **Plants** and **animals** living in tropical rainforests are adapted to **moist conditions**, so many species die in dry weather. **Frequent** or **long periods** of drought could lead to **extinction** of some species. **Drought** can also lead to **forest fires**, which can **destroy** large areas of forest.
3) Scientists predict that a **4 °C** temperature rise could **kill 85%** of the Amazon rainforest.

Poaching and Overexploitation Impact Biodiversity

1) **Poaching** and **overexploitation** (overhunting and overfishing) leads to the **decline** and **extinction** of some species, which reduces biodiversity (see p. 70). For example:

   In **Malaysia** the tiger, Malayan tapir, Asian elephant and clouded leopard have all become **endangered** as a result of **poaching**.

A clouded leopard.

2) Many organisms are **highly adapted** to their environment and **rely** on symbiotic relationships for survival (see p. 61). This means that the **loss** of a **species** can impact **other species** and the ecosystem as a **whole**. For example:

   The **brazil nut** is an important food source for the **agouti** (a rodent native to Central America) — the agouti breaks open the hard seed pod to eat the nut inside. Sometimes the agouti bury the nuts and forget about them — these **germinate** and **grow**, which is only possible because the nut has been removed from its **thick pod**. If the agouti became **extinct** the brazil nut would be **severely affected**.

Practice Questions

Q1 Give four causes of deforestation.

Q2 Give two environmental impacts of deforestation.

Q3 What effect might climate change have on rainforests?

Exam Question

Q1 Assess the impacts of human activity in a biome that you have studied. [10 marks]

Why is it hard to play cards in the jungle? There are too many cheetahs...

Wow, we humans really aren't doing the rainforest any favours. The stuff on these pages can be pretty disheartening, but you still need to learn it. Make sure your know all the different human activities in the rainforest and their impacts. Luckily there are some solutions to these problems so it's not all doom and gloom — turn over to the next page to find out more...

Tropical Ecosystems — Sustainable Management

These two pages are packed with great ideas about how we can make the most of the rainforests without destroying them. Unfortunately carrying out these ideas isn't always as straightforward as it sounds...

There are Ways to Make ***Human Activity*** *More* ***Sustainable***

1) It's important to **conserve** tropical rainforests in order to protect the **environment**, enable **native people** to survive and preserve **renewable resources** (p. 71).
2) However, many **people** living in tropical rainforests **rely** directly on them for **food** and **shelter**. In addition, many **developing countries** depend on **resources** produced from the **rainforest** or from **deforested land** (e.g. agriculture, logging, mining) to boost their **economies** and fund **development**.
3) Rainforests need to be managed in a way that's **sustainable**. Sustainability is about **balancing** social, economic and environmental needs so people **today** can get the things they need, **without stopping** people in the **future** from getting what they need. There are lots of ways this can be done.

Deforestation *can be* ***Managed More Sustainably***

Selective Logging

1) Only **some trees** (e.g. just the oldest ones) are **felled** — most are left standing.
2) This is **less damaging** to the forest than felling **all the trees** in an area. If **only a few trees** are taken from each area the **forest structure** is kept — the canopy is still there and the soil isn't exposed. This means the forest is able to **regenerate**.
3) **Dragging** felled trees **out** of the **forest** using **horses** or removing them with **helicopters** is less damaging than using heavy lorries.
4) For example, Greenpeace sponsor schemes in **Papua New Guinea**, where landowners are trained to select, fell and transport trees with as **little damage** to the surrounding **environment** as possible. It's estimated that these projects give local people **ten times more profit** than **commercial logging** operations.
5) However, **selective logging** can still **damage** the rainforest:
    - When a **single** tree falls it can damage as many as **30 others**.
    - **Selective logging** can cause a **patchy canopy**, which doesn't give the same **protection** to the soil as a **full canopy**.

Replanting

1) **New trees** are planted to replace the ones that are **cut down**. For example, **Peru** plans to replant more than **100 000 km²** of forest before 2018.
2) It's important that the **same types of tree** are planted that were cut down, so that the **variety of trees** is kept for the future.
3) However, these projects can be very **expensive**. They tend to be used more in **developed countries**, where more funds are available for conservation. For example, in **Australia** replanting projects are taking place in **Queensland**.

Ecotourism *can Benefit the* ***Economy*** *and the* ***Environment***

1) Ecotourism is tourism that **doesn't harm** the **environment** and **benefits local people**.
2) Only **small numbers** of **visitors** go to an area at a time, and staff and visitors are encouraged to **minimise** environmental impact by, for example, **conserving water** and disposing of **waste properly** to prevent **pollution**.
3) It provides a source of **income** for **local people**, e.g. they act as guides, provide accommodation and transport. It also raises **awareness** of conservation issues in tropical rainforests, which can bring **funding** for rainforest **conservation**.
4) When local people are employed in tourism they **don't have to log** or **farm** to make **money**. If a **country's** economy relies on **ecotourism**, there's an **incentive** to **conserve** the environment.
5) In some places ecotourism has been very successful, e.g. in **Costa Rica** ecotourism brings in about US$1.6 million a year and provides jobs for local people. As a result of ecotourism, **25%** of the country is **protected** from development.
6) However, **ecotourism** does **not necessarily** help with the development of the **local community** or the **host country**:
    - **Ecotourism** is often run by companies in the home countries of the visitors, so only a **small amount** of the money is actually **received** in the **host country**.
    - Many jobs in tourism are **menial** and low-paid.

Ecotourism lodges are designed to have a low environmental impact.

Tropical Ecosystems — Sustainable Management

Areas of Rainforest can be **Legally Protected**

Environmental Law

1) **Environmental laws** can help **protect rainforests**. For example:
   - Laws that **ban** the use of wood from forests that are not managed **sustainably**.
   - Laws that **ban excessive logging**.
   - Laws that control **land use**, e.g. the **Brazilian Forest Code** says that landowners have to keep 50-80% of their land as forest.
2) However, enforcing these laws can be difficult — it's hard to monitor **large areas** with **scattered populations**.

Protection

1) Many countries have set up **national parks** and **nature reserves** to protect rainforests. For example, the **Central Amazon Conservation Complex** in Brazil (see p. 74) is a UNESCO World Heritage Site.
2) Within national parks and nature reserves, **damaging activities** such as logging, hunting and poaching can be **monitored** and **prevented**. **Local people** can be employed as rangers to enforce the restrictions. This provides them with jobs and money, and educates them about the **importance of conservation**, so they're less likely to **overexploit** the rainforest's **resources**.
3) However, it's difficult to **enforce** restrictions, particularly over **large areas** of **dense rainforest**. Many of the people living in the rainforest depend on the rainforest for their **livelihood**, so unless they can make money in another way they will continue to **exploit** its resources.

The **International Community** Can Help **Rainforest Conservation**

Reducing Demand for Hardwood

1) **Hardwood** is wood from **certain tree species**, e.g. mahogany and teak. The wood is used to make things like **furniture**.
2) There's a high **demand** for hardwood in more **developed countries**, which means that some **tropical hardwood trees** are becoming **rarer**.
3) Some richer countries are trying to **reduce demand** so fewer trees are cut down.
4) Strategies to reduce demand include charging lots of tax on **imported hardwood** or **banning its sale**.
5) Some countries with tropical rainforests also **ban** logging of hardwood species. E.g. **Brazil banned** mahogany logging in **2001**, and **seizes timber** from illegal logging companies.

Reducing Debt

1) A lot of tropical rainforests are in **less developed countries**.
2) Less developed countries often **borrow money** from richer countries or organisations (e.g. the World Bank) to fund **development schemes** or to **cope with emergencies** like floods.
3) This money has to be paid back, with **interest**.
4) These countries often allow **industrial activities** in rainforests to help to pay back the debt.
5) Debt can be **cancelled** by countries or organisations. This would mean countries wouldn't have to rely on exploiting the rainforests, so they could be **conserved** for the future.
6) However, a system is needed to make sure the money is spent on **conservation**. In a **conservation swap** part of a country's debt is paid off by someone else in **exchange** for investment in **conservation**. For example, in 2008 the **USA** reduced **Peru's debt** by $25 million in exchange for conserving its rainforest.

Practice Questions

Q1 What is ecotourism?

Q2 Give three ways that environmental law can help protect rainforests.

Q3 Give two strategies that can reduce the demand for hardwood.

Exam Question

Q1 Discuss methods of sustainable management and their effectiveness in a biome that you have studied. [10 marks]

Conversation swap — you talk about ducks, I'll talk about biscuits...

That word 'sustainable' keeps popping up all over the place — it seems to be the answer to everything. If you manage your revision sustainably you'll do well in your exams now, whilst preserving exam success for future generations. Or something.

Urban Ecosystems

The Big Smoke. Concrete jungle. The Bright Lights. Cities don't sound like they'd be very comfortable places for wildlife to set up shop. But urban areas, and the areas surrounding the city, can be a home to loads of plants and animals.

*The **Expansion** of **Urban Areas** Creates **New Niches***

An organism's '**niche**' is its **role** in an **ecosystem** — it includes its habitat, what it lives off and what it's eaten by. As a city gets bigger, and the urban ecosystem gets more complicated, there are **more niches** for organisms to occupy. Some examples of organisms and their **urban niches** include:

- **Plants** growing in **cracks** in the pavement, on **wasteland** and in **gardens**. They're eaten by **insects**, **mammals** and **birds**.
- Invertebrates such as **woodlice** living **under paving stones** and in rubble. They eat dead plant material and provide a food source for **small mammals** and **birds**.
- **Birds** (e.g. herring gulls) living near **waste dumps** feed on human food waste.

*The **Growth** of **Urban Areas** Supports **Small-scale Ecosystems***

Urban areas are home to lots of different **small-scale ecosystems** or '**distinctive ecologies**'. For example:

Urban Gardens and Parks

Exotic species are plants and animals that have been introduced to an area.

1) Gardens and parks have a large variety of plants (e.g. **grass**, **flowers**, **shrubs** and **trees**). Gardeners increase **biodiversity** by planting both native and exotic species.
2) Lots of **invertebrates** (e.g. insects, slugs and bees) live in or feed off the plants.
3) Birds feed on **invertebrates** and **plant seeds**, and **nest** in shrubs and trees.
4) Some gardens and parks have **ponds**. Aquatic insects, fish and amphibians (e.g. **frogs** and **newts**) live in these.
5) **Mammals** (e.g. **squirrels** and **hedgehogs**) live in or visit urban gardens and parks.

Sports fields

1) Sports fields are **dominated** by **grass** because they're mowed, but there are also small plants (e.g. **daisies** and **dandelions**).
2) Lots of invertebrates (e.g. **insects**, **spiders**, **worms** and **butterflies**) live off the plants.
3) **Birds** visit to feed on seeds and insects.

Roads

1) **Plants** grow by the roadside. Cars carry seeds to **verges**, and **exhaust fumes** are rich in nitrogen, which boosts **growth**.
2) Vegetation is often **managed**. **Mowing reduces** biodiversity, but **planting** trees as noise screens or flowers to make the road more attractive can **increase** biodiversity. The plants support **invertebrates** (e.g. insects and butterflies).
3) **Birds** often **nest** in the vegetation. Birds of prey may **hunt** along the roadside, and carrion birds (e.g. crows) **scavenge**.
4) Insects, birds and mammals feed by the roadside and some animals use the verges to **travel** between different areas. This is called a **wildlife corridor**.

Roads and railways are routeways. Routeways are man-made paths and tracks that host ecosystems.

Railways

1) Many different **plants** are found along railways (e.g. **Oxford ragwort** and **clover**) because trains bring seeds from a wide area as they travel.
2) Patches of **wetland plants** (e.g. **rushes**) grow along the sides of the railway. This is because railway beds **drain water** away from the tracks, creating mini wetlands.
3) **Hardy shrubs** (e.g. **gorse**, **hawthorn** and **brambles**) grow at the side of the tracks. This is because **railway companies** cut vegetation back, and these shrubs **grow back quickly**.
4) The variety of plants supports lots of different **invertebrates**, which act as food for **birds**.
5) Lots of **mammals** live along the railway (e.g. **mice**, **hedgehogs** and **badgers**). They feed on plants, invertebrates or smaller mammals. Railways are **fenced off**, so animals are rarely disturbed, and they can use the railways as **wildlife corridors**.

Urban Ecosystems

Urban Growth **Affects Ecosystems** in the **Rural/Urban Fringe**

1) The '**rural/urban fringe**' is where an **urban area** meets a **rural** area.
2) It has a variety of **land uses** — e.g. **residential** (housing estates), **commercial** (out of town shopping centres), **industrial** (factories), **agricultural** (farmland), **recreational** (golf courses, nature reserves), and **routeways** (roads, railways).
3) The variety of land uses means there's a **variety of ecosystems**. Both **rural ecosystems** (e.g. woodland, grassland, farmland) and **urban ecosystems** (e.g. gardens, sports fields, routeways) can be found in the rural/urban fringe.
4) As urban areas **grow**, ecosystems in the rural/urban fringe are affected:

- As the **population** of urban areas increases there is often **new development** in the rural/urban fringe, which can destroy ecosystems. E.g. a higher demand for **water** might mean that grassland is **flooded** to create a **reservoir**.
- Rural ecosystems can be **broken up** by new developments. For example, new developments may gradually surround a wood, **cutting it off** from other rural areas. This can **separate populations** of organisms from each other, and from important feeding grounds.
- Increased human populations cause more **air** and **water pollution**, which can damage ecosystems. E.g. **water pollution** from industrial or domestic waste **reduces biodiversity** in water courses, which can affect bird populations because it reduces their food supply.
- Lots of people **visit** the rural/urban fringe to do **recreational activities** (e.g. nature walks, mountain bike trails). Visitors can disrupt ecosystems by **disturbing wildlife** and **increasing soil erosion** along paths and trails. Some visitors cause more serious problems:
  - **dropping litter** and **fly-tipping** (dumping big bits of rubbish, e.g. mattresses) — animals and birds can be injured or killed if they get trapped in pieces of litter.
  - **destroying wildlife** — e.g. picking flowers means their seeds are not distributed, so the plant can't reproduce.
  - **vandalism** — e.g. knocking down dry stone walls can disturb birds' nest sites.
  - **starting fires** — e.g. barbecues can start accidental forest fires which damage large areas of woodland.

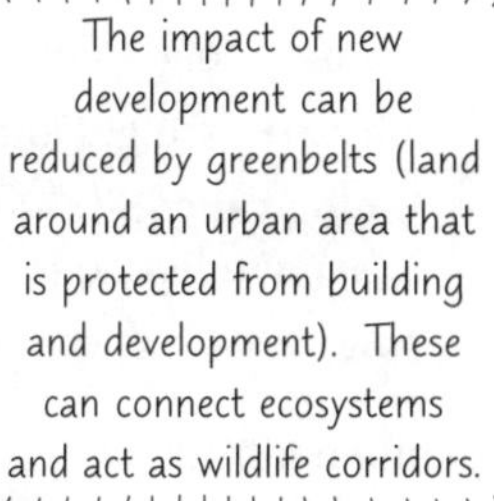

Cheryl was starting to regret asking the hairdresser for a rural/urban fringe.

5) Some developments can create **new** ecosystems, e.g. the creation of a **wetland** on a **derelict industrial site**. Others have a **positive effect** on existing ecosystems, e.g. the creation of a **wildlife trail** that preserves the ecosystem along an **old railway line**.

Practice Questions

Q1 What is a niche?

Q2 Give three examples of organisms and their urban niches.

Q3 Describe one small-scale ecosystem that could be found in an urban area.

Q4 What is a wildlife corridor?

Q5 Give four land uses that are typically found in the rural/urban fringe.

Exam Questions

Q1 Describe the distinctive ecologies of routeways and explain how they support wildlife. [8 marks]

Q2 Outline the impacts of urbanisation on ecosystems in the rural/urban fringe. [8 marks]

I found a small-scale ecosystem after I didn't brush my teeth for a week...

*Think of an ecological niche as what an organism does for a job. Instead of being a butcher, baker or candlestick-maker, an organism's niche is more about the role it plays within its ecosystem and how it being there is important for other species in the ecosystem. My niche is to make a marvellous revision guide so you can pass your exams — I know *sigh* I'm just give, give, give...*

Urban Ecosystems

Introduce a species of spider to the new environment of your mum's living room to see these pages in action. No, don't really...

The **Introduction** of **New Species** in Urban Areas Can **Cause Havoc**

1) **Introduced species** (also called **exotic** or **non-native** species) are organisms living in an ecosystem that's not their natural home. The introduction of new species can be **planned** (deliberate) or **unplanned** (accidental).
2) In the UK, species have been **deliberately introduced** for lots of reasons, for example:
    - **Farming** — e.g. wheat was introduced from the Middle East as a food crop about 5000 years ago, and American mink were introduced from the USA for fur farming in the 1920s.
    - **Game** — e.g. rainbow trout and Canadian geese are from North America.
    - **Forestry** — e.g. Douglas fir was introduced as a timber crop.
    - **Biological control** — e.g. the Japanese knotweed psyllid (an insect that feeds on the plant) is being released in parts of the UK to control the spread of Japanese knotweed.
    - **Novelty** — e.g. grey squirrels were introduced from North America in the 19th century because they were a curiosity.
3) **Unplanned** introductions can occur in various ways, e.g.:
    - **Spreading from gardens** — e.g. Oxford ragwort was introduced as an ornamental plant but has spread to the wild.
    - **Escaped animals** — e.g. ring-necked parakeets in south east England are descended from escaped pets.
    - **Imported** — e.g. the harlequin ladybird is thought to have arrived on imported flowers.
4) The introduction of species can have **negative impacts** on **ecosystems.** These harmful species are called '**invasive**':
    - **Non-native** species can **out-compete native** species. E.g. **grey squirrels** out-compete native **red squirrels** — they are bigger, hardier and less timid than red squirrels, so they can gather more food and survive through winter.
    - Native plants can be **damaged**, e.g. grey squirrels **strip bark** off trees and **eat shoots** before they can grow.
    - **Farm ecosystems** can be **disrupted**, e.g. Canadian geese can damage **crops**, and Oxford ragwort is **toxic** to livestock.
    - Non-native species may **eat** native species, e.g. American mink eat water voles and birds.
    - They may **transfer diseases** to native species, e.g. the grey squirrel carries **Squirrel Pox**, which is fatal to red squirrels.
5) However, many introduced species have **no significant negative impacts**, and some might even have a **positive impact**, e.g. Buddleia (a flowering shrub which colonises wasteland) provides a food source for butterflies and bees.

Wasteland in Urban Areas is Quickly **Colonised**

1) **Wasteland** is an area of land that has been **abandoned**, e.g. because of **deindustrialisation** (decreased industrial activity). Wastelands are often in **poor condition** with no water supply, high pollution levels and very acidic or alkaline soil.
2) Wastelands can provide a base for **ecosystems** to form through **succession**. The **characteristics** of the wasteland can affect the **sere** that develops on it, e.g. **drainage** (water availability), **acid/alkali conditions** and **pollution** levels. For example:

Succession in a disused quarry or an abandoned car park:

See p. 56-57 for more on succession.

- **Mosses and lichens** start to grow on **bare rock, rubble** or **concrete** as they can cope with very little water. They extract nutrients from the bare material, and energy from photosynthesis, and form a thin soil.
- The next stage is **flowering plants** such as **Oxford ragwort**. Seeds blow in on the wind, and germinate in **cracks** in the rock (cracks retain water and soil). As the plants die, they rot down and produce **humus**, which slowly makes the soil more **nutrient rich**.
- Bigger, taller plants can grow in the soil, e.g. **Rosebay willowherb**. **Grass** also starts to grow at this stage, and over time the area becomes a weedy grassland, with invasive plants like Japanese knotweed.
- As the soil thickens, weeds and grass are replaced by **shrubs** and **trees**, e.g. **sycamore** and **rowan**. Plants like **brambles** that can put roots into deep cracks in the rock below the soil also thrive.

3) Roadside verges and railway sidings are **colonised** in much the same way, except the succession usually starts at a **later stage** because the **soil** is already **established**. Seeds are blown in by passing vehicles.

Urban Ecosystems

Some Cities Have **Ecological Conservation Areas**

Ecological conservation areas are areas of land that have been granted a **protected** status to ensure that the ecosystems that exist there are **preserved** and **enhanced**. Developments in ecological conservation areas are **strictly controlled**. For example:

1) The **Mersey Forest** is a network of **woodlands** and **green spaces** in Cheshire and Merseyside.

- It's managed by a partnership of **public**, **private** and **voluntary** organisations, including 7 local authorities, landowners, The Forestry Commission, charities and local community groups.
- The Mersey Forest includes a **range of habitats** — oak and pine woodlands, grasslands, coastal salt marshes, coastal mudflats and rivers. These varied habitats are home to a **huge number of species**.
- The aims of the Mersey Forest are to provide **green space** for local people to enjoy, to **protect** the ecosystems in the area and preserve **biodiversity**, and to bring **money** to the local area through sustainable forestry and tourism.

2) There are many **conservation projects** in and around the Mersey Forest. For example:

- An introduced species, the **Spanish Bluebell**, is **out-competing** the native **British Bluebell** throughout the UK. The **Bluebell Recovery Project** has been **protecting** and **replanting** the native bluebell population of the Mersey Forest since **1996**, using **bulbs** that have been grown from **local British Bluebell seeds**.
- The **Friends of the Woodlands** initiative funds and advises **10 community conservation groups** in Merseyside and North Cheshire. These groups do voluntary work in the Mersey Forest area, e.g. clearing litter, running woodland art workshops and setting up projects to produce woodland products.

3) The Mersey Forest also runs projects in **urban areas** to get **people** involved in conservation and to bring local **communities** together. For example, the **Green Streets** programme sets up **community groups** to plant and care for **trees** in their neighbourhood. The trees improve air quality, make streets more attractive and provide habitats for birds.

4) Altogether, the Mersey Forest projects have created **3000 hectares** of new woodland by planting more than **8 million trees**. This conservation effort has benefited the local environment and the community in various ways:

Environmental benefits:

- Protecting woodland and planting trees **creates habitat** for woodland wildlife, and increases **biodiversity**.
- **800 hectares** of **non-woodland habitats** have been created, including **90 km of hedgerows**.
- A **reduction** in **pollution** (e.g. urban tree planting improves air quality).
- Planting trees **reduces soil erosion**.
- **Wildlife corridors** are created.

Social benefits:

- **60%** of the 1.5 million **local residents** use the woodlands for **recreation**. This improves **health** by promoting exercise and reducing stress.
- A range of environmental **education** activities are offered, encouraging people to explore the forest.

Economic benefits:

- An **improved image** of the area has **boosted** the **economy** — e.g. house prices in St Helens have increased by a total of £15 million.
- **Sustainable forestry** has created **150 new jobs** since 1994.
- An increase in **tourism, leisure** and **recreation** creates jobs and brings money to the area.

5) The Mersey Forest has been **very successful** so far, but some urban areas in the north west still lack green space, e.g. parts of **Liverpool**. The Mersey Forest wants to improve the **landscape** in the city by planting trees on **derelict sites**.

Practice Questions

Q1 What is an introduced species?

Q2 Give two negative impacts of introduced species on ecosystems.

Q3 Briefly describe the process of succession on wasteland in the UK.

Exam Question

Q1 For an ecological conservation area you have studied, discuss how effective the conservation strategies have been. [10 marks]

A little less conversation, a little more conservation please...

You don't need to go off to the rainforest to experience an ecosystem — it seems urban areas provide habitats for all kinds of wildlife. So keep your eyes peeled when you're out and about in town and you may be treated to an urban safari...

Global Ecosystem Issues

Now you've had an introduction to some of the smaller ecosystems it's time for the big boy. All the ecosystems on Earth are part of the global ecosystem. Human activities have an impact on the global ecosystem and conserving it is a tricky business.

Human Activity Generally Reduces Biodiversity

1) **Biodiversity** means the **variety** of organisms living in a particular area — all the different **species**, **habitats** and **ecosystems**.
2) Globally, biodiversity is **not evenly distributed**. It generally increases from the **poles** towards the **equator** — around **50%** of all the world's **plants and animals** live in tropical rainforests. This is because closer to the equator the climate is **warmer**, more **moist**, and more **stable**. This means **plants grow better** and can support more species higher up the food chain.
3) **Human activities** tend to reduce biodiversity. For example:
   - **Deforestation** (e.g. for farming) results in habitat loss.
   - **Draining wetlands** (e.g. for building) results in habitat loss.
   - **Pollution** can damage habitats and harm species.
   - **Global warming** changes the abundance and distribution of species.
   - **Rising sea levels** due to climate change leads to habitat loss.
   - **Overexploitation** (e.g. overfishing, overhunting and overharvesting) reduces the population of certain species.

Litter left by humans causes water pollution.

4) It's important for **ecosystems** to maintain a **high level** of biodiversity:
   - **Having** a range of species helps **maintain** the **ecosystem** — e.g. insects pollinate plants and animals disperse seeds. If **one species dies out**, it affects the **whole ecosystem**.
   - Biodiversity helps ecosystems **adapt** to **changing physical conditions** — e.g. if the **climate changes** in an ecosystem with low biodiversity all the species may die. When biodiversity is **high**, there's a better chance that some of the species in an ecosystem will be able to **adapt** to the **new conditions** and survive.
   - Biodiversity creates **feedback loops** that maintain biodiversity. For example, high biodiversity increases the **fertility** of the **soil** because there's a greater **variety** of **decaying matter**. Fertile soil means that a greater range of plants can grow, so the ecosystem remains biodiverse. If these feedback loops **collapse** the ecosystem may not be able to recover.
5) **Reducing biodiversity** threatens ecosystems and can be **unsustainable**. Humans rely on ecosystems to supply important **natural resources** such as food and fuel — when **biodiversity** is **reduced**, ecosystems are **less able** to **produce** these resources. This means that **future generations** will not be able to make use of them to meet their needs.

Lots of Fragile Environments on Earth are Being Damaged

1) **Fragile environments** are ecosystems that are **easily disturbed** and **can't adapt** to change, e.g. coral reefs, coastal wetlands, polar environments, savanna grasslands (p. 72) and tropical rainforests (p. 74).
2) Fragile environments are easily **damaged** by changes brought about by **human activities**, e.g. loss of habitat due to deforestation, species loss due to overfishing or damage to habitats due to water pollution.
3) Changes in the **natural environment** also affect fragile environments, e.g. extreme weather events like floods and droughts, or longer term changes such as increasing or decreasing erosion or sedimentation.
4) **Small changes** can cause **a lot of damage** to fragile environments, for example:
   - **Coral reefs** are sensitive to changes in **water temperature** and **quality** — they grow in salt water between 21 and 29 °C. If temperatures increase the coral can become **'bleached'** — this is when the coral can't provide enough nutrients to support the algae that live in it, and forces them out instead. The coral needs these algae to provide oxygen and nutrients — without them the coral will eventually **die**.
   - **Polar environments** are sensitive to **temperature changes** — small increases can **melt** vast areas of **ice**, which can **destroy habitats** and **threaten species**. E.g. polar bears need sea ice to hunt seals, which are their main food source. As ice melts, polar bears cannot feed and their numbers **decline**.
   - **Coastal wetlands** are sensitive to **changes in sea level** and **sedimentation** — species are adapted to live in certain depths of water and soil, and small changes can **destroy** many species' **habitats**.
5) Once a fragile environment is damaged, it is **extremely difficult** to **repair** the damage.

Global Ecosystem Issues

Managing Fragile Environments *Isn't Easy*

1) **Fragile ecosystems** are often rich in **natural resources**, e.g. ingredients for medicines, and often have high biodiversity. There is a conflict between using natural resources (**exploitation**) and preserving them for future generations (**conservation**).
2) A single **ecosystem** often has many uses. For example, the Amazon rainforest:

- Provides the resources to feed **subsistence farmers** and **native people** who hunt and fish.
- Provides **renewable resources** for export, such as rubber and ingredients for medicines (e.g. the periwinkle plant is used to treat cancer).
- Is important for countries that depend on **exploiting** its resources to develop their **economies**.

3) Managing fragile environments involves striking a **balance** between **conservation** and **exploitation**. This can be very **difficult** because:

- Some fragile environments cross **international borders**. For example, the Amazon rainforest covers an area which includes parts of **nine** different countries — this makes it very **difficult** to agree on and carry out a **management strategy** across the whole area.
- Many fragile environments are located in **less developed countries** that **lack** the **money** or the **expertise** needed to conserve them properly.
- Countries that depend on **natural resources** from **fragile environments** for income are reluctant to stop these activities, because it would damage their economy and slow development. E.g. in Brazil the mining industry damages the rainforest, but brings money to the country — the leading mining company brought in almost $9 billion in 2006.
- People who live in a fragile environment may exploit it because they have **no alternative**, or because they **don't understand** the need to conserve it.
- In some areas there is a need to introduce **non-native species** (e.g. as a food crop), but these can **out-compete** native species, and be extremely difficult to remove. For example, in Arizona an invasive plant, Tamarisk, was introduced as a windbreak, but it out-competes native plants and is difficult to control, making it a threat to the desert ecosystem.

Marcus was pretty sure he could sort out these fragile ecosystems given half a chance.

4) In some cases people are trying to **restore** fragile environments, for example the Indonesian government has invested in **replanting** areas of rainforest, and the Coral Restoration Foundation has set up **coral nurseries** and **restoration projects** in many areas where reefs have been damaged. However, restoration of fragile environments can be **difficult**:
   - Some fragile environments **cannot be restored** because they have already been so **badly damaged** by human activity. For example, clearing land in a rainforest causes **soil quality** to decline. Even if the land is replanted, the degraded soil means that rainforest vegetation **can't easily regrow**.
   - **Natural hazards** (e.g. floods, droughts, volcanic events) can cause **damage** to fragile environments which will only fully recover over long timescales. For example, the **Indian Ocean Tsunami** in 2004 destroyed areas of **coral reefs** and **mangrove swamps**. Although some countries affected by the tsunami are undertaking schemes to **replant mangroves** it could take hundreds of years for the ecosystems to fully recover.

Practice Questions

Q1 What is biodiversity?

Q2 Give three examples of human activities that reduce biodiversity.

Q3 What is a fragile environment?

Exam Question

Q1 Discuss the difficulties associated with the management of fragile environments. [8 marks]

Biodiversity — it's the spice of life...

Ecosystems supply us with all sorts of useful things and it's sometimes too easy to take advantage of them. Managing ecosystems requires a balance between making the most of the resources and preserving the ecosystem for future generations. Many ecosystems are already in decline due to human activities, so we're at a critical time in global ecosystem management.

Global Ecosystems Case Study — Serengeti

It's time for another case study — hurrah. Pack up your binoculars and your safari hat because we're off to the Serengeti...

Poaching *is a* ***Big Problem*** *on the* ***Serengeti***

The **Serengeti** is a **savanna grassland ecosystem** covering 30 000 km² in Tanzania and south west Kenya. The plantlife is dominated by grasses and shrubs with occasional trees (e.g. acacia). It supports herds of **grazing animals** (wildebeest, zebra, buffalo etc.) and their **predators** (lions, leopards, cheetahs). There are four main **environmental problems**:

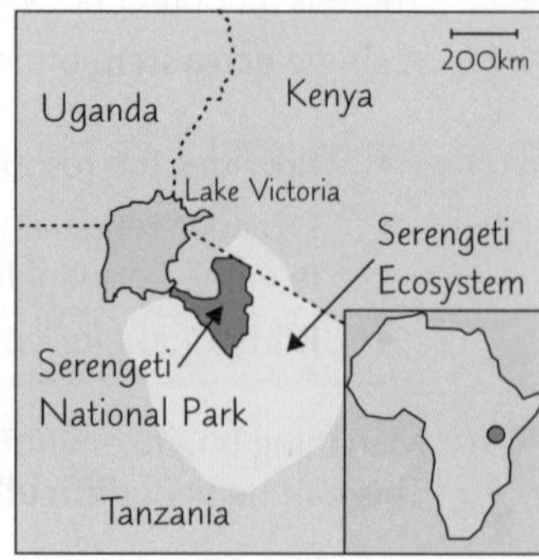

HUNTING AND POACHING

1) Historically animals have been **hunted** by visitors for **sport**, as well as by local people as a **source of food** or for products like **ivory** and **rhino horn** to sell.
2) During the 1970s and 1980s poaching for ivory and rhino horn was a huge problem and caused the **black rhino** population in the Serengeti to fall to **two animals**.
3) **Legislation** like the **1989 ban** on the **international trade of ivory** has helped to reduce elephant poaching in recent years, but **local people** hunting illegally for meat is still a problem.

INCREASING POPULATION

1) The human population in the Serengeti is increasing. This creates **land use** conflicts. Land is needed for **settlements**, for growing **crops** and for **grazing** farm animals.
2) As areas of the Serengeti have been colonised and farmed, natural **habitats** have been **lost**.
3) **Increasing population** has also led to increased **hunting**.

FIRE

1) **Controlled fires** during the dry season help to sustain the savanna environment.
2) Fire **prevents woodland** growth, burns off **dead grass** on the surface, leaving the **roots** intact, and **fertilises** the soil. **New shoots** grow through in the **wet season** and are a source of **food** for grazing animals.
3) However, **uncontrolled fires** (sometimes started to clear land for farming) can **damage** trees and destroy grass roots, so grasses can't grow back.

INVASIVE SPECIES

1) **Invasive plant species** can cause damage. For example, the **Mexican poppy**, which was accidentally introduced with imported wheat, **out-competes native plants** and **crops**, making some areas **unsuitable for farming**.
2) **Animal species** can spread **disease**, e.g. in 1994 canine distemper virus spread from **domestic dogs** killed **a third** of the population of **Serengeti lions**.

Managing *the* ***Serengeti*** *involves* ***Working*** *with* ***Local People***

The **Serengeti National Park** covers an area of around **15 000 km²** in northern Tanzania. It was established in 1951 to **preserve wildlife** and **reduce environmental damage**. The park is managed by **Tanzania National Parks** (TANAPA). The management strategy aims to balance conservation of biodiversity with the needs of local people, through a number of different schemes:

1) **Monitoring** the **ecosystem** through aerial wildlife surveys, water quality monitoring and monitoring of invasive species.
2) Protection of **priority species**, e.g. rangers monitor the black rhino population and carry out **anti-poaching patrols**.
3) **Disease monitoring** and **vaccination programmes** — domestic dogs in a zone around the park are vaccinated against rabies and canine distemper virus to try to stop these diseases spreading to wild animals.
4) **Controlled burning** is carried out to stop a build-up of dry grass, which could cause damaging wildfires.
5) **Conservation education projects** — the park supports conservation clubs in 74 local primary schools, holds teacher training workshops, and informs local people about work in the park. Involving local people in conservation means they are more likely to **protect the ecosystem** themselves.
6) Four **Wildlife Management Areas (WMAs)** were created, which have a **community based conservation approach**. For example, the **Ikona Community WMA**, an area of **450 km²**, is managed by communities from five villages. They work together to manage the wildlife, and are allowed to use the resources from the area within sustainable limits — either through hunting for their own use, or making money from tourism (e.g. selling local produce or guiding safaris).
7) **Tourism** brings **money** to the local area, but strict **regulations** are in place to make sure it doesn't **damage** the ecosystem, e.g. driving is only permitted in designated areas, and access into the park is only allowed at certain points.

Global Ecosystems Case Study — Serengeti

Management Strategies have Helped the **Environment** and **Local People...**

Local **conservation education** projects have improved **understanding** between local people and the National Park:

1) The **WMAs** have been successful in lots of ways. They provide local people with a **food source** and **income** from **legally traded** animal products and tourism, and help to **reduce** illegal **poaching**.
2) **Poaching** has **declined** in recent years, and the populations of **most species** are steadily **increasing** — e.g. the elephant population increased from 500 in 1990 to 2100 in 2011.
3) Money from tourism goes back into the National Park to help pay for conservation projects. It also **boosts** the **local economy** by creating jobs and a market for local produce. The increased **ranger presence** for tourism has also helped **reduce poaching**.
4) **Disease monitoring** and vaccination has helped **prevent** damaging outbreaks of disease. E.g. in 1996 an outbreak of rinderpest (a disease which affects hooved animals like cattle) was stopped from entering the Serengeti due to a programme of cattle vaccination in the districts of the Park closest to the affected area.

...but there are still **Threats** to the **Ecosystem**

It's still proving difficult to balance **wildlife conservation** with the **needs of local people**:

1) The **human population** around the park is still growing, and more settlements and farms are built near the park each year. There can be **conflicts** between agriculture and conservation, e.g. elephants sometimes raid crops such as sorghum and maize, which can make conservation **unpopular** with local people.
2) Some **local people** are reluctant to become part of a **WMA**, because they have **doubts** about what they'll gain from it. Others have **refused** to stop **farming** or **hunting** within the WMAs, so some areas are still being over-exploited.
3) Outside the WMAs, **poaching** is still a **problem** in the Serengeti — **40 000 animals** are killed each year for **meat** and other **products**. These are mostly wildebeest and zebra, but other animals often get caught in poachers' snares or traps. If the human **population** around the park continues to **increase**, it could lead to a **rapid decline** of the **wildebeest population**.
4) **Tourism** can have a number of **negative impacts**:

- **Construction** and use of roads, trails, campsites, hotels and other buildings have an **environmental impact** through increased erosion and loss of habitat.
- Road **vehicles** and **aeroplanes** cause air and noise **pollution**.
- **Waste disposal** from accommodation can be a problem, e.g. if food waste isn't disposed of properly it can attract pests such as rats and cockroaches.
- Tourists can **disturb** and sometimes **distress** animals.
- Tourism increases the **demand** for **water**, which can lead to **water shortages**.

A traffic jam of safari vehicles in the Serengeti.

A clear **code of conduct** and **limits** to **tourism** have been set by the National Park to try and reduce these impacts.

Practice Questions

Q1 How has poaching damaged the Serengeti ecosystem?

Q2 What effect has human population growth had on the Serengeti ecosystem?

Q3 What are Wildlife Management Areas (WMAs)?

Q4 Give two positive and two negative impacts of tourism on the Serengeti ecosystem.

Exam Question

Q1 Discuss the effectiveness of a management strategy in a fragile environment you have studied. [10 marks]

Right, time to geti your head down and learn some stuff...

The Serengeti is a great example to pull out in your exam — there's a lot of stuff to talk about and examiners love answers that are backed up by a truckload of facts. Unfortunately that also means there's a lot to remember, so make sure you know it really well.

Global Ecosystems Case Study — Amazon

The Amazon Rainforest is another example of a fragile environment. You have to know two case studies for your exam, so you need to learn these pages as well as the ones on the Serengeti. Just thinking about it makes me feel a bit fragile to be honest...

The **Amazon Rainforest** is under **Threat**

1) The **Amazon** is the world's largest **tropical rainforest** and covers 40% of the South American landmass.
2) It's one of the most **biodiverse** regions on **Earth** and is home to up to **1 million plant species**, over **500 species** of **mammals** and over **2000 species** of **fish**. The Amazon is also home to many **endangered species**, including the Amazonian manatee (an aquatic mammal), black caiman (a reptile) and the pirarucu (a fish).
3) There are two main threats to the environment:

Climate change is also a serious threat to the Amazon. It could lead to drought, forest fires and species extinction.

Deforestation

1) **Deforestation** is the single biggest **threat** to the rainforest — **13%** of the original forest has been **cleared.**
2) There are a number of **reasons** for **deforestation** (see p. 62). In the Amazon, mining, logging and subsistence agriculture all contribute to deforestation, but **cattle ranching** is the biggest problem — it was responsible for **more than 60%** of all deforestation between **2000** and **2005**.
3) The impacts of deforestation are **wide** (see p. 62). In the Amazon there have been problems with increased **forest fires** and **soil erosion**, and decreased **biodiversity** caused by habitat loss.

Overhunting and overfishing

1) Most of the **local people** still live a **traditional lifestyle** and rely on hunting, fishing, foraging and small-scale farming for food.
2) **Population growth** in recent years has caused an **increase** in **subsistence hunting** and **fishing** by local people.
3) Hunting primates for **bushmeat** is a big problem — in the Brazilian Amazon **local people** consume between 2.2 and 5.4 million primates per year. This is **unsustainable** because primates **reproduce slowly** and many species are **endangered.**
4) The loss of certain species can have knock-on effects on other species (see p. 63).

The **Central Amazon Conservation Complex** is in the **Brazilian Amazon**

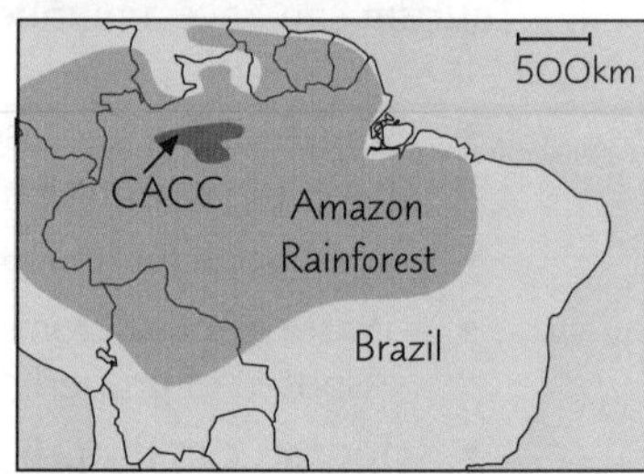

1) The **Central Amazon Conservation Complex** (**CACC**) was established in **2003** by bringing together four reserves in the Brazilian Amazon — **Jaú National Park**, **Anavilhanas Ecological Station**, **Mamirauá Reserve** and **Amana Reserve**.
2) It aims to protect the **biodiversity** of this area of rainforest, with a focus on protecting endangered species, and to maintain the various **ecosystems** while allowing local people to continue using the forest for their livelihood in a **sustainable way**.
3) The complex covers an area of **49 000 km²** and it includes a **variety of habitats** — dry (unflooded) rainforest, rivers, lakes, seasonally flooded forest and dry grasslands.
4) The complex is managed by several organisations, including the **Brazilian Institute of the Environment and Natural Resources** (IBAMA), local government, research institutes and representatives from the mining and tourism industries.
5) The management approach uses a number of **schemes** to try to balance **conservation** and **sustainable development**:

1) The complex is divided into zones — **total protection**, **buffer zones**, **sustainable use**, **rehabilitation** and **experimental use**. Activities within these areas are **strictly controlled**:
   - In areas of total protection access is heavily restricted — for example only **researchers** and **authorised visitors** are allowed in **Jaú National Park**.
   - In areas of sustainable use there are **quotas** to limit **logging**, **hunting** and **fishing**.
2) Two **Sustainable Development Reserves** (SDRs) have been created where **hunting** and **logging** is only allowed for **subsistence**, and there are **limits** to the numbers of **animals** and **fish** that can be caught.
3) **Economic Alternatives Programs** have been set up. These are **sustainable schemes** run by **local people** who receive a **direct income** from their work — communities are involved in **fisheries management**, **ecotourism**, **sustainable agriculture** and **handicraft** production. For example, the Fibrarte Project supports local people who use natural fibres to make handicrafts, which they can **sell**.
4) **Education projects** have been set up to educate local people about the environment and how to manage it.
5) Projects have been set up to **increase community involvement** with conservation. In Mamirauá, **60 communities** take part in **monitoring wildlife. Local representatives** meet every two months with local government and non-government organisations to discuss ways of **managing** the environment and **conserving biodiversity**.

Global Ecosystems Case Study — Amazon

Sustainable Development Initiatives have been **Successful**...

A black caiman lurking in shallow water.

1) The creation of the **conservation complex** has protected the surrounding area from **major developments** that might have impacts on the CACC — there are no dams, pipelines, mines or commercial logging activities and currently **none are planned** for the future.
2) The **SDRs** have improved **biodiversity**. Populations of many key species have increased — since the creation of the CACC the **black caiman** population has **increased by 100%** and the **pirarucu fish** population by over **300%**.
3) **Economic Alternatives Programs** promote **sustainable activities** and have **reduced poverty** — average **household income** has **increased** by 50-99% in some areas. Local farmers and craftsmen belong to **producer's associations**, which means they can sell their goods directly to buyers, rather than trading through 'middle men' who charge a commission.
4) **Ecotourism** provides a **source of income** for locals and promotes **conservation** — in **Mamirauá** a low environmental impact **ecotourism lodge** has been built, which recycles waste and uses solar power. The lodge brings **jobs** and **money** to the local community, and invests money into **conservation** and **community** projects.
5) **Local education** and **health improvement** projects have been **successful**:

- Local people have been trained as **health workers**, and better **rainwater collection technology** means local communities have access to clean drinking water. These changes have **improved** the **quality of life** of the local population, shown by a **53% drop** in **infant mortality**.
- **80 teachers** from local schools have been trained to educate children about the **environment**. As a result, around **1800 children** have had classes on conservation.

...but **Protecting** such a **Large Area** is **Difficult**

1) The reserves are **large** and **understaffed**, which makes it difficult to **monitor** and **control illegal activities**, e.g. hunting. 150 people are employed in the Amana and Mamirauá reserves and there are 100 volunteer guards, but more **volunteers** are **needed** to cover the large area effectively.
2) **Restricting access** to areas of **total protection** is very difficult because of the size of the zones and the **limited number** of staff. For example, in **Jaú National Park** there are only **four permanent staff**, so poaching of fish and turtles is still a problem. **26 volunteer guards** have been trained, which may **improve** the situation.
3) **Population growth** in the area puts **stress** on the **ecosystem**, and some areas still suffer from **intensive fishing** and **hunting**, especially of monkeys and manatees.
4) Population growth across the region means **deforestation** around the edges of the CACC **continues**. **Deforestation** around the **edges** of the complex results in **habitat loss** and **fragmentation** (when forested areas are split up so animals can't move between them). It also makes the complex more **accessible**, which increases the risk of illegal overhunting and overfishing in the complex.

Practice Questions

Q1 Name two threats to the Central Amazon Conservation Complex.

Q2 What are SDRs?

Q3 Give one example of how SDRs have been successful.

Q4 Give one reason why restricting access to the zones of total protection is difficult.

Exam Question

Q1 Compare and contrast the management schemes in two different fragile environments you have studied. [40 marks]

Well you can't say conservation isn't Complex...

So there you have it — another jolly little case study, if you can call the largest protected area in the Amazon basin 'little'. The trouble with the Central Amazon Conservation Complex is that it's such a large area, with so many different habitats, that it's very difficult to come up with a management scheme that addresses all the issues. That's what makes it great to write about in the exam.

Urban Areas and Urbanisation

Ahh cities, at last. This is the section that I know you've all been waiting for. Now don't get too excited and rush on to the best bits (retailing will still be there when you get to it), you need to get a few basic things into your brain first...

*You Need to Know About **Millionaire, Mega** and **World Cities***

More than **50%** of the world's population live in **urban areas**. This number is increasing, particularly in **developing countries**. Population growth in urban areas has increased the number of **big cities** in the world:

1) A **millionaire city** is an urban area with **over a million people** living there, e.g. Budapest in Hungary.
2) A **mega city** is an urban area with **over 10 million people** living there, e.g. Mumbai in India.
3) A **world city** is a city that has an **influence** over the **whole world**. World cities are centres for **trade** and **business**, and they also tend to be hubs of **culture** and **science**, e.g. London, New York and Tokyo.

Millionaire, mega and world cities are more common in the northern hemisphere and are often located on a coastline or large river.

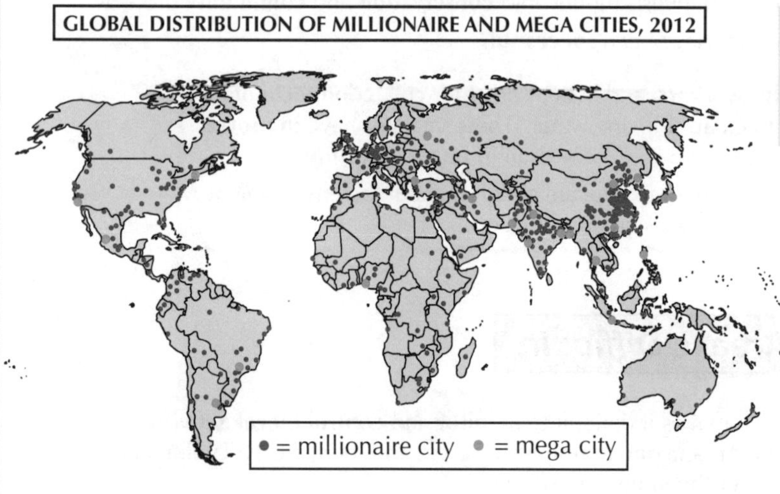

Millionaire cities — there are more than **400**. In the past, millionaire cities were mostly found in the **developed world**, but **increasingly** they are found in the **developing world**.

Mega cities — there are more than **20**. More than two thirds of **mega cities** are in **developing countries**.

The exact number of **world cities** is hard to define. World cities tend to be in **developed countries**. Over time it's likely that more cities in **developing countries** such as India and China will become world cities.

*Four **Processes** Affect the **Populations** of **Cities***

1) There are **four processes** that involve the movement of people in and out of **urban areas**:

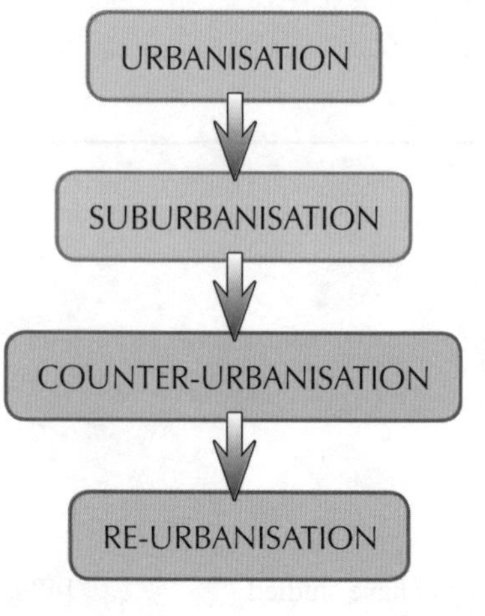

Urbanisation (see p. 77-79) is the **growth** in the **proportion** of a **country's population** that lives in urban areas.

Suburbanisation (see p. 80-81) is the movement of people from the **city centre** to the **outskirts**, or **suburbs**.

Counter-urbanisation (see p. 82-83) is the movement of people from **cities** to **rural areas**.

Re-urbanisation (see p. 84-85) is the movement of people **back** to the **city centre**.

As people move from one area to another, economic activities (services and industry) move with them.

2) These processes may happen **one after the other** as a country **develops** — this is called the **cycle of urbanisation**.
3) However, in many cities **all four processes** are happening at the **same time** but in different parts of the city.

Urban Areas and Urbanisation

Urbanisation is Mainly Caused by Rural-Urban Migration

1) Urbanisation is caused by **rural-urban migration** and a **naturally increasing population**.
2) As people migrate to cities the **urban population** increases. The migrants tend to be **young people** looking for work. They may then have **children**, which **further increases** the urban population.
3) Rural-urban migration takes place because of **push** and **pull factors**.
   - **Push factors** are the things that push people **away** from a rural area. In **developing countries**, push factors are often linked to **poverty**.
   - **Pull factors** are the things that **attract** people to an urban area.
4) At the moment rural-urban migration is taking place in many **developing countries**. Here are the reasons why:

Every day Cilla dreams of rural-urban migration.

In developed countries, rapid urbanisation occurred in the 18th and 19th centuries, and now the processes of suburbanisation, counter-urbanisation and re-urbanisation are more important.

PUSH FACTORS

1) Human activity and changes in climate can cause **desertification** (when fertile land becomes barren desert). If land becomes **unproductive** it **cannot** provide enough food to support the population, and people are forced to **move away**.
2) Some farmers take out **loans** to help them **improve their yields** (e.g. by buying fertiliser or building irrigation systems). If their **crops fail** they may be **unable** to pay these loans back, and may **lose their land**.
3) **Conflict** and **civil war** may cause people to **flee** their homes. If many people are **killed** or **injured** in a war, there will be less people to work the land and there could be food shortages.
4) **Natural disasters** such as earthquakes and floods may damage homes and farmland, which people cannot afford to **rebuild** or **repair**.
5) **Changes in land use** in rural areas can drive people out. E.g. farmland may be flooded when **dams** are built to generate **hydro-electric** power.
6) **Mechanisation of agriculture** means fewer people are needed to work the land, so there's a lack of jobs.

PULL FACTORS

1) There are **more jobs** available in urban areas.
2) **Jobs** in urban areas are usually **better paid** than jobs in rural areas.
3) There may be better access to **health** and **education** services.
4) **Other family members** may have already moved to the city. They may be able to help migrants find **homes** and **jobs**.
5) There is often a **perception** that **quality of life** will be better in a city.

The expectation of a better quality of life in a city is often wrong — see p. 78-79.

Practice Questions

Q1 What is the difference between a millionaire city and a mega city?

Q2 What is meant by the term 'urbanisation'?

Q3 What are push and pull factors?

Q4 Give one pull factor which attracts people to urban areas.

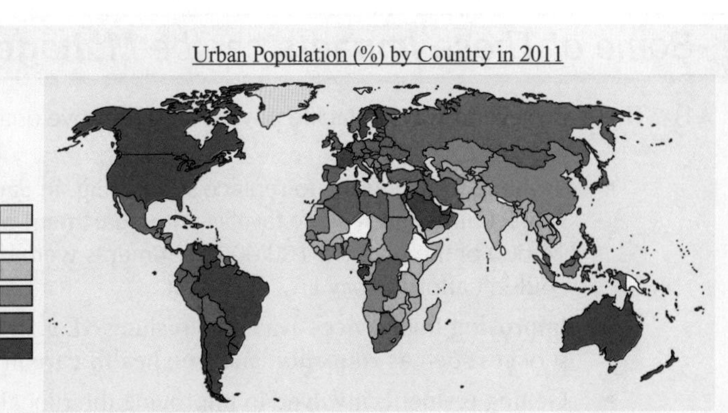

Exam Questions

Q1 Look at the map showing urban population by country. Describe and comment on the pattern of urbanisation shown. [7 marks]

Q2 Discuss the causes of urbanisation. [8 marks]

Pull factors — quality of dance moves, use of deodorant etc...

As developing countries, errr, develop, people ditch country living and flood to cities. It's well worth knowing the push and pull factors that convince them to make the move — don't turn over until you can rewrite the lists above while standing on your head.

Urbanisation

You might've already worked out that loads of people migrating to a city is going to cause a few issues...

Urbanisation has Impacts in Urban Areas

1) As **urban populations** grow there is increased **demand** for space (e.g. for houses), **resources** (e.g. water), and **services** (e.g. schools). If these increased demands **cannot** be met, it can lead to **poor quality of life** for the people living in the area.
2) Many **developing countries cannot afford** to meet these extra demands or cannot **keep up** with the **rapid** rate of urbanisation, so urbanisation has a number of **negative impacts**:

A shanty town (favela) in São Paulo.

©iStockphoto.com/AM29

1) When migrants move to a city there are often **not enough houses** for them, or they **cannot afford** to rent or buy.
2) Some migrants are forced to **live on the streets** or in **shelters**, e.g. in 2009 there were more than 13 000 homeless people in São Paulo, Brazil.
3) Migrants often **build their own houses**, leading to the unregulated growth of **slums** or **shanty towns**. The houses are often **poorly built** using cheap materials. Shanty towns have a number of problems:
   - They're often built on land that isn't suitable for construction, e.g. **steep hillsides** at risk of **landslides**, or **flood risk** areas.
   - There is often a **lack of basic services** like clean water and sewage disposal. This means that there is a **high risk of disease** (e.g. dysentery and typhoid).
   - Children growing up in a shanty town often **don't** have access to **education**, or need to **work** to earn money for their families. This makes it **difficult** for them to get a **well paid job** and **move out** of the shanty town as they grow older.
   - The **difference in wealth** between people living inside and outside the shanty town can cause tension and lead to **social problems** (e.g. crime and violence).
4) There is often high **competition** for good jobs in the **formal sector** (where workers receive regular wages from an employer and have set hours of work). Migrants may have to accept **low wages**, **poor working conditions** and **little job security** (e.g. not being on a contract, so they could be dismissed at any time).
5) Migrants who can't find formal work may be forced to work in the **informal sector**, doing unskilled jobs (e.g. car washing), that **don't** tend to **pay well**, offer **no job security** and can be **dangerous**. People dependent on this type of irregular income often live in **poverty**.
6) Rapid population growth increases the pressure on **roads** and **railways**, increasing **congestion** and **air pollution**.

Some of These Impacts can be Managed

1) There are **several ways** to tackle poverty and improve quality of life in **urban areas**. Here are some examples:

- **Building new housing** to replace slums. E.g. in **São Paulo** in 1995 the government-run **Cingapura Housing Project** aimed to **replace** favelas with **apartment blocks**, which locals could rent **cheaply**. However, only 14 000 of the planned 100 000 apartments were built — the scheme was **scrapped** because many people couldn't afford to pay any rent at all.
- **Improving the services** available in slums. E.g. in **São Paulo** the Monte Azul Community Association provides services such as **education** and **free health care** in the Monte Azul favela.
- Getting **residents involved** in improving their local areas. E.g. in Rio de Janeiro, the **$300 million Favela-Bairro** project made improvements in 73 favelas across the city (e.g. supplying electricity and clean water, and running adult education classes to improve adult literacy). **Residents** chose what improvements they wanted in their own favela, so they felt **involved** with the development. New services (e.g. daycare centres for children) were **staffed by local people**, which gave them an **income** and an opportunity to **learn** new skills.
- **Redeveloping** whole areas of slum into new **independent townships**, e.g. in **Dharavi**, Mumbai (see next page).

2) Although schemes like this can help to **decrease poverty** and **increase quality of life**, the **scale** of the problem is so large that tackling it can be extremely **difficult**.

Urbanisation

Mumbai in India has Experienced Rapid Urbanisation

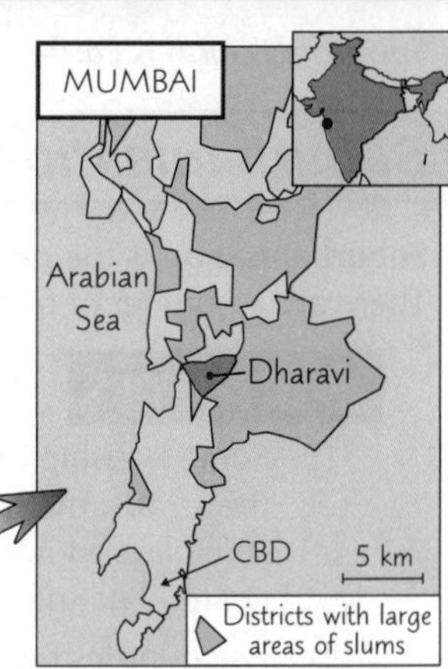

Dharavi is one of the largest slums in Mumbai and is home to more than 1 million people.

1) **Mumbai** (formerly Bombay) is a **mega city** (see p. 76) on the west coast of **India**.
2) Mumbai is **globally important** — it is a major **port** on the Indian Ocean, India's **financial centre** and a hub of **industry** and **services**. The city is also a **cultural centre** — it's home to the **Bollywood** movie industry.
3) Migrants from **rural** areas all over India have moved to Mumbai in search of jobs. As a result, the population of Mumbai **increased rapidly** from **5.9 million** in 1971 to **12.5 million** in 2011.
4) The city has struggled to handle the **rapid urbanisation** caused by immigration — **more than half** of the population live in **poverty** in slums, which cover large parts of the city.
5) Urbanisation has created a number of **issues**:

IMPACTS

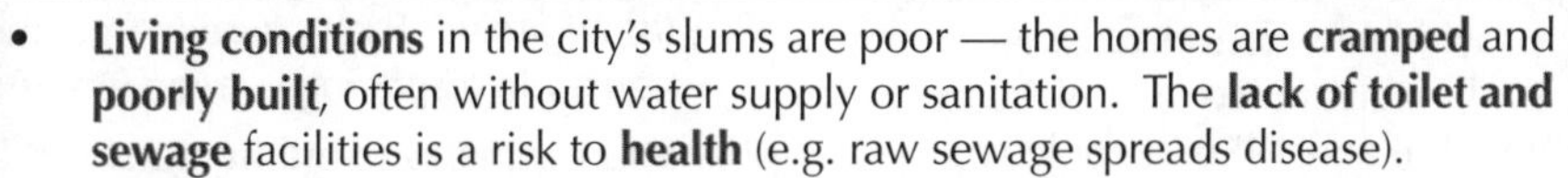

- **Living conditions** in the city's slums are poor — the homes are **cramped** and **poorly built**, often without water supply or sanitation. The **lack of toilet and sewage** facilities is a risk to **health** (e.g. raw sewage spreads disease).

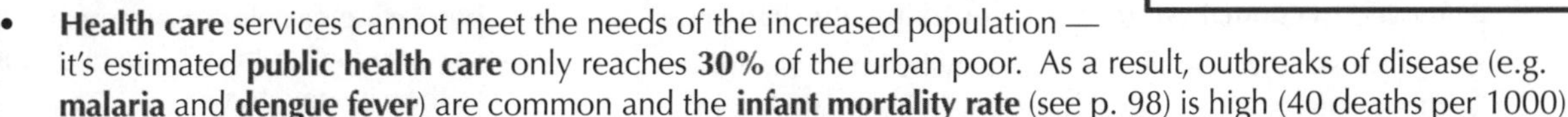

- **Health care** services cannot meet the needs of the increased population — it's estimated **public health care** only reaches **30%** of the urban poor. As a result, outbreaks of disease (e.g. **malaria** and **dengue fever**) are common and the **infant mortality rate** (see p. 98) is high (40 deaths per 1000).
- The increased population adds to the **demand** for water. Mumbai's water supply is dependent on the **monsoon rains**, and in dry years water has to be strictly **rationed**.
- The **road network** in Mumbai carries **millions** of people each day. It cannot cope with this level of traffic and there are problems with **long journey times**, **congestion** and **air pollution**.
- An increasing population produces **more waste**. This can cause problems, e.g. in the eastern neighbourhood of Chembur waste on open rubbish dumps is burnt, which causes **air pollution**. This has health impacts on local residents — **25%** of deaths in Chembur between 2007 and 2008 were caused by **respiratory problems**.

Steps have been taken to **manage** some of these issues:

MANAGEMENT

- In 2004 the government first announced a **redevelopment project** to clear the Dharavi slum and create a new **independent township**. Plans include **building new apartments**, a water and sewage system, hospitals and schools. Some residents of Dharavi are **strongly against** the redevelopment — it's an established community with successful industries, e.g. **recycling rubbish** from all over the city. Residents are worried that the redevelopment will destroy their **livelihoods** and the **community spirit** of the area.
- The **Slum Sanitation Program** was started in 1995 by a group of Non-Governmental Organisations (NGOs). It built 330 new **communal toilet blocks** in slums in Mumbai.
- To try and reduce the demand for water, the local authority has made **rainwater harvesting** systems (collecting rainwater from rooftops) compulsory on all **new residential buildings** in Mumbai on plots larger than 300 m^2. However, since 2007 only **half** of the eligible buildings have actually installed rainwater harvesting plants.
- People are using **alternative forms of transport** (e.g. scooters and mopeds) to avoid being stuck in traffic and reduce their journey times. This helps to reduce congestion, but these vehicles add to the poor air quality.
- The **public transport** system is being upgraded — a **Metro system** with over 140 km of new rail lines is being developed in the city. The first line is set to open in **2013**, but the system will not be completed until **2021**.

Practice Questions

Q1 Give two impacts of urbanisation.

Q2 Give one management strategy used to tackle the impacts of urbanisation.

Exam Question

Q1 "For every problem caused by urbanisation there is an effective solution."
To what extent do you agree with this view? [40 marks]

Poverty management strategy #12 — win 'Who Wants to be a Millionaire'...

Phew — the first case study of the section and it's a bit of a whopper. Mumbai is a big city with some big problems — make sure that you learn the issues and management strategies off by heart. Oh, and everything else on the pages as well...

Suburbanisation

Suburbanisation is caused by cheaper housing on the edges of cities, better transport links and dreams of home grown veg.

Suburbanisation *is Taking Place in the* ***Developed World***

Suburbanisation is the movement of people from **city centres** to the **outskirts** (see p. 76).
There are a number of reasons **why** people move:

PUSH FACTORS

1) Some **housing** in cities is **poor quality**, e.g. in the UK in the 1940s, many houses in inner cities were small and some **lacked basic services** like indoor bathrooms and central heating.
2) As countries develop, governments often **clear** low quality city centre housing and provide **new houses** outside the city for residents. E.g. **slum clearance** took place in much of **England** between **1950 and 1970**. People were moved to **council estates** on the **outskirts of urban areas**.
3) **Deindustrialisation** in city centres (when manufacturing moves out of an area) leads to people losing their jobs.
4) As **unemployment** increases in the city, people have **less money** to spend there, so local shops and services may be forced to close (see p. 86). This means there are **fewer local services** for people living in the city centre.

PULL FACTORS

1) Planning laws may be **more relaxed** outside city centres, so it's **easier** to build houses. In the UK, until the 1950s developers took advantage of relaxed planning laws and built **new housing estates** on the edge of urban areas. They offered large, modern houses in a **spacious, green environment**.
2) Improvements in **public transport** and **increasing car ownership** mean that people can live further from work and **commute** in to the city each day.
3) As **businesses** and **shops** move out of city centres to take advantage of **cheaper rents** on the outskirts, more **jobs** and **services** become available in the suburbs.

Suburbanisation *has* ***Impacts*** *on the* ***City Centre*** *and the* ***Suburbs***

IMPACTS ON THE CITY CENTRE

- As people and businesses **move out** to the suburbs, buildings in the city centre are **abandoned** and may become **derelict**. These processes can lead to the city centre becoming **run down**.
- As businesses leave **unemployment** increases, which leads to **lower living standards** and **poverty**.
- **Wealthier middle class people** may move to the **suburbs** where there is a **better quality of life**. The people left behind are **poorer** and are often **foreign immigrants**. This can lead to economic and ethnic **segregation**.
- Some people from the suburbs may still **commute** into the city to work, which increases **congestion** and **pollution**.

IMPACTS IN THE SUBURBS

- **New housing estates** are often built on open countryside, which affects **wildlife habitats**.
- As **urban areas** spread, more ground is **concreted over**. This can increase **surface run-off** and the risk of **flooding**.
- Most people who live in the suburbs **own cars**. This means that the number of cars on the roads **increases**, causing **congestion** and **air pollution**.

There are Ways of ***Managing the Impacts*** *of Suburbanisation*

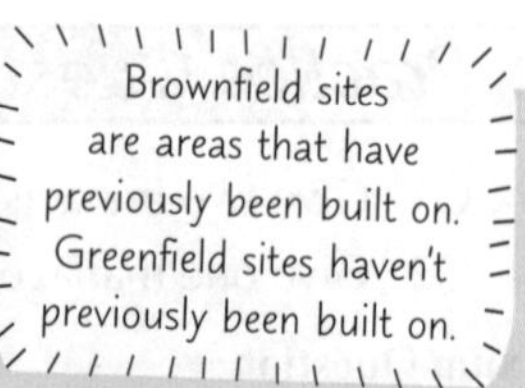

1) **Redevelopment schemes** encourage some **people** and **businesses** to move back to city centres (re-urbanisation — see p. 84-85) by improving **brownfield sites** in the city centre. E.g. the Birmingham Big City Plan, launched in 2011, aims to redevelop five inner city areas of Birmingham. The proposals include space for businesses, shops and cultural uses, as well as 5000 new homes and 50 000 new jobs.
2) Many urban areas are surrounded by a **greenbelt** (an area of countryside with restrictions on land use and development) to prevent the **urban areas** getting too large. This protects the countryside from **development**.
3) Some schemes have aimed to **reduce traffic congestion** in the **city centre**. For example, after the London congestion charge (see p. 44) was introduced in 2003, the volume of traffic in the congestion charging zone fell by 15%.
4) Some towns have improved their **flood defence schemes**, e.g. in Shrewsbury in Shropshire, the council has built a system of **flood barriers** and **pumping stations** to reduce the flood risk to newly developed urban areas close to the River Severn.

Suburbanisation

Surbiton is a *London Suburb*

GREATER LONDON AREA

SURBITON

Kingston upon Thames

1) **Surbiton** is an area of **south west London** in the borough of **Kingston upon Thames**. The population of the borough increased from 141 000 in 1971 to 160 000 in 2011 as a result of suburbanisation from the centre of London. **Surbiton** has been the focus for much of this **growth**.
2) People move to Surbiton because:
   - **Transport links** into the **centre of London** are excellent, so it is popular with commuters — the fastest trains reach London Waterloo in **18 minutes**. It is also close to the **A3** — one of the main road routes into the city.
   - There is a variety of **good quality housing**, e.g. semi-detached houses and flats.
   - It is a wealthy area with plenty of **shops** and **restaurants**.
   - The area has good state **schools** and a number of **parks**, so it's popular with families.
3) Suburbanisation has caused **problems** in Surbiton:
   1) Lots of people **own cars** (about 70% of households own at least one car), and roads often have a large number of parked cars. This causes congestion and can make it difficult for **larger vehicles** (e.g. buses) to get through.
   2) Surbiton is currently in **London travel zone 6**. This means that fares into central London are **expensive** and many commuters choose to **drive** — about **40%** of the working population in **Surbiton** drive to work. This further increases congestion and air pollution, especially along the roads connecting Surbiton to the A3.
   3) **House prices** are **high** in Surbiton — the average selling price in **April 2012** was **£406 000** (compared to a UK average of £226 000). This makes it **harder** for people on **lower incomes** to **move** to the area, which could lead to **economic segregation** — people on higher incomes living in different areas from those on lower incomes.

The train stations in London are divided into six zones. Zone 1 is in the centre of the city and zone 6 covers stations on the edge of London.

4) There are some strategies in place to **manage the problems** in Surbiton:
   1) The **Improvement Strategy for Surbiton Town Centre** was launched in **September 2009**. It proposed **widening roads**, building a **new access road** to Surbiton station and having **set delivery times** for local shops, so that delivery bays in the town centre can become **parking bays** at other times of the day. These measures will help **combat congestion** and make it easier for traffic to **pass** parked cars.
   2) The **Surbiton Neighbourhood Committee** has been set up to involve the residents of Surbiton in **local decision making**. The committee can make decisions about how to make **improvements** (e.g. traffic management) within the area.
   3) There is currently a campaign to **reclassify Surbiton station** as being in London travel **zone 5**. This would mean that commuters would **pay less** to travel into **central London**, which would encourage more people to use the train.
   4) **Secure bicycle storage units** have been installed at the station and there are plans to **improve pedestrian access**, which should **encourage** more people to cycle or walk to the station rather than driving.

Josh and Pierre had their own way of clearing congestion in Surbiton.

Practice Questions

Q1 Give two reasons why suburbanisation occurs in developed countries.

Q2 Give two strategies that have been used to manage problems caused by suburbanisation in Surbiton.

Exam Question

Q1 Outline the impacts of suburbanisation. [8 marks]

I think it's time to rename the town Suburbiton...

Poor Surbiton is often the butt of jokes about suburbanisation, but that's just because it's such a great example. So get it learnt.

Counter-urbanisation

You might think counter-urbanisation is when you build a LEGO® house on your kitchen work top — well, you'd be wrong. It's the movement of people away from large urban areas to smaller settlements and rural areas.

There are **Lots of Reasons** for **Counter-urbanisation**

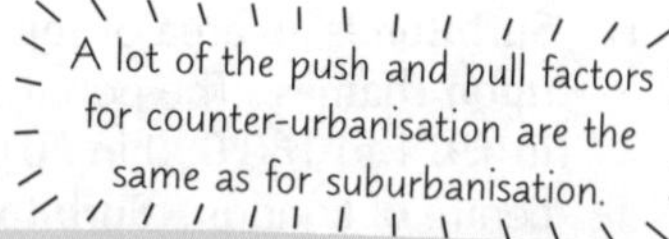

PUSH FACTORS

- Many people move out of urban areas to escape the **air** and **noise pollution** of towns and cities.
- Suburbs and city centres often have problems with **congestion** and **parking**.
- As **suburban** areas become more popular **house prices** rise. People feel they are not getting **value for money** and move further from the city. E.g. in Surbiton **£300 000** would only buy a **two** bedroom house, but in St Ives (see next page) it would buy a **four** bedroom house.

Bob enjoyed country living, but he couldn't shake off his craving for a skinny caramel latte.

PULL FACTORS

- **Houses** in **smaller settlements** and **rural areas** are often less **densely packed** than those in city centres and the suburbs. This means houses are often **bigger** and have more **outside space**.
- People think that living somewhere **quieter** and with **more open space** will improve their **quality of life**. This is especially true for **retired** people and **families** with children.
- Improved **communication services** (e.g. high-speed internet connection) make it easier for people to live in rural areas and **work from home**. E.g. workers can remotely access their office computer at home.
- **Technological improvements** also mean that some companies **no longer** need to be in a city centre to do business and can move to **rural areas** where land is **cheaper**. This creates **jobs** in rural areas.
- As in suburban areas, increased **car ownership** and improved **rail services** mean that people can live **further** from the city and **commute** to work.

Villages with key services and good access to commuter routes are sometimes called suburbanised villages.

Counter-urbanisation has **Impacts** on **Rural Areas**

There are **positive** and **negative impacts** of counter-urbanisation in rural areas:

POSITIVE IMPACTS

1) Some services see an **increase in business** (e.g. pubs that have restaurants). This is because the newer residents are often **professionals** or **retired people** who have **higher disposable income**.
2) In some villages the existing houses are **improved** as farm buildings are **renovated** and **upgraded**. Farmers are able to make money by **selling unwanted land** or **buildings** for housing developments.
3) In some rural areas schools have **closed** due to a lack of pupils. If **families** move to a rural area then schools can **stay open**, and children of existing residents can continue to go to school locally.

NEGATIVE IMPACTS

1) Development (e.g. unattractive new housing developments) can affect the **character** of rural settlements.
2) Some **rural shops** and **services** (e.g. bus services) **may close** — wealthier residents who own cars are more likely to travel to use **shops** and **services** in **urban areas**.
3) **Rural roads** and **infrastructure** may struggle to cope with the **additional traffic**. This can cause **congestion** and **increase air pollution** in rural areas.
4) **Schools may close** if the new residents are **older people** rather than families with **children**.
5) There is more demand for houses, so **house prices increase**. Younger people **may not be able to afford** to buy a house, which can mean the **population** is dominated by older people.

Have a look back at the impacts of suburbanisation (p. 80) — counter-urbanisation has similar impacts.

There are things that are being done in rural areas to **manage** the negative impacts:

1) In some areas, developments are only allowed if they're **in keeping** with the **rest of the area**, e.g. the houses must be built using certain materials.
2) Some companies offer **mobile services** that visit **rural areas**. E.g. NatWest Bank has mobile banking units that visit rural communities in Cornwall, Devon, Cumbria and South Wales each week.
3) In some rural areas there are **local occupancy clauses** on houses. E.g. in parts of Cumbria some relatively low-cost houses can only be bought by people who have lived in the area for **at least three years**. This means that local people on **low incomes** can stay in the area.

Counter-urbanisation

St Ives is a Great Example of Counter-Urbanisation

1) **St Ives** in Cambridgeshire is about **70 miles north of London**. The town has grown through counter-urbanisation. In 1961 its population was just **3800**, by **2010** it had reached **16 400**.
2) It has good **road access** and **rail links** to Cambridge and London. Many people commute into **Cambridge** and around a **quarter** of the working population **commute into London** each day.

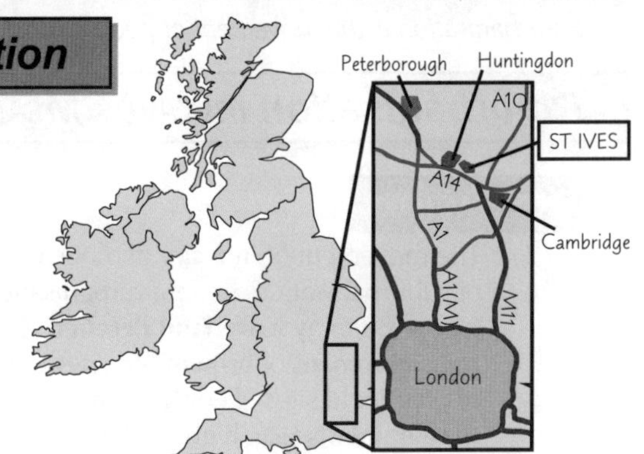

Counter-urbanisation has had Impacts in St Ives

- **Traffic congestion** is a problem, particularly during rush hour on the **A14** (the main **commuter** route from St Ives to Cambridge).
- The **average price** of a detached house in St Ives **rose from £130 000** to **£291 000** between **2000** and **2010**. Commuters often earn **higher wages** than people **working locally**, so they are better able to **afford** higher prices.
- St Ives is on the River Great Ouse and has a history of flood problems. As the **demand for housing** has grown, new developments have been built on the south **river bank** in the centre of town, and on the **floodplain**. This puts more residents at risk of flooding — **1000 properties** in St Ives are at risk of flooding from a 1 in 100 year event.
- There are now more **shops** and **services** in the town. For example, in addition to everyday food and grocery stores there are shops selling other goods, e.g. clothes and antiques, as well as more cafés and restaurants.
- The movement of families to St. Ives has changed its **population structure**. The original population was **ageing**, but the influx of younger people means that there are now more people under the age of 16 than over the age of 65. This has put **pressure on schools**, and **more pre-school** and **primary school places** are needed in the town.

Management Strategies Include More Affordable Housing and Better Transport

- Plans were approved in 2010 to build **200 new homes** in St Ives. At least **75** of these will be **affordable housing** aimed at people on lower incomes, e.g. **social rents** (houses that are rented out at low rates by councils or housing associations) and **low-cost ownership** (which enables people to e.g. buy a house at a discounted price or buy a share in a house and rent the rest).
- There are plans to expand **primary schools** in St Ives to make **240 more places** available.
- After flooding in 1998 and 2003, **flood protection works** costing **£8.8 million** were completed along the River Great Ouse in 2007. **New embankments** and **flood walls** were constructed in St Ives.
- A **£116 million guided busway** which links St Ives to Huntingdon and Cambridge has been built. It's hoped that this will **reduce congestion**, as many commuters no longer need to drive along the A14. There are also plans to **extend the busway** to a new train station in Cambridge, from which journey times to London will be quicker than from Huntingdon. This should **reduce** the number of London commuters who use Huntingdon station.

A guided busway is a track for buses to drive on.

Practice Questions

Q1 What is counter-urbanisation?

Q2 Give three reasons for counter-urbanisation.

Exam Question

Q1 With reference to at least one example, discuss the impacts of counter-urbanisation. [8 marks]

It sounds like a St Hive of activity...

Hopefully you know the drill with these pages by now. Learn the causes and impacts of counter-urbanisation and the management strategies that have been used to deal with it. Don't turn over until you can repeat the whole lot off by heart.

Re-urbanisation

Re-urbanisation is the movement of people back into urban areas — and it's the last of the urbanisation processes.

Re-urbanisation Involves Movement Back to City Centres

PULL FACTORS

1) The movement of industry and businesses **out of** cities as a result of suburbanisation, counter-urbanisation and deindustrialisation (see p. 80) may leave **land derelict**. **Government policies** often **favour redevelopment** of **brownfield sites** in city centres over development of greenfield sites. People are **attracted** back to the city by **new developments** (e.g. high quality apartments).
2) **Urban Development Corporations** (**UDCs**) were set up in the UK to regenerate derelict urban areas and provide a more attractive environment for people to live and work. They have the power to **buy land in a city** and plan how the land should be used in order to encourage businesses and people to **move back** into the regenerated areas.
3) Most **universities** are based in urban areas, so young people move there for **education**.
4) **Young single people** often want to live **close to their work** in areas with **good entertainment services** (e.g. bars and nightclubs). For example, Notting Hill in London has been **gentrified** (see p. 86) and attracts young, affluent workers because it is a **lively area** that is well connected to the city centre. Young couples may choose to **stay** in the urban area where they have settled when they have **children**.
5) Once re-urbanisation has **started** it tends to **continue** — as soon as a few businesses invest and people start to return, it encourages other businesses to invest.

PUSH FACTORS

1) There may be a **lack of jobs** in some rural or suburban areas.
2) Rural areas provide fewer **leisure** or **entertainment** facilities (e.g. nightlife).
3) Counter-urbanisation may cause high **house prices** in rural areas (see p. 82).

There's more information about regeneration on pages 86-89.

Re-urbanisation has Impacts on the City Centre

POSITIVE IMPACTS

1) As people move back into the city centre, **new shops** and **services** open, which **boosts the economy** in the city.
2) As shops and businesses return, **jobs** are created. This means there is **less unemployment**, which can help to **reduce** certain types of **crime**, e.g. theft.
3) **Tourism** in the city may **increase** if the city centre is improved. Increased tourism brings **money** into the city which can be spent on **improving** the area even more, e.g. building new attractions or improving public transport.
4) Local state **schools** can benefit from the increased number of students. However, **wealthier people** moving into an area may choose to send their children to **private schools** or **better-performing schools away** from the city centre.

NEGATIVE IMPACTS

1) Original residents in the area being re-urbanised are often on **low incomes** and may not be able to **afford housing** as prices increase. They may have to move to **cheaper areas** of the city.
2) There may be **tension** between the **original residents** and the **new residents**, which could lead to crime or violence.
3) **Jobs** created in new businesses may not be **accessible** to the original residents, many of whom are **unskilled** or **semi-skilled**.
4) **Shops** and **services** catering to the newer, more wealthy residents (e.g. cafés and designer clothes shops) may **replace** shops and services **targeted** at **original residents** (e.g. grocery stores and launderettes). For the original residents, the new shops may be **too expensive** or not stock the products they want, which means they may have to go **elsewhere** to shop.

Re-urbanisation can impact rural and suburban areas too, e.g. as young people move out, an ageing population may be left. Services can also be affected as demand for them falls.

Some of the Impacts can be Managed

1) Re-urbanisation projects can include **guarantees** to bring **affordable housing** to an area. For example, a redevelopment programme in Camden (North London) guaranteed that 25% of the new homes on the site would be made **affordable** for council tenants and people on low incomes.
2) Some charitable projects aim to improve the **skills** of the existing population to increase employment levels. E.g. **City Gateway** is a charity set up in the **London Docklands**. They work with disadvantaged young people from the area, running training courses to help them learn **new skills** so they can get into **employment**.

Re-urbanisation

Redevelopment Caused **Re-urbanisation** in the **London Docklands**

1) The **London Docklands** are on the **River Thames** in the east of the city. During the **19th** and **early 20th centuries**, the docks were **globally important** and there was a lot of **economic activity** in the area, e.g. warehouses and shipping offices.
2) From the **1960s** onwards the docks began to **decline** because of changes in the shipping industry — larger container ships became common and the London docks were not **large** or **deep** enough to accommodate them.
3) By **1980** large areas of the Docklands were in a **derelict state**. **150 000 people** had lost their jobs and **20%** of the housing was **not suitable** for living in. The Docklands had **poor public transport**, so it wasn't well linked to the rest of the city.
4) The **London Docklands Development Corporation** (LDDC) was a UDC that was set up in 1981 to redevelop the area. The LDDC redevelopment plan focused on a number of key areas, and had **positive impacts**:

Enterprise Zones are areas where taxes are lowered and planning restrictions are relaxed to encourage businesses to locate.

- **Economy** — part of the area was made an **Enterprise Zone** from 1982 until 1992. By 1998, there were **2700 businesses** trading in the Docklands and the area had attracted **£7.7 billion** of **private investment**. The new businesses created **jobs** — by 1998 **85 000 people** worked there.
- **Housing** — **24 000 new homes** were built, including **6250** housing association or local authority houses.
- **Transport** — the **Docklands Light Railway** opened in 1987, which cut journey times to **Central London** to less than 20 minutes. New **pedestrian** and **cycle routes** made travel within the area **easier** and **safer**.
- **Community** — new **public facilities** were built, including a **sailing and watersports centre** and the **Surrey Quays** shopping complex. Five new **health centres** were built and existing ones were **refurbished**.
- **Education** — **new schools** and colleges were built and existing schools were **improved**, e.g. by buying new IT equipment.
- **Environment** — the docks were **refurbished**, providing a pleasant environment for local residents. New **outdoor spaces** were created, including an ecology park at Bow Creek and a wildfowl sanctuary at East India Dock.

5) **Redevelopment** of the Docklands caused **re-urbanisation** — since 1980 the population has **doubled**.
6) However, re-urbanisation has had some **negative impacts** in the Docklands:

- There was some **conflict** between **original residents** and **newer, more affluent residents**. This was because some of the original residents felt that the LDDC **favoured** luxury developments rather than affordable housing.
- Many of the original residents were **unable** to find work in the new businesses. This was because the jobs on offer were often **skilled** positions in the service industry (e.g. banking) and many of the original residents were not qualified for this type of work (e.g. in 1981, **36%** of people in the Docklands were either **unskilled** or **semi-skilled**).

7) There have been attempts to **manage** these impacts:

- In some areas of the Docklands (e.g. Shadwell Basin and Wapping), the LDDC asked for **40% of new housing** to be sold at an **affordable price** to the original residents.
- Centres were set up to provide **training** in **basic literacy**, **numeracy** and **IT**, e.g. **£1.5 million** was spent on an IT centre, which opened in 1984. It trained **unemployed 16-18 year-olds** in basic electronics and computer programming, giving them **work experience** with local businesses and a **qualification** at the end of the course.
- The LDDC also supported **Skillnet** — a **job agency** which worked with training providers and employers to provide people with the **skills** they needed to find work in the area (e.g. in construction).

Practice Questions

Q1 Give two positive impacts of re-urbanisation.

Q2 Give two impacts of re-urbanisation in an area you have studied.

Exam Question

Q1 Look at the photograph. Comment on the evidence that re-urbanisation has occurred in this area. [7 marks]

Redeveloping the Docklands was Quay to re-urbanisation...

Talking about re-urbanisation seems like a great way to impress someone on a date — you can point out high density buildings and improved transportation links as you stroll around a newly-created public space. There's a reason I've never had a girlfriend.

Urban Decline and Regeneration

People piling out of cities can lead to urban decline. But fear not my urban-dwelling friends — regeneration can turn it around.

Urban Decline Usually Starts with a Decline in Industry

Urban decline is when a **decrease** in economic activity in an **urban area** causes it to become **run down**.
There is often a **pattern** to the decline:

Urban decline usually only takes place in part of the city (e.g. the inner city).

1 DECLINE IN INDUSTRY

1) The **movement of manufacturing overseas** (see p. 108) causes industry to close.
2) Industry may also **move** to sites **outside of the city centre** where rent is cheaper.

2 INCREASE IN UNEMPLOYMENT

1) If **industry declines** there will be a **loss of jobs** and an **increase in unemployment**. Some unemployed people will move **out** of the area to **find jobs** elsewhere.
2) The **jobs** available to the unemployed people who are left behind may be **unskilled** or **low paid**.

3 SHOPS AND SERVICES DECLINE

1) If **lots of people** leave the city, there will be **fewer people** to use the **shops** and **services** (e.g. public transport or leisure facilities). The people who remain in the city have **less money** to spend there.
2) The **shops** may be forced to **close down** and **services** may go into **decline**.

4 THE PHYSICAL ENVIRONMENT DECLINES

1) As industry, people and services move out, they leave **empty buildings** (e.g. factories, houses and shops), which may become **derelict**. Derelict buildings have problems with **vandalism** and **graffiti**.
2) **Recreational areas** (e.g. parks) are **neglected** and may develop problems with crime (e.g. drug dealing).
3) As the area becomes **unattractive**, **decline continues** because fewer people want to live there.

There are **three different processes** that **regenerate** urban areas — **gentrification**, **partnership schemes** and **property-led regeneration schemes**.

These processes are covered in more detail on the next few pages.

Gentrification is Regeneration by a Wealthier Group

1) **Gentrification** is when **wealthier people** move into a **run down area** and regenerate it by improving their **housing**.
2) It often causes **social changes** in the area — **lower income groups** are **replaced** by more affluent people.

POSITIVE IMPACTS

1) **Housing** is **improved** as wealthy newcomers regenerate old buildings.
2) The **value of housing** in the area **increases**. This means that **existing homeowners** in the area are able to sell their homes for **more money**.
3) **New businesses** (e.g. bars and restaurants) move into the area to cater for the **wealthier newcomers**. This creates **jobs**.
4) **Crime rates** may **fall** — as housing is improved there are **fewer derelict buildings** that attract graffiti and vandalism.

Max had completed the gentrification process.

NEGATIVE IMPACTS

1) The **high demand** for housing can cause problems. E.g. **tenants** in the area may be **forced out** of their homes because **landlords** want to sell the house while its value is **high**.
2) Increased house prices mean that the **children** of the original homeowners may be **unable to afford** to buy or rent nearby, and may be forced to **move** elsewhere.
3) Original residents may **lose** the shops and services they **need** (e.g. launderettes and charity shops) as these are **replaced** by **up-market shops** aimed at the wealthier residents (e.g. coffee shops).
4) All of these problems can contribute to **tension** between the **local people** and the **new residents**.

Urban Decline and Regeneration

Islington in London has Been Gentrified

Georgian Housing along Regent's Canal in Islington.

1) **Islington** is a borough in **north London**. There are lots of **large Georgian** and **early Victorian houses**, which were originally occupied by **wealthy residents**.
2) In the **late 19th century**, the railways expanded and made access to the city easier, so the wealthier residents left Islington and **moved out** to the **suburbs**.
3) **Poorer residents** from central London **moved into** the area, which became overcrowded. They couldn't afford to **maintain** the housing and the area became **run down**.
4) In the **1960s middle class** people began to buy properties in Islington because:
   - Across the city, there was an **increase in jobs** in the **service** sector (e.g. in law and the media) and a **decrease in jobs** in the **manufacturing** sector. People working in the service sector tended to be young, well paid and work long hours, so they wanted to live **close to the city centre**.
   - Islington was **well connected** to the city centre by nearby Angel underground station.
   - Houses in Islington were **large** and **attractive**, and much **cheaper** than in wealthier areas of the city. Many of the houses were in a poor state, so people could **renovate** them to suit their own tastes.
   - Once the gentrification process **began, more and more** wealthier people were encouraged to move there.

Gentrification has had a Number of Impacts on Islington

1) The impacts of gentrification have been both **positive**...
   - Improved **housing** — wealthier residents **renovated** and **improved** many of the Georgian and Victorian properties (e.g. restoring original features and repainting exterior walls).
   - New **businesses opened**, e.g. wine bars and restaurants, bringing **money** and **jobs** to the area.

   ... and **negative**:
   - Increased **house prices** — the average house price in Islington increased from around **£130 000** in 1996 to **£430 000** in 2008. This made it difficult for people on **lower salaries** to live in the area. Many people were forced out of the area or into **social housing** (which accounted for nearly **50%** of housing in 2008).
   - There is **wealth gap** between the **richest** and the **poorest** residents, e.g. the richest 20% earn more than £60 000 a year while the poorest 20% earn less than £15 000 a year. In 2007, Islington was the **8th most deprived area** in England — it had the second-highest rate of child poverty in England, a high crime rate and high unemployment.
   - Some **businesses** have **closed**, e.g. traditional pubs and convenience stores.
2) The negative impacts of gentrification are being **managed** by projects that aim to **tackle deprivation** in the area:
   - Islington businesses are being encouraged to pay all of their staff the **London living wage** of **£8.30 an hour**. This gives low-skilled workers a **larger income** and helps them to cope with the **high cost of living** in Islington.
   - **Charities** work in poorer neighbourhoods to **improve education**. E.g. Light Project International run practical maths classes for unemployed people over the age of 16 and adult education classes in languages.

Practice Questions

Q1 Name the four stages of urban decline.

Q2 What is gentrification?

Exam Question

Q1 With reference to an area you have studied, discuss the changes that have taken place due to gentrification. [10 marks]

My favourite regeneration programme is Dr Who...

It seems to me that people just can't make up their minds. First they move to the city, then they realise they want to live outside of the city, and then they move back again to get another taste of urban living. Still, I guess it's good news for removal men.

Urban Regeneration

Two more urban regeneration schemes to learn I'm afraid — partnership schemes and property-led regeneration. Alright, we both know they don't sound like they'll be a barrel of laughs but don't give me that look — I'm only a book.

Partnership Schemes Involve Councils and Businesses

Peter and Lara's partnership scheme was heading straight for divorce.

1) **Partnership schemes** involve **local councils** working with **businesses** and **local communities** to come up with a **regeneration plan** for an area.
2) The schemes often try to improve the **economy** and **environment** in the area. They also aim to make **social improvements**, e.g. by building community centres.
3) In the UK, partnership schemes such as **City Challenge** aimed to regenerate urban areas:

> **31 City Challenge Partnership Schemes** ran in deprived urban areas between **1992** and **1998**. The government provided **£1.14 billion** of funding for these schemes and they attracted a total **investment** of around **£7.58 billion**. Cities competed with each other for this funding which aimed to regenerate **deprived** areas by improving the **physical environment**, **economy** and **quality of life**.

Hulme in Manchester was Regenerated by a City Challenge Partnership

1) In the 19th and early 20th century Hulme provided housing for people working in **Manchester's industries**. By the mid 19th century it was **overcrowded**, with many people living in **poor quality housing** with few facilities (e.g. no indoor toilet). The whole area was **cleared for redevelopment** in the 1960s.
2) People were moved out of their homes into flats in new **tower blocks** and **apartment buildings**, which had problems with **pest infestation** and **poor heating**. Many residents felt **isolated** and suffered from **depression** and **poor health**.
3) By the early 1990s, many **families** had moved **out** of Hulme. Many of the flats were **unlivable**, the area was **poor** and there were problems with **unemployment** and **crime**.
4) In 1992 the **Hulme City Challenge Partnership** was formed. Manchester City Council worked with private companies to design a **£37.5 million** regeneration package to redevelop the area. It aimed to create a **strong community feel** by building a mixture of housing, businesses, shops and community spaces, and improving **transport links** to connect Hulme to the city centre and surrounding communities. The main improvements were:

- Tower blocks were **demolished** and a variety of **new houses** were built. New housing was a **mixture** of council-owned and private to provide for **existing residents** and encourage **outsiders** to buy into the area.
- The main **shopping area** was **refurbished** to include a range of shops, a covered market hall and a supermarket.
- The creation of the **Zion Centre** — an arts venue and community centre which runs arts projects for local people.
- A **business park** was built at **Birley Fields** to encourage **private investment** in the area. Several **high profile businesses** occupy the offices, including the construction company Laing O'Rourke and Colgate Ltd. This has created **jobs** and brought **outsiders** working for these companies into the area.
- **Hulme Park** was created to provide a safe, outdoor green space for residents.

The Hulme City Challenge Partnership has been Successful in Some Ways

1) The new housing and services have made Hulme a much **more attractive place to live** — its population **grew** by an estimated 3.3% between 1992 and 2002, compared to 0.2% across the city as a whole.
2) From 1997 to 2002 Hulme and neighbouring Moss Side received around **£400 million** of private and public **investment**. **Jobs** were created in **new industries** and **services** that moved to the area. Unemployment fell from 32% in 1989 to 6% in 2010.
3) However, not all Hulme's problems have been resolved:

Social housing is owned and rented out by councils or housing associations.

- Hulme is still a **poor area** and 47.5% of the population live in **social housing**.
- **House prices** have **increased**, which has made private housing **unaffordable** for local people on low incomes.
- Unemployment is still **high** compared to the rest of Manchester.

Urban Regeneration

Property-led Regeneration** is being used in the **London Thames Gateway

1) **Property-led regeneration schemes** involve **building** or **improving property** in an area to change its **image** and improve the local **environment**. These changes encourage further investment and the return of **people** and **business**. They are often set up by **UDCs** (see page 84), who plan and coordinate the development.
2) The **London Thames Gateway** is a **large area** stretching for 40 miles along the Thames to the **east** of London.
3) The area was once important for **manufacturing**. However, manufacturing industries **declined** from the 1960s onwards, and the area became **run down**. The London Thames Gateway Development Corporation (**LTGDC**) is a **ten-year programme** that was set up in **2004** to regenerate the part of the Thames Gateway to the **north** and **east** of the London Docklands. Its **aims** are:
   - To make sure **land** and **buildings** are being used and not left derelict.
   - To **encourage** existing and new **industry** and **business** to **develop**.
   - To create an **attractive environment**.
   - To **improve housing** and **social facilities**, so people want to live and work in the area.

4) The LTGDC is supporting a number of projects across East London, and has invested **£209.6 million** up to April 2011. Projects include:
   - Building **new town centres** in Canning Town and Custom House with retail, business and leisure space, an improved **road network**, improved **pedestrian** and **cycle access**, and a new **crossrail** station.
   - Renovation of schools and improvements in **education services** — the University of East London and Birkbeck (part of the University of London) are working together to establish a **new campus** in Stratford, which will open in 2013.
   - A sustainable housing development at **Barking Riverside** to provide more than 10 000 new homes along with health centres, schools, leisure facilities and extensive green space, including an ecology park. **Barking train station** and **local roads** are being upgraded and existing bus routes will serve the area to make it more accessible.
5) The project is **ongoing**, but it's had a number of **successes** so far:
   - The **population** of the area is **growing**, e.g. between 2001 and 2011 the population of the borough of Barking and Dagenham rose by **12%**.
   - **Renovation of schools** has led to **improvements** in pupils' educational achievement. E.g. a **£40 million** renovation at St Pauls Way Trust School has improved science, drama and sports facilities. As a result, the number of students at the school getting **5 A* to C grades at GCSE** improved from **29%** to **46%** in one year.
6) However, there are some **concerns** about the **redevelopment**:
   - The LTGDC has been accused of **not listening** to residents' **opinions**. For example, the LTGDC gave planning permission for a temporary **nightclub** to be erected close to the Olympic Park during the summer of 2012, despite objections about noise and disruption from local residents and Tower Hamlets Council.
   - There were **objections** to a proposed tower block at Virginia Quay, which local councillors thought didn't provide enough **affordable housing**, would cause **over-crowding** of the area, **parking problems** and **loss of open space**.

Practice Questions

Q1 What is a property-led regeneration scheme?

Q2 Give the aims of a property-led regeneration scheme that you have studied.

Exam Question

Q1 Evaluate the success of a partnership scheme you have studied which has tried to promote urban regeneration. [10 marks]

Maybe it's because I'm a Londoner, that I love the LTGDC...

Mmm, tuneful. The LTGDC is certainly my favourite example of a property-led regeneration scheme — all those wonderfully exciting aims, projects, successes and concerns. If you learn it well it may become yours too, you lucky badger...

Retailing

We all love to shop, but the way that people are shopping has changed over time — that's what these pages are all about.

Retailing and Other Services are Decentralising

1) In the 1950s and 1960s shops selling **high-order goods** (e.g. furniture, jewellery) were in **town** and **city centres** and attracted customers from a wide area. Shops selling **low-order goods** (e.g. food) provided for customers **locally** within their neighbourhoods.
2) This traditional shopping pattern began to **change** in the **1970s** — shops (e.g. supermarkets and DIY stores) began to move to the outskirts of towns. This process is called **decentralisation**. Nowadays most cities have large **out-of-town retail** complexes.
3) There are a number of **reasons** for the growth of **out-of-town** retailing:

High-order goods are expensive items that you only buy occasionally. Low-order goods are inexpensive items that you buy regularly.

- Increased **car ownership** means more people **drive** to the shops. Out-of-town locations are often close to **motorways**, so they are easy to get to by car, and usually have fewer problems with **congestion** than town centres.
- **Parking prices** are **high** in city centres — at out-of-town shopping complexes customer parking is usually free.
- The use of cars and **home freezers** also means people can do **one weekly food shop** rather than only buying what they can carry home and use immediately. This means people are more likely to shop at out-of-town supermarkets where they can **park directly outside** and get **everything** they need under one roof.
- **Increased road building**, particularly of motorways and bypasses, makes out-of-town shopping centres easy to access and attracts **customers from further away** because driving on motorways reduces journey times.
- It's **cheaper** to build retail parks out-of-town than it is to rent or buy premises in the city centre. Retail parks are often built on **reclaimed derelict land**, so it's easy for developers to get **planning permission**.

"Sure you can do a week's shopping here. You like grapefruit, right?"

4) It's **not just shops** that have moved to out-of-town retail parks. Many large retail centres also offer **services**, e.g. **leisure facilities** such as bowling, cinemas and restaurants. This helps them to attract **more customers** by making a trip to a shopping centre a **social** and **family** activity. It also encourages people to spend **more time** there.

Decentralisation Affects City Centres and the Rural-Urban Fringe

Out-of-town retail parks have impacts on nearby **city centres**:

Negative impacts

- Out-of-town shopping centres **compete** with city centre shops, so **fewer people** shop in the city centre. This can force shops in the city centre to **close**, so people **lose their jobs**.
- The **decline** in the number of people coming to the city centre to **shop** also **decreases** the number of customers using **services** (e.g. restaurants and cafés), and may force them to **close**.
- A **decline** in **business** and **retail** can lead to a more **general decline** in the area — **investment** in the city centre **decreases** and it becomes run down. This can increase problems like **vandalism**.

Positive impacts

- Local councils and the government sometimes **invest** money to **improve** the city centre and **attract customers** back (see p. 92). Improvements may include creating **pedestrian zones**, **renovating** older shopping malls and **organising events** (e.g. festivals).
- **Congestion and pollution** may **decrease** as fewer people drive to the city centre to shop.

They also have impacts on the **rural-urban fringe** (see p. 67) where they are located:

Negative impacts

- Out-of-town complexes require a lot of **construction**, e.g. building tramways to improve transport connections. Although this provides **jobs** in the short term, it creates **noise pollution** and could add to **congestion** if roads are disrupted.
- Most people drive to out-of-town retail centres, which causes **congestion** and air pollution.

Positive impacts

- Out-of-town shopping complexes **create jobs** for people living in the suburbs.
- Retail parks are often built on **brownfield sites** that would otherwise be left empty. E.g. Bluewater in Kent is built in a **former quarry**.
- Houses that have easy access to the shopping centre may **increase in value**.

Retailing

The Trafford Centre is a Large Out-of-town Retail Park near Manchester

1) The **Trafford Centre** opened in **1998**. It was built on a brownfield site in the industrial area of Trafford Park, 5 miles west of Manchester. The site covers 150 acres and it cost **£600 million** to complete.
2) The Trafford Centre has the **largest catchment area** of any shopping centre in the UK — **5.3 million people** (more than 8% of the UK population) live within a **45 minute drive**. More than 30 million people visit the Trafford Centre each year.
3) The Trafford Centre is popular for a number of reasons:

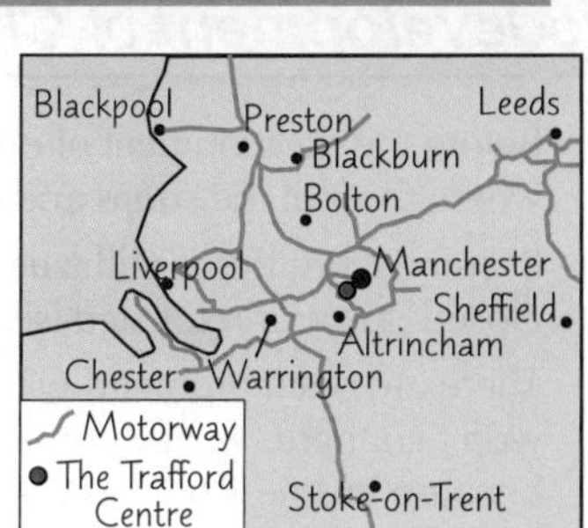

The Trafford Centre is close to many large towns and cities in northern England.

- The Trafford Centre offers a **range** of activities. As well as **over 200 shops**, there is a **1600 seat food court**, a **20 screen cinema**, **crazy golf**, **ten pin bowling**, **laser quest** and an indoor **climbing wall**.
- It is **well connected** by road. The centre is close to the **M60** for customers coming from outside of Manchester, and to the M602 into the **city centre**. There are lots of **buses** that go **direct** from Manchester to the Trafford Centre.
- It has **11 500 free parking spaces** and a **traffic control system** to reduce congestion and car park waiting times.
- It is **indoors** and **air conditioned** to protect customers from the weather all year round.
- It has **long opening hours** — shops are open until 10pm Monday to Friday, 8pm on Saturday and 6pm on Sunday.

The Trafford Centre has had an Impact on the Surrounding Area

Negative impacts

- Most visitors drive to the centre, which causes **congestion** and **pollution**, particularly at **busy periods**, e.g. Christmas.
- The Trafford Centre has had an impact on shopping in **surrounding towns**. **Fewer people** go to these **town centres** to shop or for leisure activities, because they cannot compete with the **advantages** offered by the Trafford Centre (e.g. free parking). Altrincham has suffered particularly badly — **37%** of shops were **vacant in** 2010 (nearly 3 times the **national average** of 13%).

Positive impacts

- The Trafford Centre supports **local community projects** and charities, e.g. Royal Manchester Children's Hospital, through fundraising and donations.
- The centre provides **work experience** for local school students studying Retail Business.
- **8000 people** are **employed** at the Trafford Centre — they receive **benefits** such as health care and childcare vouchers.
- The Trafford Centre is growing, so that it offers a wider **range** of services, which attract more customers and bring **more economic benefits** (e.g. jobs). For example, LEGOLAND® Discovery Centre opened in 2010.

There are some schemes in place to help **manage** the **negative** impacts:

- The centre is investing in **improving public transport**, **cycle** and **pedestrian** routes to help **reduce** traffic. There are now **40 bus services an hour** to and from the Trafford Centre and a **shuttle bus** to the Metrolink tram system.
- In 2011, **Altrincham Forward** (a board made up of local business owners, residents and councillors), produced the **Altrincham Town Centre Action Plan**. This plan outlines strategies to draw **people** into the town, including establishing an annual calendar of **events** in the town and **reducing parking charges**.

Practice Questions

Q1 Give two reasons for the growth of out-of-town shopping centres.

Q2 Give one positive and one negative impact of out-of-town retail parks on city centres.

Exam Question

Q1 With reference to at least one example, outline the characteristics of out-of-town retail centres. [8 marks]

Want a break from retail? Try some re-tell therapy...

Just because these pages are about retail it doesn't mean that going shopping counts as revision. Instead, have a good read through all this information and then tell your friends everything you can remember. It'll do you the world of good, and they'll love it...

Redeveloping Urban Centres

*These pages are all about what happens to poor city centres that fall into decline when people start shopping elsewhere *sob*.*

Redevelopment of City Centres Can Help Bring Back Shoppers

1) Before the development of out-of-town retail centres, the central business district (**CBD**) was the hub of a city — where most of the **shops** and **entertainments** were, and where many businesses had their offices.
2) In some cities this is **still true**, but in others there has been a **decline** in the CBD when shops and businesses have closed down or relocated (see p. 90). Shops are left **empty**, which is **unattractive** and can lead to **vandalism**.
3) There are often problems with **crime** (e.g. mugging), particularly at **night**. If people don't **feel safe** in an area they won't go there. As fewer people go to the city centre to shop and for entertainment, **investment is likely to decrease** because business owners don't think it is worth opening shops or services there. This leads to **further decline**.
4) **Government** and **local councils redevelop** city centres to draw people and investment back. There are different strategies for redevelopment:

- Making shopping areas **more attractive** by creating **pedestrian zones**, adding benches and planting trees and flower beds. **Pavements** are also **improved** to make it easier for people with prams and wheelchairs.
- Building **new shopping malls** (e.g. Liverpool One) or **renovating old ones** (e.g. the Arndale Centre in Manchester). These have plenty of **parking spaces** and many shops under one roof to **compete** with out-of-town retail centres.
- Opening **street markets** to improve the **atmosphere** and encourage people to shop in the city centre by increasing the range of products available, e.g. farmers' markets selling local food.
- Improving **public transport** into the town centre to decrease **congestion**, e.g. park and ride schemes (see p. 45).
- Installing **CCTV** and **security alarms** and improving **street lighting** to reduce crime and make the CBD **safer**.
- Increasing opening hours to include **late night** and **Sunday shopping**.
- Conserving **historic buildings** in the city centre to attract tourists.

Some Cities are Developing Other Functions to Revive the CBD

To compete with the **range** of facilities available at out-of-town shopping centres, some cities are investing in **entertainment** and **leisure facilities** and **cultural events** in their CBD, and others are building **new housing**. For example:

- More **cafés**, **bars**, **restaurants** and **entertainment venues** (e.g. cinemas and theatres) to bring people into the city centre. Overall, this helps to **reduce crime and vandalism** because the city centre is **busier**, but can produce **other problems** (e.g. drunkenness) that mean more police are needed on the streets at busy times (e.g. Saturday nights).
- Promoting **free cultural entertainment** in the city centre, e.g. cultural festivals or street theatre. In Liverpool, the **Liverpool Light Night** is a **cultural evening** where galleries and museums stay open late and offer free entry to visitors. There is street theatre, light displays and live music all around the city centre.
- Opening **flagship attractions** — these are major visitor attractions that draw **people** in from a wide area and act as a focal point for **tourism** and **regeneration**. For example, the Lightbox in Woking is a gallery and museum which hosts visiting art exhibitions and runs workshops for schools and community groups. People come to **visit these attractions** and then may **visit shops** and **restaurants nearby**.
- The establishment of **theme areas** such as the gay village in Manchester, where a number of **bars** and **restaurants** have opened in former cotton factories and warehouses along the Rochdale Canal. These theme areas are often attractive to **tourists** as well as local people.
- The development of more **residential property** — building new apartments and renovating old industrial buildings. If more people **live in the CBD** they are more likely to **use the facilities** there.

Canal Street in the heart of Manchester's gay village.

All these projects are helping to bring more people into the city centre, particularly when they are combined with wider **re-urbanisation** (p. 84-85) and **gentrification** (p. 86) in urban areas. Bringing more people into the CBD means **shops** and **businesses** are more likely to invest there and the **community feel** of a town or city centre is preserved.

Redeveloping Urban Centres

Manchester City Centre has been *Redeveloped*

1) Manchester was an **important industrial city** throughout the 19th and early 20th centuries. However, from the **1960s** onwards industrial activities began to decrease and people began to **move out** of the city centre.
2) The building of the **Arndale Centre** (a large shopping arcade) in **1975** brought people into the city to **shop**. However, the city centre population was still **declining** and in the 1980s it fell to **less than 1000** as people moved out to the **suburbs**. As people moved out, the centre became **run down**.
3) In **1996** an IRA **bomb** damaged much of **Manchester's CBD**, including the Arndale Centre and the Royal Exchange Theatre.
4) Redevelopment was needed to **repair the damage** done in the bombing and to bring people back into the **city centre**, particularly as the **Trafford Centre** (see p. 91) was about to open outside the city and could threaten the city's retail sector.
5) **Manchester Millennium Ltd**. was formed weeks after the bombing to **design** and **manage** the redevelopment. It aimed to:
   - **Re-design** and **rebuild** large parts of the CBD to create a **safe**, **accessible centre** for the whole north west region, where people would come to **live**, to **shop**, and for **entertainment**.
   - Make sure that the **success** of the city centre would **last** and would cause **long-term investment**.
6) The **main developments** were in the areas of the city centre damaged by the bombing:
   - Old buildings were renovated, e.g. the **Corn Exchange**, a listed building which was occupied by **temporary shops**. It was rebuilt internally and is now an **upmarket mall** selling designer clothing and jewellery.
   - **Run down** and **unattractive** buildings (including the Arndale Centre) were **rebuilt** and **restyled**.
   - **Upmarket department stores**, e.g. Selfridges, opened.
   - Large areas were **pedestrianised**, including Exchange Square, an open area where people can meet and socialise.
   - The **Printworks entertainment complex** was built on the site of an **old printing press**. It has a multi-screen IMAX cinema, a gym, restaurants, bars and a night club.
   - **Urbis**, an exhibition centre that now hosts the National Football Museum, was built in the Cathedral Gardens.
   - Other buildings were constructed or renovated, including new **shops**, **bars**, **restaurants** and **luxury apartments**.
   - Old industrial buildings (e.g. warehouses) were turned into **new residential properties**.

Redevelopment of *Manchester City Centre* has been *Successful*

1) The redevelopment of Manchester City Centre is an **ongoing process**. So far the redevelopment has been successful in many ways. For example between 2003 and 2009:
   - The population of the **city centre doubled** to over 19 000 people.
   - Manchester became the third most popular **tourist destination** in the UK — tourism contributed **£5 billion** to the economy each year.
   - Retail in the city centre made an extra **£300 million a year**.
2) However, there are still **problems** in the city centre and the redevelopment hasn't benefited everyone. In 2001, **16%** of the population were on **low incomes** — some of these people felt **excluded** from city centre living, because they **couldn't afford** to use the new facilities.

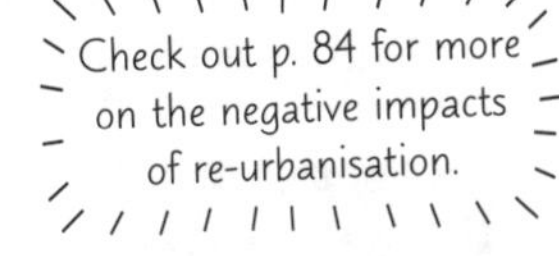

Practice Questions

Q1 Give one strategy for redeveloping city centres.

Q2 What is a flagship attraction?

Exam Question

Q1 Evaluate the success of a redevelopment scheme in an urban centre you have studied. [10 marks]

Get the defibrillator — we need to revive the CBD...

Manchester is a bit of a redevelopment fairy tale — the developers came along and gave the city the kiss of life, and it all ended happily ever after. You need to learn the ways cities can revive their CBDs and how redevelopment has happened in Manchester.

Sustainability in Urban Areas

I know, I know. It's the 'S' word again. These pages aren't rubbish, they're just about waste management...

It can be Difficult for Urban Areas to be Sustainable

Sustainability means meeting the needs of people **today** in a way that doesn't **damage** the environment or **use up** resources, so people can continue to meet their own needs in the **future**. Sustainability is often **difficult** to achieve in urban areas:

1) Urban areas have **large**, **dense populations**. This causes **environmental problems** because more people create **more waste** which has to be disposed of, drive **more cars** which cause air pollution, and use **more resources** (e.g. water, fuel).
2) The schemes that have been set up to **manage** the impacts of urban growth are often the easiest or cheapest in the **short term** (e.g. disposing of waste in landfill sites, see below) rather than the most sustainable.

Managing Waste can help Urban Areas to Become More Sustainable

1) **Managing waste** is an important way of improving urban sustainability. By generating **less waste** and **changing** the ways that the waste we do produce is **disposed** of, we can reduce the amount of resources we use and our **impact on the environment**.
2) In 2010 **each person** in the UK produced **452 kg** of waste. A lot of this waste goes into **landfill**, which is unsustainable (see below).
3) However, waste management in the UK is becoming **more sustainable** — landfill is **decreasing** and recycling is **increasing**. E.g. in 2004 **33%** of waste was recovered (e.g. recycled or composted) compared to **45%** in 2008.
4) There are national and EU targets to make waste disposal **more sustainable**, e.g. the EU wants **50%** of household waste to be recycled by 2020.
5) There are **lots** of different methods of **waste management**:

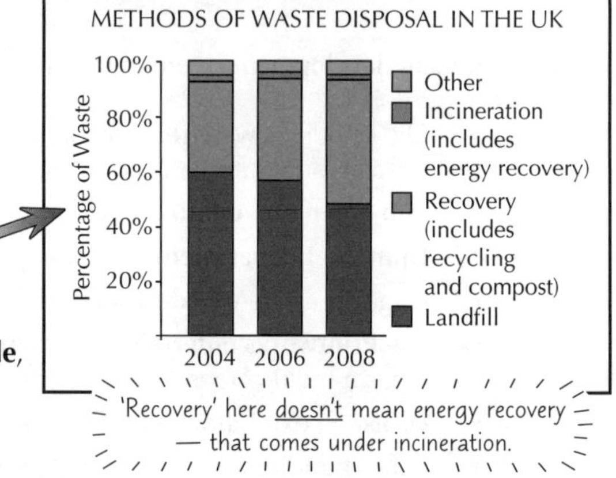

LANDFILL

Landfill is when rubbish is **buried** (often in former quarries). Landfill is **cheap** in the short term but it is **not sustainable**:

- Landfill sites release **carbon dioxide** (CO_2) and **methane** (greenhouse gases — see p. 48). In the UK, landfill sites produce 36% of all methane emissions. This is not sustainable because greenhouse gases cause climate change (see p. 48). However, there are **new technologies** that allow the gases produced to be **captured** and **used**, e.g. as a bio-fuel. In 2008, a landfill site in Mumbai, India was closed and covered — methane produced by the site is used to **generate electricity**. This scheme should reduce greenhouse gas emissions by **2.2 million tonnes** of CO_2 equivalents by 2028.
- Landfill can **pollute groundwater** — new landfill sites can be specially lined to prevent this.
- Dumping waste in landfill sites **wastes valuable materials** that could be **reused** or **recycled**.
- In developing countries, people often **live and work** on landfill sites, scavenging for materials to **sell**. E.g. in Manila, Philippines, **10 000 families** lived on or next to the Smokey Mountain dump until it was closed in 1996. Although this gives people an **income**, it's not sustainable because it doesn't **meet their needs** (e.g. it puts them at risk of disease).

COMPOSTING

In the UK, household waste contains around **38%** organic material (e.g. vegetable peelings). Organic material is **biodegradeable** (it can be broken down by micro-organisms), so it can be composted, either by **individuals** or on a **larger scale**.

- If householders compost in their own gardens it **reduces the costs** to the local authority for waste disposal.
- **Large-scale composting** involves collecting compost from people's **homes** and from **public waste** (e.g. cuttings from pruning trees in parks). The material is transported to **reactors**, where microbes break it down anaerobically (without oxygen). It produces **two useful products** — **biogas** (a mixture of methane and CO_2 which can be combusted to generate heat and electricity), and a nitrogen-rich **fertiliser**.
- Composting is **sustainable** because it **decreases** the amount of waste going to **landfill**, and biogas is a **renewable energy source** that doesn't rely on burning fossil fuels.
- Composting has to be **managed properly** to succeed, for example waste must be **sorted** properly to ensure there are no contaminants, e.g. metals. If the compost is contaminated it can't be sold on for agricultural use because it would **pollute** the soil and could be **harmful** to people eating the crops.

Sustainability in Urban Areas

RECYCLING

Recycling is when waste materials are made into **new products** or **materials**, e.g. plastic bottles are made into fleece jumpers. There are many **advantages** to recycling:

- Producing goods from recycled materials is often **quicker** and **cheaper** than making them from scratch.
- Recycling materials uses **less energy** than making new things, e.g. it uses **20 times more energy** to manufacture aluminium cans from **raw materials** than recycled materials. Some materials (e.g. glass and aluminium) can be recycled **many times**.
- Recycling **reduces demand** for raw materials. Using fewer raw materials reduces the **environmental impacts** that occur when they're extracted, e.g. deforestation. It also **reduces** the amount of waste going to **landfill** and the **problems** associated with that.

Ulrika liked this recycling lark — she'd made her favourite doily into a snazzy hat.

However, there are some **difficulties** with making recycling work well:

- Recycling **relies on individuals**, and some people don't bother. Some local councils encourage people to recycle by letting them put all their recyclable waste **in together** (so they don't have to sort it), or by offering **incentives**. E.g. residents in Windsor, Berkshire were invited to join a trial scheme which gave **rewards** (e.g. points that could be used to pay for goods) for recycling. 70% of those invited signed up to the scheme, and recycling rates for the participants increased by **35%**.
- Recycling costs money — **initial investment** is needed to set up recycling plants, and collection can be **expensive**.
- Lots of the UK's material for recycling is **sent abroad** for processing, e.g. 55% of paper for recycling was sent to China in 2007. Transporting materials **produces emissions**, but generally **less** than would be produced by making new materials.

ENERGY RECOVERY

Energy recovery is when waste that **can't** be composted, reused or recycled is burnt to generate **heat** and **electricity**.

- Energy recovery **reduces** use of fossil fuels, but it is not **fully sustainable** because it produces CO_2 and other **emissions**.
- Energy recovery is used to generate electricity from household waste in Sheffield:
  - The **Energy Recovery Facility** (ERF) provides heat for **140 buildings** in the **city centre**, including Sheffield City Hall. Without ERF, heating these buildings would produce an extra **21 000 tonnes** of CO_2 every year.
  - ERF also provides **17 MW** of electricity to the national grid and **reduces** waste going to **landfill**, e.g. only **15%** of Sheffield's waste goes to **landfill** sites.
- **Other local councils** are looking into ERF. **Leicestershire County Council** has given planning permission for the construction of an energy recovery facility that will produce enough electricity to power **42 000 homes**.

REDUCE AND REUSE

- As well as improving waste management, the overall **amount of waste** produced can be **reduced**. This can be done by **individuals**, e.g. by registering with the Mail Preference Service to reduce the amount of junk mail received, and **businesses**, e.g. by reducing packaging on food.
- Waste products can also be **reused**. This is easier for **some products** than it is for others, e.g. plastic bottles are easily reused, but aluminium cans are not.
- Reusing materials tends to be easier for **individuals** than on a **large scale**. Only certain products can be **successfully reused** on a large scale, e.g. in Germany, drinks companies charge a **deposit** for drinks in **refillable** glass or plastic bottles, which customers get back when they return the bottle to a designated collection point.

Practice Questions

Q1 Name three methods of waste disposal.

Q2 Give two reasons why it is difficult to make recycling successful.

Exam Question

Q1 Explain how different methods of waste management can improve the sustainability of urban areas. [8 marks]

Reduce, reuse, recycle, revise...

We can all do our bit towards sustainable waste disposal — you could write your revision notes on scrap paper and then recycle them once you've passed your exam. Just make sure you read them carefully in the meantime...

Sustainability in Urban Areas

Managing transport can improve the sustainability of urban areas by reducing emissions, pollution and use of fossil fuels.

Increasing Urban Populations *Mean There is* ***More Traffic*** *in* ***Urban Areas***

1) In urban areas the number of cars on the road is **increasing**:
   - As urban areas grow, more people live on the outskirts of cities and **commute** to work in the centre.
   - If businesses and offices **move out** of the city centre (see p. 90), more people are employed on the outskirts. Generally public transport is not as good outside the city centre, so more people **drive** to work.
   - In developing countries, **increasing wealth** means **more people own cars**.
   - As urban areas grow there are more vehicles delivering to a growing number of shops and businesses.
2) Driving cars **isn't sustainable** — it causes **air pollution** which can reduce people's **quality of life**, **greenhouse gas** emissions which damage the environment, and **congestion** which means journeys take longer and people's transport needs aren't met.
3) **Improved public transport** makes cities more sustainable because it produces **less emissions per passenger** than cars.
4) To encourage people to use public transport, it needs to be **reliable**, **cheap** and **easy** to use.
5) Improving public transport isn't the only way to reduce the number of cars on the road — encouraging other **sustainable methods of transport** (e.g. cycling and walking) can help too.

There are ***Many Ways*** *to Make* ***Transport More Sustainable***

Look at the schemes on p. 44-45 as well.

Lots of **different** schemes are used in cities to make transport **more sustainable**.
Most of them aim to reduce **congestion** and **pollution** by reducing the **number of cars** on the road.

Road schemes

- **Bus lanes** encourage people to use public transport because buses can **bypass traffic jams**, so travelling by bus is quicker than by car. In Curitiba (a city in Brazil), each of the **main roads** into the city centre has been widened to incorporate a two-way **express lane** for buses. This makes the bus service **reliable** and **efficient**. However, in some cities bus lanes are created without widening the road. This can **increase congestion** for other road users, as the roads are narrower.
- **Cycle lanes** can speed up travel for cyclists and make it safer to cycle in cities. In 2005, 6 towns in the UK became **Cycle Towns**, which received extra government funding to provide facilities for cyclists (e.g. signed cycle routes, cycle storage) and start cycling initiatives (e.g. events in schools to encourage children to cycle more). Across these towns there was a **27% increase** in cycling between 2005 and 2008.
- **High Occupancy Vehicle** (HOV) lanes can only be used by vehicles with a **minimum number** of occupants (usually **two** or **three**). They tend to operate during rush hour, and encourage **car sharing**, e.g. in **Toronto, Canada** the opening of HOV lanes on Highway 403 led to an increase in car sharing from 14% to nearly **40%** in three years.

Integrating transport systems

- **Integrating transport systems** means **coordinating** different types of public transport, e.g. making train arrival times match bus departure times. This makes it **easy** for passengers to transfer between different types of transport. It also **reduces journey times** because people don't have to wait for a connection. These factors mean people are **more likely to use** public transport.
- Integrating public transport systems is also about making public transport **accessible** to pedestrians and cyclists, e.g. in Tempe, Arizona all the buses have **bike racks** so people can easily cycle and use the bus in one journey.
- **Curitiba** has an **integrated** public transport system. There are around 1600 buses in operation and passengers can buy **one ticket** for any journey throughout the city. **70%** of commuters use the bus system and Curitiba uses **30% less fuel per capita** than it would without it. As a result air pollution in the city is one of the **lowest in Brazil**.

Congestion charging is an important road scheme that's been used in London. Look at p. 44 for more about it.

Traffic management

- **Bypasses** can be built so people can go **around** city centres instead of **through** them.
- **Park and ride schemes** run in many UK cities, e.g. York, Cambridge. They allow people to **park outside the city** and catch a shuttle bus into the centre. This is usually **cheaper** than parking centrally.
- Although park and ride schemes and bypasses can reduce traffic in the city centre, they won't necessarily **reduce** the number of cars across the **whole urban area**.
- Bypasses and car parks for park and ride schemes are often built on **open countryside** in the rural-urban fringe. This can have environmental impacts (e.g. destruction of woodland) and cause **conflict** (see p. 122).

Sustainability in Urban Areas

Increasing the use of more **sustainable vehicles** can help to **reduce emissions** in cities:

Low carbon vehicles

- These include hybrid, hydrogen and electric vehicles, and vehicles that run on biofuels. These may run on **renewable energy** sources and produce significantly **less emissions** than standard petrol or diesel vehicles. E.g. in 2010, **Singapore** started using hydrogen-electric buses. The buses are powered by hydrogen and lithium-ion batteries, and **only emit water**.
- Using low carbon vehicles improves **air quality** because emissions of **pollutants** (e.g. sulfur oxides) are reduced.
- However, these vehicles are usually **expensive to buy** and can be **difficult to refuel** if the facilities aren't available. Although vehicles that run on electricity have fewer **environmental impacts** in urban areas where they are used, the **electricity** they use has often been generated by **burning fossil fuels**.

*The **German** Government has Made **Transport** More **Sustainable***

1) Between 2000 and 2008, Germans walked, cycled and used public transport for more than **40%** of journeys. This reduces air pollution and greenhouse gas emissions, which increases **environmental sustainability**.
2) In Germany, the government encourages people to buy fuel efficient cars and to drive less (e.g. by putting high taxes on fuel). There are also incentives to use **public transport**, e.g. significant discounts are offered on weekly, monthly and annual train tickets that make it **economical** to use public transport to commute to work.
3) **Freiburg** in south west Germany is the country's **most sustainable** city in terms of transport facilities. From the 1970s onwards the city has built up an **efficient** public transport system:
   - The transport system is **integrated**, e.g. buses are timetabled to match train times. Public transport is also integrated with **walking** and **cycling** routes, e.g. there are designated, secure bike parking spots at public transport '**bike and ride**' facilities to encourage people to cycle to train and bus stations.
   - A **unified ticketing system** means that passengers only have to buy one ticket even if a journey takes them on several routes and different types of public transport.
   - A **light rail system** (the Stadtbahn) was built that is within easy walking distance (300 m) of **65%** of residents. The light rail trains run every 7.5 minutes and are **fully integrated** with the city's 26 bus lines.

   Light rail trains are a bit like trams — they run on special tracks, often alongside road traffic.

   - Buses and light rail trains have **priority** at traffic signals, which makes journeys on public transport faster.
   - The whole city centre is a **pedestrian zone** with vehicles banned, which makes walking safer.
   - In 177 '**home zones**', the streets have low speed limits and priority is given to pedestrians and cyclists.
   - Cyclists are allowed to travel **in both directions** on half of the city's 120 one-way streets. This **shortens** journey times for bikes compared to cars.
4) These measures have had impacts on the city's **environmental sustainability**:
   - Between 1982 and 2007, the **proportion** of journeys travelled by **car** fell from **38%** to **32%** — **68%** of all journeys in Freiburg are done on foot, by bike or on public transport.
   - The **distance** each person travelled **by car declined** by **7%** on all roads and **13%** on residential roads from 1990 to 2006.
   - Between 1992 and 2005 **CO_2 emissions** per capita from transport **fell** by **13%**.
5) The public transport system requires **little financial input** from the state — passenger fares cover **90%** of the running costs.

Practice Questions

Q1 Give three reasons why the number of cars is increasing in urban areas.

Q2 Give one benefit to passengers of an integrated transport system.

Exam Question

Q1 With reference to specific examples, discuss the ways that transport systems in urban areas can be made more sustainable. [10 marks]

Life would be so much easier if someone would just invent teleportation...

Sustainable transport is about getting people out of their cars and walking, cycling or using public transport. Talking of public transport, I heard a great joke about a bus driver, a flamingo and a pot of emulsion — shame there isn't enough space to tell you it...

Development Basics

When a country develops it basically gets better for the people living there — their quality of life improves (e.g. their wealth, health and safety). Right, that's development done... oh wait, there's a bit more you need to know about...

As a **Country Develops** Lots of **Things Change**

1) **Economic changes** — the **wealth** of a country **increases** as it develops. **Gross Domestic Product** (GDP) and **Gross National Income** (GNI) are two **measures** of a country's **wealth**:

GDP is the **total value of goods** and **services a country produces** in a **year**.

GNI is the **total value of goods** and **services people of that nationality produce** in a **year** (i.e. GDP + money from people living abroad).

GNP (Gross National Product) is very similar to GNI and is usually used in the same way.

As a country becomes **wealthier**, the number of **people living in poverty** (without basic human needs like water, food and shelter) usually **decreases**.

2) **Social changes** — these affect people's **quality of life**. Social change can be measured by the **infant mortality rate** (IMR) and the **number of people per doctor**. These both **decrease** with development:

IMR is the number of **babies** who **die under 1 year old, per thousand babies born**.

People per doctor is the **average number** of people **for each doctor**.

An **increase** in **access to safe water** and **literacy rate** shows an **increase** in **development**:

Access to safe water — the **percentage** of people who can get **clean drinking water**.

Literacy rate is the **percentage** of adults who can **read and write**.

3) **Demographic changes** — **birth rate** and **death rate** are measures of development. They both **decrease** with development:

Birth rate is the **number of live babies born per thousand** of the population **per year**.

Death rate is the **number of deaths per thousand** of the population **per year**.

Development can also be shown by an **increase** in **life expectancy**:

Life expectancy is the **average age** a person can **expect to live to**.

4) **Political changes** — changes to a country's political system can also be a measure of development:

For example, a country is **developing** if it **changes** from a **dictatorship** (where a leader makes all the decisions for a country) to a **democracy** (where the people decide on things, e.g. by voting).

5) **Cultural changes** — as a country develops, the way people live their lives (e.g. their **behaviour** and **beliefs**) may change:

For example, in some cultures **women** are **not treated as equal** to men, e.g. they're **not** allowed to be **educated** or their **only job** is to **provide children**. As a country **develops**, the **role** of women **changes**. This can be shown by an **increase** in the **female literacy rate** (which shows women are **being educated**) and a **decrease** in the **birth rate** (which can show that women are **working** and they have **less time** to **raise children**).

Development Measures have **Limitations** When **Used On Their Own**

1) The different measures of development can be **misleading** when used **on their own** because they're **averages** — they don't show up **elite groups** in the population or **variations** within the country.
2) They also shouldn't be used on their own because as a country develops, **some aspects develop before others**. So it might seem that a country's **more developed** than it **actually is**.
3) Using a compound measure called the **Human Development Index** (HDI) **avoids these problems**:

HDI is a **number** that's calculated using **life expectancy, literacy rate, education level** (e.g. degree) and **income per capita**. As a country **develops**, its **HDI** gets **higher**.

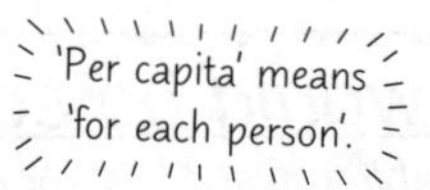

Development Basics

There are Lots of Ways to Classify How Developed a Country is

1) In the late 1960s, countries were classified into the **First**, **Second** and **Third Worlds**:
   - The **First World** included the developed **capitalist countries** such as the **USA** and western European countries.
   - The **Second World** included **communist countries** such as the **former Soviet Union** and eastern European countries.
   - The **Third World** included **every other country**.

In a capitalist country resources belong to individuals — only they can profit from what they own. In a communist country, the ownership of resources and any profit that comes from them is shared between everyone.

2) In the 1980s countries were classified into two categories based on how **economically developed** they were.
3) **Richer** countries were classed as **More Economically Developed Countries** (MEDCs) and **poorer** countries were classed as **Less Economically Developed Countries** (LEDCs).
4) **MEDCs** were generally found in the **north**. They included the USA and European countries, but also Australia and New Zealand.
5) **LEDCs** were generally found in the **south**. They included India, China, Mexico, Brazil and all the African countries.

Brandt line
MEDCs
LEDCs

6) In the **1980s** the **Brandt Report** discussed the **north/south divide** — the **Brandt line** was used to show the divide.
7) But this simple classification **can't** tell you which countries are **developing quickly** and which **aren't** really developing at all.
8) Nowadays, countries are classified into **more categories** to show the **continuous spectrum** of economic development between the least developed countries and the most developed countries — this is the **development continuum**:

Rich industrial countries — these are the **most developed** countries in the world. For example, the UK, Norway, USA, Canada, France.

Former communist countries — these countries **aren't really poor**, but **aren't rich either** (they're kind of in the middle). They're **developing quickly**, but not as quick as NICs are. For example, the Czech Republic, Bulgaria, Poland.

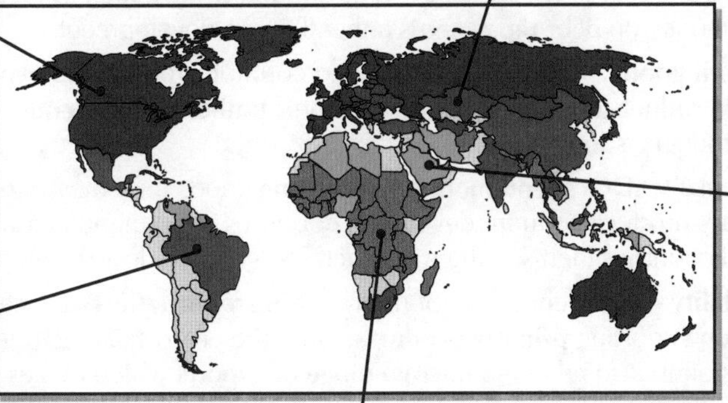

Oil-exporting countries — these are **quite rich** (they have a high GNI) but the **wealth** often **belongs to a few people** and the rest are quite poor. For example, Qatar, Kuwait, Saudi Arabia.

Newly Industrialising Countries (NICs) — these are **rapidly getting richer** as their **economy** is moving from being based on **primary industry** (e.g. agriculture) to **secondary industry** (manufacturing). For example, China, India, Brazil, Mexico, South Africa.

Least Developed Countries (LDCs) — these are the **poorest**, **least developed** countries in the world. For example, Ethiopia, Chad, Angola.

Practice Questions

Q1 What is the Human Development Index?

Q2 What is an NIC?

Q3 Name two examples of LDCs.

Exam Question

Q1 Outline the changes associated with the development of a country. [8 marks]

Exams — the most feared measure of memory development...

What a delightful pair of pages — get all this learnt because it'll help make the rest of this development stuff easier to handle.

Least Developed Countries

The LDCs are the poorest, least developed countries in the world. You need to know all about their characteristics and the issues they face. I'm afraid that means these aren't the cheeriest pages in the world.

Life Isn't Easy in the Least Developed Countries

1) A lot of the Least Developed Countries are found in **Sub-Saharan Africa**, e.g. **Ethiopia**, **Gambia**, **Rwanda**, **Uganda** and **Zambia**. A few are found outside Africa, e.g. **Afghanistan** (in Asia), and **Haiti** (in the Caribbean).
2) There's a massive **gap** in **development** between the LDCs and the most developed countries, e.g. in terms of the global economy, the richest fifth of the global population have 80% of the world's income and the poorest fifth have only 1%.
3) The **difference** in the level of development between **more** and **less developed countries** is called the **development gap**.
4) To understand **how big** the gap is and **why** there is one, you need to know all about the **characteristics** of the LDCs and the **issues** that they face...

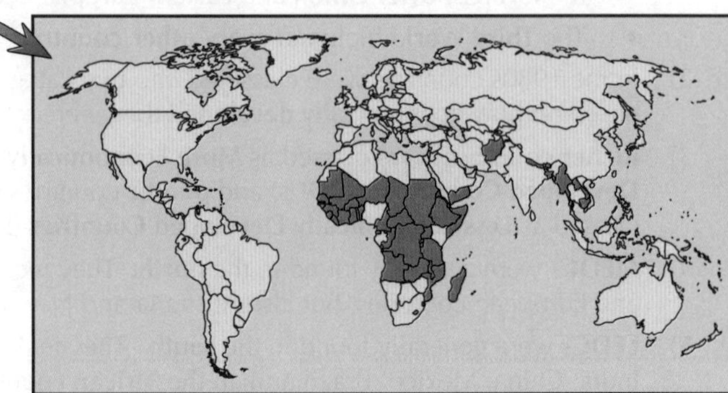

1 ECONOMIC

Take a look at the causes of poverty on pages 136-137 — it's also pretty relevant to this development gap stuff.

- **Low incomes** — in LDCs the GNI per person is less than $745, e.g. in **Ethiopia** in 2010 the **GNI** per person was **$380**.
- **Poor trade links** — many LDCs have **little involvement** in world trade — the poorest 49 countries make up **10%** of the world's population, but only account for **0.4%** of world trade.
- **High levels of debt** — many LDCs **borrow money** from more developed countries for development projects, e.g. building dams and roads. The loans are large and many have **high interest rates** — lots of LDCs are forced to spend money on **debt repayments** rather than on development.
- Trade in **low profit goods** — many less developed countries rely on the **export** of **primary products** — e.g. **agricultural products** (such as sugar and cotton), **timber** and **minerals** (such as iron ore). The price paid for these products is **low**.
- **Trade deficit** — many LDCs **spend more** on **importing** goods than they **earn exporting** goods. They sell **low profit** primary products to more developed countries, who manufacture goods from these products. More developed countries then sell the manufactured goods to less developed countries at **high prices**.
- **Economic instability** — the economies of many LDCs are **unstable** because they're **based on agriculture** and dependent on exporting **primary products**. So if the crops **fail** (e.g. due to drought), so does the economy. LDCs often also rely on a **narrow range** of exports which makes them **vulnerable** if the price falls. E.g. Ghana heavily relies on the export of cocoa.

2 SOCIAL

- **Limited health care** — in LDCs there are thousands of patients per doctor. E.g. in Ethiopia there are over 30 000 patients for every doctor compared to around 360 patients for every doctor in the UK.
- **High IMR**, e.g. in Ethiopia in 2010, there were 75 deaths per 1000 live births compared to 5 deaths per 1000 live births in the UK.
- High levels of **malnutrition**, e.g. in Ethiopia, between 2004 and 2005, 46% of the population was undernourished, and malnutrition was responsible for over half of all deaths of children under 5.

Benny wasn't worried about high levels of debt — he knew he looked hot and that was what really mattered.

- High numbers of people **infected by diseases**, e.g. an estimated 9 million people in Ethiopia contract malaria every year (around 10% of the population).
- **Low levels of education**, e.g. primary school attendance in Ethiopia was 45% between 2005 and 2010.
- **Low literacy rates**, e.g. the adult literacy rate in Ethiopia in 2010 was 30%.
- Lack of access to **clean water** and **sanitation** (toilets and safe disposal of human waste), e.g. in Ethiopia in 2006 only 42% of people had access to clean water and 11% had access to sanitation.

Least Developed Countries

3 DEMOGRAPHIC

- **Low life expectancy**, e.g. life expectancy at birth in Ethiopia in 2012 was 56, compared to 80 in the UK.
- Many LDCs have a much **higher birth rate** than **death rate**, e.g. the birth rate in Ethiopia in 2012 was 42 per 1000 people per year and the death rate was 11 per 1000 people per year. Having a much **higher** birth rate than death rate causes **rapid population growth** which can lead to other problems, e.g. food shortages.

4 POLITICAL

- Many LDCs don't have a **democratic** government, e.g. up until 1994 Ethiopia was a communist state.
- **Political corruption** is a problem in many LDCs, e.g. at general elections in Ethiopia in 2005, allegations of vote rigging led to hundreds of people being arrested and imprisoned for treason. Some governments of LDCs have also been accused of **keeping money** the country has received as **loans**, rather than spending it on **development**.
- Many LDCs are badly affected by **war** and **conflict**, e.g. tens of thousands of people were killed between 1998 and 2000 in the conflict between Ethiopia and neighbouring Eritrea. During times of conflict, **less money** is spent on **development** (as so much is spent on the conflict itself).

Don't be absurd — I paid for both my gold house and my rocket car with my own money.

5 CULTURAL

Inequality — between **men** and **women**, or between other **social** or **ethnic groups**. E.g. in Ethiopia men and women are not treated equally — between 2005 and 2010, **30%** of **males** were attending secondary schools compared to only **23%** of **females**.

All these characteristics contribute to a **low quality of life** for the **people** living in LDCs. The **HDI** (see p. 98) is a good indicator of quality of life. HDI is much **lower** in LDCs than in more developed countries, e.g. Ethiopia is ranked **174th** in the world with an HDI of 0.363 (1 is the maximum). In comparison, the UK is ranked **28th** with an HDI of 0.863.

Practice Questions

Q1 What is the development gap?

Q2 Give an economic characteristic of an LDC.

Q3 Give a social characteristic of an LDC.

Q4 Give a political characteristic of an LDC.

Q5 Give a demographic characteristic of an LDC.

Exam Question

Q1 The table shows data for three countries. Use the data to comment on the level of development of the countries shown. [7 marks]

	Angola	South Africa	Denmark
Birth rate (per 1000 people)	39.36	19.32	10.22
Literacy (% men over 15 years)	82.7	87	99
Literacy (% women over 15 years)	58.1	85.7	99
% of GDP from agriculture	9.6	2.5	4.5

Please mind the gap — it really is massive...

The characteristics of LDCs show you why there's such a huge gap between them and the most developed countries. There are a whole load of characteristics to get your head around here so it's a lot of work, but believe me, examiners love asking about LDCs and the development gap so no skiving off now. Never mind, you're nearly at the end of the section... really you are...

Global Groupings and Development

Nations get together in groups for mutual benefit (and because everyone likes to have friends).

Nations Group Together *for a few* ***Different Reasons***

1) Nations group together because it will **benefit** all of their **economies**:

- Groups can agree to **reduce barriers to trade** (e.g. import or export taxes, known as tariffs) between the member states, which helps to **increase** the **amount of trade** between members. For example, the USA, Canada and Mexico make up the North American Free Trade Agreement (NAFTA). They've agreed to abolish many tariffs which has increased trade and benefited all three economies.
- Being in a group where there's free trade between members also means there's a **larger market** for businesses, which allows them to **increase trade**.
- **Comparative advantage** — countries can **specialise** in producing the things they're good at making and trade for the things they're not good at making (it's easier to trade for all the different things a country needs, because trade is less restricted). **Production will increase** in each member country because they're concentrating on what they do **best**.

2) Nations group together because it can help to **promote development**:

Countries in a group can **work together** to tackle **development issues**, e.g. disease epidemics, poverty, education issues etc. This can benefit the **members** of a group, or the group can work together to tackle issues of **global concern**. For example, the UN is an international organisation with 193 member states. In 2000 it set eight Millennium Development Goals (MDGs), which highlighted the key global development issues and allowed progress in the development of lots of countries to be measured.

See page 138 for more on the MDGs.

3) Nations group together to **increase security** and **promote peace**:

Countries that are working together in a group are **less likely** to go to **war** with each other as it will badly affect their **economies** and **development** (see above). Countries in a group can also **agree policies** between them that increase **regional** and **global security**, e.g. the Association of South East Asian Nations (ASEAN) is a group of 10 countries that have made agreements to ban nuclear weapons.

There are ***Consequences*** *to* ***Global Groupings***

Check out the next page for an EU case study...

Positive consequences

1) **Increased economic development** for the nations in a group, e.g. due to **increased trade** (see above).
2) Increased economic development can lead to **increased quality of life** for many people in a group.
3) The group can **provide support** for **declining regions** or **industries**, e.g. the EU's rural development policy gives funding to member states to be spent in rural areas to improve the rural economy and the quality of life of people living there.
4) Within some global groupings people looking for **work** can move freely **between member countries** to **find a job**.
5) There can be **better global representation** for smaller nations who join a larger group. E.g. some of the tiny islands of the Caribbean have a greater global presence because they're members of the **Caribbean Community** (CARICOM).
6) Reduced **risk of conflict** (see above) and **better international relations** between nations.
7) Also, groups of nations can **improve global security**, e.g. NATO (the North Atlantic Treaty Organisation) has an international force of soldiers who carry out various duties including peacekeeping in conflict zones.

Negative consequences

1) In some groups, decisions are made **centrally** so member states may **lose control** over some aspects of how they **run their country**.
2) Individual countries may **lose out** when they have to **share resources** with other member states, e.g. fishing grounds.
3) Trade agreements made within a group increase trade between member countries, but can **reduce trade** with countries **outside** the group. This is particularly damaging for **LDCs**, whose **development** can be affected by lost trade.
4) Sometimes being a member of a global group can **damage** a country's economy — **richer member states** may have to support **poorer member states** financially if they are in economic crisis, e.g. the UK contributed around £4 billion to the EU bailout of Portugal in 2011.

Global Groupings and Development

Case Study — the European Union (EU)

1) European nations first formed a group to help Europe to **recover** after the **Second World War**. Their aims were to **ensure peace** and improve **economic development** by making the countries more closely **integrated**.
2) This group has grown from **6 members** in 1957 to **27 members** in 2007. It was **named the EU** in 1993.
3) It's a closely integrated **economic** and **political** group. For example:
    - **Goods**, **services**, **people** and **money** can move **freely** between most member states without barriers.
    - 17 of the 27 members of the EU have adopted a **single currency** — the **Euro**.
    - Member states have agreed to have **common laws** and **policies** on things like agriculture and fisheries.
4) There are **positive** impacts of the EU:
    - **Trade has increased** between European countries. E.g. in 1970 just over 12% of the UK's GDP came from trade with European countries. After the UK joined the EU in 1973, this percentage increased rapidly — in 2002, around 23% of the UK's GDP came from trade with EU countries.
    - The **Euro** has made **trade easier** between some countries because there is no need to **exchange money**. Prices are more **consistent** because there is **no uncertainty** in exchange rates.
    - The EU **supports** some industries. E.g. the **Common Agricultural Policy (CAP)** includes **subsidies** for EU farmers and adds **import tariffs** and **quotas** on agricultural products from outside the EU. This gives farmers a reasonable standard of living, secures food supplies and ensures a good price for consumers.
    - Being in the EU gives members **increased security** from **external threats**. E.g. the EU counter-terrorism policy protects all member states from the threat of terrorism by measures such as introducing biometric passports to increase border security.
    - Most EU residents are **free to move around** the EU — they can **work** or **live** in most other EU countries.
5) There are also **negative** impacts of the EU:
    - **Joining** the EU can be **expensive**. To become an EU member state a country must meet **certain criteria**, e.g. high standards of environmental protection. Meeting these criteria can require a **lot of investment**.
    - Countries have to **share some resources** with other member states. For example, countries joining the **EU** come under the **Common Fisheries Policy**, which means their **fishing grounds** become **open** to fishing by **other member states**.
    - Policies like the **CAP** can have a **negative impact** on the economies of countries **outside** the EU. EU countries may trade with other countries **less**, because it's cheaper for them to trade with **each other**.
    - Increased immigration **within** the EU has resulted in a **lack of skilled workers** in some eastern European countries because so many have moved to Western Europe to seek better wages.
    - Joining the EU can **reduce independence** — EU countries agree to **obey** EU policies even if it **conflicts** with their **national policies**.

Brian was getting his catch in early — he'd heard about the Common Fisheries Policy and he wasn't taking any chances.

Practice Questions

Q1 Give three reasons why different countries might group together.

Q2 Give three examples of global social and economic groupings.

Exam Question

Q1 Discuss the consequences of the grouping of nations, with particular reference to the EU. [10 marks]

Countries form groups for the same reason ageing rockers do — money...

For a long time being a member of the EU was seen as a golden ticket to success — it provided better trade opportunities and helped its members to develop socially and economically. However, since the start of the 2008 economic crisis things have started to go up the spout. Now the future of the EU and particularly the Euro is a bit uncertain — oh heck...

Development Issues

The next four pages cover three important development issues and there's a stunner of a case study for each one.

Becoming Economically Sustainable *can be* ***Disastrous*** *for the* ***Environment***

1) **Sustainable development** means **developing** to meet the **needs** of people **today**, without **affecting** the ability of people in the **future** to meet their **own needs**. Here's how **economic** and **environmental** sustainability fit in to the whole idea:
   - **Economic sustainability** means making sure the economy keeps running and growing in the future, even if resources **run out** or the **population grows**.
   - **Environmental sustainability** means using the environment in a way that doesn't permanently **damage** or **alter it**, so that future generations can still get what they **need** from it.
2) Becoming economically sustainable often **reduces** environmental sustainability because **economic activities** often have **negative environmental impacts**. For example, many industries will:
   - **Use resources** — industry relies on **natural resources**, e.g. burning fossil fuels for energy. Using up natural resources **faster** than the environment can **replace** them means they won't be **available** to future generations.
   - **Produce waste** — industrial waste can cause **pollution** which can **irreversibly alter** the environment — so it isn't the same for future generations.

Case Study — Sarawak

Sarawak is a state in Malaysia which has experienced **rapid economic growth** since the 1980s, but this growth has come at an **environmental cost**:

TIMBER INDUSTRY

1) Sarawak is one of the **world's largest** exporters of **tropical hardwood** timber. Timber exports rose from 4.2 million m^3 in 1971 to 18.8 million m^3 in 1990, and the timber industry became very important to the **Malaysian economy**.
2) **Intense logging** in the 1980s and 1990s caused **large scale deforestation** — an estimated **70%** of Sarawak's original forests **disappeared**. This caused **habitat loss** and other problems such as **soil erosion** and **flooding**.
3) By the 1990s the rate of logging was both **economically unsustainable** (the timber would run out and the industry would collapse) and **environmentally unsustainable** (the forests were being totally destroyed).
4) Since the late 1990s the Malaysian government has taken **action** to improve the **sustainability** of the industry. They have created **forest management plans** to control the logging and promote **sustainable management**, e.g. felling trees in a 25 year cutting cycle which allows the forest to **recover**. These actions are **helping** to increase sustainability, but illegal **deforestation** is still continuing.

COMMERCIAL AGRICULTURE

Commercial agriculture is large-scale farming of crops or livestock to be sold in bulk around the world.

1) Since the 1990s there's been a rise in **commercial agriculture** in Sarawak. **Palm oil** is the main commercial crop — in 2008 it accounted for nearly **6%** of Sarawak's exports. It's used to make processed food and biodiesel.
2) The **palm oil** industry has a number of **environmental impacts**. It causes **deforestation** because forests are cleared to make room for plantations. **Monoculture** (growing just one plant) **reduces biodiversity** and the use of **agricultural chemicals** and the **waste** from palm oil production causes **water** and **soil pollution**.
3) Despite the environmental issues, there is continuing **investment** in commercial agriculture. There are plans to **raise** agricultural productivity because the **demand** for **palm oil** is **rising** (for use as a **biofuel**). This means the **palm oil industry** could aid **economic sustainability**, but may continue to **harm** environmental sustainability.

OTHER INDUSTRIES

1) Since 2000, there's been **increased investment** in **manufacturing**, **construction** and **high tech industries**. E.g. aluminium and steel industries, shipbuilding and marine engineering.
2) Many of these industries require **power**. In 2011 construction of the Bakun hydroelectric dam was completed and a number of **coal power stations** are being built. These projects are environmentally damaging — the dam has caused **habitat loss** and **disrupted river ecosystems**, and the power stations will increase **air pollution** and **use up resources**.
3) Many industries also **deplete raw materials** (e.g. aluminium ore) and **create waste products** that pollute.
4) The growth of these industries promotes **economic sustainability** because they provide a source of income **now** and in the **future**, but they are not **environmentally sustainable**.

Development Issues

Some people think **Sustainable Tourism** could be the **Answer**

1) Tourists come to experience the **environment** and **culture** of a place (e.g. a tropical rainforest or a city centre).
2) Too many tourists can **damage** or **permanently alter** an area though, and spoil it for **future generations**. E.g. building hotels and other tourist facilities can destroy the habitats of plants and animals that the tourists have come to see.
3) **Sustainable tourism** is tourism that **doesn't damage** the environment people have come to see, e.g. by **limiting** the number of tourist developments or only permitting tourist activities in **designated areas**. It also benefits **local people** by generating **employment**, and **allows** income to be put back into **conservation** to protect the area.
4) Some people think that tourism can **never** be **truly** sustainable. Tourism is about attracting people to an area to **generate profit** or **income** for the **local economy**, so the more tourists there are, the **better** it is for the local economy. But, more tourists makes it **more difficult** to reduce the **environmental impact** the tourists have.
5) For sustainable tourism to **succeed** certain things need to be done, e.g. **tourist numbers** may need to be tightly controlled and tourist activities **carefully monitored** to make sure they don't damage or alter the environment.

Case Study — The Great Barrier Reef

1) The Great Barrier Reef is the **largest coral reef system** in the world. It lies off the **NE coast** of **Australia** and supports a range of wildlife including many **vulnerable** and **endangered** species.
2) In the 1980s and 1990s improved access led to a **rapid rise in tourism** — visitor numbers increased by about 30% every year in the 1980s.
3) Today, tourism is the **largest commercial activity** around the Great Barrier Reef — it accounts for **87%** of the reef's **economic output**. It is a major source of income for the **local** and **national economy**, generating over **AU$5 billion a year**.
4) Tourist activities can have **negative impacts** on the Great Barrier Reef area:

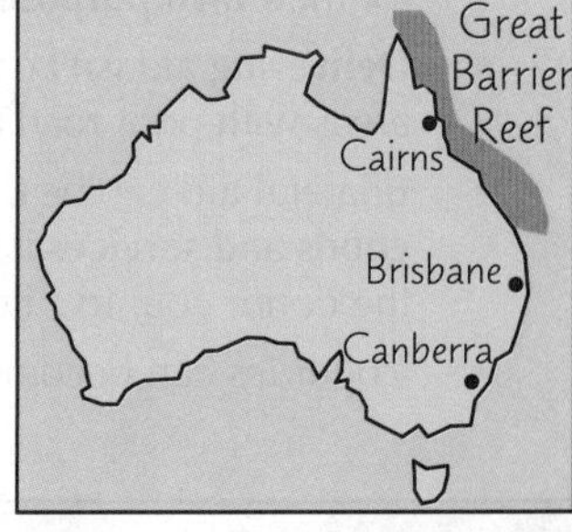

The Great Barrier Reef is an example of a fragile environment. See pages 70-71 for more on these.

- Coral reefs are easily **damaged** by **pollution**, which also affects the species dependent on them. The tourist industry creates pollution in several ways, e.g. through waste disposal, litter and pollution from boats.
- Coral can be **damaged** by **boat anchors** and by **poor diving practices** (e.g. divers stepping on coral and breaking pieces off).
- Tourists can **disturb wildlife**, e.g. by disturbing nesting sea birds. Many seabirds nest on the ground and when disturbed the parents leave the nest, exposing the young or eggs to predators.
- The reef is **culturally** and **economically** important to **local indigenous islanders**. Tourism limits where these people can fish or carry out ceremonial activities.
- Developments for tourism along the coast damage **coastal ecosystems** (e.g. mangrove forests and estuaries) which are important for **maintaining** the reef (estuaries feed important nutrients into the reef from land).

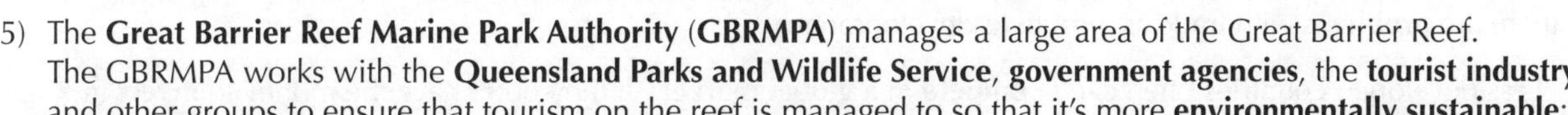

5) The **Great Barrier Reef Marine Park Authority** (**GBRMPA**) manages a large area of the Great Barrier Reef. The GBRMPA works with the **Queensland Parks and Wildlife Service**, **government agencies**, the **tourist industry** and other groups to ensure that tourism on the reef is managed to so that it's more **environmentally sustainable**:

- In 2003 the GBRMPA established a **zoning system** that describes where certain tourist activities can take place. This helps to protect the **most sensitive areas** and limits all tourism activities to more sustainable levels.
- Some activities, such as **fishing**, are **strictly regulated**. Tourist operators have to obtain **permits** from the GBRMPA for them. The number of permits is capped and there are restrictions on **group numbers** and **boat sizes** in sensitive areas.
- Most tourist operators **pay** an **Environmental Management Charge (EMC)** of around AU$3.50 per visitor per day to the GBRMPA. This money funds **research**, **education** and **management** of the marine park.
- Tourist operators and tourists are **encouraged to contribute** to **research** and **monitoring** of the reef — such as reporting on the extent of coral bleaching (see page 70). This encourages tourists to take interest in the **protection** of the reef and helps to monitor any **decline** in the reef ecosystem so that something can be done to **repair** any damage that's being done.

Development Issues

Trade and aid are two ways of helping a country to develop. Increasing trade in (and with) a developing country helps encourage economic growth. Giving aid allows it to invest in its own social and economic development. How marvellous...

Aid can help *Developing Countries* Improve People's *Quality of Life*

1) Aid is given by one country to another country in the form of **money** or **resources** (e.g. food, doctors).
2) There are **two** main **sources** of aid from donor countries — **governments** (paid for by **taxes**) and **Non-Governmental Organisations** (**NGOs** — paid for by **voluntary donations**).
3) **Governments** can give aid directly to the recipient country (**bilateral aid**) or **indirectly** through an **international organisation** that distributes the aid (**multilateral aid**).
4) There are different types of aid:

International organisations include the UN and the World Bank.

Short-term aid — money or resources to help recipient countries cope with emergencies, e.g. earthquakes.
Long-term aid — money or resources to help recipient countries become more developed, e.g. to improve health care.
'Top-down' aid — when an organisation or government receives the aid and decides where it should be spent. This is usually the case on large infrastructure projects, e.g. building dams for hydroelectric power.
'Bottom-up' aid — when money is given directly to local people, e.g. to build a well — this is often used by NGOs.

5) **Aid** is important for **development** because it allows recipient countries to invest in things that improve people's **health** and **quality of life**, e.g. improving access to drinking water. There are **problems** with aid as a route to development though:
   - Some recipient countries don't use aid **effectively** because they have **corrupt governments**, who spend the money for their **own purposes**. The money doesn't get to the people who **need** it, so it doesn't help development.
   - **Delivering** aid isn't easy, particularly in countries with **poor infrastructure**, e.g. establishing education projects in rural areas with poor road access is difficult. If the distribution of the aid is patchy, then only some areas benefit from it.
   - Bilateral aid can be **tied** — this means it's given with the **condition** that the **recipient country** has to **buy** the **goods and services** it needs **from** the **donor country**. However, if the goods and services are **expensive** in the donor country, the aid **doesn't go as far** as it would if the goods and services were bought **elsewhere**.
   - Countries can become **dependent** on aid so that they aren't able to function or develop without it.

Trade can *Stimulate Economic Growth* and *Development*

1) Trade is the **exchange** of **goods** or **services** (both buying and selling). Increasing trade **within** a developing country and **between** it and other countries **promotes development** by:
   - Increasing **economic growth** — increased trade creates **employment** and generates **wealth**, which leads to a rise in the **GDP** of the country and the **living standards** of the population.
   - Increasing the amount of money a country has to spend on **social development**, e.g. health and education.
   - Increasing the amount of money a country has to spend on **development projects**, e.g. transport infrastructure.
2) But there are **problems** with trade as a route to development:
   - Less developed countries often can't **compete** in a **global market**. If they don't have the money to **invest** in **technological developments** that reduce the cost of production, they can't **match** the prices of countries that can.
   - Less developed countries may also struggle to trade in a global market because of **other problems** such as **HIV/AIDS** or **conflict**. E.g. money has to be spent on these issues, so there's less money available to invest in developing trade, and things like conflicts can make the supply of goods unreliable.
   - Trade can have **negative** social impacts. E.g. to keep **prices low**, wages and working conditions may be very **poor**. This means that increased trade won't necessarily improve **quality of life** for everyone.
   - Less developed countries often export **primary products** (see p. 100). This can be an **unreliable income** because things like crop yields **vary**, i.e. because of the weather. These products are also very **low profit**, so don't produce a huge amount of income to improve development.
   - Countries are often dependent on trading one thing, e.g. coffee or cotton. If the demand for that commodity falls the producer country has **nothing** to fall back on and **development** is stalled.

The general opinion is that most countries need a **combination** of **AID** and **increased TRADE** to promote **development**.

Development Issues

Case Study — Sudan

As a result of ongoing conflict a new country, South Sudan, formed in July 2011.

Sudan

South Sudan

1) Sudan is one of the **poorest countries** in **Africa**. It has experienced long periods of **civil war** and **conflict** is still one of the biggest challenges to its development (see p. 128-129).
2) The Sudanese economy has been **growing** rapidly in recent years (the country's GDP grew by 4.7% in 2010), but these changes haven't led to increased **living standards** for everyone.
3) **Poverty** is **widespread** — 46.5% of the population live below the poverty line of $1 a day.
4) Sudan receives **large amounts of aid** each year:

- In 2007 Sudan received **over $2 billion of aid** (equivalent to 4.7% of its GNI). **70%** of this aid was **humanitarian** — to help cope with severe **food shortages** caused by **conflict** and **droughts**.
- Aid comes from different sources — **individual governments** (e.g. US, UK), **international organisations** (e.g. the UN), and **NGOs** (e.g. Save the Children).
- Sudan receives a lot of **food aid** — in 2008 the World Food Programme provided food aid to 6 million people in Sudan. This helps people to **survive** in the short term, but doesn't help the country to **develop** in the long term.
- Some aid is used to **promote development** by attempting to **prevent conflicts, rebuild infrastructure** and invest in **education** and **health services**. E.g. the US Agency for International Development has funded the construction or refurbishment of 140 primary schools and 5 secondary schools in Sudan.
- There are **lots of problems** getting aid to where it's needed though, because of **conflicts** and **corruption**.

5) Growth of the oil industry is boosting **trade** and **economic growth**:

- In the 1990s, lots of Sudan's exports were **low profit agricultural goods**, e.g. cotton, nuts and livestock. Sudan had a **trade deficit** (it **spent more importing** goods than it **earned exporting** them). **Production** and **trade** of these goods has **decreased** due to conflicts and droughts.
- In 1999 Sudan started **exporting oil** and as a result the country had its **first trade surplus** (it **earned more** from exports than it **spent** on imports). Over the last decade oil has become the **main export**, and the trade surplus reached $1.4 billion in the first few months of 2011.
- The growth of the oil industry has helped development because it brings **economic growth** and **improves international relations** (e.g. trade agreements have been made with the US, the EU, Egypt and Libya).
- There are concerns that profits from the oil industry **aren't funding development** though, because of **corruption** in the government.
- **Agriculture** is still **important to the economy** — it accounts for 40% of GDP, and 80% of people are employed in agriculture. However, agricultural trade is **low profit** and **unreliable** (see previous page) so it is **difficult** for Sudan to develop while it is still highly dependent on it.
- It's difficult for Sudan to make a lot of **profit** because of **barriers** to trade, e.g. in 2012 average import tariffs were around **20%**. However Sudan is in the process of joining the **World Trade Organisation** (WTO) which will make international trade easier, and give the country access to a **wider market** for its **exports**.

Practice Questions

Q1 What is sustainable development?

Q2 Give three problems with aid as a route to development.

Q3 Give three ways that trade helps promote development.

Exam Question

Q1 Below are three development issues. With reference to a country you have studied, discuss **one** of the issues.
either "Economic sustainability versus environmental sustainability"
or "Sustainable tourism, myth or reality"
or "Trade versus aid" [40 marks]

And the winner is... Traid. The secret love child of both aid and trade.

Nobody knows for definite the best way to promote development, but a combination of both trade and aid is a good bet. It makes answers easier to write too — you can weigh up the pros and cons of both before concluding that a mixture of the two is best. Hooray!

Globalisation Basics

In the last few decades it's become a lot easier to communicate with people around the world, and a lot easier to move around. This is causing globalisation, and it affects pretty much everyone. Including you. Yes, you... with the hair...

Globalisation** is the **Process** of **Countries** becoming more **Closely Integrated

1) Globalisation is the process of the world's **economies**, **political systems** and **cultures** becoming more strongly **connected** to each other.
2) If there was **no** globalisation there wouldn't be any **interaction** between different countries. If there was **complete** globalisation, the whole world would act like **a single community**. The real world is somewhere **in between**, but countries are becoming more and more **closely integrated**.
3) Globalisation is caused by the **movement** of **capital** (money that's invested, see below) and **people** between different countries, as well as **businesses** locating their operations and selling their **products** and **services** in more countries.
4) People have been **moving between countries** and **international trade** has been going on for ages, but most people think that globalisation as we know it today really started to **accelerate** in the **1980s**. Here are a few reasons why:

Globalisation rocks Jamie-Lou's world.

- Improvements to **telephone networks** have made **global communications** cheaper and easier. **Mobile** and **satellite phones** allow people to communicate even when they don't have access to a telephone line.
- The development and rapid spread of **e-mail** and the **internet** allow large amounts of information to be exchanged instantly across the globe. This makes working across long distances very efficient.
- **Global transport** has been improved by the development of high speed rail networks, larger and faster ships, larger cargo planes and low cost airlines. These developments have made it easier for **people** and **goods** to move quickly and cheaply around the world. They have also meant that companies can get **supplies** from all over the world, and **sell their products** to people all over the world.

*There are **Four Factors** which **Promote Globalisation***

Flows of Capital

1) Capital is money that's **invested** — it's spent on something so that you get an **income** or **increased profit** from it.
2) Historically, capital was mostly invested **within a country**, e.g. companies would expand by doing things like building new factories, or setting up new branches within their country of origin.
3) Over time though, the amount of capital invested in **foreign countries** has increased — this is **Foreign Direct Investment** (FDI). E.g. global FDI increased from $3000 billion in 1996 to $12 000 billion in 2006.
4) Improvements in **information and communications technology** (ICT) have encouraged flows of capital round the world — it can **instantly** be moved around the world via the internet.
5) Increasing **flows of capital** are making the world more **interconnected**, e.g. most countries' economies are now **dependent** on flows of investment to and from other countries.

Have a peek at the next page (and below) for more on how companies divide up the parts of their business round the world.

Flows of Production

1) Historically, manufacturing industries were located in **more developed** countries.
2) The products being produced were also **sold** in the country where they were **made**.
3) In recent decades, manufacturing has **decreased** in **more developed countries**, e.g. the number of people employed in manufacturing in the UK fell from more than 5 million in 1985 to less than 3 million in 2009.
4) Lower labour costs overseas have caused many companies to **relocate** the production **side** of their business **abroad**, they then **import** the products to the countries where they're **sold**. E.g. the vacuum manufacturer Dyson moved the production and assembly part of its business to Malaysia in 2002, but the vacuums are still sold in the UK.
5) As a result of these changes, **international trade** in manufactured goods is **increasing**, e.g. the UK imported £200 billion of manufactured goods in 1990, and £550 billion in 2008.
6) Changing **flows of production** are making the world more **interconnected**, e.g. many of the manufactured products we now buy have been produced in other countries, and then imported to the UK.

Globalisation Basics

Flows of Services

1) Services are economic activities that **aren't** based around producing any **material goods**, e.g. banking and insurance.
2) Improvements in **ICT** have allowed services to become **global industries** in recent decades. Things like banking and insurance depend on **communication** and **transfer of information**. Improvements to ICT mean that services can **locate anywhere** in the world and still be able to serve the needs of **customers anywhere else** in the world.
3) During the 1970s and 1980s there was also **deregulation** (removal of rules to increase competition) and **opening up** of national financial markets to the rest of the world, e.g. in the USA and UK. This meant that it was made **easier** for banks and other financial institutions to **do business** in other countries.
4) Services can be split into **low level** (e.g. customer service) and **high level** (e.g. financial services). **High level services** tend to be concentrated in cities in **more developed countries** (e.g. London and New York). Companies are increasingly **relocating** low level services to **less developed countries** where labour is **cheaper**, e.g. call centres (see p. 116).
5) Increasing **flows of services** are making the world more **interconnected**, e.g. people are connected to other countries just through having a bank account — many banks are huge international organisations.

Flows of People

1) More people are **moving** to different countries, e.g. **international migration** has doubled since 1975.
2) Some people move because they **have to** (e.g. to escape conflict zones) but many people choose to move for **work**.
3) Some migrants are **highly skilled workers** (e.g. ICT and medical workers), moving to more developed countries where **wages** and **working conditions** are **better**. Others are **unskilled workers** who move to more developed countries to look for work because of **unemployment** or **poor wages** in their own countries.
4) Increasing **flows of people** between different countries is making the world more **interconnected**, e.g. people bring aspects of their **culture** with them when they move, and countries are connected together because people have **family** all over the world.

Marketing is Becoming More Global

1) Marketing is the process of **promoting** and **selling products** or **services**.
2) Nowadays, many products and services are sold **all over the world**, rather than just in the country where they are produced. So marketing has had to become **global**.
3) Global marketing involves treating the world as **one single market** (a fully globalised world, see previous page) and using **one marketing strategy** to advertise a product to customers all over the world.
4) Global marketing gives **economies of scale** — it is **cheaper** to have one marketing campaign for the whole world, rather than having a different campaign for every country.
5) Marketing needs to be **adapted** to regional markets though — different populations still have **different laws** and **cultural attitudes**, e.g. different countries have different laws and attitudes about consuming alcohol.

Practice Questions

Q1 What is globalisation?

Q2 Give one example of something that has caused globalisation to accelerate since the 1980s.

Q3 What is global marketing?

Exam Question

Q1 Discuss how changes in patterns of production have promoted globalisation. [10 marks]

Imagine by John Lennon — an ode to globalisation if ever I've heard one...

Don't believe me? Check out the lyrics... Let me simplify these two pages for you — basically globalisation makes some things in life easier... it's easier to talk to your pal in Argentina and easier to flog rubber ducks to your man in Hawaii. If only globalisation made it easier to pass exams...

Trans-National Corporations (TNCs)

Trans-National Corporations (TNCs) are worldwide companies that are bringing countries together by spreading themselves, and their cash, all over the world. Unfortunately, they don't seem to have spread any cash into my bank account.

TNCs** are **Companies** that Operate in **Two or More Countries

1) TNCs are companies that **produce**, **sell** or are **located** in **two or more** countries, e.g. **Sony®** manufacture **electronic products** in **China** and **Japan**, and **sell** many of them in **Europe** and the **USA**.
2) They play an **important role** in the **global economy** — in 2010, TNCs accounted for around a **quarter** of **global GDP**.
3) TNCs operate in **all types** of industry:
   - **Primary industry** (extracting natural resources) e.g. Shell extracts and trades oil and gas.
   - **Secondary industry** (making material goods) e.g. Toyota manufactures vehicles.
   - **Tertiary industry** (providing services) e.g. Aviva™ provides insurance services.
4) TNCs bring lots of **investment** into countries, spread **new technologies** and can promote particular **cultures**, e.g. McDonald's brings Western-style fast food to other countries.
5) **Potential investment**, the **creation of jobs** and access to **new technology** means TNCs can have **political influence**.
6) They're one of the **main driving forces** behind globalisation because of the economic, political and cultural **interactions** that occur **between** the countries where they operate.
7) TNCs also **connect** countries together because of how they are **structured**:
   - **Headquarters** are usually located in **big cities** in more developed countries (e.g. New York). These cities are well connected in terms of global **transport** and **communications**, and there is a supply of **highly skilled workers**.
   - **Research and development** (R&D) facilities tend to be located in cities and towns where there's a supply of **highly educated** people, e.g. scientists, engineers and technicians. They are often in the **same country** as the headquarters.
   - Some TNCs have **regional R&D** facilities located closer to the markets they are selling to, so they can make products that are specifically **for that market**. E.g. South Korean TNC Samsung has an R&D centre in Warsaw, Poland.
   - **Factories** are often located in NICs where **production costs** (e.g. labour, materials, land etc.) **are lower**, e.g. Samsung has factories in China.
   - Many TNCs also have **factories** in the country where **their market** is, e.g. Nissan™ have a factory in the UK. If a product is made in the country where it is **sold**, the TNC can avoid paying **import** and **export taxes** and can **reduce transport costs** (especially on large items, e.g. cars).

McDonald's and Starbucks in Chiang Mai, Thailand.

*TNCs have **Grown Rapidly** In Recent Years*

1) TNCs have increased in **size**, **wealth** and **number** since the **mid 20th century**, e.g. in 1970 there were 7000 TNCs, in 2012 there were more than 80 000.
2) Increasing numbers of companies have **grown** to become TNCs. Here are a few reasons why:
   - TNCs can make products **cheaply** because they can move production to countries where **costs are low**, e.g. they can take advantage of cheap labour in less developed countries.
   - TNCs can take advantage of differences in **government policies**, e.g. they can move where **taxes are low**, or where **subsidies** and **grants** to promote manufacturing are available.
   - They can operate in countries where **labour** or **environmental laws** are **less strict**, so they can carry out higher intensity production.
   - A TNC can expand to access new **growing markets** in developing countries.
   - By growing internationally they can reach a size where they can gain from **economies of scale**, which increases **profit**.
   - They can get around **trade barriers** by manufacturing in the **same country** that they are selling (see above).
   - TNCs can **shift** production between locations to **maximise profits**, e.g. they can move production from one country to another if it will save them money.
   - TNCs can control their **supply chain** to maximise profits. E.g. they can **buy** companies that supply them with components, or make components themselves to **cut costs**.

Economies of scale is where companies produce lots more of an item, so the cost of producing each individual item is reduced and they make more profit.

Trans-National Corporations (TNCs)

TNCs have **Positive** and **Negative Impacts** on their Country of **Origin**...

Economic

- **Profits** from activities abroad come back to **shareholders**. Money from **taxes** on the TNC's income also goes to the government of the country of origin.
- **Skilled employment** — even if the TNC moves some activities elsewhere, **highly skilled jobs** (e.g. in R&D and finance) remain in the country of origin.
- Some TNCs move **manufacturing** abroad. In the country of origin, this can cause **unemployment** for employees of the TNC and for the TNC's suppliers.
- Increased unemployment can lead to **wider decline** in an area — people have a **smaller disposable income** so they spend less money, causing shops and businesses to **close**.

Social

- Increased **range of products** available in shops. Large retail TNCs produce many things in **bulk**, which means that they can stock products which smaller companies **couldn't afford** to produce or stock.
- **High unemployment** caused by the closure of factories can lead to **social problems**, e.g. increases in **crime**.

Environmental

Decline in local **manufacturing industry** may **reduce pollution**.

...and on their **Host** Countries

Economic

- Increased employment creates **increased wealth** for local people and the local economy — people have more to spend in local shops.
- Increased economic activity can generate even **more** economic activity (called the **multiplier effect**). E.g. the creation of jobs brings wealth to a region, so more businesses are attracted there and even more jobs are created.
- TNCs can cause local businesses to **shut down** by out-competing them.
- A lot of the **profits** can be sent back to the **country of origin**, so they don't reach the host country.

Social

- TNCs may invest in **social development** (e.g. education), in host countries to create a **more skilled workforce**.
- They may bring **new technologies** and **working methods** into the country, which will also create a more skilled workforce.
- TNCs are sometimes accused of **exploiting** their **workforce**, particularly in developing countries where the workers are prepared to work for **low wages** in **poor conditions**.
- **Managerial positions** are likely to be filled by candidates from the **country of origin**.
- TNCs can cause **urbanisation** as people come from rural areas to work in urban factories.
- **Decisions** made by the TNC are often made in the country of origin with **little consideration** for the needs of the host country.

Environmental

- TNCs may use or invest in **environmentally friendly technologies**, e.g. renewable energy sources.
- Manufacturing can cause **pollution**, particularly in some less developed countries where **environmental laws** are often **less strict**.
- **Agricultural land** or **wildlife habitats** can be lost when TNCs buy areas of **land**, e.g. for building factories.

Practice Questions

Q1 What is a TNC?

Q2 Give three reasons for the growth of TNCs.

Exam Question

Q1 Discuss the social, economic and environmental impacts of TNCs on their host countries. [10 marks]

TNCs — aka Terribly Nasty Companies...

TNCs are often seen as the big baddies of globalisation, but in reality they're not all bad. For your exam you need to know the positive impacts of TNCs as well as the negatives ones — A2 Geography examiners love nothing more than a balanced argument.

TNC Case Study — Wal-Mart

Get over here y'all. It's time for a case study and we're heading stateside (and beyond — that's kinda the point of TNCs...)

Wal-Mart® is a Retail TNC with Headquarters in the USA

Wal-Mart is a chain of discount **department stores** (including ASDA in the UK). It's one of the **largest** TNCs in the world and the largest **retail** TNC (many of the top TNCs are **oil companies**).

1) Wal-Mart began in 1962 when **Sam Walton** opened the first store in **Arkansas, USA**.
2) More stores opened across Arkansas, then across the USA, and more recently across the globe via the **acquisition** of other retail companies. E.g. **Seiyu** in Japan, **ASDA** in the UK and **Bompreço** in Brazil.
3) Some Wal-Mart stores continue trading under their **own name**, e.g. ASDA, while others are **re-branded** as Wal-Mart.
4) Wal-Mart **divides** its **labour** across different countries. Its headquarters are still in Arkansas, but most manufacturing is carried out where costs are **lower** (cheaper labour and resources), e.g. electronic goods are made in China and clothing is made in India.
5) Wal-Mart is starting to **expand** into **NICs** like India, which have huge **new markets**. For example, Wal-Mart and an **Indian** company called **Bharti Enterprises** are opening new retail outlets **together** in the **style** of Wal-Mart stores.

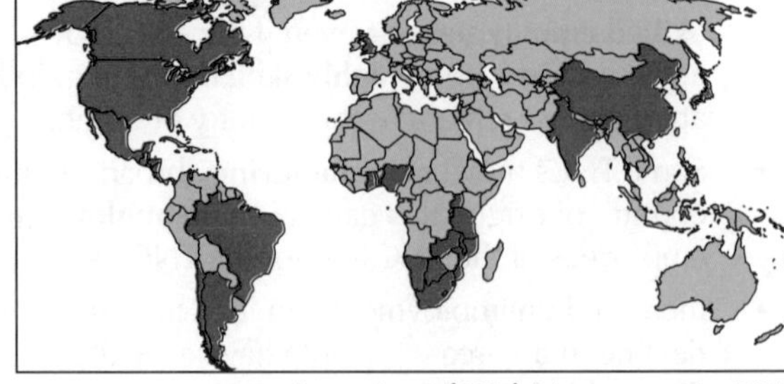

■ = Location of Wal-Mart stores in 2012

Wal-Mart® Helps to Accelerate Globalisation

Like other TNCs, Wal-Mart helps to **accelerate globalisation** — it **links** countries together through the flow of **money**, **people**, **trade** and **information**. It also brings the **culture** of its country of origin (**USA**) to other countries.

In the USA, Wal-Mart gives customers all they need in **one building** at **low cost**. They've **successfully** introduced this in other countries, e.g. ASDA now stocks more non-food items. This hasn't been **successful** in all countries. They're trying a **different approach** in **India** where people like to shop in **traditional markets** rather than supermarkets.

Although Wal-Mart is a global brand it's retained a **local approach** by buying **local companies**. Its stores **aren't** all exactly the **same**, though many of the **products** are, e.g. **George** clothing supplies ASDA in the UK and Wal-Mart in the USA. Selling the **same products** globally helps to create **common patterns of consumption** between different countries.

Wal-Mart® has Impacts in the USA...

Social

- Wal-Mart provides consumers with a **wide choice** of goods, e.g. the 'supercenter' stores sell things like garden furniture and car tyres as well as food and clothing.
- Many Wal-Mart stores are open **24 hours a day**, so consumers are able to shop **when they like**.
- Many jobs at Wal-Mart stores are **poorly paid** with **few benefits** (e.g. health care), so employees have to rely on **state benefits**. E.g. in California in 2004, it's estimated that the state paid $86 million to support Wal-Mart employees.
- Wal-Mart has been accused of having **poor working conditions**. E.g. in 2005 Wal-Mart had to pay $172 million compensation because employees had been denied meal breaks.

Economic

- **Employment** — each **new store creates jobs**, e.g. Vineland (USA) opened in 2009, creating 700 jobs.
- **Low prices** — Wal-Mart is one of the **cheapest supermarkets** in the USA.
- **Decline** in **manufacturing industry** — Wal-Mart buys a lot of products from suppliers outside the USA, e.g. electronic goods are made in China and Malaysia, which has caused a loss of manufacturing jobs in the USA.
- **Loss of local businesses** — Wal-Mart stores can cause smaller shops in the area to **shut down** as they can't **match** the low prices.
- This can cause the loss of **local jobs**, e.g. it is estimated that for every **100 jobs created** at a new Wal-Mart, **50 retail jobs are lost** from local businesses over the next 5 years.

Environmental

- Wal-Mart produces huge amounts of **greenhouse gases** but it has opened '**green stores**' that run on **renewable energy**.
- **Domestic stores** are often **very large and out-of-town** — building them takes up **large areas of land** and people **driving** to them **causes traffic** and **pollution**.

TNC Case Study — Wal-Mart

...and in its **Host** Countries

Because Wal-Mart is such a large TNC, it has a **lot of host countries**, with **stores** and **factories** based **all over the world**. It has **positive** and **negative** impacts on these host countries:

Economic

- Wal-Mart creates lots of jobs in **construction**, **manufacturing** and **retail services**. E.g. in Mexico, Wal-Mart employs over 209 000 people.
- **Local companies** and **farmers** supply goods to Wal-Mart. E.g. in Canada, Wal-Mart works with over 6000 Canadian suppliers, creating around $8 billion of business for them each year.
- **Local suppliers** to Wal-Mart may be able to expand their business by starting to **export** their goods to Wal-Mart stores in other countries.
- Wal-Mart has been criticised for forcing its suppliers to accept **low prices** for their products.
- **Local companies suffer** in **competing** with Wal-Mart. Wal-Mart stores cause **smaller shops** in the area to **shut** — they **can't compete** with the **low prices** and **range of products** on sale.
- People from the host country spend their money in the Wal-Mart stores, but **most** of the **profits** are sent back to the **USA** rather than contributing to the host country's economy.

Environmental

- Wal-Mart invests in **environmentally friendly technologies** and **sustainable development**. E.g. in Puerto Rico, 23 Wal-Mart stores are having solar panels fitted on their roofs to generate electricity.
- Wal-Mart stores use **large areas of land** for factories and stores. For example, the largest Wal-Mart store in Hawaii covers over **29 000 m^2**.

Wal-Mart might have low prices but Glenda's customers receive a unique shopping experience.

Social

- Wal-Mart offers **skilled jobs** in **less developed countries**. E.g. all the Wal-Mart stores in China are managed by local people, not by candidates from the USA.
- In its poorest host countries, working for Wal-Mart can offer a **more reliable** wage than other jobs, e.g. subsistence farming.
- **Working conditions** may be **poor**. For example, some Wal-Mart suppliers have **long working hours** — Beximco in Bangladesh supplies clothing to Wal-Mart and although Bangladesh has a **maximum 60 hour working week**, it's claimed that Beximco employees **regularly work 80 hours** a week.
- Wal-Mart **donates** hundreds of millions of dollars to improve things like **health** and the **environment** in countries where it operates. E.g. in 2008, Wal-Mart in Argentina **donated $77 000** to local projects focusing on reducing hunger, and supported **29 soup kitchens** feeding nearly **12 000 people** across the country.

Practice Questions

Q1 Explain one way in which Wal-Mart has accelerated globalisation.

Q2 Give three social impacts that Wal-Mart has had on the USA.

Exam Questions

Q1 The map shows the location of the operations of a TNC that makes designer sportswear. Describe and comment on the distribution shown. [7 marks]

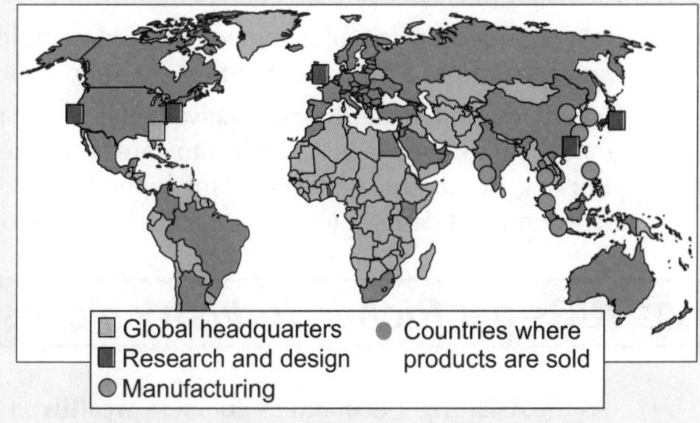

Q2 With reference to at least one example, assess the impacts TNCs have on their countries of origin and their host countries. [8 marks]

Is it a bird? Is it a plane? Nope it's yet another Wal-Mart...

Wal-Mart is a great example of a TNC that has grown all over the world. Whatever you choose as your case study for a TNC, make sure you pick up lots of facts and details to use in the exam — that's the whole point of case studies. Most of the positive and negative impacts for TNCs will be the same, but the specifics will be <u>different</u>. There's nothing for it but to learn, learn, learn. Fun, fun, fun...

Newly Industrialised Countries (NICs)

Newly Industrialised Countries are exactly what it says on the tin...

NICs are Countries that have **Recently Undergone Rapid Industrialisation**

1) NICs are countries that are **rapidly getting richer** as their economies change from being based on **primary industry** (e.g. agriculture) to **secondary industry** (e.g. manufacturing) and in some cases to **tertiary industry** (e.g. IT services).
2) **Hong Kong**, **Singapore**, **South Korea** and **Taiwan** were the first generation of NICs. They began to rapidly industrialise in the 1960s, and were later nicknamed the **Asian Tiger** economies (see below).
3) The Asian Tigers have since become **more wealthy** and **developed** — many people **no longer** consider them to be NICs.
4) In 2012, the countries that most people considered to be NICs were Mexico, Brazil, South Africa, Turkey, India, China, Malaysia, the Philippines and Thailand.

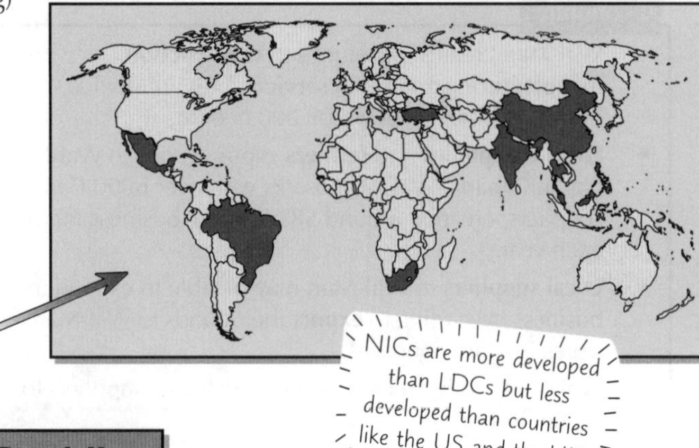

NICs are more developed than LDCs but less developed than countries like the US and the UK.

The **Asian Tiger Economies** grew very **Rapidly**

1) An **important** factor in the growth of the Asian Tigers was **investment** from **TNCs**.
2) **TNCs** (particularly from Japan) set up the **manufacturing** parts of their business in the Asian Tigers because there was:

- A **cheap** workforce.
- **Low cost** and **availability** of raw materials and land.
- A reasonable standard of **infrastructure**, e.g. roads and ports.
- Favourable **government policies**, e.g. subsidies or grants to attract investment.
- **Reduced trade tariffs**, making importing and exporting cheaper.
- Less strict **environmental**, **labour** and **planning** laws than in developed countries.
- **Expanding domestic markets** — the populations of the NICs were becoming wealthier so the **demand** for material goods within the NICs was **increasing**.

3) The first manufacturing industries had **low production costs** (cheap raw materials and low technology production) and were **labour intensive**, e.g. manufacturing toys.
4) As manufacturing became **successful**, companies invested in **developing** the industries, e.g. improving **technology** to make the manufacturing process more **efficient**. Manufacturers then started to produce **higher value goods** that were more **expensive to make** but more **profitable when sold**. For example, Hong Kong started manufacturing electronic goods.
5) The Asian Tigers became **specialised** in these industries — the workforce became **highly educated** and **skilled**.
6) The continued success of manufacturing led to **rapid economic growth** and **development**, e.g. Hong Kong's GNI per capita grew from $1800 in 1973 to $32 950 in 2008.
7) There have been **benefits** and **disadvantages** of this rapid growth. The **wealth** and **living standards** of the population have generally **improved** (e.g. better health care and access to education). However in some places working conditions are **poor** (e.g. South Korea has one of the highest accident at work rates in the world), and rapid industrialisation has caused **environmental damage** (e.g. Victoria Harbour in Hong Kong is badly polluted).

As **NICs** get **Richer**, **Industry** moves to **Cheaper Places**, **Creating New NICs**

1) As the Asian Tiger economies got more **wealthy**, it became more **expensive** to produce things there, e.g. because wages became higher.
2) To continue keeping costs **low**, the TNCs began to **move** their production to other, **less developed** countries, e.g. Malaysia, Thailand and the Philippines.
3) Also, **new TNCs** grew out of the Asian Tiger economies, e.g. Samsung originated in South Korea. These TNCs set up their manufacturing in less developed countries as well.
4) The growth of manufacturing into **less developed countries** from both new and established TNCs created a **second wave** of NICs.

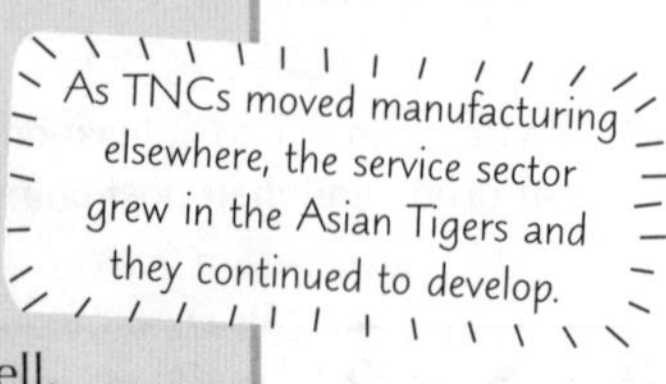

Newly Industrialised Countries (NICs)

China is a Rapidly Growing NIC

1) Since the 1970s there has been **rapid economic growth** in China — GNI per capita rose from around $180 in 1978 to $2940 in 2010 with a growth rate of around 10% a year.
2) Until 1978, the government **controlled** all of China's productive assets (e.g. agricultural land, mines and factories). Since 1978, a number of **economic reforms** and changes in **government policy** have led to economic growth:

- Encouraging **imports** and **exports** by reducing tariffs and taxes — exports rose 19% per year between 1981 and 1994.
- Encouraging the growth of **private business**, e.g. agriculture was partly privatised, allowing farmers to sell their own produce (rather than giving it to the state to sell).
- **Foreign investment** was encouraged — **special economic zones** were set up where foreign companies would receive tax breaks if they invested in manufacturing (e.g. by building factories).
- There was greater **investment** in **education** to create a workforce that is more attractive to TNCs.
- There was greater **investment** in **infrastructure** to make it easier for manufacturers to operate.
- In 2001 China joined the **World Trade Organisation**. This further opened China's markets to foreign investors and allowed Chinese businesses to export more easily.

3) As a result of these reforms (and the large supply of **cheap labour**), both **Chinese** businesses and **foreign TNCs** invested in manufacturing in China.
4) Manufacturing industries (e.g. textiles, toys, electronics, cars) **boomed**, which brought **rapid** and **continuing** economic growth for the whole country.
5) This growth has led to increased **wealth** and **improved living standards** in China.
6) However, there have been **negative consequences** of this rapid industrialisation:

- A wider **gap** between the rich and the poor. Much of the development has been in big **cities** along China's coast (where it's easiest to import and export goods), leaving the **agricultural interior** of the country relatively **poor**.
- **Environmental problems**, e.g. air pollution and acid rain in industrial areas because of increased emissions.
- **Working conditions** are poor in some areas. E.g. in 2010, over 130 workers were injured by a toxic chemical at a factory in Suzhou (near Shanghai) making products for Apple Inc.

Some NICs have Developed into Service Centres

1) Many service industries such as **financial services** (e.g. banks and insurance companies), **IT services** (e.g. software development) and **sales services** (e.g. marketing) have become **globalised** (see p. 109).
2) Because many services can be located **anywhere** in the world, the economic growth in some **NICs** (e.g. India, see next page) is based on investment in **service industries** (rather than manufacturing) by TNCs. Here are a few things that make some NICs attractive to investment in services:

- They have a **skilled**, **educated workforce**, particularly in terms of technically skilled workers (e.g. computer programmers) or workers that speak different languages (e.g. to work in international call centres).
- **Low labour costs**, especially of skilled workers compared to more developed countries.
- Good **communications** links, e.g. improved telephone networks and internet availability.
- Favourable **government policies** that attract businesses.
- Expanding **domestic markets** — as wealth increases there is a demand for more services, e.g. advertising, personal financial services and the media.

Skilled... educated... I'm good looking too by the way.

Newly Industrialised Countries (NICs)

India's Growth has been Based on Service Industries

1) There has been **rapid economic growth** in India in recent years, e.g. the economy has grown by an average of 7% per year since 1997.
2) In the 1990s India made **economic reforms** to reduce barriers to trade and encourage Foreign Direct Investment. Unlike in other NICs though, growth has focused on **service industries** rather than manufacturing.
3) Growth in the service industries **succeeded** in India for a number of reasons:
   - There are plenty of **highly educated** and **technically skilled** workers, e.g. at present, around 3 million people graduate from Indian universities every year, including 500 000 engineering graduates.
   - English is **widely spoken** and **understood** — this is important for many TNCs from English-speaking countries, e.g. they can establish customer service call centres in India.
   - **Low labour costs.**
   - There is an extensive **communications network**, e.g. for telephones and the internet.
4) There are two main ways the service industry has grown in India:

1 **Local companies** in the **service industries** (e.g. IT services) grew as they **supplied foreign TNCs**.

- In the 1980s and 1990s, some young Indian **IT professionals** migrated to the UK or US to work for western companies. When they came back to India, they understood the **IT needs** of more developed countries, and set up their own businesses to **supply** those needs.
- The **low cost of labour** in India meant that these Indian companies could provide the same service as their competitors in developed countries, but at a **lower price**.
- As the service industries grew in India, more and more western TNCs began to **outsource** (give contracts to outside businesses rather than do the work themselves) to Indian companies because it was **significantly cheaper**.

2 **TNCs** relocated **service areas** of their business to India (e.g. telephone call centres).

- The availability of a **skilled**, **English-speaking** workforce means India can offer a range of other office-based services (so called 'back-office functions') to foreign TNCs, e.g. customer service call centres.
- By moving their services to India, TNCs can save a lot of money — the average salary in an Indian call centre in 2003 was **£1200 a year** compared to **£12 500 a year** in the UK.
- Other examples of services transferred to India include **IT technical assistance** and **financial administration**. E.g. KPMG is a financial consultancy TNC. It employs people in ten cities in India, including Delhi and Mumbai.

5) The service sector has become an **important** part of the Indian economy — in 2011 it accounted for around 56% of GDP.
6) The growth of service industries in India has increased **wealth** and **employment** and improved **living standards**.
7) However the growth of the service industries has had **negative** impacts too:
   - A large proportion of the growth is from foreign investment by TNCs so the **profits leave the country**.
   - The benefits and employment opportunities are mostly only available to the **educated middle classes**, which increases the **poverty gap** between them and the lower classes.

Practice Questions

Q1 Which countries are the Asian Tiger economies?

Q2 Give three reasons why NICs attract manufacturing industries.

Q3 Give two reasons why India has experienced growth in the service sector.

Exam Question

Q1 With reference to one or more countries you have studied, explain the economic growth of NICs. [10 marks]

Awww, I really love Newly Industrialised Countries — they're just so NICe...

You like them, I like them and examiners really like them. Your exam board thinks NICs are the bee's knees, so make sure you learn all the stuff on these pages, then when you write a fabulous answer in your exam you'll be the bee's knees too...

Growth in the 21st Century

Economic growth is a continuous process, so don't think for a second that it'll stop in the 21st century...

New Markets are Emerging

1) The opening up of **new markets** is an important factor driving economic growth in the 21st century.
2) **New** (or **emerging**) **markets** are countries which are **opening up** to international trade and investment, e.g. by removing trade barriers such as tariffs. Examples of new markets include **NICs** (e.g. China, India and Brazil), wealthy **oil-producing** countries (e.g. the United Arab Emirates (UAE) and Saudi Arabia) and countries that have recently shifted from a closed market to an **open market** (e.g. Russia).
3) Some new markets, e.g. China, India and Brazil, have very **large populations**. As these countries **develop** and become more **open** to **international trade**, the **wealth** of their populations increases.
4) This creates a **growing demand** in these countries for **material goods**, e.g. luxuries such as electronic goods and cars, and **services**, e.g. entertainment and leisure facilities such as restaurants and cinemas.
5) This has allowed **more developed countries** such as the UK to grow economically — new markets provide opportunities for companies from these countries to increase profits.
6) New markets are increasingly important for the **global economy**, e.g. China has been responsible for 20% of global economic growth since 2000. As new markets become more and more important in world trade and investment, some people think the balance of **world power** could move **away** from North America and Europe into **new market countries**.

New Technologies give Opportunities for Investment

1) **New technologies**, especially in IT and communications (e.g. the internet), have also been one of the main driving forces behind **world economic growth** in recent years.
2) New technologies have led to **growth** in many areas of the world economy. E.g. improved computer hardware such as **CAM** (Computer Aided Manufacturing) has increased **manufacturing efficiency** — work done by computers and robots is faster and more consistent than people doing the same job.
3) Huge profits have been made from the **production** of new technologies and their **sale** and **distribution** to existing and new markets, e.g. laptops, tablet computers and smartphones.
4) There are high levels of **investment** in **creating** new technologies (e.g. 3D televisions), which creates growth in areas such as research and development.
5) There are many new technologies currently **being developed** that could create **more economic growth** in the future, e.g. wireless power transmission, robotics (e.g. the automation of transport) and new energy sources (e.g. fusion reactors).

Mitch wasn't interested in new technology. He had his reliable old desktop and that was just fine thank you very much.

Practice Questions

Q1 What is a new market?

Q2 Give three examples of new markets in the 21st century.

Q3 Give three examples of new technologies in the 21st century.

Exam Question

Q1 Outline the impact of new markets and new technologies on global economic growth in the 21st century. [8 marks]

Maybe in a few years time we'll all be flying to school...

Sadly this book doesn't have any extra technological functions — it won't play music, show videos or text your friends, but it will help you pass your exam. All you have to do is read the stuff on this page again and again until it's as fixed in your head as your smartphone is in your pocket. Just make sure your phone isn't still fixed in your pocket when you go into your exam though.

Causes of Conflict

If you think that a thumb war with your brother is a serious conflict, then I'm afraid you've got a fair bit to learn...

Conflict is Disagreement between People

1) People often have **different interests**, **needs** and **points of view**.
2) This can lead to **disagreements** (**conflicts**).
3) Unless conflicts are **resolved** they can lead to **tension**, **violence** or **war** (see page 120).

No doubt about it, Petal and Bob were in serious conflict.

There are Many Causes of Conflict

Identity

1) **Identity** is the set of **characteristics** that makes **you who you are** — they might include **where you're from**, your **language**, your **religion** and your **culture**.
2) If **groups** of people have **different identities** it can lead to **conflict**. A common **reason** for conflict is the level of **power** and **independence** each group has — conflicts are often about **political** power and independence.
3) Identity conflicts can be caused by **nationalism**, **regionalism** and **localism**. **Nationalism** is having a strong identity related to the **country** you're from. **Regionalism** relates to a **regional identity** and **localism** relates to a **local identity**. For example:

A region is a large area within one or more countries (e.g. a county). A local area is a specific place (e.g. a village or a town).

- **Nationalism** — **Scottish nationalists** want Scotland to have **greater political independence** from the **UK**. In **1998**, some **powers** were given to a newly-created **Scottish parliament**, but nationalists still want **full independence** from the UK.
- **Regionalism** — in **France**, the **Mouvement Région Savoie** campaigns for Savoie and Haute Savoie (small administrative divisions) to come together as a **larger political region** within France. They used to make up the region of **Savoy**, and at present are part of the larger Rhône-Alpes administrative region.
- **Localism** — in 2012, a **holiday chalet** was proposed close to **Ullswater** (a lake in the Lake District, UK). This caused conflict locally with **environmental groups** who believed that the area should **remain undeveloped**.

Ethnicity

1) **Ethnicity** is a part of **identity**. It can include things you're born with (e.g. **nationality** and **race**) as well as things that are **passed down** from one generation to the next (e.g. **language**, **culture** and **religion**).
2) Your ethnicity **doesn't** have to be the **same** as your **nationality**. For example, people **born** in the **UK** have a **British nationality** but they can belong to many **different ethnic groups** (e.g. Black Caribbean, Indian, Chinese, etc.) Some people with a **mixed family background** belong to **more than one** ethnic group.
3) **Ethnic conflict** is conflict between **ethnic groups**. It can be the result of an ethnic group wanting **more political power**. Sometimes it can be the result of a **belief** that one ethnic group is **superior** to another.

For example, in **Rwanda** there's a long history of conflict between the **Tutsi** and **Hutu ethnic groups**. In **1994** this led to a **genocide** (the mass killing of people belonging to a particular national, ethnic, racial or religious group). Around **800 000 people** (mostly Tutsis) were **killed** (mostly by Hutus) within **100 days**.

Culture

1) **Culture** includes many things that relate to **how you live your life**, e.g. foods, customs, clothing, traditions, language, art, attitudes, beliefs and values.
2) For example, culture can be **linked** to **ethnicity** (e.g. African culture), **religion** (e.g. Jewish culture), **gender** (e.g. male or female culture), **age** (e.g. youth culture) or **where you live** (e.g. urban or rural culture).
3) **Cultural differences** can result in **conflicts** — especially when people from different cultures don't fully **understand** or **respect** each other's differences.

For example, **whale meat** is considered to be a **traditional food delicacy** in **Japan**. This causes **conflict** with people who are worried about whales becoming **extinct** because **too many** are being caught.

Causes of Conflict

Resources

Conflicts can occur when people are **competing** for the same **resources**, such as:

1) **Territory** — e.g. **sovereignty** (authority) over the **Falkland Islands** in the South Atlantic Ocean has been **disputed** for a long time. In **1982 Argentina** and the **UK** fought over the islands in the **Falklands War**.
2) **Water** — e.g. the **Nile River** is a source of water for **10 countries** in North East Africa. There's conflict between the **downstream countries** (Egypt and Sudan) that use **most** of the **water**, and the **upstream countries** (including Uganda, Rwanda, Ethiopia and Tanzania) that **want to use more water**.
3) **Buildings** — e.g. the **Dome of the Rock** in **Jerusalem** was constructed by **Muslims** on the site of a **Jewish Temple** in the 7th Century. There's been a long conflict over the Dome, as it is **important** to **both religious groups**. Non-Muslims currently have limited access to the Dome and items such as Jewish prayer books are banned.
4) **Oil** — e.g. there's been a conflict between **Russia** and **Norway** over polar oil rights for over 40 years. Recently the countries made an **agreement** that **divided** the **Arctic Ocean** into **zones** where each country can **extract oil**.

Ideology

1) An **ideology** is a **set of ideas** about how **society** should be. For example, an ideology might include ideas about the **form of government**, **economic system**, **education system**, **social welfare system**, **health care system**, **justice system** and **environment**.
2) Groups of people with **different ideologies** can have different ideas that can result in **conflicts**.

For example, the governments of **North Korea** and **South Korea** have different ideologies, which have led to a long history of conflict. **North Korea** has an **authoritarian government** (all political power is held by a few people) and a **communist economic system** (property and production is controlled by the government). **South Korea** has a **democratic government** (there are several political parties and elections) and a **capitalist economic system** (property and production is privately controlled).

*Usually There **Isn't** Just a **Single Cause** of **Conflict***

Most conflicts **don't** just have a single cause — they actually have a **mixture** of **some** (or **all**) of these causes.
For example, the causes of the **war** between **Iran** and **Iraq** between 1980 and 1988 included:

- **Resources** — there was conflict over **control** of the **Shatt al-Arab** (the **river** that forms the **boundary** between Iran and Iraq). Both countries were also **major oil producers** — this led to **economic competition** between the two.
- **Identity** — the **religion** of Iran was mainly the **Shia** branch of Islam, and the leaders of Iraq followed the **Sunni** branch of Islam.

Practice Questions

Q1 What is conflict?

Q2 What is meant by nationalism?

Q3 Give an example of regionalism.

Q4 Give an example of an ethnic conflict.

Q5 What is ideology?

Exam Question

Q1 Describe how resources can be a cause of conflict. [8 marks]

Look, we can argue over these pages forever...

...but there'll still be lots of stuff on them to learn. Looking at this list of things to disagree about, it's amazing anyone's speaking to each other at all. It's important to realise that conflict doesn't always have to end in wars and violence — many conflicts are resolved by peaceful protests and discussion. In fact, you'll find lots more about that just over the page...

Characteristics and Resolution of Conflict

You may think that conflict is part of everyday life... well, you'd be right. Don't panic though, it can all get sorted in the end.

Conflict can be ***International, National, Regional*** or ***Local***

Conflicts occur on **different scales** — from small **local disputes** to large-scale **international wars**:

- **International level** conflicts involve **more than one country**, e.g. the **Iran-Iraq war** from 1980 to 1988 (see page 119).
- **National level** conflicts occur within **one country**, e.g. the conflict that began in **Syria** in March 2011 has been fought between the **authoritarian government** and **anti-government** forces who want **democracy**.
- **Regional level** conflicts occur within a region of one or more countries, e.g. in the **Kunar Province** of **Afghanistan**, many rural communities rely on **mountain springs** for **water**. These springs occasionally run **dry**, which can lead to **tension** between the communities as they **compete** for **water resources**.
- **Local level** conflicts occur within **small areas of a country**, e.g. in **2002** a plan to build 27 **wind turbines** on the **Isle of Skye** was approved. Many locals were concerned the wind farm would create **noise pollution**, harm the **tourist industry** and pose a threat to **golden eagles**. Local people who were campaigning **against** the wind farm had their property **vandalised** by people who **supported** the wind farm.

Conflict is ***Expressed*** in ***Many Different Ways***

1) **Non-violent** conflicts **don't** involve **violence** (no, really). For example:
   - **Political activity** includes supporting, opposing or creating a political party.
   - **Debate** is formal discussion to exchange opinions — and it often ends in a vote to make decisions.
   - **Boycotts** involve refusing to do something (e.g. refusing to buy a product).
   - **Strikes** involve refusing to work.
   - **Protests** and **demonstrations** involve groups of people publicly making their opinions heard and drawing attention to issues. They include protest marches (walking through areas) and picketing (gathering in one place).
2) **Terrorism** involves using violence to **intimidate people** — usually with the aim of achieving a **political goal**.
3) **Insurrection** is an organised **rebellion** with the aim of **overthrowing** a government. Insurrection **often** (but not always) involves **violence**.
4) **War** is a **violent conflict** between two or more groups.

And just at that moment, Jimmy decided to go on strike...

Groups that use violence to achieve a political goal might be considered terrorists by some people and freedom fighters by others. These groups are sometimes called 'militant groups' — it's a more neutral term.

There are Lots of Ways to ***Resolve Conflict***

Negotiation

1) Negotiation involves **discussing** issues with the aim of producing an **agreement**.
2) Negotiation is used to try to resolve many **different kinds** of conflict — for example, **business** negotiations (businesses and suppliers may negotiate with each other to agree on prices) and **government** negotiations (community groups may negotiate with local government to agree on development plans for an area).
3) Negotiations can be **formal** or **informal**. They may involve **trained negotiators** acting on behalf of a group (e.g. a lawyer may represent a group in legal negotiations).

Diplomacy

1) **Diplomacy** is **negotiation** between countries. It usually involves **trained negotiators** called **diplomats** or **ambassadors**.
2) Most countries have a **diplomatic service** to maintain **international relations** and negotiate **agreements** (e.g. trade agreements), **alliances** (e.g. political alliances where governments work together to solve problems) and **peace treaties** (e.g. to prevent or resolve violent conflicts).
3) **Cultural differences** (e.g. diplomats from different countries following **different rules** and **methods** of discussion, or having **different negotiation styles**) may affect diplomacy, so diplomats are **trained** to act reasonably and follow certain **rules of behaviour** — so they don't cause **offence**.

Characteristics and Resolution of Conflict

Mediation

1) **Mediation** involves the groups at conflict meeting with a mediator (an **independent third party**).
2) Mediators aim to make sure groups **listen to** and **understand each other**. They try to find ways of reaching an **agreement**.
3) **All sorts** of conflicts involve mediators — from **local disputes** to **international disagreements**.
4) Mediators of **international conflicts** include **countries** (e.g. Norway mediated the Sri Lankan Civil War), **non-government organisations** (e.g. 'International Alert' is a mediator in Liberia) and **inter-government organisations** (e.g. the UN is a mediator in the Middle East).

Planning Laws can Help Resolve Conflicts Over Local Resources

1) **Proposed developments** (building projects) often cause conflict over **available space** and **local resources**.
2) When a development is proposed, **planning officers** first make sure that the development **sticks to planning laws**. If it doesn't, they can ask for the proposal to be **changed**.
3) Then, **planning committees** discuss the proposals. They must consider:
   - The views of **all** of the **interested parties**. This often involves the **people** or **organisation** that made the proposal, and the **local community** who may be affected by the plans.
   - Whether the **gains** from the development **outweigh** the **negative impacts** it may cause.
   - Whether the proposed development has **wider benefits** outside of the local area (e.g. developing an industrial plant in an area can be good for other companies who will supply materials and components to the plant).
4) The committees take all of these factors into account and then make a **decision** about the proposed development. The plans may be **accepted** or **rejected**, or they may ask for the plans to be **modified** and resubmitted.
5) If plans are **rejected**, the developers can go through an **appeals process** against the decision.

The Newbury Bypass (see next page) is an example of a proposal with positive and negative impacts.

Conflict Resolution May Not Make Everyone Happy

Unfortunately, **not everyone** can **win** all the time when it comes to conflict resolution.
There are **three** possible outcomes when a conflict is resolved:

- a **win-lose outcome** (one side gains while the other loses).
- a **win-win outcome** (both sides gain).
- a **lose-lose outcome** (both sides lose out).

For example, a conflict about **trade** between two countries could result in a **win-win outcome** (e.g. a trade agreement that benefits both countries), a **win-lose outcome** (e.g. a trade agreement that involves applying taxes that benefit one country and penalise another) or a **lose-lose outcome** (e.g. trade sanctions are applied that reduce trade between the countries).

Practice Questions

Q1 What is a national level conflict?

Q2 Give three examples of how non-violent conflicts can be expressed.

Q3 What is insurrection?

Q4 What is a win-win outcome when a conflict is resolved?

Exam Question

Q1 Outline the different ways to resolve a conflict. [8 marks]

When it comes to diplomacy, it's best not to say exactly what you think...

Oh dear, conflict resolution is tricky stuff — the problem is that everyone tends to have very strong views and no one wants to lose. Think about how tricky things can get between football fans on a Saturday evening — scale it up a few thousand times and you've got some idea of how difficult things can be when whole countries are in conflict.

Local Resource Conflict Case Study — Newbury Bypass

Ah, the Newbury Bypass case study — a staple component of any decent Geography course...

*The **Newbury Bypass** was Proposed to Solve **Traffic Problems***

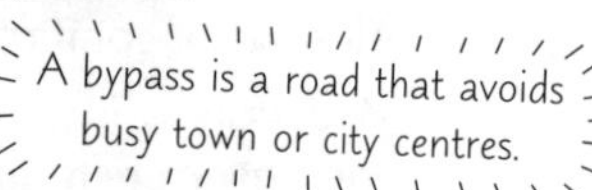

1) In the 1980s the **volume of traffic** passing through **Newbury** in Berkshire was around **50 000 vehicles per day** and **congestion** was a serious **problem** (even though Newbury already had a bypass called the A34).
2) In **1982** four possible routes for a **new bypass** to reduce traffic through the town centre were **proposed**.
3) A **public consultation** was undertaken which included **exhibitions** of the possible routes as well as the distribution of **brochures** and **questionnaires**.
4) In **1984** the UK Government's **Department of Transport** announced its recommendation of the **western route** — this would involve building an additional **13.5 km long** section of the **A34** to bypass the town.

*There Were Many **Objections** to the **Proposal***

1) Many local people believed the bypass **wouldn't solve** the **traffic problems**, partly because **a lot** of the traffic was **local** (travelling within the Newbury area). They thought that **other methods** could solve the traffic problems, e.g. traffic calming measures, bus lanes, and park and ride schemes.
2) There were many **environmental concerns** over the **route** and its **construction**. For example:
   - The proposed route crossed **three Sites of Special Scientific Interest** (SSSIs) — Snelsmore Common, the River Kennet and the River Lambourn.
   - It crossed **six county wildlife sites** and the Rack Marsh **nature reserve**.
   - **10 000 trees** would be felled.
   - The **habitats** of protected species such as the **dormouse** and the rare **Desmoulin's whorl snail** would be **destroyed**.
3) The bypass also crossed two **civil war battle sites** and 12 **archaeological** sites.

Newbury, Berkshire

*People **Campaigned Against** the **Bypass** in Different Ways...*

- A group of **local residents** formed the Society for the Prevention of the Western Bypass (SPEWBY). They submitted a **report** to the public consultation in 1982 which described the case against the western bypass, and they also **raised public awareness** of the case using the media.
- In 1994 some local residents formed the **Third Battle of Newbury Group**. This group gained the support of **national organisations** including Friends of the Earth, WWF® and Greenpeace. They raised awareness of the case **nationally**, and got many people across the country to **write protest letters** to the **government**.
- This group also made **formal complaints** to the **EU commission** — they claimed that the **UK government** was **breaking European laws** by approving the bypass without doing an **Environmental Impact Assessment** (EIA). However, **no laws** were **broken** because the bypass was proposed just **before** the law about EIAs was made.
- **Direct action protests** began in **1994**. **Protesters** from all over the country began to set up **camps** along the **route** of the bypass. Some built **tree houses** and others lived in **tents**. There were a few incidents of criminal damage and violence, but the protests were **mostly peaceful**.
- By **February 1996** there were **hundreds of people** in over **30 camps**. Protestors tried to **stop work** to clear the bypass route by **living in the trees**, digging and living in **tunnels**, and **blocking** the path of **heavy machinery**.
- That month, the protest became the **biggest ever anti-road protest** in UK history — **8000 people** marched along 3 km of the route of the bypass.

*...But the **Bypass** Also Had **Supporters***

- A **large number** of local residents **supported** the building of the bypass and a group of them formed the **Newbury Bypass Supporters Association**. They gathered a **petition of 6000 signatures** of people who **supported** the bypass.
- The **four local councils** in the area **supported** the bypass (although some objections were expressed, e.g. Berkshire County Council's archaeological officer raised concerns about the route going through the Kennet River Valley SSSI).
- The **local MP** (David Rendel, a Liberal Democrat elected in 1993) was a **strong supporter** of the building of the bypass.

Local Resource Conflict Case Study — Newbury Bypass

A **Public Inquiry** and a **Review** Were Held

To try to resolve the conflict, the government held a **public inquiry** and a **review**.

1) The public inquiry was held in **1988**. This involved **147 witnesses** giving evidence to a **government appointed inspector**.
   - **Support** for the bypass was expressed by the **four councils** and the **Newbury Bypass Supporters Association**.
   - **Opposition** to the bypass was expressed by **SPEWBY**, a group of **local farmers**, a **parish council**, the **National Trust** (who owned one of the woodlands) and the **National Rivers Authority**.
2) In **1990**, following the inquiry, the **government** announced the bypass would **go ahead** despite the opposition.
3) The conflict continued, so in **1994** the transport minister announced a **review** by the **Highways Agency** where **alternatives** to the bypass would be considered. Again it was decided that the bypass would **continue**.

Work Began on the Bypass in **1996**

1) After the review, **preparations** to clear the bypass route **began**.
2) The **Highways Agency** obtained **eviction** orders to remove the direct action **protestors** from their camps. The evictions began in 1996.
3) Two **police forces** (Thames Valley and Hampshire), over **600 security guards** and professional **climbers** were used to remove the protestors and their camps.
4) It took around **five weeks** to evict all the protestors.
5) **Security costs** on the bypass reached over **£30 million** — originally only £7 million had been allocated for security.
6) Over **900 protestors** were **arrested**.

The **Bypass** was **Built** But the **Conflict** Goes on

Jonny protested by making the Newbury Bypass Bypass.

1) The bypass was **completed** in **1998** but the anti-bypass campaign continues and there have been several **reunion rallies** at Newbury.
2) Campaigners still work to **raise awareness** of the **negative impacts** of the bypass. E.g. some people say the bypass has actually **increased** the amount of traffic in the area.
3) There is ongoing **environmental assessment** of the impacts of the bypass. For example, **pollution** in habitats along the bypass route is **monitored**.
4) Although the bypass was built, the **anti-bypass campaign** had some **successes**:
   - The campaign highlighted **environmental issues**. As a result nearly **200 000 trees** and **shrubs** were planted and attempts were made to **relocate wildlife** such as dormice, snails, bats, slow worms, voles and badgers.
   - The campaign also **raised awareness** of the fact that road building may not be the solution to **traffic problems**. As a result, many new **road building schemes** were **scrapped**.

Practice Questions

Q1 What was the cause of the conflict in Newbury?

Q2 What groups were involved in the conflict?

Q3 Why did some people object to the bypass?

Q4 What was the outcome of the conflict?

Exam Question

Q1 Give an example of a conflict over a local resource you have studied and evaluate the processes which operated to resolve it. [10 marks]

If only they could have bypassed the conflict...

There's loads to learn here, I'm afraid — the Newbury bypass conflict is an example of a local dispute that just ran and ran. It became a national campaign and even made some of its main campaigners household names around the UK.

International Conflict Case Study — Gaza and the West Bank

This is the first of three case studies about international conflicts. Ready, get set, go.

Israel, the *West Bank* and *Gaza* Were Created from *Palestine*

1) **Palestine** was an area in the **Middle East** that used to cover the area that is now Israel, Gaza and the West Bank.
2) Historically, this area has been settled by both **Jews** and **Arabs**.
   - The **Jews** hadn't had their **own state** for around 2000 years.
   - They saw the **biblical land** of **Palestine** as their natural home.
   - Many Jews **set up communities** in Palestine in the early part of the 20th century. Jews also **fled Europe** and moved to Palestine around the time of **World War 2** (due to anti-semitism — the hatred of Jews).
   - Conflict developed between the **Jews** and the **Arabs** who lived there (called **Palestinians**) over who had the **right to the land**.

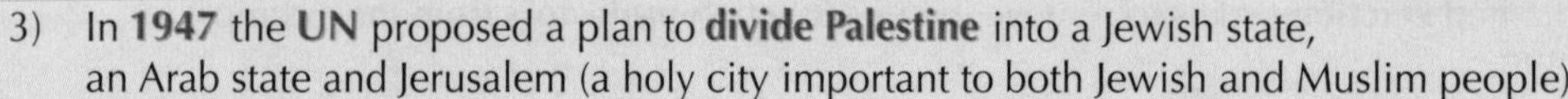

3) In **1947** the **UN** proposed a plan to **divide Palestine** into a Jewish state, an Arab state and Jerusalem (a holy city important to both Jewish and Muslim people).

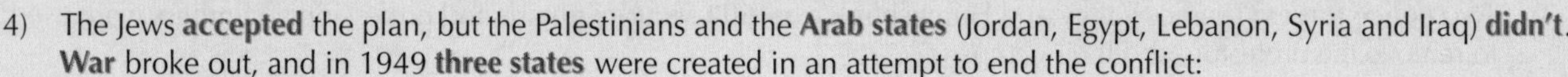

4) The Jews **accepted** the plan, but the Palestinians and the **Arab states** (Jordan, Egypt, Lebanon, Syria and Iraq) **didn't**. **War** broke out, and in 1949 **three states** were created in an attempt to end the conflict:
   i) the **State of Israel** including Jerusalem (a national home for the Jewish people),
   ii) the **West Bank** (an Arab territory controlled by Jordan),
   iii) **Gaza** (an Arab territory controlled by Egypt).

As a result of the conflicts between 1947 and 1949, hundreds of thousands of Palestinians living in Israel became refugees and fled to the West Bank and Gaza.

5) Many Palestinians still **did not agree** with this solution. In the **1960s** the **Palestinian Liberation Organisation** (PLO) was formed with the aim of making the whole former area of **Palestine** an Arab state. An armed conflict began between the PLO and Israeli forces.
6) In response to attacks from the PLO, **Israel invaded** and **seized control** of the **West Bank** and **Gaza** in 1967.
7) **Conflict** between **Israelis** and **Palestinians** continued. E.g. in 1987 Palestinians began **demonstrating** against the Israeli occupation of the West Bank and Gaza in an uprising called the **First Intifada**.
8) There were peace talks in 1993 to end the First Intifada. They resulted in the **PLO** recognising **Israel's right to exist** and Israel giving **control** of the **West Bank** and **Gaza** to **Palestine**.
9) However, this **didn't end the conflict**. Between **2000** and **2005** there were more violent conflicts in a Second Intifada (Palestinian uprising against Israel).
10) In 2006, **elections** were held in Gaza and the West Bank — they were won by **Hamas**, a Palestinian group with a **history of violence** against Israel. They **refused** to accept Israel's right to exist and **fighting continued**.

The *Conflict* is *Ongoing*

1) There have been **many peace talks** to **try to resolve** the conflict, e.g. the 1993 peace talks (see above). These have been **mediated** by **countries** and **international organisations** including the **USA**, the **EU**, the **UN**, the **Arab League** and **Russia**.
2) Issues that are proving **hard to agree on** include:
   - **Control of Jerusalem** — e.g. some people are concerned that access to holy places may be restricted.
   - The **location of certain settlements** — e.g. some people would like Israeli settlements removed from Palestinian areas, and vice-versa.
   - The **rights of the Palestinian refugees** from the 1947-1949 conflicts (and their descendants) to return to Israel. This includes at least 4 million people currently living in refugee camps.
   - **Freedom of movement** of Palestinian people. E.g. the borders around Gaza are tightly controlled — Palestinian people are not allowed to pass freely into Israel or Egypt.
3) In **2010 new peace talks** began, mediated by the USA.

International Conflict Case Study — Gaza and the West Bank

The Conflict Over **Israel**, the **West Bank** and **Gaza** Has Had Many **Impacts**

Social Impacts

- **Hundreds of thousands** of people live at risk of **military attacks**.
- **Since 1948** there have been **tens of thousands** of **deaths** caused by the conflict. There were an estimated **50 000-100 000 military deaths** and **10 000-50 000 civilian deaths** between **1948** and **1997**.
- **Tens of thousands** of people have been **injured** as a result of the conflict.
- During the **1948 war**, around **700 000 Palestinians** were forced to leave their homes and become **refugees**. These people and their descendants (now at least 4 million people) still live in refugee camps (mostly in Jordan, Lebanon, Syria, the West Bank and Gaza).
- Some people have **human rights concerns**, e.g. over the treatment of civilians and political prisoners.
- There have been many **cultural losses**, e.g. places of worship have been destroyed (both Jewish synagogues and Muslim mosques).
- Many **unexploded land mines** litter the landscape. They pose a risk to civilians and livestock.

Environmental Impacts

- Large **military structures** have been **built** that have **affected the environment**. E.g. Israeli military bases and large security walls in the West Bank and Gaza have damaged agricultural land, affected drainage patterns and destroyed natural habitats.
- The **loss of agricultural land** has led to **overgrazing** in some areas, which has led to **desertification**.
- Some areas have been **damaged** and **polluted** by **explosions**, e.g. a wastewater plant bombed in 2009 contaminated water resources and the surrounding land.
- The **Mediterranean sea** is being **polluted** as 80 000 m^3 of partially treated or untreated **sewage** is being pumped out from the Gaza strip **every day** (caused by a lack of investment in infrastructure due to the ongoing conflict).

Economic Impacts

- It's difficult to estimate the cost of such a long conflict but it's likely to have cost many **trillions** of US$ since **1948**.
- The conflict has **hindered economic growth** in the region, e.g. because large amounts of money are spent on security instead of development.
- The **majority of Palestinians** live in **poverty** — around 40% are unemployed.
- Because the **Palestinians** have no country, they **can't trade internationally**.
- The **Palestinians** rely on large amounts of **international aid**. E.g. at least 4 million people currently living in refugee camps are supported by a UN refugee fund.

Practice Questions

Q1 What was Palestine divided into in 1949?

Q2 What is the PLO?

Q3 Who won the election in Gaza and the West Bank in 2006?

Q4 Give four social impacts of the conflict.

Exam Question

Q1 Describe the economic and environmental impacts of a major international conflict you have studied. [8 marks]

Hmm, Gazza and Jordan — what can go wrong...

You'll probably have heard about this conflict in the news, but you may not have known the social, economic and environmental impacts of it. Get those details learnt — it's all about using facts and figures to back up your point when it comes to case studies.

International Conflict Case Study — Afghanistan

Here's another case study about an international conflict — this one's about the ongoing war in Afghanistan.

There's a **History** of **Conflict** in **Afghanistan**

1) In **1979**, the **Soviet Union invaded Afghanistan** and supported the installation of a communist government.
2) At the time, the **US** was in a **conflict** with the **Soviet Union** — so the US began **funding** rebel groups opposed to the Soviet Union (the Mujahideen).
3) In **1989** the Soviet Union **left** Afghanistan — but **conflicts continued** between the Mujahideen and the government, and between different groups **within** the Mujahideen.
4) In **1996** the **Taliban** (one of the Mujahideen groups) took **control** of the **government**.
5) **Al-Qaeda** (an extreme Islamic group from the Middle East) had links with the Taliban and a base of operations in **Afghanistan**. In **1998**, the US launched **missile attacks** on bases that they believed were used by **Osama Bin Laden** (the leader of al-Qaeda).

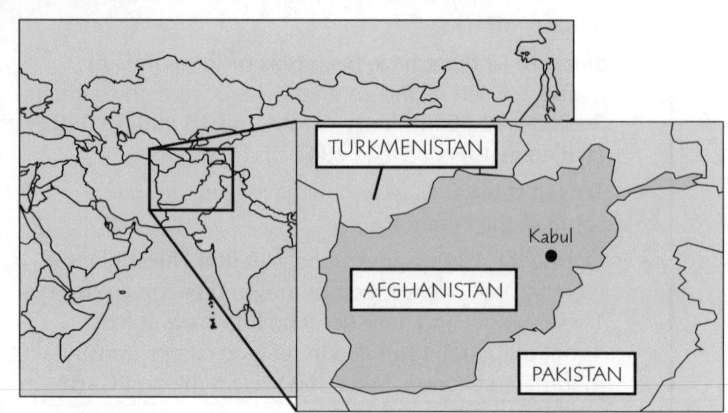

The **US Invaded** Afghanistan in **October 2001**

1) On **September 11th 2001** there was a **terrorist attack** in the **US** — hijacked planes were flown into the **World Trade Centre** and the **Pentagon**. The attacks are widely believed to have been carried out by **al-Qaeda**.
2) The **US** wanted to bring **Osama Bin Laden** to **trial** for the attack. They issued a series of **demands** to the Taliban government of **Afghanistan** (including the immediate handover of Osama Bin Laden), but they were **refused**.
3) In **October 2001** the **US invaded Afghanistan**. They were supported by an **international coalition** that included the UK, Canada, Australia, Germany and France, as well as an Afghan opposition force (the Northern Alliance).
4) The coalition wanted to **prevent further terrorist attacks**, so their **aims** in Afghanistan were:

    - To bring **Osama Bin Laden** (and other leading members of al-Qaeda) to **trial**.
    - To destroy **al-Qaeda**.
    - To ensure that Afghanistan could no longer be used as a **safe haven** for **terrorists**.

5) By **December 2001** the **Taliban** government had been **removed** from power and a **new government** had been set up. **US** and **coalition troops** remained in Afghanistan in conflict with al-Qaeda and Taliban forces.
6) In **2006 NATO** took over the command of the **US-led coalition force**, which included soldiers from more than 40 different countries.
7) On the **2nd May 2011**, a **US-led** operation stormed a compound in Pakistan and Osama Bin Laden was shot and **killed**. Both al-Qaeda and the Taliban vowed to **avenge** his death.
8) In **2012**, there were around **130,000** coalition troops still serving in Afghanistan.

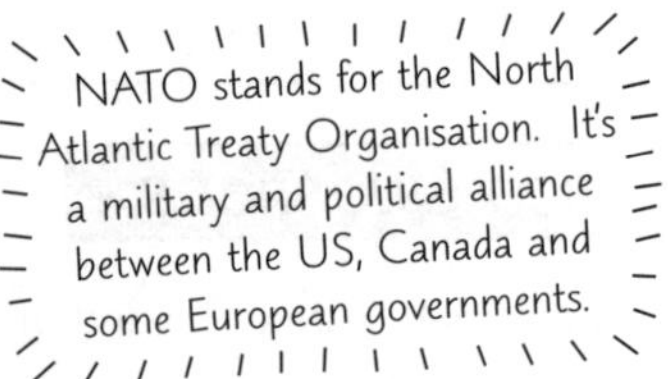

There's Lots of **Debate** About How to **Resolve** the **Conflict**

1) Many people think that **military action isn't** the **best way** to resolve the conflict — they want **diplomatic talks** that include the Afghan government, the Taliban, other groups in Afghanistan and the neighbouring countries.
2) Others think that **military action** is **necessary** to prevent civil war and to **prevent** the Taliban returning to **power**. Some believe that the Taliban would create a regime that abuses human rights.
3) In 2009 **President Obama** (of the US) described a **new strategy** in the war — sending **33 000 more US troops** to Afghanistan to **train** the **Afghan army** and **police forces**. The US and the UK plan to **fully withdraw** their troops from Afghanistan by the **end of 2014**.

International Conflict Case Study — Afghanistan

The War Has Had Many **Impacts**

Social Impacts

- An estimated **11 000 Afghan civilians** were **killed** between 2001 and 2009 — both the Taliban and the coalition troops were responsible for the deaths.
- **1832 coalition troops** were **killed** between 2001 and 2010 (including 1115 US troops and 300 UK troops).
- Many soldiers suffer from **Post Traumatic Stress Disorder** — an anxiety condition which can cause sleep problems and feelings of isolation.
- By 2010, an estimated **3 million refugees** had fled Afghanistan to neighbouring countries, e.g. Iran and Pakistan. Many ended up living in **refugee camps**. There was a **lack** of **basic supplies** (e.g. tents and food) for the refugees and there were outbreaks of **disease** within the refugee camps (e.g. cholera and tuberculosis).
- The ongoing conflict has contributed to widespread **poverty** and **malnutrition** in Afghanistan.
- The war also **prevented** the growth of **health** and **education** services (that were already limited before the conflict).
- The **availability** of **safe drinking water** has **decreased** due to damage to infrastructure and contamination — this has caused **health problems**.
- The presence and behaviour of **coalition troops** has caused **distress** to many people — for example, air strikes and night raids spread **fear**.
- **Many groups** in Afghanistan have been accused of **human rights abuses** — e.g. the Taliban, local security forces and US soldiers have all been accused of **torturing prisoners** and treating them inhumanely.
- There are **safety** and **security problems** in many areas — this can lead to high levels of crime.

Environmental Impacts

- **Explosives** have **polluted** the air, soil and water with chemicals that are **toxic** to both humans and wildlife.
- The area of Afghanistan covered by **forest** has **halved** during the last few decades of conflict. The forests have been cleared by **illegal logging** as well as logging for fuel and cooking purposes.
- **Water supplies** from rivers and groundwater have been **polluted** due to a lack of adequate sanitation and waste management. Years of conflict have **destroyed** much of the **infrastructure** and reduced the country's ability to **manage waste**.
- **Hunting** of wild animals for **meat** and **furs** has increased.

Economic Impacts

- **Many countries** are **paying** for the war — especially the **US** who had spent an estimated **$740 billion** by the end of 2010. The **UK** spent **£11.1 billion** on the war up to March 2010.
- Fears over **terrorist attacks** as a result of the war have led to **increased spending** on **security** in countries like the US and UK (e.g. on **airlines** and at large **political** and **public events**).
- The conflict has **prevented** the **economic growth** of **Afghanistan**. It's one of the **poorest countries** in the world and it relies heavily on **international aid**.
- **Rebuilding** the **infrastructure** of Afghanistan following the conflict will have a **high economic cost** — e.g. roads, water and communication infrastructure, health services, manufacturing and agricultural industries all need investment.

Practice Questions

Q1 When did the US invade Afghanistan?

Q2 Give two reasons for the US invasion of Afghanistan.

Q3 Give three environmental impacts of the conflict.

Exam Question

Q1 With reference to at least one case study, discuss the social impacts of international conflict. [10 marks]

So, Afghanistan — nope, nothing funny here at all...

Even though those lists of impacts are pretty long, you really need to store the lot in your memory so you can write a stonking answer in the exam. And that's well worth doing if you want your Geography teacher to be as proud as your Mum on results day.

International Conflict Case Study — Darfur

This is the last of the three case studies. Once again, get stuck in with learning those details.

Rebel Groups** Attacked the **Government in 2003

1) **Darfur** is a region in the west of **Sudan** in Africa.
2) For **many decades** there have been tensions and **conflicts** between **nomadic Arabs** in the region and **black African farmers** over land and grazing rights.
3) In **February 2003** rebel groups attacked government troops. The main rebel groups were the **Sudan Liberation Army** (SLA) and the **Justice and Equality Movement** (JEM). They accused the government of **oppressing black Africans** in favour of Arabs.
4) **Sudan's government** responded to the attacks using **official military** and **police forces**. A **war** began between the **government** and the **rebel groups**.
5) However, a **third faction** was also involved in the conflict — the **Janjaweed**. They are pro-government **nomadic Arabs**.
6) The **Janjaweed** have been accused of **murdering** black Africans and trying to **drive them out** of large areas. Some groups believe that **genocide** has taken place (the killing of people belonging to a particular national, ethnic, racial or religious group).
7) The Sudanese **government** has been accused of **financially supporting** and **working with** the Janjaweed — but the government **denies** this.
8) A **peacekeeping force** from the **African Union** entered the region in **2004** — but they had little success preventing conflicts.
9) The **UN** had tried to get peacekeepers into the region — but the **Sudanese** government initially **rejected** the offer. In **2007** they **accepted** and a combined **UN-African Union** peacekeeping force (called UNAMID) began working in the region.
10) The **conflicts** and the **accusations of genocide** have continued. In **2008** the International Criminal Court (ICC) issued an **arrest warrant** for **President Bashir** (the head of the government) for **war crimes** and **crimes against humanity**. He strongly **denies** the charges and the ICC has **no power** to arrest him unless he leaves Sudan.

As a result of a wider national conflict, Sudan was split into South Sudan and Sudan in 2011.

Libya
Egypt
DARFUR
Chad
SUDAN
Ethiopia
Central African Republic
SOUTH SUDAN

The African Union is a group made up of 54 African countries.

***Peace Deals** and **Ceasefires** Haven't Worked*

1) Since the conflict began many groups have helped to arrange **peace negotiations** — including the **African Union**, the **Arab League**, **Chad** and the **UN**.
2) In **May 2006** a **ceasefire** between the **government** and the **SLA** was agreed — but **JEM** rejected the deal.
3) In **February 2010** a **ceasefire** between the **government** and **JEM** was agreed. Shortly afterwards, JEM accused the government of **breaking** the **ceasefire** by carrying out air strikes and they **boycotted** further negotiations.
4) In **April 2010 elections** were held. **President Bashir** won but there were accusations of **fraud** and **election rigging**.
5) In **July 2011** the **government** signed a peace deal with the **LJM** (Liberation and Justice Movement) — a collection of rebel groups. Some refugees **left** refugee camps and began to **return** to villages in Darfur. However, JEM and the SLA **did not sign** the deal, and outbreaks of fighting have **continued**.

The **conflict in Darfur** was caused by disagreements over **local resources** (land and grazing rights). However, it's also part of a wider **national conflict** related to **political power**, **control of natural resources** (especially oil), and **religious and ethnic differences** between people in different parts of the country.

©iStockphoto.com/Claudia Dewald

A refugee camp in Sudan.

International Conflict Case Study — Darfur

The War Has Had Many ***Impacts***

Social Impacts

- An estimated **300 000 people** had been **killed** in the conflict by **2008** due to the combined effects of **war**, **famine** and **disease**.
- By 2010, **2.7 million people** had become **refugees** — many living in camps near Darfur's main towns. Around **200 000** of these **refugees** fled to neighbouring **Chad**, where they live in camps along the border.
- Many **villages** and **refugee camps** have suffered **violent attacks** involving murder, rape and theft.
- The murder of farmers and the destruction of farming communities has led to a **decrease in food production** in the region. As a result, lots of people have suffered from **malnutrition**.
- People living in refugee camps have **limited** access to **clean water** and **health facilities** (the camps are **massively overcrowded** so local resources cannot meet the demand).

Environmental Impacts

- **Desertification** (which causes land to become unsuitable for growing vegetation) is happening **around refugee camps**. Refugees are **stripping the land** of vegetation to use as fuel — the soil then becomes more **exposed** to wind and rain and is **eroded away**.
- Refugees are also putting **increased pressure** on **local resources** as they use up the available **firewood**.
- **Refugee camps** are **polluting water resources** (as they generally have poor waste disposal infrastructure).
- **Uncontrolled deforestation** is taking place as different groups participate in **logging** to **fund the conflict** and for **construction**. E.g. the UN estimate that 52 000 trees are being felled each year to be used in the production of bricks (wood is used as a fuel in brick kilns).
- **Wildlife** has been **killed**, **injured** and **disturbed** by weapons (including bombs).

Economic Impacts

- The **total cost** of the war to Sudan is difficult to estimate — it is likely to be many **billions of dollars**. This is especially damaging because Sudan is such a **poor country** (see p. 107) and this money could have been spent on **development**.
- The **trade of livestock** in Darfur is important to Sudan's economy. **Millions of pounds** of livestock have been lost due to the effects of conflict in the region.
- The conflict has **prevented** the **economic growth** of the region, e.g. productive farmland has been abandoned and many of the available natural resources haven't been developed.
- The conflict has contributed to widespread **poverty** and **slowed the development** of Sudan's **infrastructure**. **Rebuilding** the infrastructure that has been damaged during the conflict will also have a **high economic cost**, e.g. water infrastructure, health services and agricultural industries all need investment.

Practice Questions

Q1 Why did rebel groups first attack government troops?

Q2 Name the rebel groups involved in the conflict.

Q3 What has been done to attempt to resolve the conflict?

Q4 Give three social impacts of the conflict.

Exam Question

Q1 For an international conflict you have studied, examine the impacts of the conflict on the area involved. [40 marks]

... or here

These last few pages haven't really been the cheeriest, but then I don't suppose you read the conflict section for a bit of light-hearted jollity. If that's the kind of thing you're after, I can only recommend that you hire a bouncy castle.

Separatism

Not everyone wants to follow the crowd, you know. Some people are separatists...

Separatism Involves Breaking Up a Group

No amount of separatism could break up this group.

1) **Separatists** support the **separation** of a **smaller group of people** from a **larger group**.
2) The **groups** involved in separatist movements can **vary in size**. For example, the larger group could be a **single country** or **several countries**.
3) Separatism often involves **smaller groups** wanting **more political independence** from the larger group, so they can meet the needs of their people.
4) Separatism occurs because small groups feel **alienated**, **discriminated against** or **oppressed**. It can also occur if they feel they are at risk of **losing their identity**.
5) There are a number of **possible reasons** for these feelings:

- **Economic independence**. E.g. the state of Western Australia is rich in minerals such as iron ore. It accounts for a high percentage of Australia's GDP, but has a smaller population than the eastern states. Some people think that Western Australia would be much more wealthy if it was an independent country.
- **Historical allegiances**. E.g. Quebec is a province of Canada colonised by the French in the 17th century. It has a French speaking majority and a French-influenced culture. Quebec separatists want it to become a separate country.
- **Peripheral location**. E.g. Scotland and Wales are located away from the political centre of the UK (London), which can make some people living there feel that the government doesn't look after or understand the specific needs of the regions. Scottish and Welsh nationalists campaign for greater independence from the rest of the UK.
- **Religious differences**. E.g. India and Pakistan used to be one country. On the basis of the two main religions (Islam and Hinduism), it was split into an Islamic nation (Pakistan) and a Hindu nation (India) in 1947.
- **Cultural differences**. E.g. Chechen people mostly live in Chechnya — a region of the Russian Federation. They have a unique culture which has been shaped by living in isolated farming communities in a mountainous region. Chechen separatists want political independence from Russia.
- **Language differences**. E.g. Catalonia is a region of Spain with a unique language (Catalan) and culture. Catalan separatists want greater political independence.

GDP is the total value of the goods and services produced by a country in a year.

Separatism is almost always caused by a combination of several of these reasons.

Separatism Can Have Serious Consequences

The **consequences** of separatism can be **peaceful** or **non-peaceful**. For example:

PEACEFUL

1) **Establishing or maintaining a separate cultural identity**. E.g. the Bretons (people who live in the region of Brittany in France) maintain a separate culture to the rest of France through traditions, customs, festivals, foods and music.
2) **Language preservation**. E.g. the Welsh language is being preserved in several ways — a Welsh TV channel (S4C) was launched in 1982 and most road signs are in both languages. Laws made in the 1990s ensure that public sector literature is published in Welsh and English, and since 1999 it's been compulsory to teach Welsh in schools.
3) **Greater political independence**. E.g. devolution of the UK government in 1998 gave some political powers to the newly-created Scottish Parliament, National Assembly for Wales and Northern Ireland Assembly.
4) **Settlements that redistribute land, wealth and resources**. E.g. the Maori Party is a political party that seeks to support and protect the rights of the indigenous people of New Zealand. The Maori people lost a lot of land when Europeans began settling in New Zealand in the 18th century. Since the 1990s government negotiations have resulted in the Maori being given financial compensation and large areas of forest land.
5) **Civil disobedience** (refusal to obey certain laws or government demands). E.g. Lithuanian separatists in the 1980s ignored Soviet Union leaders and held mass meetings (rallies) and protests before gaining independence in 1990.

NON-PEACEFUL

1) **Terrorism**. E.g. the Baloch Liberation Army (BLA) is a separatist group that seeks to establish the independence of Balochistan (a region that spans parts of Pakistan, Iran and Afghanistan). The group has admitted using terrorist methods — such as bomb attacks in markets and on railway lines.
2) **Civil War**. E.g. the Sri Lankan Civil War (1983-2009) involved a separatist group (the Tamil Tigers) that wanted to establish an independent Tamil state. The military defeated the Tamil Tigers in 2009.
3) **Genocide**. E.g. Russia has been accused of committing genocide against the Chechen people.

Separatism

There's a **Separatist Movement** in the **Basque Country**

The Basque Country is a region that includes parts of **south western France** and **northern Spain**. Basque separatists want the **region** to become an **independent state**.

FRANCE

BASQUE COUNTRY

SPAIN

Basque Separatism has Many **Causes**

The Basque people have a **unique identity** which they want to **protect**:

- The Basque people have a **long history** going back to before Roman times.
- The Basque people have a **unique culture** and **language** that's different to **French** or **Spanish**.
- The language (**Euskera**) is one of the **oldest** in Europe and has **no clear links** with other **European languages**. Today, around **30%** of the 2.5 million Basque people speak the language.
- The Basque region occupies a **distinct geographical area** on the borders of **France** and **Spain**.

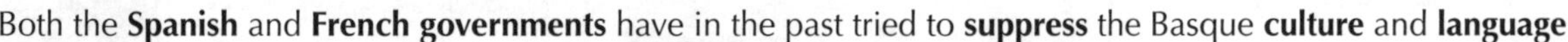

Both the **Spanish** and **French governments** have in the past tried to **suppress** the Basque **culture** and **language**.

There have been **Peaceful** and **Non-Peaceful Consequences**

PEACEFUL CONSEQUENCES

- The Basque people **preserve their culture** through traditions, clothing, foods, festivals, marches and public storytelling sessions.
- The **language** is being **preserved** through **school policies** and the **media**.
- **Political parties** (e.g. the Basque Nationalist Party) have formed — they aim to get **greater political independence** for Basque.
- **Some** political independence has been **gained**. **Areas of Basque** that are in **Spain** have their own **parliament** and **police force**, control over **education** and **collect** their own **taxes**. While some Basque separatists are happy with this, others want **full independence**.

NON-PEACEFUL CONSEQUENCES

- The **separatist group ETA** (Euskadi Ta Azkatasuna) has used **violence** in its campaign for independence, e.g. assassinations, sniper attacks and bomb attacks.
- It formed in **1959** to **oppose** a **dictatorship** in **Spain** that banned the Basque language and suppressed their culture.
- ETA have **killed over 800 people** since they formed, including policemen, politicians, journalists and businessmen.
- They were **most active** in the **1970s**. But **terrorist activities** have occurred in **recent years** — in **1997** ETA kidnapped and killed a politician and in **2006** they were responsible for a **bomb** in **Madrid Airport** that killed 2 people.
- In 2010, ETA declared a **ceasefire** and in 2011 it announced that it had decided to **end all armed activity**. However, ETA have **broken** ceasefires in the past and the Spanish government still want ETA to **disband** completely.

Practice Questions

Q1 What is separatism?

Q2 List three possible causes of separatism.

Exam Question

Q1 With reference to at least one case study, discuss the possible consequences of separatism. [10 marks]

They also preserve their culture through sport — Basquetball...

There are loads of examples of separatism out there. Although separatist movements can involve relatively small numbers of people, the consequences can be pretty big — just look at what's going on in the Basque Country.

The Challenge of a Multicultural UK

Over the years, there's been a flurry of people moving to the UK from all over the world, and there are lots of reasons why.

*The **UK** is a Fairly **Multicultural** Place*

1) A **multicultural society** contains people from many different **national**, **cultural**, **religious** and **linguistic** backgrounds.
2) The **UK** is an **example** of a multicultural society.

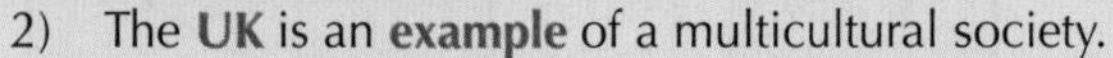

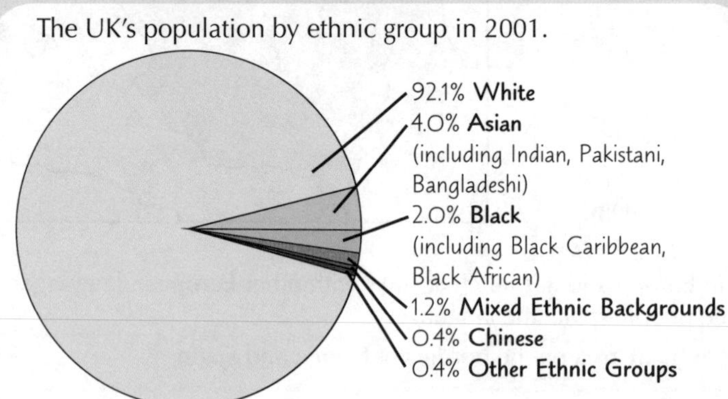

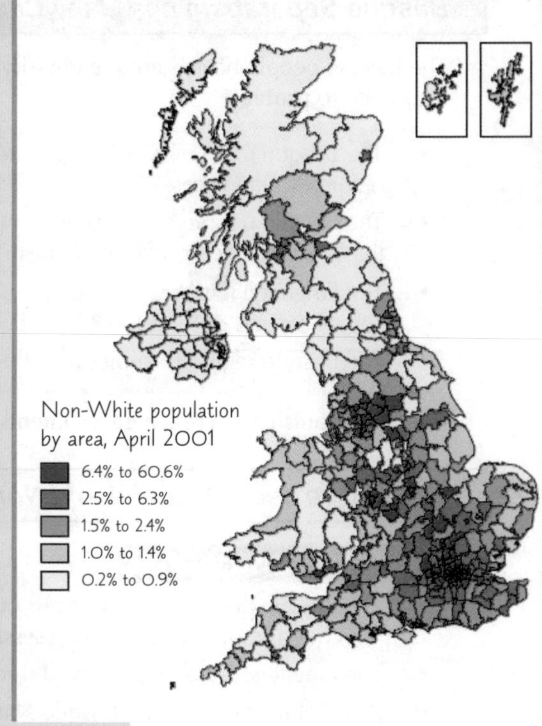

3) Ethnic groups **aren't evenly distributed** across the UK. For example:
   - **More** people from ethnic minority groups live in **England** than in **Scotland**, **Wales** or **Northern Ireland**.
   - **Ethnic minority groups** tend to live in **larger urban areas** such as London and Birmingham. E.g. 45% of the UK's ethnic minorities live in London, where they make up 29% of the population. But less than 4% of the UK's ethnic minorities live in the south west of England, where they make up only 2% of the population.
   - Different **ethnic minority groups** have **different distributions** — e.g. 78% of the UK's Black Africans and 54% of the UK's Bangladeshis live in London.

***Immigration** Has Been **Encouraged** In The Past*

The UK is a **multicultural society** because of **immigration**:

1) The **British Empire** existed from the **17th century** to the early **20th century**. During that time there was some **immigration** from British **overseas colonies** to the UK.
2) Between the **1940s** and **1960s** there were **large waves** of **immigration** to the UK:
   - Around **World War Two** there were **labour shortages** so the government **encouraged immigration**.
   - New **laws** allowed people from countries of the **former British Empire** to **live** and **work** in the **UK** without a visa. This included people from India, Pakistan, the Caribbean, South Africa, Kenya and Hong Kong.
   - As a result, many people came to the UK. For example, more than **60 000 Indians** and **Pakistanis** had moved to the **UK** by **1960**.
3) Since the **1960s** there have been other **waves** of immigration. For example:
   - In **1972** the **Ugandan dictator** General Idi Amin **expelled 80 000** African Asians from the country. Uganda had been part of the **British Empire** until 1962 so many Ugandans held **British passports**. **28 000** of those who were expelled came to the **UK**.
   - In the **1970s** and **1990s** many **Ethiopians** and **Somalians** came to the UK **fleeing civil war** in East Africa.
   - Since **2004** there has been an **increase** in immigration from **Eastern Europe** after several **new countries** joined the European Union. This is because **EU citizens** can live and work in **any EU country**.

The Challenge of a Multicultural UK

Most Immigrants Move to **Urban Areas**

Retail therapy — yet another reason to move to an urban area.

1) The vast **majority** of **immigrants** to the UK have settled in **industrial cities** and towns where there is a **demand for workers**. For example, in the 1950s and 1960s many immigrants moved to **Birmingham** (where there were jobs in **manufacturing** and **engineering** industries) and other cities and towns in the **Midlands** and **northern England**, e.g. Manchester, Liverpool, Nottingham, Leicester and Coventry.
2) **Few** immigrants have settled in **rural areas** because there **aren't** as many **jobs** available.
3) Immigrant workers have found **employment** and **accommodation** and then **helped others** from their family or community abroad to **join them** in the UK. They often move to the **same areas** and set up **communities** of ethnic minorities (see p. 134). This is known as **'chain migration'**.
4) **Large numbers** of immigrants have always settled in **London** because it is a **global hub** — a place that lots of people visit, pass through and where many international organisations and businesses operate. There are also jobs in **manufacturing**, **transport**, **hospitals** and the **tourism** industry.

Some **Ethnic Minority Populations** Have **Spread Out** a Bit More

Take a look back at the previous page to see the distribution of ethnic minority populations in the UK.

1) Many ethnic minority populations are still **concentrated** in certain **urban areas**.
2) However, some ethnic minority populations have **spread out** more across the UK.
3) This is mainly due to the **children** and **grandchildren** of immigrants **moving away** from their **place of birth**. Here's a bit about **why** this has happened:

- The **decline** of many **traditional industries** in the late 20th century has led to **high unemployment** in many **old industrial towns**. As a result, people have **moved** to areas where **employment prospects** are **better**.
- Many children and grandchildren of immigrants have lived in the UK all their lives — so they often feel **more comfortable** moving to areas with **lower ethnic minority populations** than their parents or grandparents might have done.
- Many have gone to **universities** in towns or cities away from their place of birth, then **settled** in their **university town**, or in a town or city where more **graduate jobs** are available.
- **Inter-marriage** between people from **different ethnic groups** can cause them to leave their established communities and move to a **new area**.

Practice Questions

Q1 What is a multicultural society?

Q2 Why were there large waves of immigration to the UK in the 1940s, 1950s and 1960s?

Q3 Why do many immigrants settle in London?

Exam Question

Q1 The graph shows the percentage of the UK's ethnic minority population that live in different regions.

Describe and comment on the graph. [7 marks]

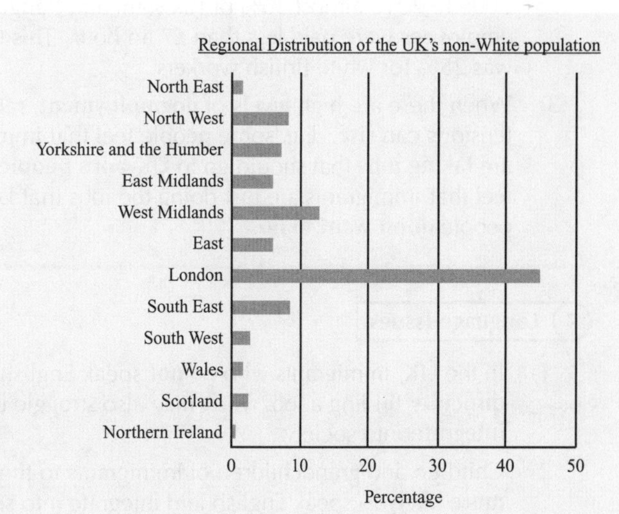

Waves of immigration — surfboards not usually involved...

When you look outside and it's bucketing down, it's hard to think why so may people actually want to end up living in the UK. The reasons behind the spread of immigrants throughout the UK are a lot more logical though — so no excuses for not learning the lot.

The Challenge of a Multicultural UK

There aren't any challenges associated with the UK's multicultural society, surely... oh, alright, there are a couple then...

*There are **Issues** Associated with **Multicultural Societies***

1) Racial, Ethnic and Religious Tensions

1) **Racial**, **ethnic**, **religious** and **language differences** can lead to **tensions** between groups — often because groups **lack understanding** of each other.
2) **Racial violence** can be a problem. E.g. after the London bombings on 7th July 2005 **assaults** on Muslims increased in the **UK**.
3) Sometimes there's **opposition** to certain **customs** and **religious practices**. E.g. in the UK there has been some debate about **banning** the **burqa** (the full Islamic face veil) in some public places. Some people say wearing it violates **women's rights**, but others believe that a ban **violates** the **human right** to **freedom of expression**.

2) Housing and Assimilation Issues

1) Many immigrants have **low paid** jobs in **inner city** areas. As a result, many immigrants live in **low cost housing** where **poor living conditions** and **overcrowding** are an issue.
2) The **children** of immigrants can become **trapped** in low cost housing and find it **difficult** to **move away**. It's often much easier for them to rent housing **cheaply** within the community, e.g. in Rochdale 96% of the Pakistani community live within the central area, which is among the most deprived areas in the North West.
3) Many ethnic minority populations prefer to **live in communities** where they can **socialise** with members of their own ethnic group and have **access** to **facilities** important to their culture (e.g. **places of worship** and **shops** that sell ingredients required for traditional cooking). **Individuals** may also feel **safer** and **less isolated** in these communities.
4) However, ethnic minority populations living in groups can create **ethnic segregation** within an area — and this can result in **racial tensions** (see above).
5) When ethnic minority groups **spread out more** it can lead to them **adopting** the culture of a **larger group** — this is called **cultural assimilation**. The members of an ethnic minority group can feel like they're **losing** their **own culture**.

3) Economic Issues

1) Immigrants claiming **state benefits** for unemployment and housing and putting increased pressure on **public services** can cause **resentment** among other members of the population.
2) In the UK, many immigrants work **long hours** for **low salaries** compared to UK-born people. E.g. from 2008 to 2010 almost 50% of Pakistani and Bangladeshi employees were paid less than £7 an hour. This figure was 25% for white British workers.
3) When there are high levels of **unemployment**, racial tensions can **rise**. E.g. some people feel that immigrants are **taking jobs** that should go to **UK-born people**. Others feel that immigrants are just doing the jobs that UK-born people **don't want to do**.

4) Language Issues

1) In the UK, immigrants who **do not** speak English often have **difficulty** finding a job. They may also struggle to fully **integrate** into society.
2) Children and grandchildren of immigrants to the UK are **more likely** to speak English and integrate into society. This can cause **tension** within the ethnic group as older members of the group may feel their culture is being **eroded**.

5) Education Issues

1) At some schools (e.g. in inner city areas) **most** of the children come from one or more ethnic minority groups, and these students may need **extra help**. E.g. some ethnic minority **children** do not speak English and schools may need to provide special **English** lessons for them.
2) **Faith schools** have developed in some areas to teach children according to a particular **religion**. Some people argue that this can cause **segregation** between different groups.
3) **Holiday patterns**, **school meals** and **school timetables** may need to be altered for ethnic minority groups. E.g. some schools in Manchester and London have had to close to allow **Muslim** pupils to have time off to celebrate the festival of **Eid**.

Cultural challenges for Gordon and his chums were all about who could stay awake for the longest in the art gallery.

The Challenge of a Multicultural UK

Bradford is a UK City with a **Multicultural Society**

Bradford is a city with a **diverse mix** of **cultures**. There are **places of worship** for **many** different religions and a large number of different **cultural** and **religious festivals** are celebrated in the city. There are also shops and markets that sell many **international foods**.

The pie chart shows the **population** of Bradford by **ethnic group** in 2001:

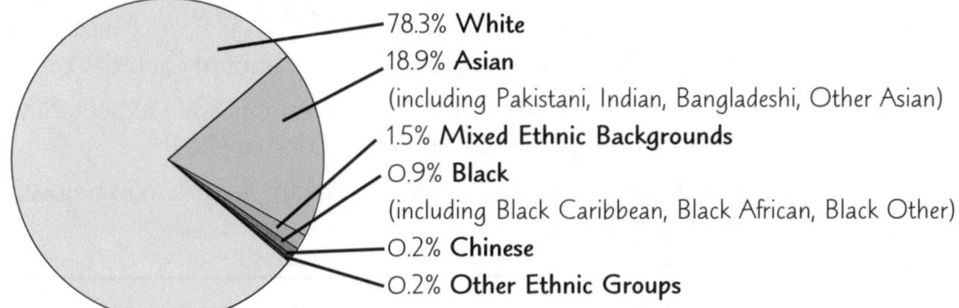

There are Lots of **Reasons** for this **Ethnic Mix**

- Bradford became an important international centre for the **textile industry** in the **19th century**. There was lots of **immigration** as people came to work in the **mills** — especially **white workers** from **Europe**.
- From the **1940s** to the **1960s** the government encouraged immigration to meet **labour shortages**. Immigrants came to **Bradford** to work in the textile industry (where there was a **high demand** for **workers**). Many people came from **Pakistan**, the **Caribbean** and **East Africa**.
- Around **70%** of the ethnic minority population in Bradford is **Pakistani**. This is largely due to **chain migration** (see p. 133) — early settlers from Pakistan helped other Pakistanis to come to Bradford.

There are Many **Issues** with Bradford's **Multicultural Society**

- Economic issues — Bradford's employment rate is **76%**, but only **49%** of ethnic minority **men** and **23%** of ethnic minority **women** are employed.
- Housing issues — Ethnic groups in Bradford are **concentrated** in particular areas. E.g. many Pakistanis living in Bradford live in the **Manningham** area, where **overcrowding** is a problem.
- Racial, ethnic and religious tensions — Relations between ethnic groups are **generally good**, but in **2001** there were **riots** after a demonstration by the Anti-Nazi league against the National Front.
- Education issues — Some schools in Bradford, with a **mix** of children from **different ethnic backgrounds**, have to have **specialist language** staff to help teach students who can't speak English.

The National Front is a political party that is against immigration of non-white people to the UK. The Anti-Nazi league was set up to oppose groups like this.

Practice Questions

Q1 Give one reason why Bradford has a multicultural society.

Q2 Give one issue caused by Bradford's multicultural society.

Exam Question

Q1 Using examples from the UK, discuss the issues related to multicultural societies. [10 marks]

Multicultural Challenge — your starter for ten...

Nothing in Geography ever seems to come without issues and multicultural societies are no different. Start by learning the bread and butter issues on the left hand page and then add the lovely jammy filling that is the Bradford case study. Is it lunchtime yet?

The Challenge of Global Poverty

These final few pages are all about global poverty. First up there's the distribution and causes to get your head around.

Poverty is Unevenly Distributed Across the World

The international poverty line used to be less than $1 a day. In 2008, the World Bank set it at less than $1.25 a day.

1) Poverty means being **unable** to **afford basic things** such as safe drinking water, food, shelter, sanitation, health care and education.
2) There are **different** ways of **measuring poverty** worldwide. For example:
   - **Economic indicators** can be used, such as gross domestic product (GDP) or the international poverty line (the percentage of the population living on less than a certain amount each day).
   - Indexes such as the **Human Poverty Index** can be used — it includes several measures such as life expectancy, adult literacy, access to safe drinking water and the proportion of children who are underweight.
3) All of the measures of poverty show that it is **unevenly distributed** across the world. For example, the map below shows the **percentage** of people living on **less than $1 per day** in 2004.

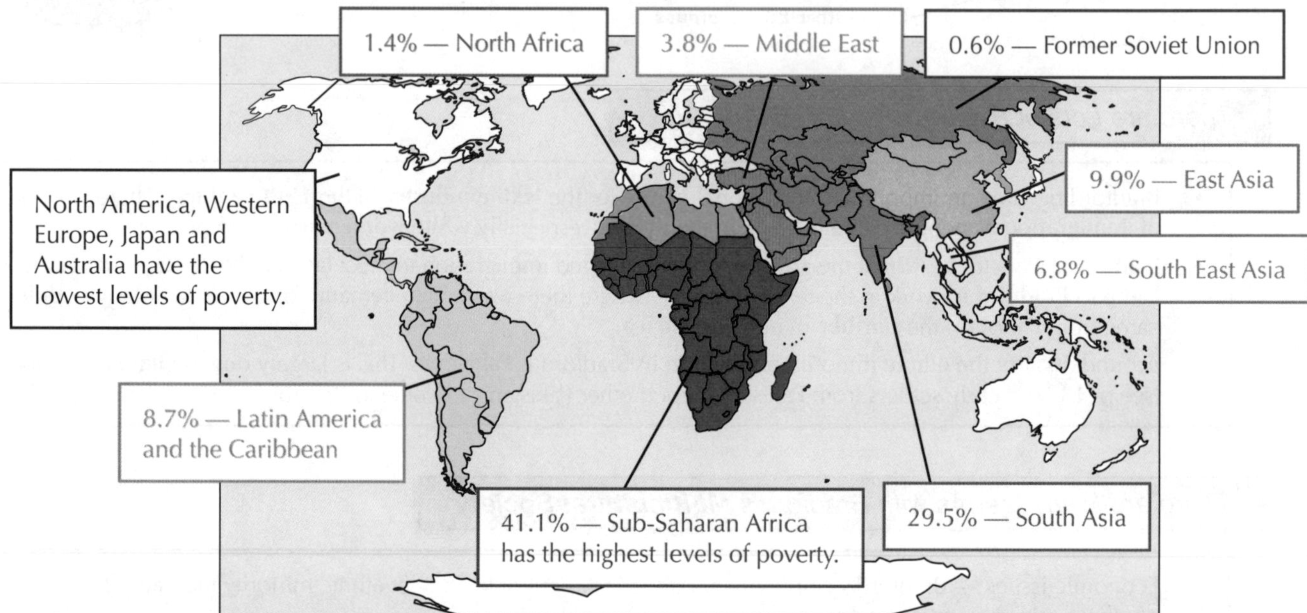

There are Many Causes of Poverty

These pages cover a few examples of things that can cause poverty, but take a look at pages 100-101 as well — there's a bit more on why entire nations are in poverty.

Here are a few of the things that can **cause poverty**:

BAD GROWING CONDITIONS

- **Physical factors** affect how easy it is to **grow food.** Plants need **water** and **fertile soil**, and animals need plants to graze on.
- Many poor countries have **low quality soil**, which can be made worse by **bad farming practices** (e.g. overgrazing). These **degrade** the soil, reduce **agricultural productivity** and **increase poverty**.
- Many of the **poorest countries** in the world have climates with **little** or **seasonal** rainfall, which makes it difficult to grow crops and rear animals. If it **doesn't rain**, or if it rains **less than usual**, it can lead to **food shortages** or **famine**.

Famine is when a large percentage of the population doesn't get enough food and they become malnourished.

SUBSISTENCE FARMING

- **Subsistence farmers** only produce enough food to **feed themselves** and their **families**. They are particularly at **risk of poverty** because they depend on the food they produce to **survive**.
- The growth of their crops relies on the **climate**, so they're **vulnerable** to extreme weather events that **reduce production** (see next page).
- Subsistence farmers usually **don't have surpluses** which they can sell or trade — so they have **no income**. This means they are unable to **escape poverty** because they **can't afford** adequate health care, education or better technology to **increase food production**.
- Subsistence farming occurs in **Sub-Saharan Africa**, **South East Asia** and parts of **Latin America**. E.g. in **Zambia** most of the population relies on subsistence farming to survive. There are **few irrigation systems** so most farmers rely on seasonal rains. However, **droughts** in the 1980s and 1990s **reduced production** and resulted in **famine**.

The Challenge of Global Poverty

OVERPOPULATION

- Overpopulation is when there **isn't** enough **space, food, water** or other **resources** to support the population.
- It can result from **population increase**, the **reduction of resources** — or from a combination of **both**.
- Overpopulation causes **poverty** because there is too much of a strain on **resources** (e.g. water, food and housing). E.g. **India's population** is over **1 billion** and increasing rapidly. 35% of people in India are living on less than $1 a day. The number of people living in poverty may **increase** as the population continues to **grow**.
- The areas with **high levels** of **overpopulation** (e.g. Sub-Saharan Africa, and South Asia) also have the highest levels of **poverty**.

WAR

- War can **damage** or **destroy property, infrastructure** and **crops**. This can cause poverty by creating **shortages** of safe drinking water, shelter, food, sanitation, health care and education.
- When a country is at war, **productivity** often **decreases**. **Industrial** and **agricultural activity** can be **disrupted** and **trade** with other countries may **decline or stop**. E.g. because of the First Gulf War (1990-1) the **GDP** of Iraq **fell** from $2304 per capita in 1989 to $938 in 1990.
- People become **refugees** during times of war when they **flee their homes**. Many end up in **refugee camps** which often have a limited supply of food, water, shelter and health care.
- **War** in parts of the **Middle East** and **Africa** in recent years has **increased poverty** in these areas.

NATURAL HAZARDS

- **Natural hazards** (e.g. floods, droughts) can **cause poverty** by **damaging or destroying** property, infrastructure and crops.
- **Floods** can reduce access to **clean water** and **sanitation**. They can also cause **loss of property** and **reduce crop yields**. E.g. floods in Bangladesh in 1998 made 25 million people homeless. 2 million tonnes of rice were lost, clean water became scarce and diseases (e.g. cholera) spread.
- **Drought** reduces **water supplies** and can increase **soil erosion**. This can result in reduced crop yields, crop failures and the death of livestock. For example, drought and crop disease contributed to a famine in Ethiopia in 1984 that left 8 million people starving.
- Many of the **poorest** areas of the world are **heavily affected** by natural hazards, e.g. Sub-Saharan Africa, South Asia and South East Asia. Some hazards can occur **every year** (e.g. tropical cyclones in Bangladesh), which means people struggle to break out of poverty.

Poverty Usually Has a Mixture of Causes

Poverty is usually the result of a **combination** of **causes**. The causes of poverty are often **linked to each other** and can create a **cycle of poverty** that becomes difficult to break. For example:

1) **Drought** can lead to **famine** and **poverty** as water and food resources decline.
2) This can cause a **war over natural resources**. War increases poverty (e.g. by causing destruction and reducing productivity).
3) War can also result in **refugees**, who may move to an area where they contribute to **overpopulation** and put further pressure on resources.

Practice Questions

Q1 What is poverty?

Q2 Give three causes of poverty.

Exam Question

Q1 The map shows the percentage of children who are less than five years old and underweight. Using the map, describe and comment on the global distribution of poverty. [7 marks]

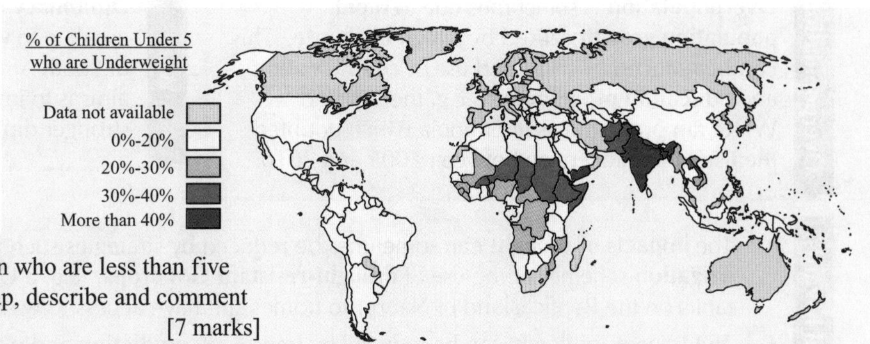

Poverty — pretty serious stuff, I'm afraid...

Nearly half the children in the world live in poverty and one third of deaths in the world are due to poverty — that's 50 000 people every day. You need to have a good grip on what's causing it all, so scribble the points on these pages out a few times.

The Challenge of Global Poverty

Poverty is a global problem — it affects people in countries all over the world. So, it needs some international solutions...

International Agencies** can help to **Reduce Poverty

1) **International agencies** play an important role in **reducing** global poverty. For example:

In 2000, the UN agreed eight Millennium Development Goals (to be achieved by 2015) to tackle global poverty:

- Eradicate extreme poverty and hunger
- Achieve universal primary education
- Promote gender equality and empower women
- Reduce child mortality
- Improve maternal health
- Combat HIV/AIDS, malaria and other diseases
- Ensure environmental sustainability
- Develop a global partnership for development

The MDGs are intended to highlight the areas that need to be addressed, and to give the UN a way of measuring the progress that's been made in reducing global poverty.

To date, the success of the MDGs has varied. Some progress is being made, e.g. in Sub-Saharan Africa there has been an 18% increase in primary school enrolment between 1999 and 2009. But little or no progress has been made in other areas, e.g. in Africa the number of children with stunted growth due to malnutrition has actually increased between 1990 and 2010.

The last goal basically means that countries need to work together to help each other develop.

2) Other **international agencies**, such as the World Bank and the World Health Organisation, and **international charities** (e.g. Oxfam and the Red Cross) are also working to **reduce global poverty**.

Poverty** can be **Reduced** in a **Number of Ways

To **reduce poverty**, international organisations are doing things to address the **causes of poverty** (see pages 136-137).

Bad growing conditions

- Growing crops that can **withstand** harsh environmental conditions helps to **increase crop yields**. For example, the $39 million Water Efficient Maize for Africa (WEMA) project aims to develop drought-tolerant types of maize to be grown in Sub-Saharan Africa.
- Reducing overgrazing helps **maintain soil quality**. For example, in central Tanzania the HADO project encouraged farmers to grow hay to feed cattle. This reduced grazing and provided reliable food for animals all year round.

Subsistence farming

- Subsistence farmers need to **improve productivity** so they can **generate an income**.
- **Loans** could enable farmers to increase productivity by **buying equipment or animals**. E.g. as part of a UN programme, a Kenyan business is offering small loans to 100 000 farmers in Kenya to help them buy livestock, seeds and equipment which they can use to improve their farming methods and produce more food.
- Increased agricultural productivity also reduces the risk of **famine** by **improving food security**. Food security is when **all people** have access to **sufficient food** at all times. E.g. a UN programme in 2012 aimed to increase the area of irrigated farmland in Afghanistan by 15% (by upgrading old irrigation systems) and increase crop yield by 20%.

Overpopulation

Overpopulation is sometimes due to **rapid population growth** caused by a **high birth rate**. This can be reduced by increased use of **contraception** and **education programmes**. E.g. the UN and WHO ran programmes in Ethiopia which doubled the use of contraception between 2005 and 2010.

War

Diplomacy could resolve many conflicts before they escalate to **war** (see page 120). For example, the Union of South American Nations was set up in 2008. One of its aims is to improve security in South America by building stronger diplomatic links between the nations.

Natural hazards

- The **impacts of drought** can sometimes be reduced by strategies such as **water collection and storage** schemes, **irrigation** schemes or the use of **drought-resistant GM crops**. E.g. a UN-led programme has installed water storage tanks on the Pacific island of Nauru, so homes still have access to water during a drought.
- The impacts of **floods** can be reduced by improving **prediction and warning systems**, e.g. UNESCO (part of the UN) has set up a project to improve flood prediction and warning systems in Pakistan following the 2010 floods. This allows people to make better **plans** to prepare for floods, and to **protect their property** when floods occur.

The Challenge of Global Poverty

Poverty, Security and Development are all Tied Up Together

1) Poverty is **closely linked** to the **level of development** of a country (see pages 98-99). **More developed** countries tend to have **lower levels of poverty**.
2) So a country **needs to develop** to reduce its level of poverty.
3) In order to develop, countries need **security**. This means a few **different things**:

- **Economic security** involves a country's economy being **stable** and **sustainable**, as well as all individuals having a reliable **basic income.**
- **Food security** involves having access to a reliable source of **sufficient food**.
- **Health security** involves having **protection from diseases** and access to **health care**.
- **Personal, community** and **political security** involves being **protected** from violence, crime and human rights abuses.

I know, I know, it's confusing. But think how upset you'd be if CGP hadn't explained this stuff so well.

4) Countries **can't develop without security**. For example, if a country has a low level of economic security, (e.g. because it has a high level of debt), then it can't afford to invest in development.
5) But, countries **can't get security without development** either. For example, if a country is at a low level of development, then it can't generate the money it needs to pay off debts and create economic security.
6) If you thought we'd forgotten about a case study for this stuff... think again.

Poverty, Security and Development are Problems in Afghanistan

1) There have been **conflicts** going on in Afghanistan for a long time (see pages 126-127).
2) The conflicts have contributed to Afghanistan being at a **very low level of development**:

- It is **economically poor** — in 2011, the GDP per capita was $1000 (in the UK it was $36 600).
- The **birth rate is high** — in 2011, each woman had an average of 5.64 children.
- There are **high levels of gender inequality** — in 2000, the male adult literacy rate was 43.1%, but the female adult literacy rate was only 12.6%.

3) They've also meant that Afghanistan has **very little security**:

- **Economic security** is low — the unemployment rate was 35% in 2008.
- **Food security** is low — in 2008, 29% of the population did not get enough calories every day.
- **Health security** is low — there is 1 doctor for every 5000 people.
- **Personal security** is low — in 2008 there were 2118 civilian deaths caused by war.

4) Afghanistan can't get **security** without **investing** in projects to improve its level of **development**, such as building roads, hospitals and schools etc. These projects would create security by providing **jobs**, **health care** and **education**.
5) But money can't be **invested** in **development projects** while things like **personal** and **political security** are so low, e.g. there is no guarantee that new roads, hospitals and schools won't be destroyed by the ongoing conflict.
6) So, Afghanistan can't get security **without development**, but it can't develop **without security** either. To break this cycle Afghanistan may need **help** (e.g. money or military assistance) from **international agencies** and **other countries**.

Many countries are trapped in poverty because they can't overcome this problem.

Practice Questions

Q1 What are the eight UN Millenium Development Goals?

Q2 What is security?

Exam Question

Q1 'No development without security, and no security without development.' Discuss this statement. [40 marks]

Eight goals? One way to make sure that England finally score...

Ah, a conundrum to end the section with. You need development to reduce poverty, but you can't get development without security and you can't get security without development. It's a bit of a chicken and egg situation...

Exam Structure

Alas, the time has come my dear to prepare thyself for the examinations. The first thing to do is to know thy enemy...

You have to do **Two Exam Papers**

Unit 3 Exam — **Contemporary Geographical Issues**

1) It's a marathon **2 hrs 30 mins** long and there are **90 marks** to be had.
2) It's worth **30%** of your A level grade.
3) There are **three sections** in the paper — **A**, **B** and **C**:

Dave (far left) couldn't believe he'd picked the easiest option in the human pyramid on motorbikes exam...

SECTION A

- You have to **answer questions on ONE OPTION** out of three **physical** options — either Plate Tectonics, Weather and Climate or Ecosystems.
- There will be **three questions** worth between 7 and **10 marks** each.
- There are **25 marks in total**, so spend about **45 minutes** on this section.
- There will be questions where you have to use your **understanding** to **interpret resources** (like photos, maps and graphs) and questions that **test your knowledge** of the topics.

See pages 141-142 for advice about answering the kind of questions you'll get in this paper.

SECTION B

- You have to **answer questions on ONE OPTION** out of three **human** options — either World Cities, Development and Globalisation or Contemporary Conflicts and Challenges.
- The structure of this section is **exactly the same as Section A**, so spend about 45 minutes on it.

SECTION C

- You have to answer **ONE ESSAY QUESTION** worth **40 marks**. You get a choice of **six** — one on each topic.
- You should spend about **60 minutes** penning your finest answer.
- Annoyingly, you **can't answer the essay question on an option you've already answered in Section A or B**. For example, if you've chosen to answer questions on Plate Tectonics in Section A, and World Cities in Section B, you can't do the essay question on either of those options — you have to do a different one.
- Since the essay question is worth a whopping **40 marks** it's a good idea to **choose your essay question first**, before you decide which options you'll answer in Sections A and B.

Unit 4 Exam — **Geography Fieldwork Investigation** OR **Geographical Issue Evaluation**

1) For Unit 4 you **either** sit the **Geography Fieldwork Investigation exam**, or the **Geographical Issue Evaluation exam**. If you're not sure which one you're doing, ask your teacher.
2) Whichever one you're doing it's **1 hr 30 mins** long and there are **60 marks** in total.
3) It's worth **20%** of your A level grade.
4) Here's a bit more detail about each one:

GEOGRAPHY FIELDWORK INVESTIGATION

- There are **two sections** in this paper — **A** and **B**.
- In Section A you'll have to answer questions about **your fieldwork**. Spend about an **hour** on this bit.
- In Section B you'll have to answer **general investigation questions**, e.g. comment on a particular method used or analyse fieldwork data that you're given. Spend about **30 mins** on this part.
- You have to **answer all the questions**.

GEOGRAPHICAL ISSUE EVALUATION

- For this exam you're **given a resource booklet** to study about **two months before** your exam.
- In the exam you'll get questions on things like **data analysis, data interpretation, fieldwork to investigate the issue** and **theory** to do with the issue.
- You have to **answer all the questions**.

Answering Questions

Figuring out what an exam question is actually asking you to do is a bit of a dark art. Here are some tips to help you decipher exam speak and produce a top notch answer...

1 Make Sure You Read the Question Properly

There are loads of hints about how to answer the questions in this book in the Answers section at the back.

It's dead easy to **misread** the question and spend 10 minutes writing about the **wrong thing**. A few simple tips can help you avoid this:

1) **Underline** the **command words** in the question (the ones that tell you **what to do**):

Answers to questions with 'explain' in them often include the word '**because**' (or '**due to**').

E.g. for the question 'Explain why GDP alone is not a reliable measure of development', your answer would include '... GDP may be misleading because it is an average...'.

'Assess', 'Evaluate' and 'Discuss' all mean pretty much the **same thing**. They're all about **weighing something up**, e.g. how **successful** responses to a tectonic hazard were. You need to give a **balanced** answer — talk about all the **different viewpoints** on the subject.

Command word	Means write about...
Describe	what it's **like**
Explain	**why** it's like that (i.e. give reasons)
Compare	the **similarities AND differences**
Contrast	the **differences**
Distinguish	the **differences**
Assess / **Evaluate** / **Discuss**	the **advantages** and **disadvantages OR** the **arguments for** and **against**
Examine	**describe AND explain**
Outline	**describe AND explain**
Define	the **meaning** of the word

If a question asks you to describe a **pattern** (e.g. from a map or graph), make sure you identify the **general pattern**, then refer to any **anomalies** (things that **don't** fit the general pattern).

E.g. for the question 'Describe the global distribution of volcanoes', you first need to say that they're mostly on plate margins, *then* mention that a few aren't (e.g. Kilauea in Hawaii).

When writing about differences, use **comparative words** like '**larger**' or '**more severe**', e.g. 'Temperature has risen more steeply in the last century than at any time in the last 1000 years'.

'Examine' and 'Outline' are pretty similar. The main difference is that you do **more explaining** for '**Examine**' and **more describing** for '**Outline**'.

2) **Underline** the **key words** (the ones that tell you **what it's about**), e.g. volcanoes, conflict, global warming.
3) **Re-read** the question and your answer **when you've finished**, just to check that your answer really does address **all parts** of the question being asked. A **common mistake** is to **miss a bit out** — like when questions say 'use data from the graph in your answer' or 'use evidence from the map'.

2 Figure Out Your Structure Before You Start

1) For any **longer answers**, you need to think carefully about how to **structure** your answer. Jot down the **order** you're going to cover things in.
2) **Label** your **plan** and **answer** clearly so the examiner knows which is which.
3) **Don't cross out** your plan — the examiner might look at it to see what you've included, especially if you run out of time.

Q1 Describe how energy flows through an ecosystem.

PLAN

1. Intro — define 'ecosystem'. Energy flows through system as organisms are eaten.
2. Where energy comes from — plants (autotrophs) photosynthesise using sunlight.
3. Energy flow — primary, secondary and tertiary consumers (give examples).
4. Loss of energy — 90% at each level. Lost through waste, movement etc.

ANSWER

An ecosystem is a set of relationships...

3 Include Relevant Geographical Terms

Use the **proper geography words** for things, e.g. say 'herbivore' rather than 'plant eater', and 'aid' instead of 'help'.

Don't Forget all the Usual Rules

1) Your answer should be **legible** (you won't get many marks if the examiner can't read it), use **correct grammar**, and **everything** should be **spelt correctly** (double-check jazzy geography words).
2) **Use diagrams** where they're appropriate — drawing a diagram can be way **quicker** than describing the same thing in words.
3) If you're **running out of time** at the end of the exam, **don't panic** — just write what you can as **bullet points**. You'll still get some marks for doing this.

Answering Questions — Unit 3

There are loads of different types of question that can come up in the Unit 3 exam. If you know what they all are you'll stand a better chance of writing a cracking answer, and if you write a cracking answer you'll get a top grade. Happy days.

*You Might Have to **Interpret** a **Resource***

1) Whichever options you choose in Sections A and B of the **Unit 3** exam, one of the questions will probably include a **resource** for you to look at. This could be, for example, a graph, a map, an aerial photo or a data table.

Watch out for log scales (see p. 145).

If you're given a **GRAPH**, make sure you read the **scale** carefully — use **working lines** to help you read off values accurately. Start by looking for **general trends** in the data, e.g. whether values increase or decrease overall, and whether they change smoothly or in stages. Then look for any **anomalies** — points that don't fit the pattern.

If you're given a **MAP**, have a good look at the **key** to work out what it shows. Be **specific** when you're writing about maps — if you're referring to a particular place or feature, give the **grid reference**. Make sure you use **compass points** (e.g. west) rather than words (e.g. left). There's more about how to read maps on pages 147-148.

If you're given a **PHOTO**, study it really carefully. Scribble down a **list** of all the relevant things you spot in it, and use the list to plan your answer.

When you're writing about a graph or a data table, quote specific data to back up your points, and manipulate it if you can (e.g. by working out the difference between two values).

If you're given a **DATA TABLE**, start by looking for **patterns** in the data — e.g. if the table gives data for two different areas, look for major **similarities** and **differences** between the two places.

2) You might be given **two** resources (e.g. two maps showing the distribution of ethnic groups in an area at two different times) and asked to **compare** them. Pick out **similarities** and **differences** between the resources.
3) Read the question carefully and think about how it **relates** to the resource, and which **bits** of the resource will be helpful to you. E.g. if you're given an aerial photo and asked about the **environmental** impacts of development in the rural/urban fringe, you can **ignore** any possible **economic** and **social** impacts.

*Include Lots of **Facts** and **Figures** in **Case Study** Questions*

1) Usually, one of the questions in Section A and Section B will ask you to write about a **case study**. Case study questions won't necessarily include the words 'case study', so you need to know how to spot them. Look out for **phrases** like 'with reference to one named area' or '... that you have studied'.
2) Remember to include loads of **specific details** in your answer — place names, dates, statistics and so on.
3) Make sure they're **relevant** though — there's no point giving the exact number of people killed in a war if the question is about the **causes** of the war.
4) Drawing an **annotated map** might help you show how your points **relate** to the **area** you're talking about.

***Essay** Questions Are Worth **Lots** of **Marks**...*

Re-read the question a couple of times whilst you're answering it, to make sure you're sticking to the question.

1) The last question in your Unit 3 exam will be an **essay question** worth **40 marks**.
2) You answer a question on **one** topic, but you'll be expected to bring in your **wider knowledge** of Geography too.
3) However the question is worded, you'll need to include specific **examples** or a **case study**. Have a good read of the **advice** about case study questions above — the same tips apply to essay questions.
4) Essay questions will often use words like '**evaluate**' or '**discuss**', so you have to look at **both sides** of an issue.
5) If a question uses the phrase '**To what extent...**', you need to form a sensible **opinion** about the subject. It doesn't matter whether you agree with what the question is saying or not, as long as you give a **balanced argument** and **justify** your views.
6) Make sure your essay has a sensible **structure**, and **link** your points together so your answer **flows**. Use words and phrases like 'however', 'in contrast' and 'in addition' to link your sentences.
7) For essay questions you should **always** write a **conclusion** — **sum up** the different viewpoints and then say what **you think**. You could also briefly mention how and why the issue you're discussing may **change** in the **future**.

Unit 4A — Geography Fieldwork Investigation

Unit 4 is a detailed study of a geographical issue, and it's worth 20% of your A level. You might be doing Unit 4A, in which case you need this page, or Unit 4B, which is covered on the next page.

Unit 4A is All About **How** You Carry Out a **Fieldwork Investigation**

There are **two parts** to Unit 4A:

1) You have to come up with a **research topic** and an **issue** to investigate. Then you have to **collect**, **present**, **analyse** and **interpret** data, draw a **conclusion** and **evaluate** your project.
2) You'll also have to sit an **exam**. It's an hour and a half long, and it's split into two parts:
   - In the first part you have to answer questions about **your investigation** — you might be asked about your **aim**, **methods**, what **data** you collected and **why**, how you **presented** and **analysed** it, how you could **extend** your research and so on.
   - In the second part you'll be given some **data** (e.g. maps, data tables, graphs). You might have to answer questions about what it **means**, what different **techniques** there are for **presenting** and **analysing** data or how **useful** the different techniques are.

You Have to Come Up With a **Topic** to **Study**

1) Coming up with a **research topic** and an **issue** to investigate is probably the hardest part of Unit 4A. Think about the following things:
   - Which **areas** of Geography you find most **interesting**. Have a look through your notes and decide whether you want to do a project on **Human** or **Physical** Geography, or a **combination** of the two.
   - Where you **live**. For example, if you live in a city, you could look at urban climate and air quality and how it relates to land use, or if you live near the coast you could look at rates and impacts of coastal erosion.
   - What's **happening** in the area where you live. Maybe there's a plan to build a supermarket on the outskirts of your town — you could look at what local residents and workers think, what impacts it might have etc.
2) When you have a broad topic, come up with an **aim** and a **hypothesis**. An aim is **what you want to find out**, e.g. 'To see what effect the proposed supermarket in the Bonnet area of Wigginton will have on people in the area'. A hypothesis is a **specific testable statement**, e.g. 'The proposed supermarket in the Bonnet area of Wigginton will improve quality of life in the area'.

You Need to **Collect**, **Present** and **Analyse** Your **Data**

1) When you know exactly what you want to find out, **plan** what **data** you'll need and how to **collect** it. Think about what data would be most **useful** and what you can **realistically** (and **safely**) collect.
2) You need to collect some **primary data** (data that you collect yourself), but you can also use some **secondary data** (data that someone else has collected) if it's relevant.
3) When collecting primary data, think about your **sampling strategy** — when you're studying a large area like a city or a river, you **can't** collect data for the whole thing, so you have to select **sites** to study. Make sure these sites are **representative** of the whole area.
4) When you've collected enough data, you need to **present** and **analyse** it. Plotting data on **graphs** and **maps** and applying **statistical analyses** can help you to see **patterns** — have a look at pages 145-152 for some ideas.

Finally, **Interpret** Your Data and Reach a **Balanced Conclusion**

1) The final part of your project is drawing a **conclusion**. You need to say what your data **shows** in relation to your **original aim** and **hypothesis**, e.g. whether it supports the hypothesis or not.
2) Your conclusion needs to be **balanced** — e.g. if you've studied a potential bypass that might be built around your town, don't just write about the negative impacts of it, make sure you mention the positive impacts too.
3) Your results might not give you a **clear-cut** conclusion, but that's fine — it gives you more to write about.
4) You also need to **evaluate** your study, e.g. write about the **limitations** of the study and suggest ways that it could be **improved**. You should think about how your study could be **extended**, e.g. what extra data could be collected.

Unit 4B — Geographical Issue Evaluation

If you're not doing Unit 4A then you'll be doing 4B, the Geographical Tissue Evaluation — working out how far advanced your Geography teacher's cold is from the state of their... what? Oh. Geographical ***Issue*** *Evaluation. My mistake.*

Unit 4B is All About Analysing and Interpreting Information

1) If you're doing **Unit 4B**, roughly two months before the exam you'll be given an **Advance Information Booklet** (**AIB**) that contains loads of material about a geographical issue.
2) The issue could be based in the **UK** or **elsewhere** and could vary in **scale** from **local** (e.g. the management of a single ecosystem) to **international** (e.g. the expansion of a transnational corporation).
3) You need to study **all** the information **carefully**, work out what it all **means**, how it **fits** together and how you might **investigate**, **present** and **analyse** it.
4) In the exam you'll have an hour and a half to answer questions about the **issue**, using the **data** you're given as well as your existing knowledge of Geography.

"If only I'd studied A2 Geography," sighed Martha as the others pored over their AIB for the seventeenth lunchtime in a row.

The Information in the AIB Will All Relate to a Single Issue

1) The AIB could include several different **types** of information, such as **reports**, **data tables**, **maps** and **graphs**. All the information will be **related** in some way — e.g. you might be given a report on a proposed out-of-town shopping centre, photos of the town's high street and a data table about employment in the area.
2) The AIB might also direct you to some **secondary data sources**, such as **websites** — make sure you look at these before the exam, as questions are sometimes **directly based** on information from these sources.
3) The information you're given will give you some **clues** about the type of **questions** that might come up. E.g. if the booklet has a table of development indicators in two countries it's pretty likely that you'll have to compare them in some way.
4) As well as looking at the information you're given, have a think about how you might **collect more data** — you could get a question about what **fieldwork** or **extra research** could be carried out to investigate the issue further.

Think About How You'd Present and Analyse the Data

1) In the exam, you might have to **choose** a technique for **presenting** or **analysing** data (see pages 145-152), then justify **why** you chose that technique. Look at **each** piece of data that you're given and think about how it might best be **presented** or **analysed** — this'll save you time in the exam.
2) If the data you're given are quite **complex**, and contain lots of figures, try **different methods** of plotting them on graphs or maps before your exam. This will help you understand what the information shows.
3) You also need to think about possible **problems** with the data. For example:

- How **reliable** are the data sources? Are they **biased** or **unbiased**?
- How **big** was the sample? Is it **representative** of the population?
- Are there important points of view that are **missing**?

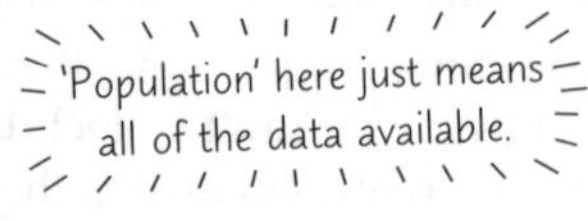

Use All the Information to Form Opinions About the Issue

1) Once you've got your head around all the information, you need to **link it all together** and form an **opinion** about the issue.
2) You're likely to be asked to **argue** a point of view using the information, e.g. suggesting how an area could best be managed to meet the needs of everyone involved. There's **no single right or wrong** answer — but you need to be able to **justify** your argument, so make sure you can **use the data** to support it.
3) Whatever your view is, you need to give a **balanced argument**. Try to think of potential **economic**, **political**, **social** and **environmental impacts** of the different sides of the argument, and how any negative impacts could be **reduced**.
4) It's likely to be a **complex** issue with lots of different parties involved, so you need to think about possible **conflicts** that your solution might cause and how they could be **resolved**.

Graph and Map Skills

The examiners could spring any type of graph or map on you in your exam (they're sneaky like that). So make sure you know all about the different types...

There are Loads of Different Types of Graphs and Maps

1) There are some types of graphs and maps that you'll have come across lots of times before. These include **line graphs**, **bar charts**, **pie charts**, **scatter graphs**, **atlas maps** and **sketch maps**.
2) Some graphs and maps are trickier than others, so the next four pages are full of tips to help you interpret the tougher ones.
3) When you're **interpreting** graphs and maps you need to remember to **read** the **scale** or **key really carefully**.
4) If you have to read from a graph **draw working lines on** to help you get an accurate figure.

Triangular Graphs Show Percentages Split into Three Categories

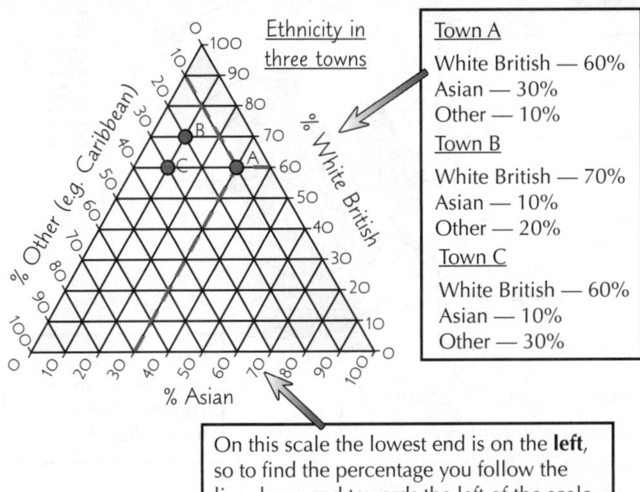

1) To read a triangular graph start by **finding the point** you want on the graph.
2) **Follow** the **line** that goes **down** from the **point** to the **lowest end** of the **scale** and record the percentage.
3) Then **turn the graph around** so that the next axis is at **the bottom**, **follow** the **line** down to the lower end of the scale and record that percentage.
4) Do the same for the **third axis**.
5) The three readings should **add up** to **100%**.
6) The graph on the left shows the ethnicity of people in three towns. There are **three ethnic groups** so a triangular graph can be used. **Each point** represents **one town**.

Logarithmic Scales are Used When the Data Range is Large

1) The **intervals** on logarithmic scales are **not fixed amounts** (e.g. they don't go up by 5 every time).
2) Instead, the **intervals** get **increasingly larger** at the top end of the scale (e.g. 10, 20, 40, 80).
3) This lets you fit a **very wide range** of **data** onto one **axis** without having to draw an enormous graph.
4) The graph on the right uses a **logarithmic scale** on the **vertical axis** to show how the population of four cities changed over 40 years.

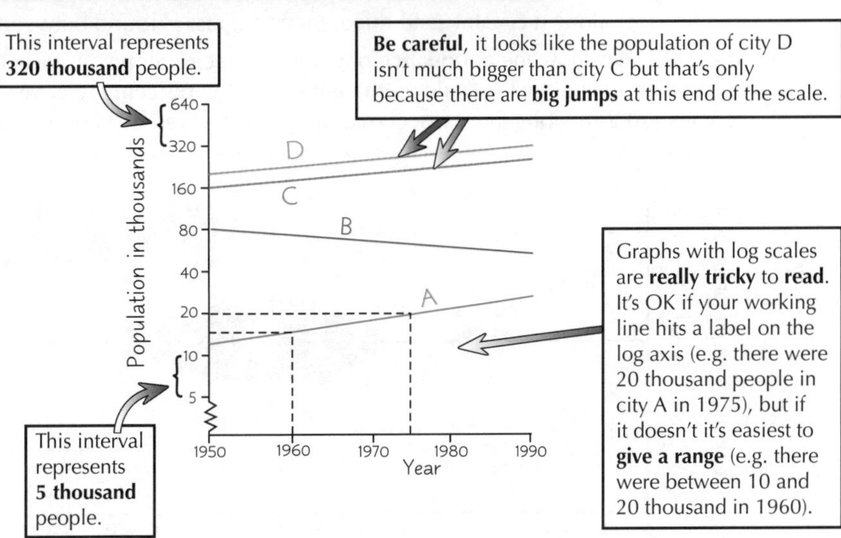

Graph and Map Skills

Dispersion Diagrams Show the Frequency of Data

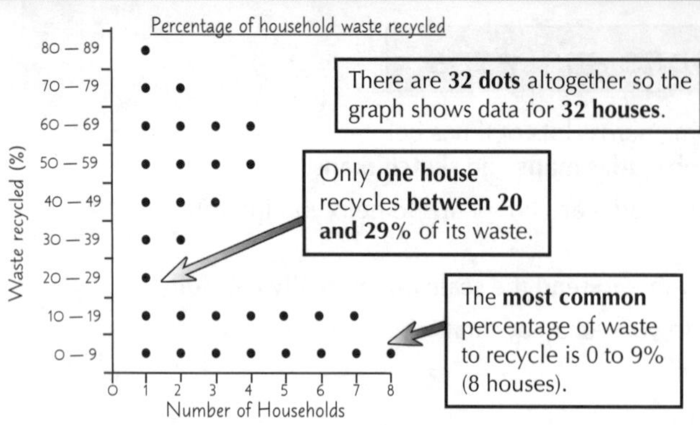

1) Dispersion diagrams are a bit like a cross between a **tally chart** and a **bar chart**.
2) The **range of data that's measured** goes on one axis. **Frequency** goes on the other axis.
3) **Each dot** represents **one piece of information** — the **more dots** there are in a particular category, the **more frequently** that event has happened.
4) The dispersion diagram on the left shows the **percentage** of **household waste** that's **recycled** for **houses** in a **particular village**.

Radial Plots Often Show Directional Data

1) **Radial plots** always appear as a **circle**.
2) The points on the **outside** of the circle usually show **direction** (compass points), but they can show other things, e.g. months of the year.
3) The **bars** coming out from the centre show another variable — the **distance** they reach from the centre shows the **size** of the variable.
4) The most common radial diagram is a **wind rose**. The bars point in different directions to show **which way** the wind is blowing **from**. How **far** the bar reaches from the centre shows how **often** winds blow from that direction.
5) This diagram also shows a third variable — each bar is split into different coloured sections to show the **frequency** of different **wind speeds** from each direction.

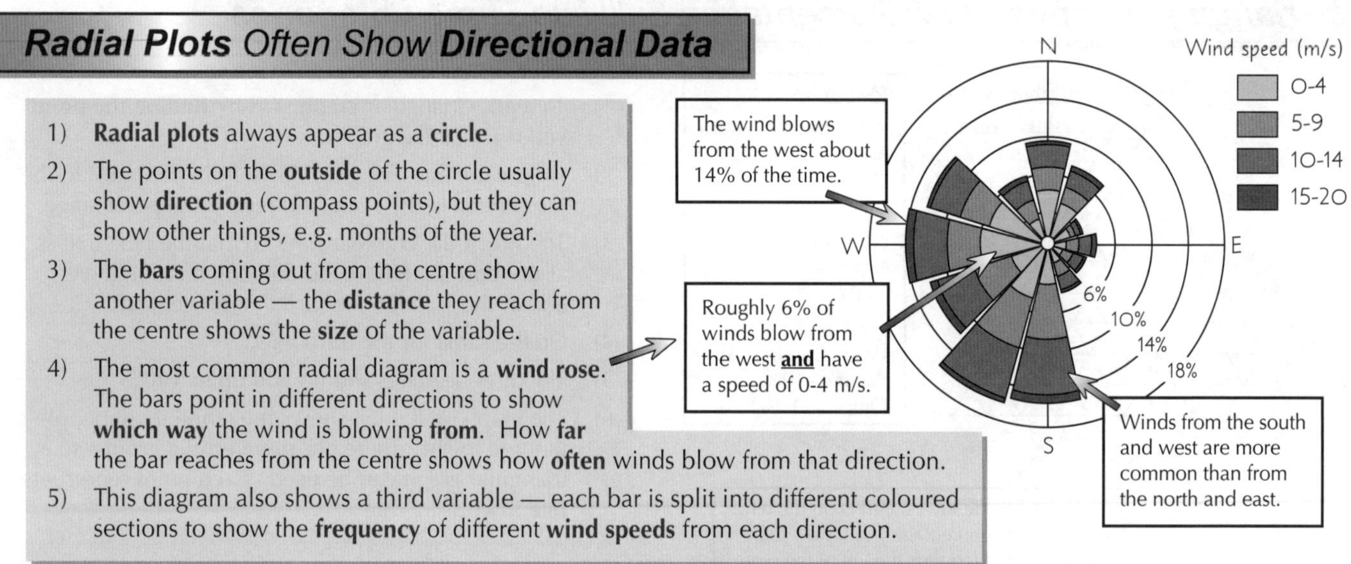

Kite Diagrams Usually Show the Distribution and Abundance of Organisms

1) **Kite diagrams** are usually used to plot **species distribution** along a **transect**, e.g. in the diagram below of a transect along a **coastal sand dune**, marram grass is found between 0 and 10 m along the transect.
2) They can also show the **abundance** of different species along a transect. E.g. in the diagram below the scale on the left shows the **percentage cover** of each species. At 2 m along the transect marram grass covered 20% of the surface.

A transect is a line — you count the number or percentage cover of organisms at fixed points along it.

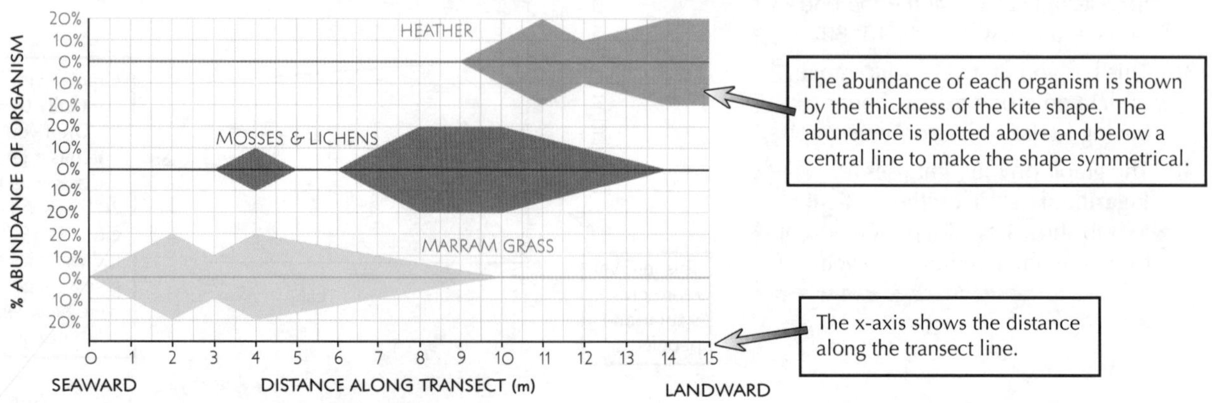

Graph and Map Skills

Choropleth Maps Show Information Using Colours and Patterns

1) Choropleth maps show how something **varies** between **different areas** using **colours** or **patterns**.
2) The maps in exams often use **cross-hatched lines** and **dots**.
3) They're straightforward to read but it's **easy to make mistakes** with them as the patterns can be very similar.
4) If you're asked to talk about all the parts of the map with a **certain type of hatching**, look at the map carefully and put a **big tick** on each part with that hatching, to make them all **stand out**.

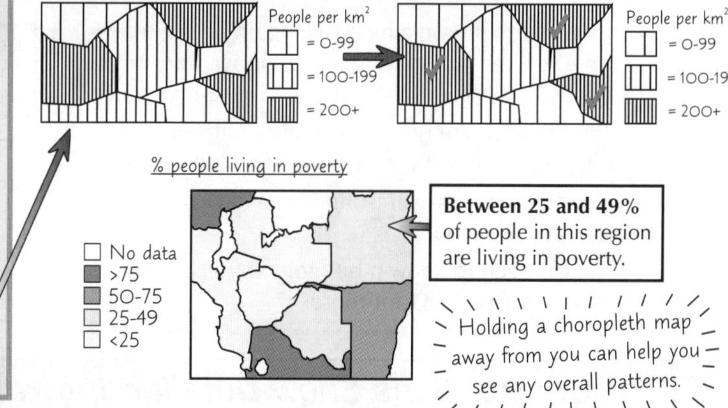

Dot Maps Show Distribution and Quantity Using Identical Symbols...

1) Dot maps use **identical dots** to show how something is **distributed** across an **area**.
2) Use the **key** to find out what **quantity** each dot represents.

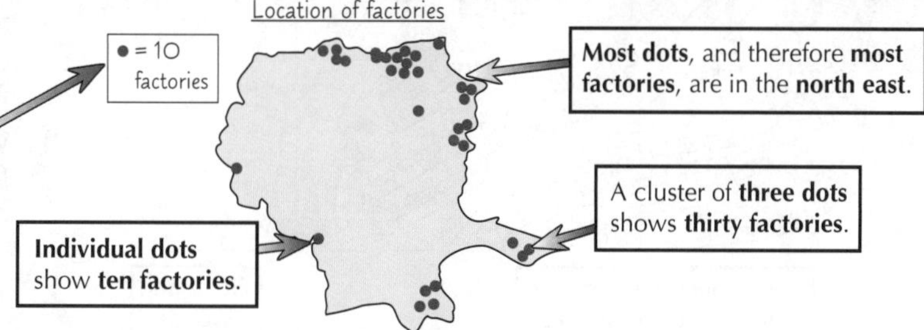

...Proportional Symbol Maps Use Symbols of Different Sizes

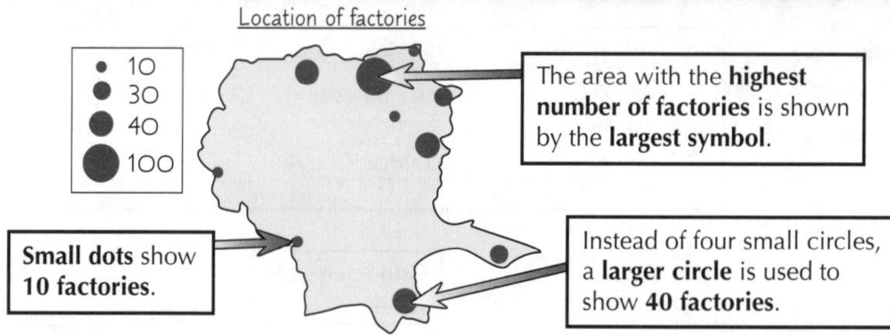

1) **Proportional symbol maps** use symbols of **different sizes** to represent **different quantities**.
2) A **key** shows the quantity each symbol represents. The **bigger** the **symbol**, the **larger** the **amount**.
3) The symbols might be **circles**, **squares**, **semi-circles** or **bars**, but they're always read the **same way**.

Flow Line Maps Show Movement

1) Flow line maps have **arrows** on, showing how things **move** (or are moved) from **one place to another**.
2) The map on the right shows the movement of people **into** and **out of a region**.
3) It's also a **proportional symbol map** as the size of the arrows show **how many** people are moving.

The **largest flows** of people are **to Region A**, as these are the **largest arrows**.

Roughly the same number of people are **immigrating to Region A from Regions B and C**. This is shown by the arrows, which are the **same size**.

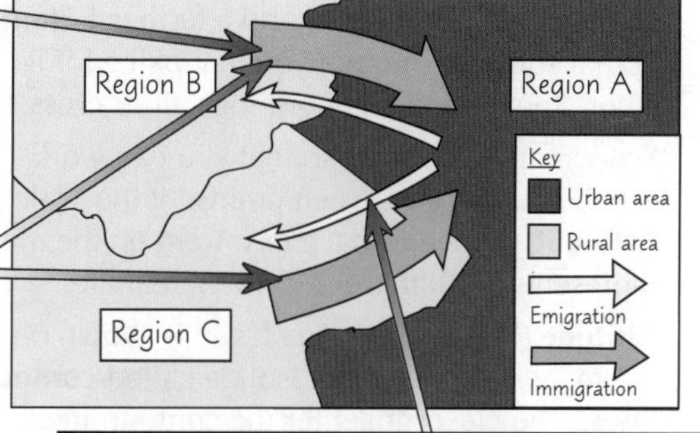

The **smallest flows** of people are **out of Region A**, as these are the **smallest arrows**.

Graph and Map Skills

Isoline Maps Show Where Conditions are the Same

1) **Isolines** are lines on a map **linking** up all the **places** where something's the **same**, e.g. on **weather maps** isolines show places that are the **same air pressure**.
2) If the place you're being asked about lies **on** an isoline you can just **read** the value off the line.
3) If the place is **between** isolines you have to **estimate** the value.
4) You also need to know a bit more about **weather maps** — see page 31 for more.

Helsinki and Lecce both lie **on** this line so both have a pressure of **996 mb**.

Madrid lies **between** the lines for **988** and **992**. It's pretty much in the middle of the lines, so has a pressure of roughly **990 mb**.

Map of low pressure system

996
992
988
984
980
LOW
Molde
Helsinki
Frankfurt
Madrid
Bratislava
Lecce

Town Centre Plans Show Detailed Information of Urban Areas

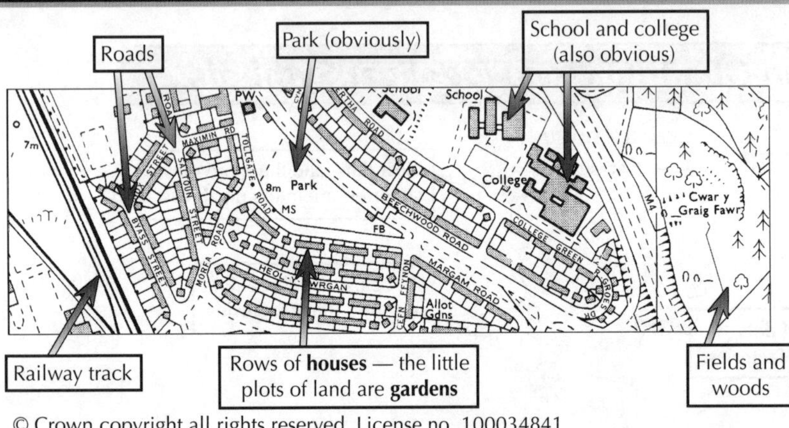

1) When you get a plan, start by looking at the **types of buildings** and what's **around** them.
2) **Small buildings** are probably **houses** or **shops**. **Bigger buildings** are probably **factories** or **schools**.
3) Work out what kind of **area** it is — lots of **car parks** and **shops** mean it's a **Central Business District** (CBD), **houses with gardens** mean a **residential area**.
4) The plan to the left shows a **residential area**.

Ordnance Survey Maps Show Detailed Information of All Areas

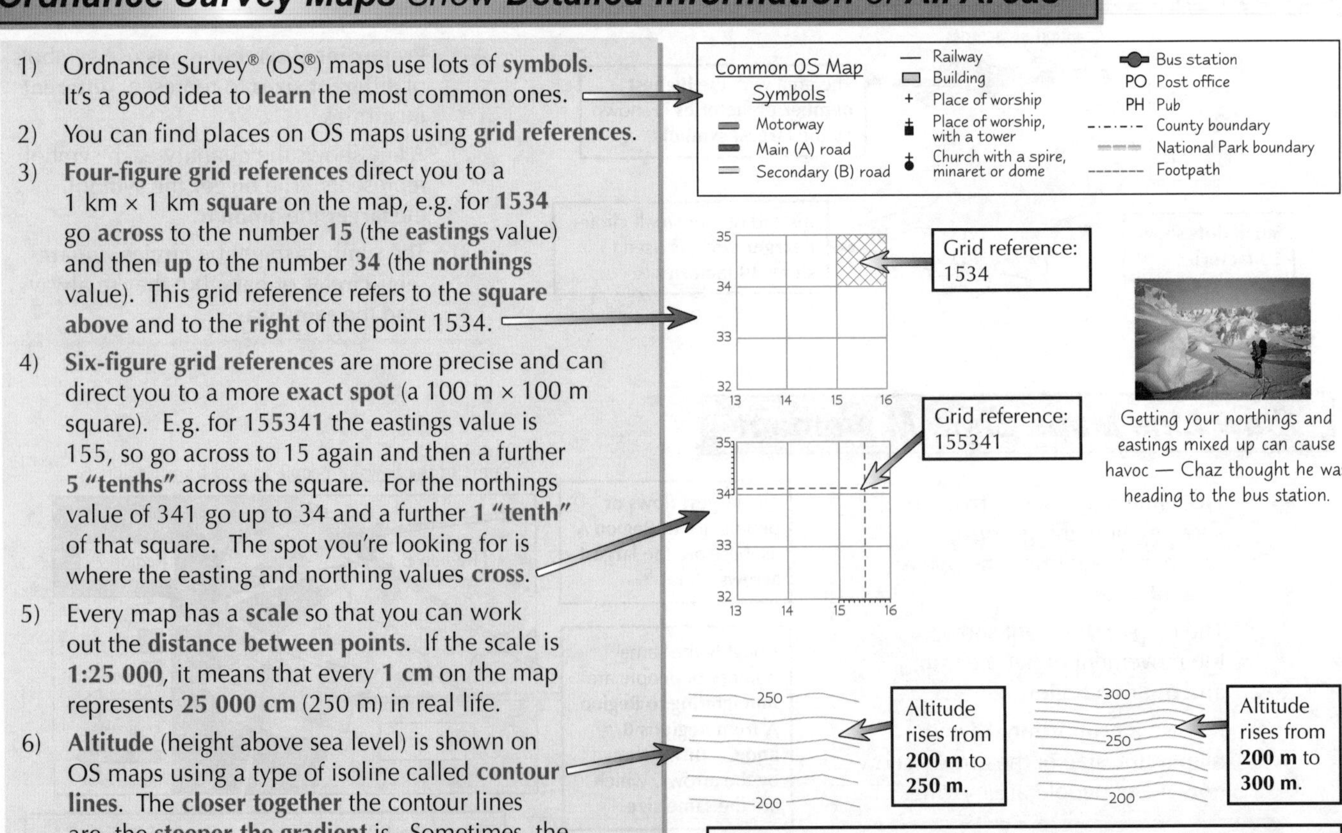

1) Ordnance Survey® (OS®) maps use lots of **symbols**. It's a good idea to **learn** the most common ones.
2) You can find places on OS maps using **grid references**.
3) **Four-figure grid references** direct you to a 1 km × 1 km **square** on the map, e.g. for **1534** go **across** to the number **15** (the **eastings** value) and then **up** to the number **34** (the **northings** value). This grid reference refers to the **square above** and to the **right** of the point 1534.
4) **Six-figure grid references** are more precise and can direct you to a more **exact spot** (a 100 m × 100 m square). E.g. for **155341** the eastings value is 155, so go across to 15 again and then a further **5 "tenths"** across the square. For the northings value of 341 go up to 34 and a further **1 "tenth"** of that square. The spot you're looking for is where the easting and northing values **cross**.
5) Every map has a **scale** so that you can work out the **distance between points**. If the scale is **1:25 000**, it means that every **1 cm** on the map represents **25 000 cm** (250 m) in real life.
6) **Altitude** (height above sea level) is shown on OS maps using a type of isoline called **contour lines**. The **closer together** the contour lines are, the **steeper the gradient** is. Sometimes, the altitude of specific **spot heights** is also given.

Getting your northings and eastings mixed up can cause havoc — Chaz thought he was heading to the bus station.

Statistical Skills

The next few pages may look as terrifying as your Geography teacher in their underwear, but I'll bet my lucky stapler that some statistics will crop up in your exams, so get learnin'.

There are **Different Ways** of Finding the **Average** Value of a Set of Data

1) The **mean**, **median** and **mode** are different ways of finding the **average** value of a set of data.
2) You find the **mean** by **adding up** all the numbers in a set of data, then **dividing** by the number of **sample points**, **n**.

Take a look at the data in this table:

Location	1	2	3	4	5	6	7	8	9	10	11
Temperature in °C	3	7	4	3	7	9	9	5	5	7	6

n = 11, so the mean temperature is: $\frac{3+7+4+3+7+9+9+5+5+7+6}{11}$ = **5.9 °C**.

3) The **median** is the **middle value** in an ordered set of data. So you need to **sort the numbers into order**, then work out which one is in the middle.
So for the data above the median is **6 °C**.

3 3 4 5 5 (6) 7 7 7 9 9

If there are an even number of sample points the median is the mean of the middle two numbers.

4) The **mode** is the **most common value** in a set of data.
So for the data above the mode is **7 °C**.

3 3 4 5 5 6 (7 7 7) 9 9

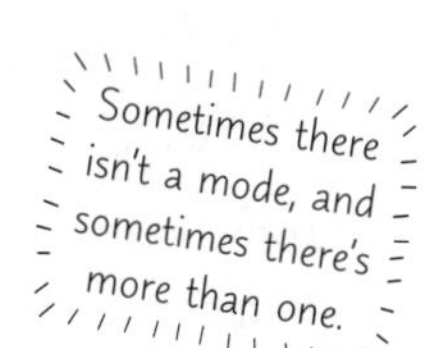

The **Interquartile Range** is a **Measure of Dispersion**...

1) The **interquartile range** (**IQR**) is the range of values covered by the **middle 50%** of a set of data.
2) To find the interquartile range you first need to find the median of the values **to the left** of the median. This is called the **lower quartile** (**LQ**). Next find the median of the values **to the right** of the median. This is the **upper quartile** (**UQ**). Then you just **subtract** the **LQ from the UQ** to give you the **IQR**.
3) So, for the data above, the **LQ** is **4** and the **UQ** is **7**, and the interquartile range is UQ – LQ = 7 – 4 = **3 °C**.

4) The interquartile range tells you about the **spread** of data **around** the **median**. If it's a **big** number, it shows that the numbers are pretty **spread out**. And yep, you've guessed it — a **small** number means that a lot of the data is pretty **close** to the **median**.

...and so is **Standard Deviation**

1) The **standard deviation** is a bit trickier to calculate than the IQR, but it's often a **more reliable** measure of dispersion (spread).
The symbol for it is σ.

The formula is $\sigma = \sqrt{\frac{\Sigma(x-\bar{x})^2}{n}}$

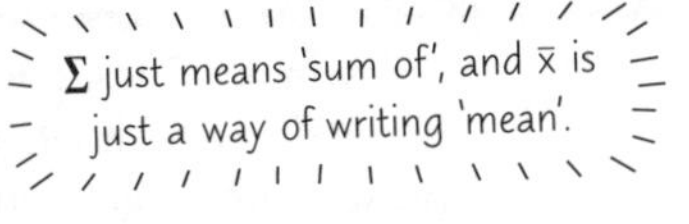

2) To calculate it, it's easiest to **work out** the **individual bits** in the formula **first**, e.g. the mean.
It's a good idea to **draw** a **table** to help you. Below is a simple example for the set: 5, 9, 10, 11, 14.

- For these numbers, the **mean** is (5 + 9 + 10 + 11 + 14) ÷ 5 = **9.8**.
This is shown in the 2nd column in the table.
- For each number, **calculate** $x - \bar{x}$ (3rd column in the table).
- Then **square** each of those values (4th column) — remember that the square of a **negative number** is always **positive**.
- Then **add up** all the squared numbers you've just worked out — this will give you $\Sigma(x-\bar{x})^2$.
- Now just **divide** your total by **n**, then take the **square root**.
- In this example, n = 5, so $\sigma = \sqrt{\frac{42.8}{5}}$ = **2.93** (2 d.p.)

x	$\bar{x}$	$x - \bar{x}$	$(x - \bar{x})^2$
5	9.8	−4.8	23.04
9	9.8	−0.8	0.64
10	9.8	0.2	0.04
11	9.8	1.2	1.44
14	9.8	4.2	17.64
		Σ	42.8

Standard deviation can be represented by σ or **s**.

3) If the standard deviation is **large**, the numbers in the set of data are **spread out** around the **mean**. If it's **small**, the numbers are **bunched** closely around the mean.

Statistical Skills

Make Sure You Know How to Find **Spearman's Rank Correlation Coefficient**

The Spearman's Rank correlation coefficient is a test to find out whether two sets of numbers are **correlated** (there's a **relationship** between them). The example below uses the test to see if **GDP per capita** ($) and **life expectancy** (in years) are correlated.

1) The bad news is that it's a bit of a pain to calculate. The first step is to give a **rank** to each number in both sets of data. The **highest** number is given rank **1**, the second highest is given rank 2... you get the idea.
2) Then you **calculate 'd'**, the **difference** between the ranks for each item, e.g. if the ranks for Country F are 4 and 6, the difference is 2.
3) Next you **square 'd'** and **add up** the **d^2 values** to give $\sum d^2$, which you use in the formula below.
4) Finally you need to work out the **Spearman's Rank Correlation Coefficient** (known as r_s).

The formula is: $r_s = 1 - \frac{6\sum d^2}{n^3 - n}$

Country	GDP per capita ($)	GDP rank	Life expectancy	Life expec. rank	d	d^2
A	14 000	5	72	5	0	0
B	19 000	4	71	6	2	4
C	9000	9	67	8	1	1
D	6000	11	61	11	0	0
E	21 000	3	75	3	0	0
F	13 000	6	74	4	2	4
G	22 000	2	76	2	0	0
H	35 000	1	78	1	0	0
I	5000	12	60	12	0	0
J	7000	10	65	9	1	1
K	11 000	8	64	10	2	4
L	12 000	7	69	7	0	0
					$\sum d^2$	14

5) So for the example above, $\sum d^2 = 14$ and n = 12. So $r_s = 1 - \frac{6 \times 14}{12^3 - 12} = 1 - \frac{84}{1716} = 1 - 0.05 = \mathbf{0.95}$.
6) The number you get is always **between –1** and **+1**.
7) A **positive number** means the variables are **positively correlated** — as one variable **increases** so does the **other**. The **closer** the number is to 1 the **stronger** the correlation.
8) A **negative number** means that the two sets of variables are **negatively correlated** — as one variable **increases** the other **decreases**. The **closer** the number is to –1 the **stronger** the correlation.
9) If the coefficient is **0**, or near 0, there probably isn't much of a relationship between the figures.
10) The value of r_s in the example above was **0.95**, which is **close to 1**, so there's a **strong positive correlation** between the **data** for GDP per capita and life expectancy.

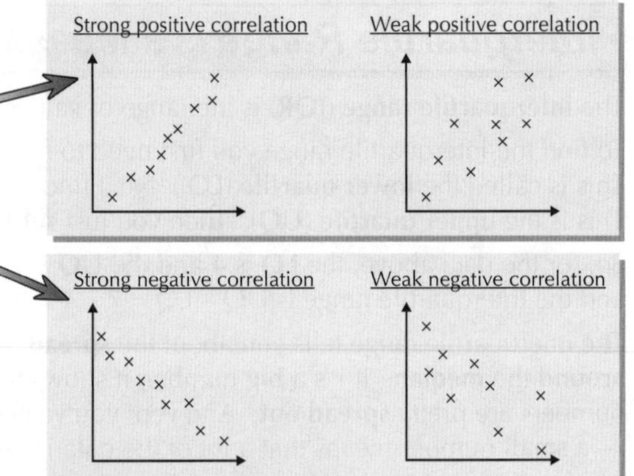

You **Have To Check** the **Correlation Is Significant** Though

1) A **Spearman's Rank correlation coefficient** might tell you that **two sets of numbers** are **correlated**. But you need to check whether this is evidence for a **genuine link** between the two quantities you're looking at. (You sometimes get correlations between sets of data **by chance**, even if there's no underlying relationship. For example, there **is** a correlation between GDP per capita and life expectancy **for the data shown above**, but this might have been a fluke and there might be **no real relationship** between the two things.)
2) You can check whether it's evidence for a genuine link by looking at the **probability** that a correlation would happen by chance. If there's a 5% (or higher) probability that a correlation is because of chance then it's **not significant** evidence for a link. If there's a **0.1% or less** chance, then it's **very significant** evidence for a link. (This is what's meant by the **significance level** of a statistical test — it's a kind of 'cut-off' probability.)
3) To test whether the value of r_s is evidence for a relationship between GDP per capita and life expectancy, you'll need a **graph** like the one on the right, or a **table** of critical values. You'll also need to know the **degrees of freedom** (in the example above this is just n – 2, so 12 – 2 = **10**). Since r_s = **0.95**, you can use the graph to find that this correlation has a **less than 0.1%** probability of being due to chance. This means you have **very significant** evidence for a **relationship** between GDP per capita and life expectancy.

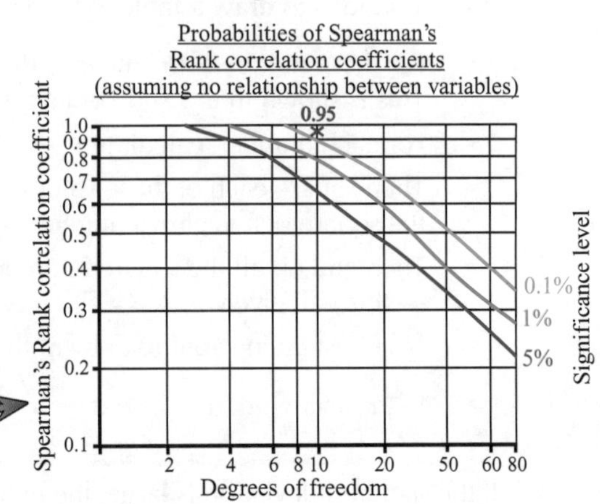

Statistical Skills

The Chi-Squared (χ^2) Test tells you whether Two Variables are Linked

1) There's no better way of explaining the chi-squared test than by showing you an example. So, here we go...

> A student is interested in finding out whether the **number of wells** in three areas of Africa is related to how much **rainfall** the areas receive each year.

2) In this case the two variables are the **number of wells** and the **amount of rainfall**.
3) You always start by making a **hypothesis** and a **null hypothesis**. The hypothesis is your theory about the link between the variables. In this example the student thinks the variables are linked, so the **hypothesis** is:

> **There is a link between the number of wells and the amount of rainfall the area receives.**

4) The **null hypothesis** is **always** that the two variables are **independent** (i.e. there isn't a link between them). E.g.:

> **There is no link between the number of wells and the amount of rainfall the area receives.**

5) First, use the null hypothesis to **predict** a **result** — this is called the **expected result**. In this example, there are 144 wells in total. If there was **no link** between rainfall and number of wells you'd **expect** that there would be an equal number of wells in each area, i.e. **48** (144 ÷ 3 = 48).
6) Next, the experiment is carried out and the **actual result** is recorded — this is called the **observed result**. The **observed** result in this case is the actual number of wells in each area.
7) The chi-squared (χ^2) **test** is then carried out and the **outcome** either supports the **null hypothesis** or allows you to **reject** it.

	Area A (lower rainfall)	Area B (medium rainfall)	Area C (higher rainfall)	
Expected	48	48	48	
Observed	64	49	31	
O – E	16	1	–17	
(O – E)²	256	1	289	
$\frac{(O-E)^2}{E}$	5.33	0.02	6.02	**11.37**

The χ^2 test uses a complicated looking **formula**.

$$\chi^2 = \Sigma \frac{(O-E)^2}{E}$$

You don't need to remember this equation — you'll be given it in the exam.

Put your observed values (**O**) and expected values (**E**) into this **equation** to work out chi-squared (χ^2) one step at a time:

- First calculate **O – E** (**subtract** the **expected** result from the **observed** result) for each area, e.g. 64 – 48 = 16.
- Then **square** each of the resulting numbers, e.g. $16^2 = 256$.
- Next, **divide** each of these figures by the **expected result**, e.g. 256 ÷ 48 = 5.33.
- Finally, **add** the numbers for Areas A, B and C together to get χ^2. 5.33 + 0.02 + 6.02 = 11.37, so χ^2 = **11.37**.

Compare Your Result to the Critical Value

1) The χ^2 value shows whether there is a **significant difference** between your observed and expected results. If there **is** a significant difference, this suggests your two variables are **linked** (and you can **reject** the null hypothesis).
2) To find out if there is a significant difference between your observed and expected results you need to **compare** your **χ^2 value** to a **critical value**.
3) The critical value is the χ^2 value that corresponds to a 0.05 (**5%**) level of **probability** that the **difference** between the observed and expected results is **due to chance**.
4) If your χ^2 value is **smaller** than the critical value then there is **no significant difference** between the observed and expected results. This means your variables are **independent** and you accept your **null hypothesis**.
5) If your χ^2 value is **larger** than the critical value then there is a **significant difference** between the observed and expected results (something **other than chance** is causing the difference). This suggests that there is a link between your two variables and the **null hypothesis** is **rejected**.
6) For this example the critical value is **5.99**. The χ^2 value of 11.37 is bigger than 5.99, so there is a significant difference between the observed and expected results and the **null hypothesis** is **rejected**.
7) Be careful with your conclusions though — your χ^2 value is **evidence supporting** your hypothesis that there is a **link** between the number of wells and the amount of rainfall. However, it **doesn't prove** this link — there could be **other factors** involved that you haven't considered in your investigation.

If you're not given the critical value, you might have to look it up in a table.

Statistical Skills

The *Mann-Whitney U Test* Shows if Two Data Sets are *Significantly Different*

1) You use the **Mann-Whitney U Test** to work out if two sets of **unrelated** data are statistically different.
2) Take a look at this example:

> A student wants to find out whether **grazing by sheep** reduces the **number** of **plant species** in a field, compared to a field that hasn't been grazed at all. She studies two fields — Field A is ungrazed and Field B is grazed by sheep.

3) The **hypothesis** is that there **is** a **significant difference** in the number of species found in grazed and ungrazed fields.
4) The **null hypothesis** is that there is **no significant difference** in the number of species found in grazed and ungrazed fields.
5) The number of species in ten quadrats in each of the fields were counted. Here are the results:

Number of species											
	Field A (ungrazed)	17	24	18	26	30	19	31	20	27	26
	Field B (grazed)	16	9	15	10	22	15	21	13	8	12

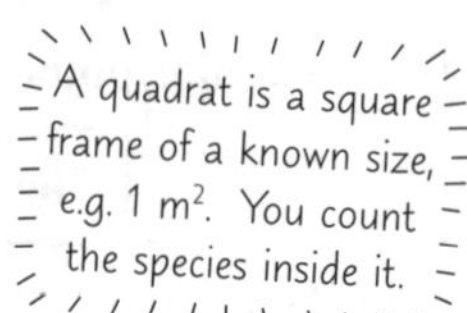

First You Need to *Rank the Data*

1) Look at **all** the data together and **rank** them regardless of what group they're in (i.e. Field A or Field B). Start with the **lowest score** (in the example it's 8) and give it a rank of '**1**'. Then the next lowest score gets a rank of '2' and so on.
2) If some of the values are the **same**, give them an **average** rank. Here there are two values of 15, so each has a rank of **6.5**.

Number of species											
	Field A (ungrazed)	17	24	18	26	30	19	31	20	27	26
	(rank)	(9)	(15)	(10)	(16.5)	(19)	(11)	(20)	(12)	(18)	(16.5)
	Field B (grazed)	16	9	15	10	22	15	21	13	8	12
	(rank)	(8)	(2)	(6.5)	(3)	(14)	(6.5)	(13)	(5)	(1)	(4)

Then *Add Up* the *Ranks* for *Each Group*

1) Add up the **ranks** for the ungrazed field group, then do the same for the grazed field group.

> Sum of ranks in **ungrazed field (Field A)** (R_A) = 9 + 15 + 10 + 16.5 + 19 + 11 + 20 + 12 + 18 + 16.5 = **147**
> Sum of ranks in **grazed field (Field B)** (R_B) = 8 + 2 + 6.5 + 3 + 14 + 6.5 + 13 + 5 + 1 + 4 = **63**

When you think about it, if the ungrazed field really did have a **greater number of plant species**, then you'd expect to see more species in the quadrats than the grazed field. This means that the **ranks** of the quadrats in the ungrazed field would also be **higher**.

2) Once you've added up the ranks for each group, you need to put your data into these scary-looking **formulas**:

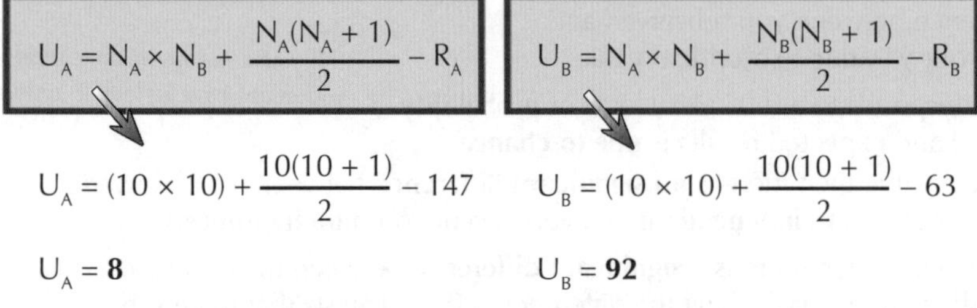

$$U_A = N_A \times N_B + \frac{N_A(N_A + 1)}{2} - R_A \qquad U_B = N_A \times N_B + \frac{N_B(N_B + 1)}{2} - R_B$$

$$U_A = (10 \times 10) + \frac{10(10 + 1)}{2} - 147 \qquad U_B = (10 \times 10) + \frac{10(10 + 1)}{2} - 63$$

$$U_A = \mathbf{8} \qquad U_B = \mathbf{92}$$

N_A is the number of quadrats in Field A
N_B is the number of quadrats in Field B
R_A is the sum of the ranks for Field A
R_B is the sum of the ranks for Field B

You might be given the critical value, or you might have to look it up in a table. For the Mann-Whitney U Test you need to use both N values (N_A and N_B) to find the critical value.

3) Take the **smaller** of these two numbers, 8, and call it '**U**'.
4) U must be **less than or equal to** the **critical value** to be **significant** and for you to **reject** the **null hypothesis**. Here, the critical value of U for a probability of 0.05 is 23.
5) U is **lower** than the critical value, so you can **reject** the **null hypothesis**.
6) Remember, this result is only **evidence** to support the **hypothesis** that there is a **significant difference** in the **number of species** in these two fields. You **don't know** whether that's down to grazing or some other factor.

Answers

Section 1 — Plate Tectonics

Page 3 — Plate Tectonics Theory

1 Maximum of 8 marks available. HINTS:
- Start by talking about the centre of the Earth — describe the structure of the core (inner and outer) and say what it's made from.
- Then describe the mantle, e.g. 'The mantle surrounds the core and is mostly made up of silicate rocks. The part of the mantle nearest the core is quite rigid. The layer above this is the asthenosphere. It's semi-molten, which means it can flow. The very top bit of the mantle is rigid'.
- Now describe the crust — make sure you mention the differences between the two types of crust. You should also describe the structure of the lithosphere, and say that it's split up into slabs called tectonic plates.
- Draw a simple, labelled diagram to help explain your answer.
- The question doesn't ask about the movement of the plates, so you don't need to talk about it.

2 Maximum of 8 marks available. HINTS:
- Start your answer by briefly saying how it occurs, e.g. 'Tectonic plates are moved by convection currents that flow in the asthenosphere'.
- Then describe and explain how a convection current is created in the mantle and core, e.g. 'Radioactive decay of some elements in the mantle and core, e.g. uranium, generates a lot of heat. When lower parts of the asthenosphere heat up they become less dense and slowly rise. As they move towards the top of the asthenosphere they cool down, become more dense, then slowly sink...'.
- Then describe how a convection current moves a tectonic plate, e.g. 'Convection currents create drag on the base of tectonic plates, which causes them to move'.
- Include a labelled diagram of the convection currents and plate movement to help explain your written answer.

Page 5 — Plate Tectonics Theory

1 Maximum of 40 marks available. HINTS:
- This is an essay question, so make sure your answer has a clear structure — you'll need an introduction, a description of each of the different types of evidence and a summary.
- In the introduction define the theory of plate tectonics, e.g. 'The Earth's lithosphere is made up of many plates that are moved around by convection currents in the mantle. This is the theory of plate tectonics'.
- Then talk about how the theory has developed over time, e.g. 'In 1912 Alfred Wegener proposed the theory of continental drift. However, he couldn't provide a mechanism that explained how the continents moved. In the 1950s and 1960s more evidence was discovered to support continental drift. Scientists developed the continental drift theory further to create the plate tectonics theory'.
- Then talk about each type of evidence in turn — aim to cover about four different types.
- Start by describing how the evidence supports the theory of plate tectonics, e.g. 'Areas of some continents have rocks of the same age and type. If you fit these continents together, the distribution of the rocks matches up. These rocks must have formed under the same conditions and in the same place in order to match so well. This would only be possible if the continents were once joined'.
- Then give an example of the evidence if you know one, e.g. 'For example, areas of South America and Africa have rocks of the same age and composition. Joining these continents together allows you to match up the distribution of the rock'.
- Then talk about another type of evidence for the theory.
- Make sure you include labelled diagrams when appropriate, e.g. for palaeomagnetism.

Page 7 — Types of Plate Margin

1 Maximum of 8 marks available. HINTS:
- Start by stating what a constructive plate margin is, e.g. 'A constructive margin occurs where two plates are moving apart'.
- Say that constructive margins can occur on land or under water.
- Then talk about mid-ocean ridges, include an example of one and explain how volcanoes form along them, e.g. 'Where diverging plates are underwater, a mid-ocean ridge forms. For example, the Mid-Atlantic Ridge is where the Eurasian plate and North American plate are moving apart. Underwater volcanoes can erupt along mid-ocean ridges. The mantle is under pressure from the plates above and when they move apart, the pressure is released...'.
- Talk about rift valleys and give an example of one, e.g. 'Where plates diverge beneath land, the crust between parallel fault lines drops down and forms a rift valley. For example, the East African Rift System has formed where the Nubian and Somalian plates are diverging. Volcanoes are found along the rift system, for example Kilimanjaro and Mount Kenya'.
- You could also describe how earthquakes occur at constructive margins, e.g. 'Earthquakes are a characteristic of constructive margins. This is because the plates don't always move apart in a uniform way, so pressure can build up. When the pressure becomes too much the plate cracks, making a fault line and causing an earthquake'.

2 Maximum of 8 marks available. HINTS:
- This question is asking about specific types of destructive plate margin, so make sure you only talk about them.
- The question asks you to compare and contrast the margins — this means you need to say how they're similar and how they're different.
- Firstly, describe what happens at oceanic-oceanic destructive margins, e.g. 'When two plates of oceanic crust are moving towards each other, the denser of the two will be subducted. This forms a deep sea trench. The subducted crust is heated by friction and contact with the upper mantle, which melts it into magma. The magma is less dense than the crust above, so it will rise back to the surface to form volcanoes. Volcanic eruptions will take place underwater and so create island arcs. These are clusters of islands that sit in a curved line, for example the Mariana Islands. As one plate moves under the other they can get stuck. This causes pressure to build up, and when the pressure becomes too much the plates jerk past each other, causing an earthquake'.
- Then point out how continental-continental destructive margins compare, e.g. 'When continental crusts converge they form fold mountains, but there's no volcanic activity as neither is subducted...'.

Page 10 — Volcanic Activity

1 Maximum of 7 marks available. HINTS:
- Start your answer by briefly describing what a hot spot is and what causes it, e.g. 'A hot spot is an area of volcanic activity found away from a plate margin. A hot spot is caused by a magma plume — a vertical column of magma that rises up from the mantle'.
- Describe the distribution of the Hawaiian islands, making sure that you include plenty of relevant details from the map. E.g. 'The oldest island is Kauai, at 6 million years old, and the islands become younger in age as you move towards the south-east'.
- Next, give reasons why the islands are distributed in this way. State that the chain of volcanic islands has formed due to the magma plume staying still, whereas the plate has moved over it in a north-westerly direction.

2 Maximum of 8 marks available. HINTS:
- Even though your answer won't be that long (it's only worth eight marks), make sure it's got a clear structure — write a short introduction and a section for each of the features.
- In the introduction state that these features are types of extrusive volcanic activity. Explain that they form when groundwater has been heated by magma underground.
- Next, describe what each of the features are and how they form. The question only mentions geysers and boiling mud pools but it'll help you to describe them if you include some information about hot springs as well. E.g. 'Springs are places where groundwater emerges at the surface. If the groundwater source of a spring flows close to an area of recent intrusive volcanic activity, the water is heated and the spiring becomes a hot spring. Geysers are a type of hot spring where hot water and steam are periodically ejected from the surface in a fountain. They form when groundwater is heated by magma deep in the crust to over its boiling point...'.

Page 13 — Seismic Activity

1 Maximum of 8 marks available. HINTS:
- Start by introducing the different types of seismic wave, e.g. 'There are three main types of seismic wave. These are P (primary) waves, S (secondary) waves and Surface waves. Two types of Surface wave are Love waves and Rayleigh waves'.
- Describe the first type of wave you introduced. E.g. 'P waves push and pull the Earth in the same direction as the wave is travelling. They can travel through both solids (e.g. rock) and liquids (e.g. sea). They travel faster than other types of seismic wave'.

Answers

- Then describe each of the other waves you introduced in turn.
- Remember, the question's only asking you to describe the types of wave, so you don't need to compare them in detail.

2 Maximum of 8 marks available. HINTS:
- Begin your answer by briefly saying what tsunamis are, e.g. 'Tsunamis are large waves caused by the displacement of large volumes of water'.
- Then describe the different causes of tsunamis. For example, start by talking about earthquakes, e.g. 'Underwater earthquakes can cause the seabed to move, which displaces water. Waves radiate out from the epicentre of the earthquake'. Then, mention other causes — e.g. volcanic eruptions and landslides.
- Finally describe the characteristics of tsunamis, e.g. 'In the open ocean where the water is very deep, the waves travel at high speeds of 500-950 km/h. They have a long wavelength of about 200 km, and a small amplitude of about 1 m'.
- Make sure you include some figures in your description of the characteristics. For example, give the wavelengths in open water and close to the shore, and say how the speed of the waves changes.

Page 15 — Managing the Impacts of Tectonic Hazards

1 Maximum of 40 marks available. HINTS:
- This is a 40-mark essay question so the structure of your answer is really important. It may help you to write a brief essay plan before you begin.
- Introduce your answer by defining what a tectonic hazard is, e.g. 'A tectonic hazard is a hazard caused by movement of tectonic plates. Earthquakes, volcanoes and tsunamis are examples of tectonic hazards'.
- You then need to describe the different strategies for managing the impacts of tectonic hazards. You should split them logically — you can do this in two ways. Either talk about a type of hazard and the different strategies used to manage it, or talk about the type of strategy (e.g. prediction or planning) and how it can be applied to the different hazards.
- After each of the strategies you describe, you should critically evaluate them. This means that you should say how successful a strategy is, e.g. 'Earthquake warning systems can detect P waves, but only after an earthquake has begun. These waves travel faster than other types of seismic wave and cause less damage so they can be used as a warning for stronger tremors. However, even far away from the epicentre the warnings may only arrive a few seconds before the strong tremors. This will not give people enough time to prepare for the earthquake or to evacuate'.
- Try to include examples of the strategies you write about, e.g. 'Japan's Earthquake Early Warning system was set up in 2007. When a P wave is detected warnings are sent out by TV and radio'.

Page 17 — Volcanic Eruption Case Study — Montserrat

1 Maximum of 8 marks available. HINTS:
- This is a case study question so make sure you choose to write about a volcanic event you know lots about.
- Give details of the volcanic event you have chosen — include what happened, where and when, e.g. 'The Soufrière Hills volcano on the island of Montserrat erupted on 25th June 1997. The eruption caused rockfalls and the formation of a massive ash cloud and pyroclastic flows'.
- Write about the economic impacts, social impacts and the environmental impacts. Make it clear in your answer what kind of impact you're writing about. E.g. 'An environmental impact of the eruption is that large areas of the island were covered with volcanic material. For example, the capital city Plymouth was buried under 12 m of mud and ash'.
- The question also asks you to talk about the responses to the eruption. Talk about a few short-term responses (e.g. evacuation) and a few long-term responses (e.g. setting up the Montserrat Volcano Observatory).

Page 19 — Volcanic Eruption Case Study — Mt St Helens

1 Maximum of 10 marks available. HINTS:
- You need to do two things in this answer:
  1) Describe how management strategies affected the impacts.
  2) Contrast this for two examples (i.e. point out the differences).
- Make sure you pick two case studies that are different (otherwise you won't have much to talk about).
- Begin your answer by briefly introducing your two examples (include when and where the eruptions happened).
- For the main body of your answer, describe the hazard management strategies for one eruption and explain how they affected the impacts. Then say how it was different in your other example. For example, 'At Montserrat, scientists had studied the volcano in the 1980s, but their report was not given a lot of attention. There was no disaster management plan and this meant that the response to the eruption was slow. This was not the case at Mount St Helens, where the USGS were monitoring the volcano prior to the eruption. Before the eruption, they issued warnings and around 2000 people were evacuated from the area'.
- Don't forget to include facts and figures to back up your points, e.g. 'Despite the Mount St Helens eruption being well managed, the eruption still caused $1.1 billion of damage and killed 57 people'.

Page 21 — Earthquake Case Study — L'Aquila

1 Maximum of 10 marks available. HINTS:
- You need to talk about at least one case study — you should have studied at least two. Whichever case study (or studies) you write about make sure you know them well enough to be able to quote facts and figures.
- Start with a brief description of the event — when it happened, where it happened, how big it was on the Richter scale.
- The question is asking you to critically evaluate the management strategies — so you need to include whether they were successful or not.
- The easiest way to do this is to describe the strategy then link it to the impacts. For example, 'There were strict building regulations in place in L'Aquila to make sure that new buildings were able to withstand earthquakes. However, some of these buildings were severely damaged or destroyed by the quake. For example, the San Salvatore hospital had been built in west L'Aquila in 2000 and was supposed to be in accordance with the regulations. But the building wasn't strong enough to withstand the earthquake and it collapsed. This hampered the efforts to treat some of the 1500 people injured in the earthquake as patients had to be treated in tents outdoors'.

Page 23 — Earthquake Case Study — Kashmir

1 Maximum of 10 marks available. HINTS:
- Begin your answer by briefly introducing the two examples you've chosen and describing some of the impacts. For example, 'L'Aquila (Italy) was struck by an earthquake measuring 6.3 on the Richter scale on the 6th April 2009. It killed around 300 people and caused an estimated $15 billion of damage. A stronger magnitude 7.6 earthquake hit the Kashmir region to the north of Pakistan on the 8th October 2005, killing around 80 000 people'.
- Write about the responses to the two earthquakes, but make sure you compare and contrast them as you go (i.e. point out where they're similar and where they're different). E.g. 'In response to the L'Aquila earthquake ambulances, fire crews and the army were sent in to rescue survivors. The immediate response to the Kashmir earthquake was much slower. Many areas did not receive help for days or even weeks. People had to be rescued by hand without any equipment or help from the emergency services'.
- Conclude your answer by briefly stating how the different responses affected the impacts. E.g. 'The slow response to the Kashmir earthquake increased the severity of the social impacts as the millions of people made homeless by the quake had little food, shelter or medical supplies. The faster response to the L'Aquila earthquake...'.

Section 2 — Weather and Climate

Page 25 — Climate Basics

1 Maximum of 8 marks available. HINTS:
- Start with an introduction where you state that the vertical structure of the atmosphere is divided into four layers — the troposphere, the stratosphere, the mesosphere and the thermosphere.
- Then describe the four layers. For each layer, give its height, then describe and explain the temperature (whether it increases or decreases through the layer, giving temperature values in °C) and the turbulence (whether the layer is turbulent or calm).
- You need to give reasons for each of the characteristics in each layer.
- You could draw a simple, labelled diagram to show the position of the four layers.

Answers

Page 27 — Climate Basics

1 Maximum of 8 marks available. HINTS:
- Write an introduction where you state that more solar radiation is received at the equator than the poles, and that winds help redistribute this energy to maintain a balance.
- Describe the way that winds are caused by differences in air pressure, and are part of global atmospheric circulation cells. Describe these cells, e.g. 'They consist of warm air rising creating low pressure zones, and cool air falling creating high pressure zones, and winds moving from the high pressure to the low pressure zones'.
- Use a simple diagram to show Hadley, Ferrel and Polar Cells — include arrows to show the direction of the surface winds.
- Starting at the Equator, describe the air circulation, e.g. 'At the Equator the sun warms the air and it rises, creating low pressure. As the air rises it cools and flows out to 30° North and South of the Equator, where it sinks, creating high pressure. When the cool air reaches the ground surface it either returns to the Equator or moves towards to the poles in surface winds'.

Page 29 — UK Climate

1 Maximum of 8 marks available. HINTS:
- Start by briefly describing the UK climate, e.g. 'The UK climate is temperate, with cool, wet winters and warm, wet summers'.
- Give the latitude of the UK, and explain how this affects climate.
- Describe the maritime location of the UK, and explain how this affects climate e.g. 'The UK is an island surrounded by water. Water gains and loses heat more slowly than land. This means that in the summer, the sea is cooler than the land, and in the winter it is warmer than the land. This causes cool winds to blow from the sea to the land in summer, and warm winds to blow from the sea to the land in winter'.
- Describe the UK's location relative to global atmospheric circulation cells, and explain how this affects climate, e.g. 'The UK is found on the northern edge of a Ferrel Cell, where south westerly surface winds bring warm air from the south. This warm air is rising, creating a zone of low pressure, causing depressions that bring rain throughout the year'.
- Describe the UK's location relative to the Gulf Stream, and explain how this affects climate, e.g. 'The Gulf Stream is a warm ocean current which passes along the west coast of the UK. It makes the UK climate warmer than other places at a similar latitude'.

Page 31 — UK Weather Systems

1 Maximum of 8 marks available. HINTS:
- Write an introduction briefly describing how a depression begins to form.
- Give a brief overview of the pressure patterns, isobars associated with a depression and say that it flows anti-clockwise.
- Describe the different stages of a depression in a sensible order (e.g. as the warm front passes, as the warm air is overhead, as the cold air passes etc.).
- For each stage of the depression describe the differences in the weather, give clear reasons for the changes and explain why they occur. E.g. 'As the warm front passes overhead temperatures increase and there is heavy rainfall. This is because the warm air rises over the body of cold air and water vapour in the warm air condenses, forming clouds and leading to heavy rain'.
- Make sure that the links between the changing weather and the reasons for it are obvious — don't just list the weather types, make sure the causes match up with them clearly.

Page 33 — UK Storms

1 Maximum of 10 marks available. HINTS:
- Introduce the storm you've studied — give the date and location of the storm. E.g. 'Between the 15th and 16th October 1987 the UK and France were hit by a severe storm'.
- Write a section on the impacts of the storm. Divide them by economic, social and environmental impacts, and make sure you've got at least one of each. Include as many specific details as you can, e.g. 'There were 18 deaths; around 15 million trees were blown down' etc.
- Write a section on the responses to the storm. Discuss the immediate responses (e.g. severe weather warnings, emergency responses by emergency services and the military etc.)
- Then discuss longer term responses after the storm (e.g. clean up operations, any improvements made as a result of the evaluation of responses).
- Be as specific as you can when giving examples of responses — include times, dates, organisations involved, relevant data etc. E.g. 'As part of the clean up operation forestry workers collected 4 million m^3 of timber from fallen trees. It took over two years for all the timber to be collected and stored'.

Page 35 — Tropical Climates

1 Maximum of 8 marks available. HINTS:
- Introduce the region you've studied — give the climate type and the location of the region. E.g. 'Monsoon climates are found in coastal regions 5–20° North and South of the Equator'.
- Describe the climate in the region — include winds, average annual temperature range, average annual rainfall and rainfall variation, and explain why the climate is like that. E.g. 'Monsoon climates are hot all year round (between 18–30 °C), and temperature varies by up to 10 °C between summer and winter. It's hot because the sun is high in the sky, so large amounts of solar radiation reach the surface'.
- Give some example data for the location you've studied. E.g. 'Chittagong (Bangladesh) has a monsoon climate. Temperature varies from 19.9–28.4 °C. Rainfall is 2796 mm a year — and it varies from 6 mm in January to 818 mm in July'.
- Describe and explain how movements of the ITCZ affect the climate of your region, e.g. 'The tropical monsoon climate is affected by the seasonal shift of the ITCZ. It moves north of the Equator in summer and south of the Equator in winter. In the wet season the ITCZ is overhead, which brings low pressure and heavy rainfall. The low pressure is over the land, and high pressure is over the ocean so winds blow onshore. In the dry season...'.

Page 37 — Tropical Revolving Storms

1 Maximum of 7 marks available. HINTS:
- Start by describing what tropical revolving storms are, e.g. 'Tropical revolving storms are huge spinning storms with strong winds and torrential rain'.
- State that scientists don't know exactly how they form, but they do know the conditions needed. Then list the conditions needed.
- Describe their distribution (including their alternative names in different parts of the world).
- Finish up by explaining why they move west, away from the Equator and why they lose strength over land.

2 Maximum of 8 marks available. HINTS:
- List the main types of responses — evacuation, planning, education, building techniques and aid.
- For each type of response explain whether it's effective or not, e.g. 'Prediction of storms is important because it allows people time to evacuate safely before the storm hits. If the prediction is made far enough in advance it can significantly reduce the number of deaths. For example, in 1997 a cyclone in Bangladesh only killed around a hundred people because there was enough time to carry out a successful evacuation'.
- Try to give a balanced evaluation of a response's effectiveness. E.g. 'Evacuation is not so effective when it's difficult to communicate the evacuation order, for example in remote areas'.
- Try to include real life examples where you can, e.g. levees breaking in New Orleans, or Burma's government initially refusing to let aid workers in.

Page 39 — Tropical Revolving Storm Case Study — Katrina

1 Maximum of 10 marks available. HINTS:
- The wording 'With reference to one example' means that this is a case study question.
- The first thing to do is briefly introduce the case study, e.g. 'Hurricane Katrina hit the south east USA on 29th August 2005. It was a category 4 hurricane when it made landfall'.
- Then briefly describe the impacts, e.g. 'More than 1800 people were killed, and hundreds of thousands were made homeless'.
- Describe the preparation and responses, and comment on how they affected the impacts of the storm. Try and give as many specific examples as you can, e.g. 'The mayor of New Orleans ordered a mandatory evacuation of the town. Around 80% of residents evacuated, which meant that the death toll was much lower than it would otherwise have been'.

Answers

Page 41 — Tropical Revolving Storm Case Study — Nargis

1 Maximum of 40 marks available. HINTS:
- The word 'discuss' means you need to weigh something up. In this question it means you need to weigh up whether (and how) the level of development of a country is related to the severity of the impacts of tropical revolving storms.
- You need to discuss why the social impacts are usually higher in less developed countries using detail from the case studies you've learnt.
- The main reason the social impacts are usually higher in less developed countries is that they don't have the money to prepare for tropical revolving storms, but don't forget other things like the fact that more people depend on agriculture in less developed countries, and agriculture is often badly affected.
- For each point you make, use examples from your case studies to either back up the point or contradict it, e.g. 'In less developed countries the buildings are poorly constructed and are more easily damaged by storms. Hurricane Katrina in the USA damaged fewer than 100 schools, whereas Cyclone Nargis (a storm of comparable strength) damaged around 4000 schools. This could have been due to poorer quality construction'.
- Include a paragraph about the fact that the economic impact is usually higher in more developed countries, e.g. 'The economic impact is usually higher in more developed countries because the buildings and infrastructure damaged are usually worth more money. For example, when Hurricane Katrina hit the USA it caused an estimated $300 billion of damage, whereas when Cyclone Nargis hit Burma it only caused an estimated $4 billion worth of damage. High value infrastructure damaged by Katrina included oil platforms and international shipping ports'.
- Finish off your answer with a conclusion, e.g. 'In general, the severity of the social impacts is much higher in less developed countries than more developed countries. However, when the storm is extremely strong even developed countries suffer badly, as no amount of preparation is enough for the force of the storm. Generally, the severity of the economic impact is...'.

Page 43 — Urban Climate Characteristics

1 Maximum of 7 marks available. HINTS:
- You need to describe the differences and suggest reasons for them.
- Take your time to study the table and pick out the differences.
- Once you've done that write about each climate characteristic at a time — say what the difference is and explain why they might be different, e.g. 'Annual average rainfall is 100 mm higher in City B than in City A. This could be because City B has more pollution than City A, so there are more condensation nuclei in the air to encourage cloud formation'.
- Try to manipulate the data if you can, e.g. 'The average number of days without cloud cover is 50% higher in City A than City B'.

Page 45 — Urban Air Quality

1 Maximum of 8 marks available. HINTS:
- Begin by stating that there are lots of different ways of reducing air pollution in urban areas. Write that road traffic emissions cause the majority of pollution in urban areas — so most pollution reduction policies focus on reducing road traffic.
- Describe in detail a few different pollution reduction schemes you have studied — e.g. congestion charging, using number plates to restrict car use, clean air acts, construction of tall chimneys, alternative fuels.
- For each scheme/strategy:
  i) Describe how the scheme reduces pollution.
  ii) Describe any problems associated with the scheme.
  iii) Give specific examples of the scheme, including data where you can.
- For example, 'Congestion charging involves charging people to use their vehicles in certain places at certain times. It aims to reduce pollution by discouraging people from driving. Problems with congestion charging include increased traffic outside the zone and difficulties enforcing the charge. Congestion charging in Central London was introduced in 2003 and has reduced traffic and emissions by up to 15%'.

Page 47 — Climate Change — Evidence

1 Maximum of 8 marks available. HINTS:
- To get full marks you need to outline (describe and explain) a number of sources of evidence for climate change, e.g. ice cores, pollen analysis and indicators of sea level change.
- Structure the answer to have an introduction, then separate sections outlining each of the sources of evidence, and finish with a conclusion.
- In your introduction, define the key terms of the question such as 'climate change', e.g. 'Climate change is any significant change in the weather of a region over a period of at least several decades'.
- For each source of evidence, describe it and then explain how it's used to determine past climate, e.g. 'Scientists can drill deep into ice sheets (huge masses of ice) to extract cores of ice. Scientists can analyse the gases trapped in the ice cores, and the chemistry of the ice to tell what the temperature was when the ice formed. For example, oxygen has two isotopes — O-16 and O-18. During periods of cold climate, water containing the lighter O-16 is more readily evaporated from seawater...'.

Page 50 — Climate Change — Causes and Impacts

1 Maximum of 8 marks available. HINTS:
- Start by describing how global warming will affect the climate in the UK — include temperature and rainfall patterns.
- Use specific examples and locations — e.g. 'Summer average temperature is expected to increase by 3.9 °C in Southern England by 2080'.
- Describe the potential impacts of climate change — e.g. rising sea levels, increased droughts, changing agriculture, and changing habitats.
- For each impact, include specific examples and locations — e.g. 'Sea level is expected to rise by 13-76 cm by 2095. The areas worst affected by sea level rise will be towns and cities on coastal estuaries (e.g. Hull, Cardiff, and London) and low lying areas near the coast (e.g. large areas of Norfolk)'.

Page 53 — Climate Change — Responses

1 Maximum of 8 marks available. HINTS:
- To evaluate the international responses you need to first explain what the responses are and then assess their impacts.
- Describe the responses, giving examples to back up your point. The Kyoto Protocol is a good example, because it has had mixed success, so there's plenty to write about.
- For each response, give as much detail as you can and then assess whether the response is effective, e.g. 'Developed countries in the Kyoto agreement have agreed to cut emissions by 5% overall. However, not all developed countries signed up to the agreement. Some of the largest polluters (e.g. the USA) chose to stay out of the Kyoto protocol because it would affect their economies. This means that the response is less effective than it could have been because the largest polluters, who have the greatest effect on global emissions, aren't trying to reduce their emissions in the same way'.
- Think about other possible problems with coordinating the international responses to global warming, e.g. problems with enforcing the agreement.

2 Maximum of 40 marks available. HINTS:
- This question is asking to what extent you agree with the statement. You need to decide whether you agree or disagree and explain why. It doesn't matter which way you argue, as long as your answer is relevant to the statement and you give reasons for each point you make.
- Start with an introduction which briefly explains what greenhouse gas emissions are and why we need to reduce them, e.g. 'Greenhouse gases are produced through the burning of fossil fuels. Greenhouse gas emissions need to be reduced because they are one of the main causes of global warming'. Go on to say that changing the energy mix of the UK to include less fossil fuels is an important way of reducing greenhouse gas emissions, but that there are other ways. Then say whether you agree or disagree with the statement.
- Go through each of the reasons why you agree or disagree in turn. Explain each point in detail, giving a balanced argument. E.g. 'There are other ways to reduce greenhouse gas emissions which could be as important as using less fossil fuels. A switch over from fossil fuels takes time and money to carry out, and in the meantime shorter term solutions are needed. Government schemes such as offering financial incentives to encourage people to insulate their homes or buy lower emissions cars can be very effective at reducing emissions. Although the impact from these changes would not be as large as the benefit gained from changing over to renewable sources of energy, it could significantly reduce greenhouse gas emissions while renewable energy sources are developed'.
- Even if you agree with the statement you should discuss a range of ways of reducing greenhouse gas emissions and say whether they are important or not (e.g. saving energy in the home, recycling waste, reducing emissions from transport, buying local produce).
- Back up your points with detail and facts where possible, e.g. 'Reducing the burning of fossil fuels in the UK is very important to reducing greenhouse gas emissions because the burning of fossil fuels is responsible for a large part of the UK's emissions. Of the reductions in emissions in the UK by 2020, around 40% will be due to a reduction in the burning of fossil fuels'.

Answers

- At the end write a short conclusion — say whether or not you agree with the statement and use a sentence or two to summarise why. It's important that your conclusion is related to the rest of your answer and that it completes your argument.

Section 3 — Ecosystems

Page 55 — Ecosystem Basics

1 Maximum of 7 marks available. HINTS:
- Discuss the diagram in order of the web's hierarchy. Start with the autotroph and move up through the trophic levels to herbivores, carnivores/omnivores and top carnivores.
- Refer specifically to the diagram, using the names of the consumers shown rather than talking about food webs and chains in general.
- Show that you know which consumer belongs to which trophic level, e.g. 'Greenfly is a primary consumer (herbivore) while a sparrow is a primary and secondary consumer because it is an omnivore'.
- Explain how energy is lost in the process of consuming as well as from the consumer themselves, e.g. 'The sparrow loses some energy through respiration and waste, and the sparrowhawk loses further energy in eating the sparrow, as it cannot digest the bones or the feathers'.

Page 57 — Succession

1 Maximum of 8 marks available. HINTS:
- Choose one of the examples from these pages. Explain what your chosen succession is and where you might find it. E.g. 'A lithosere is a succession that starts on bare rock, for example on new ground created after a volcanic eruption'.
- Describe the main stages of the succession in turn. For each stage, describe the abiotic conditions, the plants that move in and why they can grow there. E.g. 'At first the rock is dry and has no organic matter. The pioneer species are lichens — they can survive on bare rock because they require very little water and nutrients'.
- Explain the effects the plants have on their environment, e.g. 'Lichens break down the rock, and release minerals. They also hold some water, this makes the environment less hostile and enables mosses to grow'.
- Give specific examples of plants wherever you can, e.g. 'At the climatic climax, the soil is deep enough for large tree species like ash and oak trees to grow'.
- Use scientific terminology, e.g. pioneer species, decompose, organic matter, out-compete, dominant species, climax species.

Page 59 — Succession

1 Maximum of 10 marks available. HINTS:
- Describe the characteristics of the area, e.g. 'The North York Moors are heather moorland. This is a plagioclimax characterised by large areas of open country covered with heather'.
- Describe and explain how the plagioclimax was created. Say what the area used to be (e.g. 'The moors used to be an oak forest'.) and describe the activities that led to the plagioclimax. For each activity explain why it was carried out (e.g. 'Areas were deforested to make farming easier'), and how the activity prevented the climax being reached (e.g. 'Deforestation reduced soil quality').
- Describe why the plagioclimax is maintained. E.g. 'The moors are maintained because they provide grazing for sheep and grouse, and because they are an important habitat for rare plants and animals'.
- Explain how the plagioclimax is maintained. E.g. 'The heather is cleared by burning every 8-15 years — a few sections are burned each year in rotation. The oldest heather is burned because it gets tough and woody and eventually collapses. Burning encourages new heather shoots to grow (sheep and grouse graze these younger shoots). Burning also destroys other plants, which helps to ensure that the heather remains dominant'.
- Explain what would happen if the area was not maintained. E.g. 'Without burning the heather moorland would eventually become a temperate deciduous forest again, and the moorland plants and animals would lose their habitat and disappear'.
- Give specific examples of plant and animal life. E.g. grouse, sundew, golden plover.

Page 61 — Tropical Ecosystems — Characteristics

1 Maximum of 10 marks available. HINTS:
- Describe the climate of a tropical rainforest, e.g. temperature and rainfall. Where possible, give percentages or figures to back up your descriptions.
- Show that the climate creates abiotic conditions that affect animal and plant life, e.g. 'Soil moisture budget and humidity levels are high because of frequent heavy rainfall, which means that organisms have to be adapted to these conditions'.
- Concentrate your answer on explaining each climatic condition and listing the effects it has on the biotic conditions (the animals and plants living in the rainforest). Show that you understand how biotic factors change to suit the climatic conditions.
- You might do this for a paragraph on the effects of rainfall in the rainforest:
- Explain that the high temperatures encourage evaporation which increases the humidity levels in the rainforest. In turn, this promotes heavier rainfall. Give details for the amount of annual rainfall in the rainforest.
- Link the heavy and continual rainfall to plant adaptations in the rainforest. E.g. 'Plant leaves have drip-tips to funnel water, and trees have buttress roots to stabilise their very tall trunks'.
- Link the heavy and continual rainfall to animal adaptations in the rainforest. E.g. 'Pond turtles have webbed feet that let them both walk and swim on the wet forest floor'.

Page 63 — Tropical Ecosystems — Human Activity

1 Maximum of 10 marks available. HINTS:
- The question asks you to assess the impacts of human activity, so you need to write about what humans do and what effect their actions have on the tropical rainforest.
- Start with a brief introduction saying which biome you will discuss in your answer and what its main features are. Give a brief summary of the main human activities. E.g. 'Tropical rainforests are a biome with a hot, wet climate and high biodiversity. The primary human activity is deforestation, but overhunting, overfishing and climate change all have significant impacts on tropical rainforests'.
- For each human activity discuss the different impacts (environmental, social and economic) that this activity has on the rainforest, and give reasons why it is a problem. E.g. 'Deforestation can have negative impacts on the people living in the rainforest. The plants and animals they rely on to make their living may be destroyed, or they may be forced to sell their land so it can be used for commercial agriculture or logging'.
- Make sure you include some positive impacts as well as negative impacts, e.g. 'Deforestation often takes place to clear land for mining or agriculture. These activities can have a positive impact on the local economy by providing jobs for local people'.
- Give as much detail and as many examples as you can. E.g. 'Deforestation causes habitat loss. This affects biodiversity because species that can't adapt or move face decline or extinction. For example, in Brazil the number of endangered species has nearly tripled from 218 in 1989 to 628 in 2008'.

Page 65 — Tropical Ecosystems — Sustainable Management

1 Maximum of 10 marks available. HINTS:
- Start with a brief introduction that explains the idea of sustainable management and explains why it is important.
- The question asks you to discuss methods of sustainable management and their effectiveness. This means you need to give details about different methods of sustainable management and then say whether they work or not.
- For each method start by explaining how it works, and why it is sustainable, e.g. 'Many countries have established national parks and nature reserves to help protect areas of rainforest. Within these protected areas, activities like logging and hunting are banned or heavily restricted. This means that the biodiversity of that area of rainforest is preserved'. Then go on to say how successful the method is and give details of any problems, e.g. 'It can often be difficult to enforce regulations within protected areas — the parks are huge areas of dense rainforest and there may not be enough funds to employ staff to patrol the whole area'.
- For each sustainable management technique give examples and as much detail as you can, e.g. 'Selective logging is less damaging than large scale deforestation, and it is permitted in some protected areas. As well as preserving the rainforest and allowing it to regenerate, selective logging can benefit local people. For example, in Papua New Guinea it's estimated that landowners receive ten times as much profit from selective logging as from commercial logging. However, it can still have serious impacts because it leaves a patchy canopy (so soil erosion can be a problem) and felling one tree can bring down as many as thirty others'.

Answers

Page 67 — Urban Ecosystems

1 Maximum of 8 marks available. HINTS:
- Introduce the routeways you will discuss — e.g. roads and railways. You may also have studied canals in class. Discuss at least two different types.
- Write a section for each routeway.
- Describe the ecosystem — start with the plants, then the invertebrates, then birds and mammals.
- For each group of organisms, explain why they are found there. E.g. 'Many different types of flowering plants are found along railways because trains bring seeds from a wide area. A variety of mammals are found because they use the railways as wildlife corridors, have a rich food source and are rarely disturbed'.
- Use specific examples / name species wherever possible. E.g. 'Mammals might include mice, rabbits and foxes'.

2 Maximum of 8 marks available. HINTS:
- Write an introduction where you define the rural/urban fringe and describe what ecosystems are found there. E.g. 'The rural/urban fringe is the area of land between an urban and a rural area. The fringe usually has a variety of ecosystems; both rural ecosystems (e.g. woodland, grassland, farmland) and urban ecosystems (e.g. gardens, sports fields, routeways) can be found there'.
- Describe the changes that may result from urbanisation.
- For each of the changes, give a specific example and describe its wider impacts. E.g. 'Rural ecosystems can be destroyed by new developments, such as a housing estate being built on an area that was previously woodland. A housing estate would generate air and water pollution, which can damage ecosystems — for example water pollution from domestic waste can reduce biodiversity in water courses, which can affect bird populations by reducing their food supply'.

Page 69 — Urban Ecosystems

1 Maximum of 10 marks available. HINTS:
- Write an introduction — state what an ecological conservation area is, and introduce the area you will discuss. E.g. 'Ecological conservation areas have a protected status to ensure that ecosystems are preserved and enhanced. The Mersey Forest is an ecological conservation area that includes a network of woodlands and other ecosystems in Cheshire and Merseyside'.
- Describe how the area is managed. E.g. 'The Mersey Forest is managed by a partnership of public, private and voluntary organisations, who work together to protect ecosystems, preserve biodiversity and provide green spaces for local people to enjoy'.
- Describe the ecosystems and species found in the area.
- Discuss how effective conservation strategies are. List the environmental, social and economic benefits specific to the area. Try to include some percentages or figures that back up your claims. E.g. 'Over 8 million trees have been planted, which has created habitat for woodland wildlife'.
- Explain why the conservation strategies have been effective (or not effective). E.g. 'The Bluebell Recovery Project is a sustainable conservation strategy because the project team are replanting bluebells using only locally sourced bluebell bulbs. British bluebells are being outcompeted by the invasive Spanish bluebell. By planting local varieties the project is helping to protect the native British bluebell and the natural ecosystem'.
- Try to include negative points or areas where the scheme has been less successful if you can, e.g. 'The Mersey Forest has brought a huge number of benefits to the area, but there is still a lot more that can be done, especially in urban areas. For example, in Liverpool...'.

Page 71 — Global Ecosystem Issues

1 Maximum of 8 marks available. HINTS:
- Write an introduction where you describe what fragile environments are, and give a few examples. E.g. 'Fragile environments are ecosystems that are easily disturbed and not able to adapt to change. Examples include coral reefs (which are very sensitive to changes in water temperature) and coastal wetlands (which are very sensitive to changes in water levels)'.
- Describe the threats to fragile environments, e.g. loss of biodiversity, climate change, pollution, extreme weather. Mention that once a fragile environment is damaged, it is extremely difficult or impossible to repair the damage.
- Explain that in many fragile environments there is a conflict between conservation and exploitation. Give an example of this, e.g. the need to conserve the Amazon rainforest vs. the economic benefits of logging and farming.
- Describe the difficulties associated with managing fragile environments. E.g. environments crossing international borders, lack of money or expertise, economic reliance on resources from ecosystems, problems of introduced species.
- Give specific examples where you can, e.g. 'The Brazilian economy is dependent on mining (of e.g. gold and iron) — the main mining company alone brought in $9 billion in 2006. However, clearing land to extract metals damages the environment, whilst access roads open up more land for agriculture and logging'.

Page 73 — Global Ecosystems Case Study — Serengeti

1 Maximum of 10 marks available. HINTS:
- Write an introduction describing the ecosystem you have studied — where it is, what type of ecosystem it is, and why it needs protecting.
- Then describe the management strategy used in the ecosystem. E.g. 'The Serengeti National Park is managed by Tanzania National Parks (TANAPA). The management approach involves trying to balance the need to conserve biodiversity with the needs of local people. Schemes include monitoring the ecosystem, protecting priority species, disease monitoring and vaccination programmes, preventing wildfires, local conservation education projects and the creation of four Wildlife Management Areas (WMAs) where local people legally manage wildlife'.
- Discuss how effective the schemes are. Start with a brief introduction where you summarise how effective the strategy has been overall. E.g. 'The schemes have improved understanding between local people and the National Park, but it is still proving difficult to balance wildlife conservation with the needs of local people'.
- Then go into detail about the effectiveness of different aspects of the scheme — describe things that have worked well and explain why, and things that have not worked so well and explain why. E.g. 'The WMAs are having some success. They provide local people with a food source and income, and have helped reduce illegal poaching. But there are some concerns that the areas are being overexploited. Better monitoring may be needed to ensure they are sustainable'.
- Give specific examples and include data where you can. E.g. 'Poaching has declined, and the populations of most species are steadily increasing - the elephant population has increased from 500 in 1990 to 2100 in 2011. However, 40 000 animals a year are still killed by poachers, and many more are caught in traps'.

Page 75 — Global Ecosystems Case Study — Amazon

1 Maximum of 40 marks available. HINTS:
- This is a 40 mark essay question, so the structure of your answer is really important. It may help you to write a brief essay plan before you begin.
- Introduce the two management schemes you will compare. E.g. 'The Serengeti National Park in Tanzania protects a savanna ecosystem, and the Central Amazon Conservation Complex in Brazil protects a rainforest ecosystem'.
- If you're after top marks, compare the two case studies directly rather than discussing them separately.
- Compare the threats to the two ecosystems, and highlight any similarities and/or differences. E.g. 'Both ecosystems are threatened by habitat destruction from human activities (e.g. the need for agricultural land) and overexploitation of resources from hunting'.
- Introduce the management approaches in the two areas, and highlight any similarities and/or differences. E.g. 'The Serengeti National Park is managed by one organisation (TANAPA), whereas the Central Amazon Conservation Complex is managed by several public and private organisations including research bodies and local government. Both areas have a management approach that involves working with local people'.
- Describe examples of projects within the two areas. For each one discuss the similarities and differences between strategies in the two areas and evaluate how effective each scheme has been with the reasons why. E.g. 'Law enforcement and anti-poaching strategies have been implemented in both areas. In the Serengeti, there are daily anti-poaching patrols by air, vehicle and on foot. In the Central Amazon Conservation Complex rangers and guards have been employed to man entrances to the Complex and carry out patrols. These efforts seem to be more effective in the Serengeti National Park than the CACC. This is probably because the Serengeti National Park (15 000 km^2) is much smaller than the Central Amazon Conservation Complex (49 000 km^2), and has considerably better infrastructure (i.e. roads). The resources in the Serengeti (e.g. park rangers and their vehicles

Answers

and equipment) are able to cope with its size, whilst there are not enough resources and employees to cope with the size of the Central Amazon Conservation Complex'.

- *Compare the ongoing threats to the two ecosystems, and explain the reasons for them. E.g. 'Both areas are still threatened by overexploitation of resources. This is due to continued population growth within and around the protected areas — these people are generally poor and rely on poaching or fishing to feed themselves'.*
- *Finish your answer with a short conclusion. You could write a sentence or two evaluating how successful the schemes have been overall and what still needs to be done in future to ensure sustainable management.*

Section 4 — World Cities

Page 77 — Urban Areas and Urbanisation

1 Maximum of 7 marks available. HINTS:

- *Start by describing the general pattern shown. You'll really impress the examiner if you can link urbanisation with economic development. E.g. 'The lowest levels of urbanisation are found in developing countries, for example in Africa and South East Asia countries typically have an urban population of less than 60%'.*
- *Remember to use the data in your answer as much as possible and mention any anomalies (countries or areas that don't fit the general overall pattern). It will also help your answer stand out if you can identify specific countries — but only do this if you're absolutely certain that you know which one is which. E.g. 'Although the map shows that countries in the developing world typically have the lowest levels of urbanisation, many countries at lower levels of development in South America do not follow this pattern. The majority of the countries have an urban population of 60% or higher and Brazil, Argentina and Chile all have an urban population higher than 80%'.*
- *The question asks you to comment on the pattern. This means you need to give some reasons why this pattern occurs, e.g. 'Urban population tends to be high in developed countries, because the process of urbanisation has already taken place'.*

2 Maximum of 8 marks available. HINTS:

- *You could begin your answer by briefly defining urbanisation and explaining that rural-urban migration is the main cause. E.g. 'Urbanisation is the growth in the proportion of a country's population living in urban areas. It is caused primarily by people migrating from rural areas to urban areas'.*
- *Then go on to say that the reasons people migrate can be divided into push and pull factors, e.g. 'There are many reasons for rural-urban migration. These can be split into push and pull factors. Push factors are the things that drive people away from the rural area, and pull factors are the things that attract them to the urban area'.*
- *Then talk about the different push and pull factors that may cause rural-urban migration. The command word in the question is discuss, so remember to talk about the effect of that factor on the population. E.g. 'Agricultural activity can cause problems like desertification. This means that fertile land becomes unproductive. This affects the people who are dependent on the land for food, and can force them to move away to urban areas'.*

Page 79 — Urbanisation

1 Maximum of 40 marks available. HINTS:

- *It's important to structure your essay. Start with an introduction where you introduce your argument. In the main body of the answer you should go through all the points that support your argument, then finish your essay off with a conclusion.*
- *In your introduction you should define urbanisation and introduce any case studies that you're going to use, e.g. 'Urbanisation is the growth in the proportion of a country's population that live in urban areas. Urbanisation is occurring rapidly in Mumbai in India...' You also need to introduce your argument. Remember it doesn't matter which way you argue, as long as you answer the question, e.g. 'Although for many of the problems caused by urbanisation there are effective solutions, they do not always work for everyone...'.*
- *Then discuss the problems, their solutions and how successful they've been. E.g. 'More than half of the population of Mumbai live in slums. The slums are cramped and homes are poorly built. Dharavi is one of the largest slums in Mumbai and the 2004 Dharavi Redevelopment Project aimed to address the problems there, but it was not well received by residents. The project aimed to move people out of the slum and build apartments for them to live in instead. However, the scheme has been unpopular with residents who worry that they will no longer be able to run small-scale industries such as recycling, and that community spirit will be lost'.*
- *You need to relate each point you make back to the question, e.g. 'The situation in Dharavi shows that it can be difficult to find a solution that works well for everyone involved'.*
- *You could bring in information from different parts of the course. For example you could write about Curitiba (see p. 96), e.g. 'Increased congestion and pollution is often an impact of urbanisation. Curitiba is a city in Brazil where a number of different solutions have been found to reduce car use and decrease congestion and pollution, such as creating bus lanes on the city's main highways to make journeys by public transport quicker. The schemes have been successful and air pollution is lower in Curitiba than in other Brazilian cities'.*
- *In your concluding paragraph you have to say 'to what extent' you agree with the statement. Don't make any new points in your conclusion, just summarise your argument.*

Page 81 — Suburbanisation

1 Maximum of 8 marks available. HINTS:

- *The question asks about impacts so remember to talk about different areas within the urban environment, such as the suburbs and the city centre.*
- *The command word is 'outline', so you should describe the impacts of suburbanisation and explain why they occur. E.g. 'Shops and offices in the CBD may close and move to the suburbs because the rents are usually lower. This can leave empty buildings in the CBD, which can lead to the CBD becoming run down'.*
- *Even though the question doesn't specifically ask you to use a case study, you can still use one. You could use Surbiton or another example you have studied. E.g. 'Suburbanisation can also lead to congestion in the suburb as car ownership is high and lots of commuters drive into the city centre for work. This is the case in Surbiton, where the large number of commuters causes congestion on routes into London'.*

Page 83 — Counter-urbanisation

1 Maximum of 8 marks available. HINTS:

- *You could begin your answer by defining the process of counter-urbanisation. E.g. 'Counter-urbanisation is the movement of people from large urban areas to smaller settlements and rural areas'.*
- *Then discuss the impacts of counter-urbanisation. Remember to use a case study example and include lots of facts and figures. You could start with a negative impact, e.g. 'Counter-urbanisation can result in increased house prices in rural areas, which means local people are less able to afford to buy or rent houses. Commuters often earn higher wages, so they can afford to pay more for housing. This has been the case in St Ives in Cambridgeshire, where the average price of a detached house rose from £130 000 to £291 000 between 2000 and 2010'.*
- *Make sure you talk about positive impacts too, e.g. 'Some local businesses, such as pubs with restaurants, may receive more customers because the people moving to the area have a larger disposal income than the existing residents. This can help improve the local economy'.*

Page 85 — Re-urbanisation

1 Maximum of 7 marks available. HINTS:

- *Look closely at the photograph and think about anything that could be a result of re-urbanisation. For example, you could talk about buildings, public spaces and transportation links.*
- *For each piece of evidence, explain why it suggests that re-urbanisation has taken place. E.g. 'In the centre of the picture there are modern, high density tower blocks. These look newly built and could have been designed to attract businesses into the area. There are also cranes in the photograph, which shows that new buildings are still being constructed as the area is further regenerated'.*

Answers

Page 87 — Urban Decline and Regeneration

1 Maximum of 10 marks available. HINTS:
- Start your answer by defining gentrification. E.g. 'Gentrification is the regeneration of an area by a wealthier group who move into a run down area and improve their own housing'. Then introduce your case study.
- The question asks you to discuss the changes that have taken place due to gentrification, so you need to describe the changes and talk about their effects on the area. E.g. 'Middle class people moving into the area improved the Georgian and Victorian properties in Islington (for example by restoring original features). This increases the quality of the housing in the area, but it also increases house prices. An increase in house prices means that original residents cannot afford to buy or rent in the area and may be forced to move elsewhere or into social housing'.
- Remember the question is asking you to use a case study, so use facts and examples from your case study to back up your points wherever you can.

Page 89 — Urban Regeneration

1 Maximum of 10 marks available. HINTS:
- Briefly explain what urban regeneration is and why it is needed. Then explain what a partnership scheme is.
- Introduce your case study. Give details about where it is and why regeneration was needed.
- Then go on to describe the aims of the partnership scheme and how regeneration was carried out, e.g. 'The Hulme City Challenge Partnership in Manchester aimed to improve living conditions by building a range of new housing'.
- Lastly, you need to evaluate how successful the scheme has been. Make sure you give a balanced answer, e.g. 'The Partnership Scheme has had positive impacts in Hulme. Unemployment has decreased because jobs have been created in new industries that have moved to the area. However, Hulme is still a poor area, and 47.5% of the people there live in social housing'.
- Use details and facts in your answer wherever possible, e.g. 'Hulme has become a more popular place to live since its redevelopment — its population is estimated to have grown by 3.3% since 1992, compared to a 0.2% increase in the city as a whole'.

Page 91 — Retailing

1 Maximum of 8 marks available. HINTS:
- Introduce your answer by describing what an out-of-town retail centre is and state that shops have moved out of city centres. Briefly describe the general characteristics of out-of-town shopping centres and why they are popular, e.g. 'Large out-of-town shopping centres are easy to access by car, provide free parking, and have many shops all under one roof. This makes them popular with customers'.
- Then introduce your case study. Describing where it is, when it was built, how much it cost, who comes to shop there etc.
- Now describe the facilities it provides and why it is popular, giving as many details as possible. E.g. 'The Trafford Centre in Manchester has over 200 shops, but it is not just used for shopping — it also has extensive leisure facilities including a 1600 seat food court, ten pin bowling, an indoor climbing wall and crazy golf'.

Page 93 — Redeveloping Urban Centres

1 Maximum of 10 marks available. HINTS:
- Introduce your case study. Give some brief background information, e.g. where it is, why it needed redeveloping.
- Then go on to discuss the ways in which redevelopment was carried out. Give as much detail as you can, e.g. 'In Manchester city centre a number of old buildings were renovated, for example the Manchester Corn Exchange was refurbished and is now a upmarket clothing mall'.
- The question asks you to evaluate. This means you need to say how successful the scheme has been, e.g. 'In Manchester the redevelopment has had a number of positive impacts. An increase in good quality residential property has led to an increase in the population of the city centre. The population doubled between 2003 and 2009. However there are still problems in Manchester...'.

Page 95 — Sustainability in Urban Areas

1 Maximum of 8 marks available. HINTS:
- Start by explaining the idea of sustainability, and explain why improving waste management is an important way of improving sustainability in urban areas.
- Now go on to talk about different methods of waste disposal. You could start with landfill and explain why it is not sustainable, e.g. 'In the UK landfill is still an important method of waste disposal and it accounted for nearly 50% of waste disposal in 2008. Landfill is cheap in the short term, but there are other much more sustainable methods of waste management (e.g. recycling). Landfill is unsustainable for a number of reasons: landfill sites can pollute groundwater if they aren't properly lined...'.
- Then go on to give details about other types of waste disposal — make sure you say how they can make waste management more sustainable.
- Include facts and examples wherever possible, e.g. 'Energy recovery has been used successfully in Sheffield, where 140 buildings in the city centre are heated by ERF, preventing the release of 21 000 tonnes of CO_2 each year'.

Page 97 — Sustainability in Urban Areas

1 Maximum of 10 marks available. HINTS:
- Start by explaining briefly what sustainability is. Then explain why an increasing number of cars in urban areas is not sustainable, e.g. 'As populations in urban areas increase, the number of people driving cars increases too. Having lots of people travelling by car in urban areas isn't sustainable because cars produce greenhouse gas emissions and air pollutants which damage the environment. It also increases congestion, which means people's journeys are longer and their transport needs aren't being met'.
- Discuss the different ways of making transport more sustainable. You could start by saying that public transport is more sustainable than private cars because it produces less emissions per passenger.
- Then go on to give details about different improvements to transport which make it more sustainable. For each point give as much detail as you can and examples wherever possible, e.g. 'High occupancy vehicle lanes have been introduced in some places to encourage car sharing. In Toronto in Canada, the introduction of high occupancy vehicle lanes to Highway 403 increased car sharing from 14% to nearly 40% in three years. This increases sustainability of transport because people are travelling in fewer cars, so emissions and congestion are reduced'.
- You need to say how successful the schemes have been in the examples you have given, e.g. 'Some urban areas have taken specific measures to encourage residents to cycle instead of drive. In Freiburg in Germany, about half of the 120 one-way streets restrict motorists to travelling one way, while cyclists are allowed to travel in both directions. This reduces journey times for people cycling, but not for people driving, so it may encourage more people to cycle. In addition, there are designated, secure bike parking spots at public transport 'bike and ride' facilities, which makes it safer to leave your bike. These measures have been very successful — the proportion of journeys travelled by car fell from 38% in 1982 to 32% in 2007. Making cycling more popular is a good way of increasing sustainability because cycling produces no emissions and does not cause congestion'.

Section 5 — Development and Globalisation

Page 99 — Development Basics

1 Maximum of 8 marks available. HINTS:
- Start by giving a brief introduction about what sorts of things change as a country develops. Say that the changes can be economic, demographic, social, political and cultural.
- Then go on to give more detail about each type of change. You could mention how the change is measured, e.g. 'As a country develops, a number of economic changes take place, such as an increase in wealth. This can be shown by measures such as GDP (Gross Domestic Product), which is the value of goods and services that a country produces in a year. Increased GDP means that a country has become more wealthy'.
- The question is asking you to outline the changes, so you could link some of the changes together to explain why they are happening, e.g. 'An increase in wealth as a country develops can cause other social changes to take place. For example, when a country is more wealthy, fewer people are living in poverty (without basic human needs such as water and food)'.

Page 101 — Least Developed Countries

1 Maximum of 7 marks available. HINTS:
- The question is asking you to use the data. Before you start writing your answer you could jot down the key points that you notice in a short plan.

Answers

- The question is asking you to <u>comment</u> on the level of development for each of the countries shown. So, first you need to show what the data says about the level of development of each country, e.g. 'The data shows that Angola has many of the characteristics of a country at a very low level of development, such as a high birth rate. The group of countries that make up the Least Developed Countries (LDCs) all tend to have high birth rates'.
- <u>Manipulate</u> the data wherever you can, e.g. 'In Angola the birth rate is almost 4 times that of Denmark'.
- You also need to <u>link together</u> what the data says about the different countries and <u>explain</u> these differences, e.g. 'The literacy rate in Denmark (99% for both men and women) is considerably higher than in Angola (82.7% for men and 58.1% for women). There is also a discrepancy between the literacy of men and women in Angola: more men are literate than women. This is not true in Denmark, where the percentage is the same for men and women. This is because countries which are less developed tend to have inequalities between men and women...'
- Point out any data that is <u>anomalous</u>, e.g. 'As countries develop you would expect less of their income to come from agriculture. So we would expect that Angola would get the most of its GDP from agriculture and Denmark the least. The data actually show that Denmark gets more of its GDP from agriculture than South Africa, even though all the other data suggest that Denmark is a more developed country than South Africa'.

Page 103 — Global Groupings and Development

1 Maximum of 10 marks available. <u>HINTS</u>:
- Start your answer with a bit about the grouping of nations — you could <u>briefly introduce</u> the EU to show <u>why</u> it came about and <u>who</u> it involves. E.g. 'The EU is an economic and political grouping of 27 European countries. It formed to help Europe recover after the second world war, and its aims were to promote peace and economic growth for its members'.
- Now go on to <u>discuss</u> the consequences of global groupings. Make sure you support your points with <u>examples from the EU</u>. E.g. 'Global groupings can bring economic benefits to their members. For example, the EU has a free trade agreement, which allows members to trade with each other without barriers such as tariffs or quotas. This leads to increased trade and promotes economic development. You can see this in the UK by looking at figures such as the percentage of GDP made up by trade with EU countries...'.
- The question is asking you to <u>discuss</u> the consequences, so give a <u>balanced argument</u>, e.g. 'There are negative impacts of trade agreements too. Although they increase trade between member countries, they exclude countries that are not members. For example, in the EU, the Common Agricultural Policy puts quotas and tariffs on trading with countries outside the EU. This makes it more likely that EU members will trade with each other, rather than with countries outside the EU'.

Page 107 — Development Issues

1 Maximum of 40 marks available. <u>HINTS</u>:
- Remember, for this question you only have to write about <u>one</u> of the issues.
- The command word is 'discuss'. This means you need to give a <u>balanced answer</u>. Briefly plan the points you are going to make before you start writing. To get <u>top marks</u>, you should try and discuss the <u>positive</u> and <u>negative</u> points <u>together</u> rather than discussing all the positives and then all the negatives.
- Start by giving an <u>introduction</u> to the issue you've chosen, e.g. for economic sustainability versus environmental sustainability you could say, 'Sustainable development is about meeting the needs of people today, so that the economy can grow, without compromising the ability of people in the future to meet their own needs. For development to be truly sustainable there needs to be both economic and environmental sustainability...'.
- <u>Use your case study</u> to discuss the issue in the question. Give as much <u>detail</u> as you can and make sure that you always <u>link</u> the points you make <u>back to the question</u>, e.g. 'It is difficult for a country to develop in a way that makes its economy sustainable, whilst maintaining environmental sustainability. For example, in Sarawak (a state in Malaysia) one way that the economy has developed has been an increase in commercial agriculture. The main crop is palm oil which is grown for export (it accounts nearly for 6% of Sarawak's exports). Although palm oil cultivation is economically sustainable, because it can continue to bring revenue into the country in the future, it is not environmentally sustainable...'.
- For a 40 mark question like this you need to use your knowledge from the <u>whole course</u>. You could bring in what you've learnt about sustainability from the other topics.
- Finish with a <u>conclusion</u>. Give an <u>overview</u> of your discussion, and say what <u>you think</u> about the issue. Make sure that the conclusion is <u>balanced</u> though — back up what you say about both sides of the discussion with evidence from your answer.

Page 109 — Globalisation Basics

1 Maximum of 10 marks available. <u>HINTS</u>:
- Start with a <u>brief introduction</u> to your answer, e.g. 'Globalisation is the process of the world's economies, political systems and cultures becoming more strongly connected to each other. The movement of manufacturing away from developed countries has been an important factor in globalisation'.
- Then explain <u>what changes</u> in patterns of production have taken place, e.g. 'In recent decades, manufacturing has decreased in developed countries and increased in developing countries. There are a number of reasons for this. Firstly, labour costs are often lower in developing countries. By relocating manufacturing abroad companies can save money...'.
- Now discuss <u>how</u> these changes have promoted globalisation by making countries more interconnected, e.g. 'As production moves away from developed countries, these countries become reliant on goods produced abroad, so international trade increases. This means that less developed and more developed countries become more interconnected through trade'.
- Use <u>examples</u> to back up your points wherever possible, e.g. 'A variety of different products that used to be made in the UK are now made abroad. For example, the vacuum cleaner manufacturers Dyson moved their production operations from the UK to Malaysia in 2002'.

Page 111 — Trans-National Corporations (TNCs)

1 Maximum of 10 marks available. <u>HINTS</u>:
- First, write a short <u>introduction</u> to your answer, e.g. 'Trans-National Corporations (TNCs) are companies that operate in two or more countries. They start in one country (their country of origin) and as they grow, parts of the business, e.g. manufacturing, services and retail, move elsewhere (their host countries)'.
- You need to <u>discuss</u> the social, environmental and economic impacts of TNCs, so first you could write about the <u>positive</u> impacts, e.g. for economic impacts you could say, 'TNCs can provide jobs in host countries. This can create increased economic activity in the host country through the multiplier effect: higher employment means the local population has a higher disposable income which they spend locally. This increased wealth then attracts other businesses, who may provide even more employment'.
- Then you could talk about how TNCs can also have <u>negative</u> economic impacts, e.g. 'However, TNCs can also have a negative effect on employment in host countries. They may out-compete local businesses which can cause them to shut down'.
- Make sure you discuss <u>economic</u>, <u>social</u> and <u>environmental</u> impacts on the host country.

Page 113 — TNC Case Study — Wal-Mart

1 Maximum of 7 marks available. <u>HINTS</u>:
- You should describe the <u>general patterns</u> on the map, but the question is also asking you to <u>comment</u>, so you should try to explain the <u>reasons</u> for the patterns you spot. E.g. 'The manufacturing operations for the TNC are all located in South East Asia, for example, in China, India and Malaysia. It's likely manufacturing is based in these countries to take advantage of the lower labour costs found in newly industrialised countries (compared to wealthier nations such as the USA, where the headquarters are located)'.
- Make sure you describe and comment on <u>all</u> the different types of operations.
- Comment on any <u>anomalies</u> that you see in the general patterns and try to <u>explain</u> them, e.g. 'All the research and design centres are in highly developed countries such as the USA, the UK and Japan except for one which is in China. This is likely to be because the TNC needs to have a research and design centre close to the market where they are selling the products'.

Answers

2 Maximum of 8 marks available. HINTS:
- The question is asking you to write about an example, so you need to write about a case study. Give a brief introduction to your case study, e.g. 'Wal-Mart is a retail TNC which started in the USA in the 1960s. It has become the largest retail TNC in the world and operates in North and South America, Europe, Asia and Africa'.
- Discuss the impacts in the host countries and country of origin together but always make it clear which one you are talking about, e.g. 'As Wal-Mart has grown it has bought more and more of its manufactured products from outside the USA. This has had a negative impact on manufacturing in the USA, where the industry has declined and there have been job losses. However, in its host countries this change in production has had a positive impact, providing jobs in manufacturing in countries such as China'.
- Make sure you include both positive and negative impacts.
- The question is asking you to assess the impacts so you could write a short conclusion — write about whether you think the TNC has had an overall positive or negative impact on the host countries and country of origin. Whatever conclusion you reach, make sure you back it up with the points you have made in your answer.

Page 116 — Newly Industrialised Countries (NICs)

1 Maximum of 10 marks available. HINTS:
- Start your answer by briefly describing what NICs are, e.g. 'NICs (Newly Industrialised Countries) are countries that are rapidly developing as their economy moves from being dependent on primary industry to secondary or tertiary industry'.
- The question is asking you to explain the economic growth of NICs, so you need to say why they became wealthier. You could divide your answer between countries that grew because of investment in manufacturing, and countries that grew because of investment in services.
- For both of these you should make sure that you refer to one or more countries that you have studied. E.g. 'The first wave of NICs was the Asian Tiger economies (Hong Kong, Singapore, South Korea and Taiwan) who experienced massive economic growth from the 1960s onwards. For example, the GNI per capita of Hong Kong grew from $1800 in 1973 to $32 950 in 2008. One of the main reasons that NICs grew economically was investment that came from foreign TNCs, who set up the manufacturing parts of their business in these countries. TNCs invested in manufacturing in the Asian Tigers for lots of reasons. There was a large and cheap workforce available...'.

Page 117 — Growth in the 21st Century

1 Maximum of 8 marks available. HINTS:
- The question is asking you outline, so you need to describe how new markets and new technologies have affected economic growth in the 21st century and also explain a bit about why this has happened.
- Make sure you're really clear about the meaning of the terms you are using, e.g. 'New markets in the 21st century are countries that are becoming more open to international trade and investment, and are often rapidly developing as well'.
- First you could discuss the impact of new markets on economic growth, e.g. 'The emergence of new markets has been an important driving factor in the growth of the global economy in the 21st century. NICs such as China, India and Brazil are all countries that are rapidly developing and have huge populations. As these countries develop, the people who live there become more wealthy. This creates enormous opportunities for global companies to increase their profits and grow by exploiting these new markets'.
- Make sure you discuss everything that's asked for in the question — you also need to discuss the effect of new technologies on global economic growth in the 21st century.

Section 6 — Contemporary Conflicts and Challenges

Page 119 — Causes of Conflict

1 Maximum of 8 marks available. HINTS:
- Write an introduction to your answer — for example, state that conflicts can occur when people are competing for the same resources.
- Include some examples of resources that people might compete for, e.g. territory, water, buildings and oil.
- Then, for each type of resource describe a specific example of a conflict, e.g. 'The Nile River is a source of water for 10 countries in North East Africa. There is conflict between the downstream countries (Egypt and Sudan) that use most of the water, and the upstream countries (including Uganda, Rwanda, Ethiopia and Tanzania) that want to use more water'.
- Include names, facts, dates and figures where you can.

Page 121 — Characteristics and Resolution of Conflict

1 Maximum of 8 marks available. HINTS:
- The question is asking you to outline the ways to resolve a conflict, so you need to talk about a few different methods and explain how they may lead to a resolution.
- You could divide your answer between the ways to resolve different levels of conflict, e.g. international, national, regional and local conflicts.
- Introduce each method one at a time, e.g. 'Diplomacy is negotiation between countries to resolve an international conflict. Diplomats and ambassadors are trained negotiators who can represent a country to negotiate agreements, alliances or peace treaties'.
- Don't just describe the method — outline why it may or may not be successful. 'Diplomats are trained to act reasonably and respectfully, however cultural differences between countries mean that diplomats have to be aware of different negotiation styles and different protocols that countries have'.

Page 123 — Local Resource Conflict Case Study — Newbury Bypass

1 Maximum of 10 marks available. HINTS:
- Introduce the conflict you have studied — include when it started, what caused the conflict and what the local resource involved was, e.g. 'The Newbury bypass was proposed in 1982 to help solve congestion in the town after the volume of traffic had increased to 50 000 vehicles per day. There was conflict between those who supported the proposal and those who objected to it. Many people believed the bypass would not solve the traffic problems and there were many concerns about the impacts the bypass would have on the natural environment around Newbury'.
- Evaluate the processes which operated to resolve the conflict — begin by describing what was done. E.g. 'There was a public enquiry in 1988 where 147 witnesses gave evidence to a government appointed inspector either supporting or opposing the bypass'.
- Then comment on whether the process was successful. E.g. 'In 1990, following the enquiry, the government announced the bypass would go ahead. However, the groups who opposed the bypass still did not agree to its construction and the conflict continued. As a result, in 1994 there was a review by the Highways Agency to consider alternatives. Again it was decided that the bypass would go ahead despite continued opposition. As one side was still unhappy with the proposal it could be argued that the process was not a success'.
- Make sure you include lots of specific information, details, facts and dates.

Page 125 — International Conflict Case Study — Gaza and the West Bank

1 Maximum of 8 marks available. HINTS:
- Briefly introduce the conflict you have studied. The question is about the impacts of the conflict so you don't need to give lots of detail here, but you should give some background. E.g. 'There is conflict in the Middle East between Jews and Arabs over who has the right to the land that was formerly known as Palestine. In 1949 Palestine was divided into three different territories — Israel (a Jewish nation), Gaza and the West Bank (both Arab nations under the control of Egypt and Jordan respectively). Armed conflict was happening between Jews and Arabs leading up to this division, and has been continuing since 1949'.
- Split the impacts into economic and environmental and make sure you write a section for each. E.g. 'It's difficult to estimate the cost of such a long conflict, however it's likely to have cost many trillions of US$ since 1948. This has hindered economic development in the region because large amounts of money have been spent on security instead of development'.

Page 127 — International Conflict Case Study — Afghanistan

1 Maximum of 10 marks available. HINTS:
- Make sure you introduce any case studies you include in your answer, e.g. 'A major international conflict began in Afghanistan in October 2001. As a response to the terrorist attacks of September 11th 2001 (carried out by al-Qaeda), the USA and an international coalition force invaded Afghanistan. Their objectives were to prevent further terrorist attacks by ensuring that Afghanistan could no longer be used as a safe haven for terrorists, destroying al-Qaeda and bringing Osama Bin Laden (the leader of al-Qaeda) to trial'.

Answers

- You are only being asked about social impacts — make sure you discuss at least four or five of these in detail. Don't talk about economic or environmental impacts because you won't get any marks for them.
- Remember to give examples from at least one case study you have learnt and include facts and data where you can, e.g. 'The war in Afghanistan has had a wide range of social impacts on both Afghanistan and the other countries involved. For example, the conflict has led to an estimated 11 000 civilian deaths between 2001 and 2009. These deaths were the result of actions by both the Taliban and the coalition forces. Coalition forces themselves have suffered 1832 losses between 2001 and 2010'.

Page 129 — International Conflict Case Study — Darfur

1 Maximum of 40 marks available. HINTS:
- For an answer worth 40 marks it's really important that you plan the structure of your answer before you start writing.
- Begin with an introduction to the conflict you have chosen, e.g. 'Darfur is a region in the west of Sudan in Africa. An international conflict started there in February 2003 when rebel groups attacked government troops. The main rebel groups are the Sudan Liberation Army (SLA) and the Justice and Equality Movement (JEM)'.
- You could mention some of the causes of the conflict too, but you don't need too much detail here — remember that the question is asking about the impacts of the conflict.
- Then, examine the impacts of the conflict. To do this, you need to do more than just describe what the impacts are, e.g. think about how the different groups of people have been affected by the impacts.
- You should also split your answer up into the different types of impact — social, environmental and economic. E.g. you could write about the social impacts first, 'By 2010, the conflict in Darfur had caused 2.7 million people to flee their homes. Many of these people have become refugees and now live in camps near Darfur's main towns. Living in these camps has lots of negative impacts on people. For example, due to overcrowding they have limited access to clean water and healthcare. This can make other problems worse, such as the spread of disease...'.

Page 131 — Separatism

1 Maximum of 10 marks available. HINTS:
- Begin your answer by defining separatism. E.g. 'Separatism is when a smaller group of people want more independence from a larger group of people'.
- Briefly introduce your case study. E.g. 'The Basque Country is a region on the borders of France and Spain. The Basque people have a unique history, culture and language (Euskera), so many people in the region want it to become an independent state from France and Spain'.
- Then discuss the consequences of separatism. You could divide your answer up by discussing both the peaceful and the non-peaceful consequences of separatism, e.g. 'Political parties like the Basque nationalist party have formed. They aim to get greater political independence for the Basque Country and they do this peacefully. This is in contrast to the actions of ETA — a separatist group who use violence in their campaign for independence. ETA have killed over 800 people since their formation in the 1960s, and in 2006 were responsible for a bombing at Madrid Airport'.

Page 133 — The Challenge of a Multicultural UK

1 Maximum of 7 marks available. HINTS:
- You need to describe the graph, so if there's a general pattern, you should mention this first. Then you can move onto the specific features of the graph, such as any anomalies (things that don't fit the general pattern). Remember to quote figures from the graph in your answer. E.g. 'All but two of the regions of the UK are home to less than 10% of the UK's non-white population. London has by far the greatest percentage with around 45%. Next to this, the West Midlands has around 12% of the UK's non-white population. Compared to the English regions, Wales, Scotland and Northern Ireland all have very low percentages of ethnic minorities...'.
- The question is also asking you to comment on the graph, so use your knowledge to explain the reasons for the patterns shown on the graph, e.g. 'London has a high percentage of the UK's non-white population because it has always attracted high numbers of immigrants. People move to London from all over the world because it is a global hub where lots of organisations have offices. Also, there are lots of jobs in manufacturing, transport, hospitals and the tourism industry'.

Page 135 — The Challenge of a Multicultural UK

1 Maximum of 10 marks available. HINTS:
- Begin your answer by briefly explaining what a multicultural society is.
- Describe the different issues and explain how they can arise. Remember to give examples from the UK to back up your points. E.g. 'There are economic issues associated with multicultural societies. For example, many ethnic minority groups work longer hours for lower salaries than people who were born in the country. In the UK in 2011, almost 50% of Pakistani and Bangladeshi workers were paid less than £7 an hour, whereas 25% of White British workers were paid this amount'.
- You could divide up the issues you discuss into different types (e.g. economic, housing, education issues etc.) and try to link them together as you discuss them. E.g. 'As a result of many immigrants being in low paid work, a large number of immigrants live in low cost housing where overcrowding is a problem. For example, overcrowding is a problem in the Manningham area of Bradford, where there is a large Pakistani community'.

Page 137 — The Challenge of Global Poverty

1 Maximum of 7 marks available. HINTS:
- First briefly define poverty, and talk about how the map shows global poverty, e.g. 'Poverty means being unable to afford basic things such as safe drinking water, food, shelter, sanitation, healthcare and education. The map shows global poverty by showing the percentage of children under five who are underweight. A major cause of being underweight is an inadequate food supply, so areas with lots of underweight children are also likely to be areas in poverty'.
- Then describe the pattern shown on the map in detail, using names of places and figures. E.g. 'Poverty is unevenly distributed across the world. Central Africa and South Asia have the highest levels of poverty, with at least 30% of under 5s being underweight in a number of countries. India and Bangladesh are the worst affected countries, with at least 40% of under 5s being underweight. This is in contrast to countries such as the USA...'.
- If there are any anomalies to the pattern you've described, then make sure you highlight them in your answer.
- The question is asking you to comment on the global distribution of poverty, so you also need to explain your points. E.g. 'Poverty is high in countries in South Asia, such as India and Bangladesh, for a number of reasons. For example, these countries are heavily affected by natural hazards such as floods and droughts. These hazards can cause poverty by damaging or destroying property, infrastructure and crops'.

Page 139 — The Challenge of Global Poverty

1 Maximum of 40 marks available. HINTS:
- Start by writing an introduction to your answer. Introduce both the key terms ('security' and 'development') in the statement, e.g. 'Security for a country means many different things. It can include personal security, which is how at threat the population is from violence or crime, but also economic security, which is to do with how stable the country's economy is and whether everyone has a reliable income or not'.
- Write about the first part of the statement — you should use examples to back up your points wherever possible. E.g. "No development without security' means that it is difficult for a country to develop if it does not have all the different forms of security. For example, in Afghanistan there is very little personal and political security because of an ongoing war. Without this security, Afghanistan can't invest in development projects such as building roads, schools and hospitals as there is no guarantee that they won't be destroyed by the ongoing conflict'.
- Then write about the second part of the statement ('no security without development'), and discuss how it contrasts with your point about the first part of the statement.
- This is a 40 mark essay question, so, wherever it's relevant, you need to bring in your geography knowledge from other parts of the course. For example, you could talk about how lots of countries remain trapped at low levels of development because of this problem, then discuss the ways that countries can develop (e.g. through trade and aid) to break this cycle.

Index

Index

Index